Joanna & Gary Ginter
5840 West Midway Park
Chicago, Illinois 60644

Joanna and Gary Ginter
8-4-82

MAKING IT HAPPEN

A Positive Guide to the Future

Fruit as Image of the Future

For me, the world is always
*   potential,*
*   self-transforming,*
*   problematic,*
*   unavoidably creating and*
destroying itself simultaneously.

My basic image for reality is
a fruit;
*   the seed fulfilled—*
which includes the seeds
remaining to be fulfilled.
        —Donald N. Michael

For their generous financial support
we would like to thank the following:

Jay Harris,
The George Gund Foundation,
The Atlantic Richfield Foundation,
Lillian Esselstyn.

Library of Congress Catalog Card Number: 82-70504
ISBN 0-942718-00-3

Cover design—Jean Lamuniere
Book design—David Dodson Gray

Basic Questions

All too often we feel that the future is out of our control, that somebody else will make the decisions which shape our lives.

Why should we bother to learn about and try to do something about the future?
There are, after all, a lot of things to learn and do; most of us don't have much "spare time."
Here are some of the reasons which I think are important:

■ **For the long-term future, at least, our options are wide open.** There exist an incredible range of possibilities for choosing the kind of life we really want and then going ahead and making it happen.

■ **The choices we do make about**
where we live,
our lifestyles,
how we spend our income,
our employment,
voting for political leaders,
and shaping the values of those
close to us,
are already shaping our futures and theirs.

■ **So we cannot avoid choices and our choices will make a difference.**

■ **The more information we have about the consequences of our choices, the better choices we are likely to make.**

■ **What happens in the future will affect**
our health,
our standard of living,
our control over our lives,
our happiness,
and the happiness of those
we care about.
It will also affect the survival and well being of our nation, the United States of America and our species, the human race.

■ **If we don't take a positive interest in creating our future, it is certain that someone else**
with good intentions or bad,
with compassion or greed,
in wisdom or ignorance,
competently or incompetently,
(probably with combinations of these)
will create it for us.

Why read this book?
■ You will enjoy it; even if you don't, you will be challenged by the ideas it offers.
■ Its authors are interesting and creative people who have thought about this subject, and also care about it.
■ It is written in plain English.
■ Its approach is comprehensive.
■ It is concrete, practical, and action-oriented—but it tries not to preach.
■ After you have finished, you will know that you don't just have to sit there being
euphoric,
sad,
confused,
optimistic,
pessimistic,
anxious,
happy, or bored.
Instead, you can decide what kind of future you would like to create and begin to make it happen.

Painting by Richard Hess

Basic Principles

In every book, there are major themes
or organizing principles.
Often it is left to the reader to discern them.
We want to be very clear about the basic principles which
have guided us in the writing of *Making It Happen.*
For that reason,
we have stated them here,
where you will be sure not to miss them.

■ **We have the power to shape the kind of future we want—if we accept the responsibility to do so.**

Many books on the future paint a grim prospect. But they are talking about what the world might look like if we assume that the future is the responsibility of someone else—or that the task of building a better society can be left to some "invisible hand."

The first step in facing up to the future is to realize that we—every one of us—can play an important role in shaping a more decent, humane, and sustainable society. We—every one of us—have the power to do this, if only we make up our minds to exercise it.

To shape a better future, we need to recognize that we really are responsible for our own lives and futures—and that what we do (or do not do) can make a difference.

We must also accept personal responsibility for helping make the world around us be better in the future. In America and throughout the world, many people are already doing this; we can find inspiration and guidance in their example.

■ **To take control of our future, we must first have a vision of the way we would like human society to be.**

The people-oriented ideals of freedom, equity, and opportunity are the foundation of America's guiding vision. These ideals are widely shared throughout the world.

The challenge, as in the past, is to adapt them to evolving and changing conditions and to diverse cultural settings. This process of adaptation needs to be flexible, open, and democratic.

■ **Americans should not be fearful about the capacity of American society to adapt to fundamental changes; our society is adaptable and resilient.**

Throughout our history, experimentation and change have been hallmarks of American society. Nonetheless, in every era opponents have preached that change would lead to destruction of our way of life. As Henry Steele Commager has pointed out, Americans have customarily regarded change and reform as part of the natural order of things.

■ **We should keep faith with ourselves, with democracy, and with our basic ideals.**

The goals of Americans in the 1980s and 1990s should continue to build upon the strengths of a people-based system. We must ensure that, in the emerging new global order, this is preserved as an ideal for humankind.

Our highest priorities should not be economic growth and material well-being but rather, as in the past, liberty, equity, and opportunity.

Can we have an open society based on these ideals, and on the concept that individuals should participate in decisions affecting their lives? There is no evidence to indicate that such a society is inherently riskier than the other "experiments" in progress. In fact, there is a great deal of evidence to the contrary.

■ **Americans should exercise global leadership by example rather than by telling others what to do.**

Americans cannot escape the role of global leadership.

But we cannot lead by playing a role of a privileged minority whose principal objective appears to be the preservation of an affluent, unsustainable style of life. To exercise effective global leadership, we must first get our own values and priorities in order.

The process of redefining our global role in the twenty-first century must begin now and it must begin at home. Our approach must be practical, positive, and people-oriented. It must start with clear recognition that the process of change may be difficult. It must start also with optimism about the power of the United States to lead in the world by the example we set at home. We must steer clear of "thou shalt..." and "they must..." while concentrating on "we ought to and can..."

The remainder of **Making It Happen** is animated by these principles.

Ten years later: Many people will remember the appearance ten years ago of what then seemed a heretical book— *The Limits to Growth.* It was the first *Report to the Club of Rome,* elaborated at the Massachusetts Institute of Technology, brought out by a New York publisher and presented at a world premiere at the Smithsonian Institution in Washington, DC in March, 1972. This report became much better known outside the United States than inside. It was discussed widely in Europe, Japan, and many developing nations. Some hailed it as a long-awaited message. Others were sharply critical. Only much later did the media and public in America give *The Limits to Growth* their serious attention.

Now, things have changed remarkably. Several concepts expressed or implied in the pages of *Limits...* have become part of familiar usage almost everywhere in the world. This has occurred regardless of ideological convictions or economic conditions.

It is a good idea to publish on the tenth anniversary of *Limits to Growth* a volume that expands upon and updates these concepts. It blends these concepts with sound American traditions and examines how a renewal of vigor can be initiated in U.S. society. The U.S. Association for the Club of Rome is to be commended for this effort.

Making It Happen **is a book written by Americans for Americans.** To foreign ears, the overtones of American self-esteem and pride may seem implausible at a time when the entire human community—including the United States—faces unprecedented global crises and a clouded future.

But such American attitudes may— and hopefully will—reflect a new awakening. They may indicate growing awareness that even a nation as powerful as the United States must call upon its innermost energies to stem these adverse tides in our global fortunes.

MAKING IT HAPPEN:

by Aurelio Peccei _____

To be true to itself, though, the United States must not aim merely at political or economic primacy. Even more important is the task of effective and moral leadership in creating a sustainable and humane world.

It is my hope that *Making It Happen* will induce other peoples to engage in similar self-analyses and spur them to revive their own national potential in the pursuit of higher goals. The most beneficial outcome would be several such national efforts, organized in concert and pursued in the context of mutual understanding and world solidarity.

I see *Making It Happen* as a gentle but persistent invitation to explore the alternatives before us. We need to understand just how, at this turn of history, we can be self-respecting and responsible human beings. What we seek is to keep our children's options— and our own too—as open as possible.

It would perhaps be preferable that readers not go through all these pages in quick succession. Instead I would recommend that you go to one topic, or another—and then use what you find there as basis for discussion. These discussions could take place anywhere you gather with other people, at a family dinner table, a club or union meeting, a church gathering, or PTA.

Taking a global view: It is clear that, whatever our convictions, we should view the increasing interdependence of the global system and its biophysical limits as both challenge and opportunity. There are many ways in which each of us can work toward lives which are better and more rewarding for everyone.

These themes have been developed repeatedly by The Club of Rome. The Club of Rome has been wrongly considered a company of doomsayers and advocates of zero growth.

Our role is to warn humanity how foolish it is to hide from the facts. There can be no denying that, in the last decade or so, the world situation has deteriorated on many fronts. If we continue on the present course, humankind's prospects are somber.

There is not one problem of global scope today that is being attacked and resolved effectively. Meanwhile new problems are arising ceaselessly. The *world problematique* seems ever more complex and threatening.

The factors which threaten us are many. They include the demographic explosion, expected to continue well into the next century; our insane arms race; unemployment; stagflation; wasting of resources; and other economic ills. They include also devastion of the global ecosystem and neglected social problems. Also threatening and unresolved are the political-economic confrontations betwen North and South and between East and West.

Any of these factors alone is capable of forcing humankind to its knees. Reciprocally they influence and reinforce one another, creating situations from which, one day, there may be no escape.

The need for a new outlook: At the root of the problem seems to be an incapacity or unwillingness to change our world outlook, our mentality and attitudes. At the very moment when fundamental change and innovation have become indispensable, we seem frozen in our ways of being and modes of doing.

Things can be turned around. Recent works of The Club of Rome have emphasized that again and again. Solutions are possible to the problems we face. My last book, *One Hundred Pages for the Future,* was written to show that we can open up new paths. Hope and opportunity, as well as danger, lie ahead.

Building the world we wish: I have gone even farther and affirmed that— within limits—we can build the world we wish, provided we are ready to take the responsibility for doing so.

We must recognize, as we take the first steps, that the world is one integrated system. For better or worse, all peoples and nations, will share a common future. Breakdown or rot in any part of the world endangers the whole system.

Making It Happen **recognizes that interdependence, even though it addresses itself essentially to the United States. This great nation has at its disposal all the means and all the talents to shape a bright future for itself.**

But this future cannot be a happy and peaceful one, if large sections of the planet continue to live in misery or torn by war. America cannot realistically expect to forge ahead alone—or just with a few friends. It has a vital stake in the entire world. It must be committed to the attainment of satisfactory levels of welfare and development everywhere.

I am not alone in thinking that the U.S. possesses sufficient material and human resources to devote a reasonable portion of them to creating a safer and more humane global society. By doing so, it can play a leading role in building a worthy future.

This will also serve the national interests of the United States. In today's world—and the world of the future— national and humanitarian interests are not in conflict. They reinforce one another. This is the core message of *Making It Happen.*

You will also find in these pages a wealth of other core ideas on which to base future-oriented thinking and creative action. It is for readers now to take over and make good use of them.

AURELIO PECCEI

Rome, January 1982

Who This Book Is For

Most people who write or edit books have an audience in mind when they begin. My idea was to produce a book for people who don't usually read books about the future.

I had some very specific people in mind. They were my friends and neighbors in two rural communities where I have lived for the past ten years.

They are mostly farmers, shopkeepers, and local professionals. They belong to the local Ruritan or Rotary and, perhaps, to the American Legion or VFW. Their children, like mine, may be members of 4H or Future Farmers of America. Most of their time is spent providing for themselves and their families.

These Americans, like most Americans, are concerned about current events in politics, the economy and in business, and about how these events may affect their lives and the lives of their children. They are the people in America who are most concerned about and most dedicated to a good future.

In my opinion, these are also the people who create the future. The only problem is that they don't know that they do. They think that the future is made by "decision-makers," or "experts," or famous people or that it just happens. They think they don't count.

I think they do count. That's why this book has been written.

How This Book Happened.

Have you ever wondered about the process and the decisions that ultimately result in a book you hold in front of you?

By the time you see them, most books are—

neat,
well structured,
logically organized,
(and, sometimes, also
understandable and
interesting).

Linear-rational processes: One might assume that the process that produced them was also neat, well structured, and logically organized, and sometimes it was.

In such cases, the author(s) probably—

defined a *goal* or goals,
developed specific operational
  objectives,
formulated a *strategy*
  to meet the objectives,
developed a *plan*
  to implement the strategy,
marshalled *resources,*
wrote,
edited,
published,
and *sold* the book.

Scholars call such well-planned, well-organized processes *linear-rational.* The linear-rational approach to problem-solving is characteristic of engineers, scientists, planners, military officers, and the majority of men.

Organic processes: There is also another kind of process. Among its most important characteristics are—

*multiple, often competing goals,
breadth* that often seems to
  extend beyond these goals,
apparent disorganization
  (especially to linear-rational
  thinkers),
frequent reassessments of goals,
  objectives, and means,
*frequent changes of plans,
flexibility,
adaptability,
a focus on the whole*
  rather than the parts,
evolutionary development
  rather than straight-line.

This kind of process is called *organic.*

Organic approaches to problem-solving are characteristic of artists, family farmers, small proprietors, doctors of veterinary medicine, successful politicians, kindergarten teachers, mothers, the majority of women, the U.S. Association for The Club of Rome—and me.

Which kind of process works best depends upon the type of problem to be solved. *Making It Happen* is the outcome of an organic process. We describe that process in more detail in the Epilogue.

1.

Americans are natural futurists. The American experience has been an American experiment.

INTRODUCTION

The American Experiment . 12

2.

A clear picture of what's most important to you is the first step on the path to the world and future you really want.

VALUES

What Do We Want? 27

□ **Making Value Sets Explicit**
Donella H. Meadows

□ **Conscience of a Conservative**
Senator Barry Goldwater

□ **Biblical Imperatives**
John J. Weaver

□ **Are Ethics Adequate?**
Peter Henriot

□ **New Goals and Values**
Aurelio Peccei

3.

Recognizing the reality of our bonds with other human beings and with the environment is necessary as we begin our journey.

PLANET

What Do We Have
to Work with? 45

□ **Ecological Imperatives**
Anitra Thorhaug

□ **The Pressure of Human Numbers**
Anne H. Ehrlich

□ **Economic Realities
—and Ethical Choices**
Herman E. Daly

NEW VISIONS—1.

We all want security—
personal and national—
But what does that really
mean?

Security for What? 70

☐ **The Changing Agenda**
   Thomas W. Wilson

☐ **Armaments and Human Misery**
   Robert Cory

6.

Who are our real
companions on the path to
the future—
and what do we offer one
another?

7.

Why is leadership so hard
today?
And what do leaders really
need?

4.

PARTNERS

LEADERSHIP

5.

We all want more—
but of what?

The Invisible People...... 106

☐ **As If Children Mattered**
   Page Huidekoper Wilson

☐ **Women and Global Society**
   Elizabeth Dodson Gray

☐ **The Powerful Minority**
   Robert S. Browne

Growth Toward What? 82

☐ **Growth with Quality**
   Robert D. Hamrin

☐ **The Inadequacy of Economics**
   Hazel Henderson

☐ **The Search for Sustainable Futures**
   Dennis L. Meadows

The Public Sector 132

☐ **"We Are Too Great to Limit
   Ourselves to Small Dreams"**
   1981 Inaugural address
   President Ronald H. Reagan

☐ **Political Obstacles
   to a Global Perspective**
   Patsy Takemoto Mink

☐ **A View from Capital Hill**
   Senator Claiborne Pell

☐ **Leaders or Followers?**
   Donald R. Lesh

☐ **What Can Be Done
   to Improve Foresight?**
   John M. Richardson, Jr.

NEW VISIONS—2.

8.

Good health—meaningful work to do—and a vital religion are deeply personal enterprises. Yet we pursue these in organizations which have purposes of their own.

ENTERPRISE

The Private Sector 150
- ☐ Social Systems in Trouble
  Roy R. Anderson
- ☐ Organized Labor:
  "Busy Being Born"
  Glenn E. Watts and Lou Gerber
- ☐ Technology and the
  Transformation of Religion
  John Thomas Walker

9.

People make the future happen.
Here are stories of real people making a real difference.

ACTION

It's Happening 174
- ☐ Planning—and Learning from It
  Donald N. Michael
- ☐ Social Change through Listening
  Martha Stuart
- ☐ Appropriate Technology
  Harriet Barlow
- ☐ Last Rites for Smallpox
- ☐ The Hunger Project
- ☐ Other Case Studies

10.

Who are we?
—and how did we make this book happen?

EPILOGUE

Creating Global Consciousness:
   The Club of Rome . . . 212
- ☐ The U.S. Association
  for The Club of Rome
- ☐ Reports to The Club of Rome
- ☐ How *Making It Happen* Happened
- ☐ How You Can Make It Happen

Demonstration at the U.S Capitol.

Introduction:

The American Experiment

Commentary

When I started working on this book, I was much more pessimistic than I am now. I was among those who would argue that Americans should fear the future.

Recently, my viewpoint has changed. The reason is that I have returned to an old interest, long abandoned: American history. I have found it helpful to turn to the past because I had observed that many specialists in future studies are able to say much more about what is *likely* to happen in 2050 than about what actually did happen in 1750, 1850, or even 1950.

Yet what happened in history may provide us with invaluable insights into the extent of changes that have occurred in the past. It may help us understand our own resilience in coping with such changes.

The study of history also tends to cast a more favorable light on some of the accomplishments of our own era. I am thinking particularly of the progress made over the past two decades in civil rights and women's rights. To say that progress has been made does not mean, of course, that all desirable goals have been achieved. But to say that we have

made no progress in the last twenty years would be negative and wrong.

Looking at our past has had the effect of renewing my faith in the capacity of the people of the United States to confront problems, make necessary and timely choices, and to create a better future. This book is strongly influenced by my optimism that Americans are, indeed, natural futurists.

JOHN M. RICHARDSON, Jr.

MAKING IT HAPPEN:

What Can We Know about the Future?

What can we know about the future? More important, what can we, as Americans, do about the future?

The answers found in this book can be summarized briefly.

■ **Similar, but different:** We know that the future will be similar to, but different from, the present. It will also be different from what we expect. And it will be shaped to a large extent by what we are choosing to do, or not to do, right now.

■ **Range of choice:** Those of us who are fortunate enough to live in the United States have, and will continue to have, an enormous range of choice.

■ **What will happen tomorrow vs. What happens ten or twenty years from now:** To be sure, what will happen tomorrow has been shaped, in large degree, by the choices we have made already.

But what happens ten or twenty years from now is largely undetermined. Each of us can and will make a difference. Each of us has power, great power, to decide what kind of life and what kind of world we want—and to begin making it happen. There is no people and no society better equipped to transform potential future problems into opportunities.

■ **America's uniquely future-oriented tradition:** A good place to begin is by recognizing and taking pride in our uniquely future-oriented tradition. Our forebears believed that it was possible to design a fundamentally better society. Our ancestors have literally been making it happen. We are the heirs to that legacy, and we have the responsibility and opportunity to carry it forward.

■ **About fearing the future:** There are those who imply or say outright that Americans should fear the future. In another era of transition, fraught with great problems, President Franklin Roosevelt had these words for the faint of heart—

> Let me...assert my firm belief that the only thing we have to fear is fear itself—nameless, unreasoning, unjustified terror which paralyzes needed efforts to convert retreat into advance.

I can state my own view very simply: Americans are experts at designing the future. Americans are natural futurists.

We have nothing to fear from the future...provided only that we act creatively and responsibly today.

Reaffirming Traditional Principles

The beliefs, values, and practices that are most fundamental to the American tradition are also those that can best help us to create the future we want. What is needed is not fundamental change so much as a return to fundamental principles.

But not everyone is in agreement about what those principles really are. As we enter the 1980s, some would have us believe that "the business of America is economic growth" just as, in an earlier era, President Calvin Coolidge asserted that "the business of America is business."

I hold many values in common with those who believe in economic growth, a viewpoint based on my earlier experiences as a small business entrepreneur. But I do not regard any particular economic pattern as fundamental. An economic system should be viewed as a means to achieve the things that are really important. We engage in economic activity, in other words, to get the things we need and want. What is fundamental is the idea that we should be able to strive, in whatever way we choose, to create the life and the society we want.

Identifying the central values in the American tradition: Here are eight principles that I feel capture the essence of the American tradition; see if you agree:

■ *Life, liberty, and the pursuit of happiness are basic human rights;*

■ *The powers of government derive from the people;*

■ *People have a right to participate in the decisions affecting their lives;*

■ *If people are given information that is both sufficient and accurate, they are competent to make such decisions;*

■ *The proper function of government is to engage in only those functions that cannot be better done privately, and no more;*

■ *The will of the majority must be tempered by considerations of equity, civility, neighborliness, and discretion;*

■ *The exercise of liberty must be tempered by the same considerations;*

■ *Steering an appropriate middle path between valued—but sometimes conflicting—ideals requires political institutions whose powers are limited, countervailing, and adaptable.*

These principles describe the American ideal. It is a basically humane, people-based system which has made steady—if not always smooth—progress toward providing freedom and equity to its people and, at the same time, assuring them the opportunity to improve their material standard of living.

This American ideal has adapted to radical changes in its physical environment, economic institutions, global commitments, and the aspirations of its people. The basic principles of the American system were embodied in 1948 in the Universal Declaration of Human Rights as a "common standard of achievement for all peoples and all nations."

It is a system on which the American people can and should continue to rely as they make choices about the future.

JMR ☐

Facing the Future

Problems

—and Matching Opportunities

Poverty and inequity exist in our own nation and in other nations. The gap between rich and poor nations seems to be widening, rather than narrowing.

Poverty and inequity have been greatly lessened, or eliminated in the United States and in many other nations of the world.
It is clearly possible to create a world in which each human being has the opportunity to realize his or her full potential.

Many people believe we must choose between material well-being and environmental quality. We cannot have one without sacrificing the other.

Nations and regions of the world with the highest levels of material well-being also have high levels of environmental quality. Many people believe that environmental quality and material well-being are symbiotic and make each other possible. These people say there is no conflict between these goals. We can choose to have a society with both.

Knowledgeable scientists generally agree that our *present systems of production* in many sectors of the economy threaten irreversible damage to ecological support systems upon which the survival of the human race depends.

Evidence suggests that production systems which do not damage ecological support systems are both efficient and profitable. We can choose to develop such production systems.

Hunger is a present scourge and a growing threat in many parts of the world. Some 28 human beings, 21 of them children, starve to death every minute. This is equivalent to a new Hiroshima every three days.

Hunger has been banished in many parts of the world. Experts largely agree that it is lack of will, not lack of food which is the principal cause of hunger. We can choose to have a world in which every human being is nourished sufficiently and sustainably.

More Problems—

Projections provide strong evidence that *current trends of population and economic growth and the consumption of productive resources are not sustainable in the long run.*

The arms race among the great and small nations of the world continues and is accelerating. Armaments impose a major non-productive claim on economic and physical resources that could be used for the betterment of humankind. The threat of nuclear holocaust hangs over all of us and is not diminished by more armaments.

Addressing such problems and, if possible, taking advantage of the opportunities described above is probably impossible; they are unsolvable. Even to undertake the task will mean unhappiness, sacrifice, and deprivation for those involved, with the outcome by no means certain. There is little hope for the future.

More Matching Opportunities

Many alternative options exist which could lead to sustainable local, regional, and national economic and industrial systems with higher quality of life for all.

We can choose to have a world in which war is no longer accepted as an instrument of national policy and disputes are resolved by other means. The resources presently allocated to armaments can be directed toward increasing the well-being of the human race rather than the potential for destroying it.

Addressing such problems and taking advantage of the opportunities faced by our nation and the world are both possible and feasible.
Our goals are attainable.
The process of attaining them involves in large degree a reaffirmation of beliefs, values, and practices that are fundamental in our national tradition. The task of creating a future world that is sustainable, peaceful, diverse, humane, and equitable can not only be rewarding but fun.

The New Alchemy Institute

Reflections on the American Character

The lack of confidence in "the people": Much of the recent debate about the future and the way we make public policy has demonstrated a lack of faith in the underlying principles of democratic government and mistrust of the basic intelligence and common sense of the American people.

Many future-oriented scholars and intellectuals seem to accept the view that democratic institutions, guided by popular concerns, are incapable of maintaining a long-term perspective.

They imply that global issues are too complicated to be widely understood and that people, by nature, will focus on immediate gratification and short-term goals to the detriment of broader, long-term objectives.

By stressing the need for expert judgments and complex technical analysis, these experts seem to assert that Americans just don't know what is good for them. It is surprising how many activist groups and those who see themselves as liberals (especially those found in universities) adhere to this elitist view.

The arguments of those who are hostile to ideas such as limits-to-growth, sustainability, interdependence, and global responsibility, are based on essentially the same premise. The American people, they assert, will reject policies not based on a narrow, short-term conception of self-interest. Americans are irrevocably committed to continual increases in levels of material consumption. They are also likely to add that any politician who adopts a different point of view could not be elected to public office.

Here are some of the assumptions about the American people which—explicitly or implicitly—seem to have been shaping much of the debate about the future.

I believe these assumptions should be challenged and in each case I have stated why.

■ **Is materialism the dominant value in American society? Is our conception of "The Good Life" defined in terms of ever-increasing levels of consumption and material well-being?**

The values and goals of the American people have been investigated from time to time by scholars and political leaders. Recent efforts include the President's Commission on National Goals under President Eisenhower, President Nixon's National Goals Research Staff and the White House Forums on Domestic Policy, directed by Vice President Rockefeller.

> What you have to understand is that most people in this country are men and women of common sense....
>
> ...most of the people in this country are not only...decent people, they want to do the right thing, and what you have to do is tell them straight out what the right thing is.
>
> You get a real feeling of this country and the people in it when you are on a train, speaking from the back of a train, and the further you get away from that, the worse off you are and the worse off the country is. The easier it gets for the stuffed shirts and counterfeits and the fellas from Madison Avenue to put it over on the people. Those people are more interested in selling the people something than they are in informing them about the issues.
>
> HARRY S TRUMAN, 1962
>
> From *Plain Speaking*, by Merle Miller (New York: Berkeley Publishing Corp., 1974). © 1973, 1974 by Merle Miller.

In *Goals for a Global Society* (1977), Ervin Laszlo provided us with a synthesis of these investigations. He reports that the primary goal cited in these investigations was—

■ *The health of the democratic system.* In older countries, nationhood is felt in the culture, in the common ethnic heritage, and in a shared history. But the feelings of being gathered together as a nation were at the beginning of the new United States consciously stated in a constitutional system created for expressly for that purpose. "In [the Constitution] the American people have sanctified the free enterprise, representative democracy system itself...."

Laszlo goes on to list related goals and objectives distinct from, yet closely related to, this primary U.S. goal—

■ *Peace and the protection of national interests.*

■ *Prosperity—full employment and economic stability.*

■ *An orderly, just, and free society.*

■ *A healthy populace.*

■ *An aesthetic and healthy environment.*

■ *A well-educated populace.*

■ *A better world.*

■ *Good housing.*

■ *Livable cities.*

■ *Arts and culture.*

These goals reflect a broad and sensitive view of the world. Prosperity and economic growth are mentioned, but primarily as being contributory to goals of equal or higher importance.

Many analysts and opinion leaders (and especially traditional economists) believe that, for the achievement of all other goals in U.S. society, continued growth is essential. But the American people do not appear to accord growth such a dominant position.

■ **Is personal economic gain the only important motivating force in American society?**

This widely accepted belief has been refuted again and again in the literature of professional management. A variety of human considerations, among them job satisfaction and a sense of accomplishment, have been established as far more important motivators.

Important and relevant evidence about personal motivation are also to be found in Studs Terkel's remarkable book, *Working*, which is simply a collection of comments by "ordinary" American people, from all segments of society, talking about their jobs:

"Nora Wilson may have said it must succinctly. 'I think most of us are looking for a calling, not a job. Most of us, like the assembly worker, have jobs that are too small for our spirit. Jobs are not big enough for people.'

"During my three years of prospecting," says Terkel, "I may have, on more occasions that I had imagined, struck gold. I was constantly astonished by the extraordinary dreams of ordinary people. No matter how bewildering the issues, no matter how dissembling the official language, those whom we call ordinary are aware of a sense of personal worth—or more often a lack of it—in the work they do. Tom Patrick, the Brooklyn fireman,... [told Terkel] 'The fuckin' world's so fucked up, the country's fucked up. But the fireman, you actually see them produce. You see them put out a fire. You see them come out with babies in their hands. You see them give mouth to mouth when a guy's dying. To me, that's what I want to be.'

"'I worked in a bank. You know, it's just paper. It's not real. Nine to five, and it's shit. You're lookin' at numbers. But I can look back and say, I helped put out a fire. I helped save somebody. It shows something I did on this earth.'"

■ **Are Americans insensitive to the gaps betweeen rich and poor nations? Do they view the aspirations of the Third World as a threat to their own well-being?**

Americans may be as uninformed today about the global gaps between rich and poor, as many were about the severity of deprivation in their own society during the early years of the Great Depression of the 1930s. But U.S. initiation and support of the Marshall Plan following World War 2 provides evidence that, given a sense of purpose and given leadership with vision, the American people are capable of taking a larger view.

In 1975 Louis Harris conducted a number of surveys which addressed the issue of global responsibility. Here is a summary of some of the results.

An 85 to 90 percent majority felt that "most government leaders are afraid to tell it like it is—that is, to tell the public the hard truth about inflation, energy, and other subjects."

By 67 to 22 percent, a three-to-one majority endorsed the statement that "the trouble with most leaders is that they don't understand people want better quality of almost everything they have rather than more quantity."

In a survey conducted on September 16, 1975, Harris confronted the respondents with the much-cited statistic that Americans comprise 6 percent of the world population (now 5 percent) but consume 40 percent of the

Arnold Toynbee wrote that it is "not the discovery of atomic energy, but the solicitude of the most privileged people for the less privileged, as vested in Truman's Point 4 and the Marshall Plan...[that] will be remembered as the signal achievement of our age." And Winston Churchill observed that the Marshall Plan "was the most unsordid act in history."

President Truman put it more simply: "...there wasn't anything selfish about it. We weren't trying to put anything over on people. We were in a position to keep people from starving and help them preserve their freedom and build up their countries and that's what we did."

INTRODUCTION

world's production of energy and raw materials. The following responses were made to a number of questions asked in connection with this level of consumption:

Seventy-four percent said this uses up our own natural resources and those of others abroad.

Seventy-four percent said this makes products and raw materials scarce, thereby driving prices up.

By 50 to 31 percent, most thought that, sooner or later, this will turn the rest of the world's people against us.

By 55 to 30 percent, most believed that this hurts the well-being of the world.

By 61 percent to 23 percent, almost a three-to-one majority, most felt that this is "morally wrong."

In this same survey, more than two people out of three admitted that they themselves are "highly wasteful." Ninety percent thought that "we are going to have to find ways to cut back on the amount of things we consume and waste."

■ **Do Americans resist change, wanting to maintain the status quo and preserve what they have?**

Historically, experimentation and change have been hallmarks of American society. Yet, in every era, opponents have preached that change would lead to destruction of our social system. Henry Steele Commager has noted this characteristic in his essay, "The Tradition of Change and Reform":

"Americans themselves fail to realize how deeply ingrained is their habit of change and reform, but foreign observers have not failed to note this from the very beginning. Few Americans suppose their station in life fixed by the accident of birth or of education or training. They shift cheerfully from job to job, from profession to profession, from country to city, from State to State. Sons of farmers go into business; businessmen try their hand at farming; lawyers become company directors, teachers

A POSITIVE GUIDE TO THE FUTURE

turn to law. Nothing seems fixed, nothing but the habit of experiment and of change. Democracy—as de Tocqueville pointed out—made for change, for in a democracy no one took his place in society or economy as unalterably fixed, but everyone felt he could change to any work in any place at any time he pleases. In democracy, every road was clear, every door was open, and there was nothing to prevent anyone from trying them all....

"Few Americans regard the age of an institution or of a practice as, in itself, a virtue. Where in England, for example, the fact that something has always been done a certain way is sufficient reason why it should continue to be done that way, such a consideration is in America rather a challenge than a conclusion.

"Americans have not, then, in the past been afraid of change, and they have customarily regarded reform as a part of the natural, almost of the cosmic order. Certainly, they have customarily regarded with equanimity changes that enlarged the scope of democracy, either in the political or in the social and economic realms. To be sure...there have always been some who were alarmed or startled, or outraged when upstarts pushed their way into areas heretofore reserved for gentlemen, but these have never been numerous enough or powerful enough to stem for any length of time the tide of change and reform."

America's Capacity for Change in the Future

The issue is not whether the forces of conservation or the forces of change will triumph. It is rather what *should* be conserved and what should be changed.

No one group of individuals, however dedicated and well informed, has a corner on wisdom regarding the future. Much of the initiative for defining and creating the future we want must come from average people who acknowledge their responsibility.

Experts and institutions are incapable of being the sole source of initiative for shaping our future. Both experts and institutions will play a role. But that role should be one that facilitates the informed choice, diversity, resiliency, and adaptability of ordinary people.

Here are five objectives toward that end which I think are important and worth working for:

■ **Ensure that public and private institutions provide us complete and accurate information about choices that may affect our lives.**

One of the fundamental tenets of democracy is that citizens have a right to participate in decisions affecting their lives. Such participation requires, however, that sufficient information be made available about major public problems, options under consideration, current programs and policies, and anticipated consequences of present trends, policies, and programs. Elected leaders, candidates for political office, educators, and those who shape the content of the communications media must assume a particular responsibility in this regard.

As citizens, we must demand that those who make public policy and those who provide information communicate clearly, completely, and candidly on the issues. Our political institutions are far more open, accountable, and responsive today than they were fifty years ago. Further progress is possible and essential.

■ **Provide greater opportunity for informed participation in our political processes and institutions.**

In a nation with a large, geographically dispersed population, many decisions must be delegated to elected leaders rather than being decided by referenda. But an educated, informed populace, linked together by an increasingly responsive network of instantaneous electronic communication, can play a greater role in shaping the broad policies for which, ultimately, it must bear the consequences.

In the area of fiscal policy, for example, local referenda on taxes, especially in the area of education, are an established tradition. It is unfortunate that, at present, local educational programs often become a lightning rod for popular dissatisfaction with the growing burden of taxes. Communities that turn down school tax levies are not necessarily voting against expanding or improving education. Rather, they are registering a protest by cutting back on the only tax they can directly control.

The results of referenda such as "Proposition 13" have been, in my view, generally beneficial, and have demonstrated that local voters are capable of exercising informed choices on broad fiscal issues. It has not proved true, as had been predicted, that the electorate would always vote for lower taxes or stricter budget ceilings.

Broad issues in energy policy could also, I feel, be subject to referenda. I see no reason, for example, why the public should not play a larger role in determining whether taxes in combination with the price mechanism or, alternatively, government-administered rationing, should be used to conserve gasoline in time of emergency.

I am familiar, of course, with the arguments against more direct public involvement in the policy-making process. They were used to oppose the direct election of Senators and the President, and the extension of the franchise to non-property-owners, blacks, and women.

But I believe that each step towards greater public participation in governance has made our political institutions more responsive and resilient. During a period when public skepticism and alienation have been growing, there is a need for creative action to encourage broader citizen control and involvement. That is, after all, what democracy is about.

■ **Decentralize government programs, giving greater authority to regional, state, and local contexts.**

Increased public participation and increased decentralization of programs go hand in hand. Obviously, the exercise of power in the state and local context is no panacea. Local abuses and incompetence were in part responsible for the historical trend towards centralization in the first place. But the pendulum may have swung too far. The eloquent arguments for decentralization presented by David Lilienthal in 1949 merit serious consideration today, perhaps even more than then.

MAKING IT HAPPEN:

The Crisis of Centralization

By David Lilienthal (1949)

Democracy and Centralization: Democracy to be truly responsive to our aspirations for individual freedom, must increasingly develop and nourish and strengthen local institutions of government. Few precepts of American life are more deeply felt than this.

In actual practice, however, this policy has given way to its very opposite: an unbroken, and to me disquieting, increasing centralization in Washington....

The argument from complex interrelationship to centralization: Over and over again the story is repeated of the complex interrelation, the intricacies, the interdependence of American life. The comprehension of the ordinary citizen, is of a fabric no longer separable, and hence, national in its every aspect. What happens in Sacramento, California affects a transaction in Portland, Maine, and so on. The thesis is too familiar to require repetition.

Generally speaking this is all true enough, but the conclusion that is drawn from this familiar picture is that since virtually every government problem has become a national problem, therefore every phase of government action must inevitably be administered nationally from Washington.

The inevitability of Big Government: Since—so the argument runs—local administration or state administration is obviously impossible where national interrelation is so complete, therefore Big Government is inevitable.

We are told, in short, that Big Government is the price that must be paid for the wonderful technical development of this nation.

...For a long time, all of us—administrators, citizens, and legislators—have been none too clear on this point. We have assumed that, as new powers were granted to the Government with its seat in Washington, these powers must also be administered from Washington.

We have taken it for granted that the price of Federal action was a top-heavy, cumbersome administration.

Clearly this is not true. The problem is to divorce the two ideas of authority and administration of authority. Effective techniques of decentralization, not better ways to centralize, should claim our first attention.

A hazard to democracy: ...Over-centralized administration is not something simply to be made more palatable, more efficient, and better managed. It is a hazard to democracy. It is a hazard to freedom.

Centralization at the national level or in a business undertaking always glorifies the importance of pieces of paper. This dims the sense of reality. As men and organizations acquire a preoccupation with papers, they become less understanding, less perceptive of the reality of those matters with which they should be dealing: particular human problems, particular human beings, actual things in a real America—highways, wheat, barges, drought, floods, backyards, blast furnaces.

The facts of centralized institutional life: The facts with which a highly centralized institution deals tend to be the men and women of that institution itself and their ideas and ambitions. To maintain perspective and human understanding in the atmosphere of centralization is a task that many able and conscientious people have found well-nigh impossible.

Those who believe devoutly in the democratic process should be the first to urge the use of methods that will keep that administration of national functions from becoming so concentrated at the national capital, so distant from the everyday life of ordinary people, as to wither and deaden the average citizen's sense of participation and partnership in government affairs. For it is this citizen participation that nourishes the strength of a democracy.

INTRODUCTION

■ **Develop a more effective foresight capability:** Futures research and the use of computer models for long-term projections of national or global trends are relatively new ideas.

But the idea that the federal government should plan ahead is not. As early as 1911, President Theodore Roosevelt pointed out to the country that "one distinguishing characteristic of civilized men is foresight...The reward of foresight for this nation is great and easily foretold," he emphasized, "but there must be the look ahead, there must be a realization of the fact that to waste, to destroy our natural resources, to skin and exhaust the land instead of using it so as to increase its usefulness, will result in undermining in the days of our children the very prosperity which we ought by right to hand down to them amplified and developed."

With more effective mechanisms for long-range analysis and planning, the President, federal and local officials, legislators, and the American people would be better able to:
■ anticipate the long-term consequences and interactions of present trends;
■ foresee the long-term results of present policies;
■ compare the possible long-term consequences of other policy options; and
■ identify alternative courses of action and potential opportunities while there is still sufficient lead-time to take advantage of them.

Today, we are living with the consequences of our failure to develop and implement foresighted public policies in the areas of energy, transportation, and urban development. Equally important issues loom on the horizon.

To be effective, a program to improve our national foresight must:
■ involve the public in the process and inform them of the results which emerge (in the state of Minnesota this is being done right now);
■ approach the task with humility, recognizing that we can never have precise knowledge about the future, but can learn more than we know now;

INTRODUCTION

- be flexible, adaptable, and responsive to changing needs; and
- be open to experiment, with a willingness to take risks, and to learn from our mistakes.

The Global 2000 Report to the President: In May 1977 President Carter initiated a study of "probable changes in the world's population, natural resources, and environment through the end of the century." The study—called *The Global 2000 Report to the President: Entering the Twenty-First Century*—also explored the capabilities of federal government to make projections and engage in effective longer-term planning.

The Global 2000 Report was completed in July 1980. The study confirmed the findings of several previous research efforts by stressing the dangers of continuing present trends and present policies in the areas of population, resources, and environment.

Current lack of comprehensive, integrated, foresight capability: But even more important, *The Global 2000 Report* concluded that "...the executive agencies of the U.S. Government are not now capable of presenting the President with internally consistent projections of world trends in population, resources and the environment in the next two decades," and noted that "important decisions—involving billion-dollar federal programs and even the national security" are being made today at least partially on the basis of our present, seriously deficient capabilities.

- **Develop a national security policy oriented toward human survival, founded on domestic strength, and tempered by informed public discussion:** Serious questions have been raised about our present military and national security policies and how they

are made. Many are coming to believe that the concept of national security must encompass far more than military policy.

In defining national security policy, comprehensive social, economic, and political factors are equally as important to consider. Ours is an age in which threats to the security and well-being of the American people may be posed by uncontrolled growth of populations, competition for fossil fuels and other nonrenewable resources, transnational impacts upon the natural environment, and thwarted aspirations to economic and social development. These threats to the American people may, in fact, be far more serious than another new strategic weapon in the arsenal of an adversary.

The Bottom Line:

Building on Our Strengths

To build the future we want, we must recognize and build upon our strengths. We can best do that by:

- insisting on access to better information about policy choices that will affect our lives;
- demanding expanding opportunities for expressing our preferences through referenda;
- supporting decentralization of government programs to regional, state, and local settings;
- encouraging and supporting the development of a more effective national foresight capability; and
- insisting on a broadened concept of what constitutes American national security.

These proposals reflect a belief that the most important next step for our nation, and for humankind, is to improve the processes by which rational choices can be made—rather than to adopt one or another policy at a particular moment.

Continuing the American experiment: The American system is an experiment. It is a set of principles put into practice by a nation of fallible human beings. Up to this point, the experiment has worked well enough to deserve preservation as an option for a humanity that faces an increasingly puzzling, rapidly changing, and essentially unpredictable future.

To ensure that this experiment continues, we must be very clear about which elements are of fundamental importance, and which are not.

No social experiment—and certainly not ours—is free of risk. But an open society based on principles of liberty, equity, and compassion in which individuals participate in decisions affecting their own lives has greater safeguards and more flexibility that other "experiments" currently in progress.

Making it better: Americans recognize that our society is far from perfect at home and leaves much to be desired in our relations with the rest of the world. But many of our shortcomings can be traced to losing sight of what, fundamentally, we are all about.

We have the option, the opportunity, the power, and the responsibility to make things better. A very important part of this process is thinking clearly about what "better" means.

Each of us will probably define the future we want a little bit differently. The right to do that is also part of the American experiment. So is the right to do nothing, if that is our choice.

I wouldn't want it any other way.

JMR □

This Will Make You Feel Better

If you sometimes
get discouraged,
consider this fellow:
He dropped out
of grade school.
Ran a country store.
Went broke.
Took 15 years
to pay off
his bills.
Took a wife.
Unhappy marriage.
Ran for House.
Lost twice.
Ran for Senate.
Lost twice.
Delivered speech
that became
a classic.
Audience indifferent.
Attacked daily
by the press
and despised
by half the country.
Despite all this,
imagine
how many people
all over the world
have been
inspired
by this awkward,
rumpled,
brooding man
who signed his name
simply,
A. Lincoln.

How we perform as individuals will determine
how we perform as a nation. FREE: If you would like
an 8½"×11" reprint of this message, write to
Harry J. Gray, Chairman and Chief Executive Officer,
United Technologies, Box 360, Hartford, CT 06141

I wonder what combination of chance and intention has brought me to this point in my life. In *Making It Happen* I am involved in telling readers that they can create their own future; who then can I say created the future which has become my past? Was I ever in control of events? Or was I simply the instrument of a plan which I cannot understand?... or, possibly, the product of random events with no real purpose? Most of the time, I believe that I am the master of my fate. But sometimes in reflective moments I wonder.

I was engaged for two years to a lovely, gentle, and rather conventional woman. With her, I might have led an ordered, structured, and conventional life. Instead, a very different sort of wife compelled me to confront and alter the male-oriented partriarchial world view I had assumed was "normal." I had to seek answers to questions I had never thought to ask.

As an undergraduate, I trained to be—and wanted to be—a medieval historian. In graduate school for lack of a congenial faculty advisor I embarked on a path which led, almost accidentally, to faculty appointments in political science, engineering, and management. Now, I teach international affairs.

I was such a poor student in mathematics that I took only one course in college. When I attempted calculus as a graduate student I got a "D." Later I found myself writing about mathematical automata theory, directing computer laboratories and building large computer simulation models of global and environmental problems.

I hated business; that's why I chose the academic life. But I spent five years helping to run a garment shop and two years living above it. Now our home is Windy Meadows Pottery; the dining room is frequently an office; its products—in various stages of completion—are spread throughout the house as well as the small production center which adjoins it. I run seminars for businessmen, consult with businessmen and am in business myself.

As a child, I detested the weekly chore of cutting nearly two acres of lawn which surrounded our home. I vowed to live in an apartment, but I don't. Instead, I must cut fifteen acres, with a John Deere tractor. (I don't do it every week.)

I chose not to become an attorney like my father because I thought the "pressure" would be too great. Now my work weeks are typically far longer and more pressured than his ever were. When the pressure begins to let up, I find myself seeking more.

John Richardson with USACOR member, Darnell Whitt.

So the principles I say I believe in are not always reflected in my personal life. While advocating sustainability, I keep nine horses and commute by car sixty-five miles— each way—to work. I collaborated on an energy conservation report for a Presidential Commission in 1972, but have yet to caulk the windows or insulate the attic of my home. (Not infrequently, my family calls attention to this inconsistency.) I belong to the Religious Society of Friends but spend most Sundays working or going to horse shows. I wish there was more time to do things I really want to do, but, sometimes, I waste the time I have.

This March, I was forty-three—at a midpoint—and I wonder whether the next twenty years of my life will be as diverse as the last twenty. In general, I am happy to be where I am and would not choose to live any of my life over. Lately, I have been taking my work more seriously, because I really believe it could make a difference, but myself less seriously. My recent work has been more concerned with people and I have started to write poetry. I had never done anything like that before. I am firmly convinced that I can shape the future with my intentions and actions, but don't have the faintest idea what the future will actually turn out to be. Probably this parodox should bother me, but it doesn't seem to.

Creating and producing *Making It Happen* in its various incarnations has occupied much of my time for nearly three years. It has been my way of creating the future. Although the book advocates planning, I have not really planned what I will be doing next year or five years from now. (I have planned what I will be doing ten years from now.) I am more curious than concerned. I am optimistic about the future because I believe that Americans are natural futurists and that I am one of them.

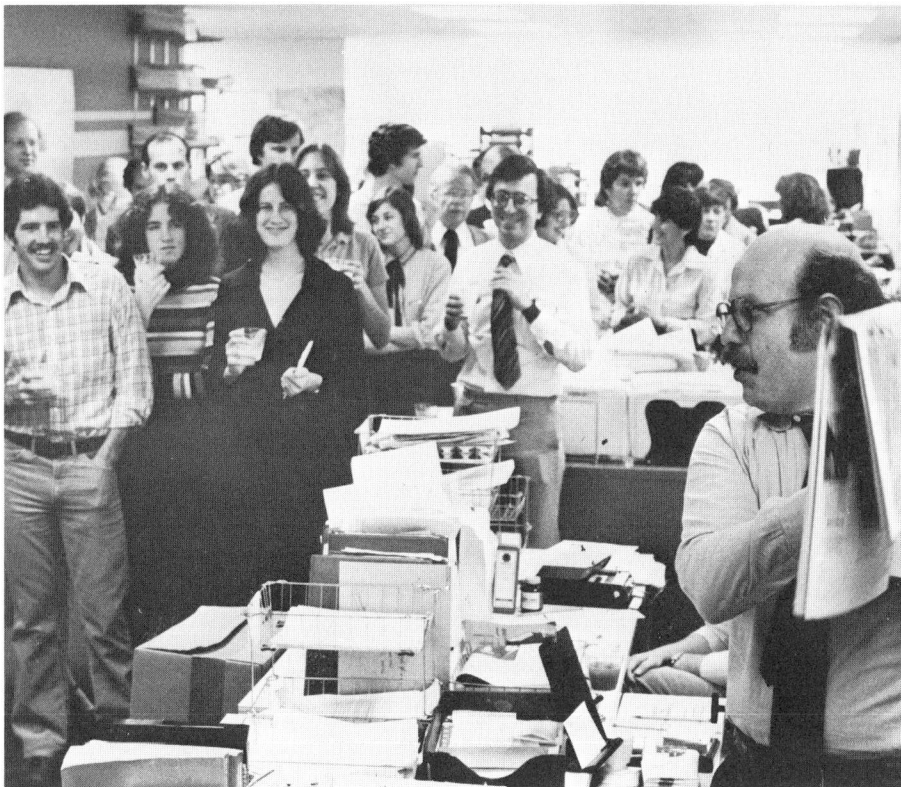

Fred Wertheimer during Common Cause staff meeting.

The Case of Common Cause

Among the organizations committed to applying and revitalizing the fundamentals of American democracy, none has been more visible and effective in achieving its goals than Common Cause.

Here are some of the achievements to which the organization has contributed:

■ Ending the Vietnam war by successfully lobbying for the first "stop the war" resolution ever to pass the House of Representatives.

■ Bringing new openness and accountability to national government by lobbying successfully for an end to the seniority system and for "sunshine laws" to publicize government activities and prevent conflict of interest.

■ Promoting legislation for the public financing of Presidential campaigns.

■ Promoting numerous reforms in state government.

In 1980 Common Cause, which has now grown to a membership of more than 250,000 with an annual budget of $5.3 million, celebrated its 10th

anniversary. A publication, *1970-1980: A Decade of Citizen Action in Common Cause,* described the achievements of the organization, the people who had made those achievements possible, and goals for the future. Some brief excerpts follow.

The Call to Revitalize Our Institutions

"Dear Friend,

"I would like to ask you to join me in forming a new, independent non-partisan organization to help in rebuilding the nation. It will be known as Common Cause...a citizen's lobby concerned not with the advancement of special interests but with the well being of the nation.... There is great urgency in ending the Vietnam war.... national

priorities must be changed.... The solutions are not mysterious.... But there has been no active, powerful, hard-hitting constituency to fight for such steps. We can provide that...."

So began John Gardner's letter seeking members for a fledgling Common Cause. It was August, 1970. The war in Vietnam dragged on. Congress did nothing to stop it. Our institutions seemed to be failing us. Most of us felt powerless to do anything about it.

But Gardner's letter contained a message of hope. If only we would focus our anger and work together, he seemed to think we could not only end the war, but could make our government more responsive and begin to solve the myriad problems facing the nation.

"We have not behaved like a great people," Gardner said. "We have not lived by the values we profess to honor. America is not the nation it set out to be. And we will never get back on course until we take some tough, realistic steps to revitalize our institutions...."

It was somehow very American: Here were problems, and it was up to us to try to solve them. There were "highly practical steps" we could learn to take. "Common Cause will keep you up-to-date," the letter said. "We want phones to ring in Washington and state capitols.... We want people watching and influencing every move that government makes...."

Skeptics laughed. Cynics said "You can't change politics and government." Columnists heaped scorn: "A sonorous organization of benignly flaccid liberal goodwill"; "a by-product of cosmetic liberalism...."

But thousands of us thought otherwise—student, schoolteacher, farmer, homemaker, government worker, executive....

Why Do We Respond?

Getting Involved

Susan Rennels of Farmington Hills, Michigan, describes herself in 1972 as "a 27-year old housewife and mother going to school part-time. Common Cause was my first effort in politics." Rennels "learned to do things I didn't know I could do," and ended up leading Common Cause/Michigan's protracted battle to pass open government laws. Now an assistant bank manager, Rennels has turned her energies to Democratic politics and passage of the equal rights amendment. Her "greatest joy," she says, "is to narrow the chasm between people who are elected and the people who elect them. Even if it's Joe next door, the minute somebody gets elected, there's this chasm. It makes a difference when you can actually get people to sit down in a living room and discuss the pros and cons." Of the laws she helped pass, Rennels says, "they've made an enormous difference."

Hugh Spitzer, a biochemist at the University of Alabama Medical School, played a key role in the successful 1973 fight to get an "ethics" law passed in Alabama. Now with the Consumer Product Safety Commission in Washington, Spitzer says he was attracted to Common Cause "because it's about working within the system. A lot of people at the time wanted to tear it all down and start at square one. I never believed in that." The ethics law Spitzer helped pass is referred to in Alabama as "a landmark." Has it had an effect? Spitzer says, "The legislature tried for three years to get rid of the law... there are now legislators serving time."

Reshaping the Machinery of Self-Government

The 1980s can be made a time of renewing our sense of common purpose, reviving our self-confidence, and rekindling the sense of individual personal responsibility for the common enterprise.

Making government work better is just as practical a problem as repairing and redesigning any other machinery— a little harder because governmental institutions and processes involve people instead of material, but just as practical because the way in which the machinery and processes are designed and operate determines the products which come out.

Our problem in the 1980s is plain. The governmental institutions and processes which worked in a simpler day are not good enough for our big government and complex society.

The challenge is to reshape the machinery of self-government so that the long-run progress of the whole enterprise is the center of attention, so that every citizen knows that his or her participation counts, so that decisions are taken, hard choices are made, and problems are solved.

Why Do They Do It?

Craig Barnes, a Denver attorney, pioneered Common Cause "open government" reforms at the state level with efforts in 1972 to enact "sunshine" laws in Colorado. Several years later he invented the concept of "sunset" laws to control bureaucracy and overregulation. "I'd just gone through a fight for a jeep driver who wanted to start a tour service of the Rockies," says Barnes. "To get a license he had to hire a lawyer. It cost him $4,000 and he lost. I was so upset by the process of keeping a kid from going into business on his own that I was fuming. I thought the whole regulatory process was out of whack. I came to think that what we ought to do is cause to be re-enacted every six or seven years the enabling legislation that created those regulations in the first place. I kind of thought the word 'sunset' would hang together with 'sunshine.'" It did, and Colorado became the first of 35 states to enact a sunset law. Barnes' current political effort: conservation.

Nancy Becker, a Trenton, New Jersey housewife and mother, had the direction of her life changed in the early 1970's. She volunteered to work on the Common Cause national campaign finance project and ended up at the center of Common Cause in New Jersey in its battles to pass "sunshine" and campaign finance laws. Becker, who now earns a living as an independent lobbyist, says, "I laugh about it now, but I had never been to the State House in my life before I got involved with Common Cause." Of the laws she helped bring to New Jersey, Becker says: "The way the legislature operates is completely different now. Information has become as important as influence, and the issues are discussed...And at the local level, zoning and school boards have to meet in the open now. That makes a difference."

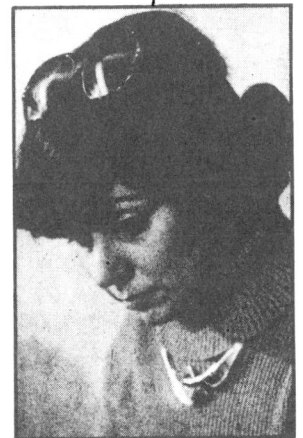

Needed: The Tonic of Social Invention

Note the enormous importance that Adams, Jefferson and their contemporaries devoted to how government works. They were practical politicans. They knew that institutions, procedures, and processes determine results. We should not forget the lesson.

ARCHIBALD COX, Chairman, *Common Cause*

We need the tonic of invention. We need to experiment with new approaches of public participation. We need to give our public servants a chance to become creative listeners.

Countless public officials share the view that, as servants of the people, their work should more clearly represent the expressed will of the people. They want and need to feel that they are implementing policies which come out of widely shared goals.

We will not solve our major problems until we find new ways to make public policy. We must exchange the narrow and hidden influence of the special interests for the broad and open expression of the public will, gained through new means of citizen involvement.

DAVID COHEN, President, *Common Cause*

"You're not alone"

"I could never be happy just being preoccupied with myself and my wants. I've got to be working for something bigger. That's what Common Cause does for me. It binds me to a lot of my fellow Americans all over the country, all working for some American ideas we care about. What is that phrase? 'You're not alone!' That's how I feel.

"It may sound pretentious but I feel some kind of connection with all the Americans of earlier days who tried to make this a better country. And it links me to following generations of Americans who will be working on the same thing. I'm proud to be a part of that.

"I don't think I'm being noble or anything like that. It's the kind of goal that keeps me in touch with my best self, and makes me feel good. It lifts me above the hard, tiring things of life that we all have to do-and I don't mind doing them—but I also like something that raises my vision.

"And it's exciting! When I think of the changes Common Cause has brought about. And maybe I helped a little.

"I'll tell you the truth. I feel as though Common Cause connects me with my country. I get real personal satisfaction in having an impact, however small, in matters crucial to my country. I was in Washington last year and saw the Lincoln Memorial and climbed the Washington Monument. I was thinking, 'I'm part of all this—Washington, Jefferson, Lincoln—I'm working on the things they would want me to be working on.'

"The problems seem awfully hard to solve. What we're really trying to do is make this country work. But maybe the problems have always been tough. I don't think Americans are afraid of tough problems if they can figure out a way to tackle them—and that's what Common Cause has supplied."

Common Cause member in California

David L. Ames

MAKING IT HAPPEN:

David L. Ames

Values:

What Do We Want?

Here you will find some personal statements and questions about goals and values. I've included them to provide a variety of examples of how people think about their own lives and the society in which they live. The purpose is not to persuade you to adopt a particular set of individual and social values. Americans prize, above all, the right to do that for themselves.

We often resist of thinking about what we really want, and instead lower our expectations to the level of what we think we can get. We then convince ourselves and others that what we really want is impossible. We're afraid that if we continue to think and talk about what we really want, we'll be considered naive and foolish. Our lowered expectations often become self-fulfilling.

Those who are specialists in time management and human potential have come to believe that the first step in getting what we really want is to identify and acknowledge it very clearly. It isn't easy to be really clear about the kind of life you would like to lead and the kind of society you would like to live in. If your experience in thinking this through is anything like mine, you may find it a bit frightening. But it will be a very important first step in the process of envisioning your future and making it happen. You will find here several exercises that may help you get started.

VALUES

Commentary

Donella Meadows is one of a small number of scientists who attempt to study the future by using computer simulation models. The popular book that she co-authored in 1972, *The Limits to Growth,* received wide attention and was instrumental in calling attention to the field of "global modeling," and to The Club of Rome.

No one can be involved in building a major global model and publishing the results of the project without having the experience change his or her life. (If I had not been involved in global modeling, for example, I would not now be working on this book.)

In Dr. Meadows' case, her experience with *The Limits to Growth* and related efforts has led her to think and write with great clarity about the relationship between values and action.

You may not agree with her values and ranking; she and I would be surprised if you did. But you may find her way of approaching the problem interesting and helpful.

This excerpt is taken from an article "The World Food Problem: Growth Models and Non-Growth Solutions," in *Alternatives to Growth,* Vol. 1, edited by her husband and colleague Dennis L. Meadows.

Making Value Sets Explicit

By Donella H. Meadows (1975)

I am not aware of any way of determining a single set of values and priorities that is applicable to all persons at all times. Yet each person readily forms an operational set of priorities that guides his or her choices and decisions.

Discussion of policy alternatives might be enhanced if people could make their value sets explicit, not to argue their relative merits, but to increase understanding of the various viewpoints within society.

What a value set looks like: To start the discussion, my own primary values in order of priority are—

■ **Survival** (of the total social and ecological system);

■ **Material welfare** (up to a level of simple sufficiency, after which this entry goes to the bottom of the list);

■ **Equity** (equal access to other items on this list);

■ **Freedom** (individual self-determination, diversity); and

■ **Efficiency** (maximum output per person-hour).

Thinking about priorities with a value set: Of course, I consider all five of these goals important and worth pursuing.

However, my mental model—my way of thinking about the world—suggests that striving for *efficiency* could undermine all four of the other values, a sacrifice I would not be willing to make.

To me, *individual freedom* would be meaningless without the first three items on this list; I would give up my personal freedom, if necessary, to obtain *survival, material sufficiency, and equity.*

Equity in poverty does not appeal to me, so I would seek *basic material welfare* before *distributional justice.*

Survival is necessary before any of the other values can be enjoyed. I would not tolerate a very high risk to *total social or ecological survival* for any reason, even for one of the other values on the list.

My value set is included here not because it is the best or only defensible one, but because I would like to show what a value set looks like, and because my own policy recommendations depend on it.

Taking Stock—What Do I Really Want Out of Life?

Time management specialist Alan Lakein suggests you begin finding the answer to this question by taking several minutes to answer each of the following questions for yourself: **What are my lifetime goals?**

How would I *like* to spend the next three years?

If I knew now that I would be struck by lightning six months from today, how would I live until then?

If you are like most people, you may never have taken stock of your life in this way, or may not have done so for many years.

After you have thought about this for a while, list on a piece of paper your seven most important personal goals.

These might include job security, a good education for your children, a home of your own, regular vacations, or whatever.

You will note that I have provided a space to do this—and filled in two of the blanks with goals that seem important to everyone, *survival—staying alive* and *good health.*

Often we take these goals for granted unless they are threatened. Then they may take precedence over all others. If they are not high-priority goals for you, feel free to cross them out and insert your own choices.

MAKING IT HAPPEN:

Some of the policy-relevant conclusions that seem consistent with my value priorities are:

■ **The long-term survival of human society, and the stability of the natural system upon which human society depends, should be the highest goal of any policy.**

Therefore, risks to the total system should be minimized, including implicit dependence on as-yet unproven technologies.

■ **Since survival has the top priority, the costs of social change are more tolerable than the risk of physical destruction of resources or physical destruction of environmental integrity.**

It is far better to develop new social norms and institutions consistent with zero growth than to risk the ecological damage that could result from desperate physical measures to sustain growth.

■ **Short-term sacrifices, especially material sacrifices, to preserve long-term stability are justified.**

In accordance with the goal of *equity*, sacrifices for the future should be borne disproportionately by the privileged of today.

■ **The quality of human life is more important than the quantity; and *material sufficiency* is more important to quality of life than is the *freedom to have more than two children.***

Therefore, the right to *sustenance* has a higher priority than the right to *reproductive freedom.*

■ **Several important aspects of quality of life cannot be measured in strictly economic terms.**

Therefore, decisions should be made on a broader basis than simple economic cost-benefit analysis.

■ **Industrialization is a means to one end that can improve the quality of life, namely *material welfare.***

It may not be the only means to that end, and it is not an end in itself.

■ **In the interests of preserving *individual freedom and diversity,* intervention by centralized government should be minimal.**

Intervention is justified only to preserve the three values prior to *freedom—survival, basic material welfare, and equity.* □

National Aeronautics and Space Administration

Launching of space shuttle, Columbia, from Kennedy Space Center, Florida.

Priority	My Most Important Personal Goals
A. _____	(Survival—Staying Alive) _____
B. _____	_____
C. _____	_____
D. _____	(Good Health) _____
E. _____	_____
F. _____	_____
G. _____	_____

Next, in the spaces to the left of your goals, try to rank them roughly in order of priority. You could do this by trying to rank them from top to bottom—or by assigning A to the most important goal, B to those goals that are less important, and C to those that are least important to you.

Conscience of a Conservative

By Senator Barry Goldwater (1960)

Many Americans would probably disagree with Donella Meadows' ranking of "freedom" as fourth in her list of priorities. Patrick Henry's famous statement "Give me liberty or give me death," placing freedom above survival, is an important part of our heritage.

One of the most influential and eloquent contemporary advocates of this point of view has been Senator Barry Goldwater of Arizona. When I first began thinking about questions of values in action, Senator Goldwater's views were among those that influenced me most. On some points, his views differ sharply from those of Meadows. There are also some surprising similarities.

This excerpt is taken from Chapter One of Senator Goldwater's book, *The Conscience of a Conservative* (1960)

Conservatives and Liberals: The root difference between the Conservatives and the Liberals of today is that Conservatives take account of the *whole* man, while the Liberals tend to look only at the material side of man's nature.

The Conservative believes that man is in part an economic—an animal—creature; but that he is also a spiritual creature with spiritual needs and spiritual desires. What is more, these needs and desires reflect the *superior* side of man's nature and thus take precedence over his economic wants.

Conservatism therefore looks upon the enhancement of man's spiritual nature as the primary concern of political philosophy.

Liberals, on the other hand—in the name of a concern for "human beings"—regard the satisfaction of economic wants as the dominant mission of society.

They are, moreover, in a hurry. So their characteristic approach is to harness the society's political and economic forces into a collective effort to *compel* "progress." In this approach, I believe, they fight against nature.

Surely, the first obligation of a political thinker is to understand the nature of man. The Conservative does not claim special powers of perception on this point, but he does claim a familiarity with the accumulated wisdom and experience of history, and he is not too proud to learn from the great minds of the past.

The Conservative understanding of man: The first thing he has learned about man is that each member of the species is a unique creature. Man's most sacred possession is his individual soul—which has an immortal side, but also a mortal one. The mortal side establishes his absolute differentness from every other human being. *Only a philosophy that takes into account the essential differences between men, and, accordingly, makes provision for developing the different potentialities of each man can claim to be in accord with Nature.*

We have heard much in our time about "the common man." It is a concept that pays little attention to the history of a nation that grew great through the initiative and ambition of uncommon men. The Conservative knows that to regard man as part of an undifferentiated mass is to consign him to ultimate slavery.

Taking Stock—
What Kind of Society Would I Like to Live in?

Now think for a few minutes about the kind of society you would like to live in. And remember—write down what you really want, not what you think you can get.

In the space below, list the social goals which, if attained, could bring that society about. Examples of such goals might be "equal opportunity for all to life, liberty and the pursuit of happiness," "preservation of the capitalist free-enterprise system," "survival of the human race," "a job for everyone who wants to work," and so on.

Again, try to rank these goals in rough order of priority.

Priority	My Most Important Social Goals
A. _____	_____
B. _____	_____
C. _____	_____
D. _____	_____
E. _____	_____
F. _____	_____
G. _____	_____

MAKING IT HAPPEN:

Second, the Conservative has learned that the economic and spiritual aspects of man's nature are inextricably intertwined. He cannot be economically free, or even economically efficient, if he is enslaved politically; conversely, man's political freedom is illusory if he is dependent for his economic needs on the State.

The Conservative realizes, thirdly, that man's development, in both its spiritual and material aspects, is not something that can be directed by outside forces. Every man, for his individual good and for the good of his society, is responsible for his *own* development. The choices that govern his life are choices that he must make; they cannot be made by any other human being, or by a collection of human beings.

If the Conservative is less anxious than his Liberal brethren to increase Social Security "benefits," it is because he is more anxious than his Liberal brethren that people be free throughout their lives to spend their earnings when and as they see fit.

The dignity of the individual human being: So it is that Conservatism, throughout history, has regarded man neither as a potential pawn of other men, nor as a part of a general collectivity in which the sacredness and the separate identity of individual human beings are ignored.... The conscience of the Conservative is pricked by *anyone* who would debase the dignity of the individual human being. Today, therefore, he is at odds with dictators who rule by terror, and equally with those gentler collectivists who ask our permission to play God with the human race.

With this view of the nature of man, it is understandable that the Conservative looks upon politics as the art of achieving the maximum amount of freedom for individuals that is consistent with the maintenance of the social order.

Freedom requires order. The Conservative is the first to understand that the practice of freedom requires the establishment of order; it is impossible for one man to be free if another is able to deny him the exercise of his freedom.

But the Conservative also recognizes that the political power on which order is based is a self-aggrandizing force; that its appetite grows with eating. He knows that the utmost vigilance and care are required to keep political power within its proper bounds.

Freedom endangered: In our day, order is pretty well taken care of. The delicate balance that ideally exists between freedom and order has long since tipped against freedom practically everywhere on earth. In some countries, freedom is altogether down and order holds absolute sway. In our country, the trend is less far advanced, but it is well along and gathering momentum every day.

Thus, for the American Conservative, there is no difficulty in identifying the day's overriding political challenge: it is *to preserve and extend freedom.* As he surveys the various attitudes and institutions and laws that currently prevail in America, many questions will occur to him, but the Conservative's first concern will always be: Are we maximizing freedom? □

Taking Stock—
How Do My Personal and Social Goals Fit Together?
"Society" does not exist apart from what we do as individuals. It is the result of what we and others choose to do.

Because of this, it is interesting to think about the relationship between personal and social goals. The following diagram, or matrix, may be helpful for this purpose.

Priority List: Social Goals

1.   2.   3.   4.   5.   6.   7.

What filling in this matrix does is force you to ask yourself about the relationship between your personal and social goals.

It might be interesting to think about whether the achievement of—or progress toward—your personal goals aids, harms, or is irrelevant to your social goals.

You should not be surprised or feel guilty if this exercise turns up some inconsistencies. All of our lives are inconsistent to some degree. The important thing is simply to be as clear as you can about what you want.

Priority List:
Individual Goals

1. _____
2. _____
3. _____
4. _____
5. _____
6. _____
7. _____

VALUES

For members of the Religious Society of Friends (Quakers), statements of ethical principles are often posed in the form of questions that are intended to assist members of the Society in their daily lives.

This particular statement is excerpted from *Faith and Practice of the New England Yearly Meeting of Friends*, adopted in 1950.

Queries of the Religious Society of Friends

■ **Christian Fellowship:** Do you live in Christian love toward one another? Have you a living concern for the welfare of each member even to the sharing of one another's burdens? Do you seek for unity in the Divine Life underlying all differences of opinion and circumstance? Do you manifest a forgiving spirit and care for the reputation of others? When contentions arise, are endeavors made to settle them speedily in a spirit of meekness and love?

■ **Personal Standards of Living:** Do you express in your daily lives the love and brotherhood, the sincerity and simplicity with which Jesus Christ lived and taught? Do you make a place for inward retirement and communion with God, cherishing the Divine Light within, that its power growing in you may rule your lives? Do you keep to moderation in your standards of living and in the conduct of your business, avoiding self-indulgence and display? Do you avoid and discourage betting and gambling and the use of alcoholic beverages and narcotics? Do you choose those recreations which will strengthen your physical, mental, and spiritual life and avoid those that may prove a hindrance to yourself and others? Do you so live that spiritual growth, family life, and interests of the church and public welfare may have their due share of your time and thought?

Young People, Education: Do you encourage and make due provision for the religious development of your children and for their understanding of the principles of our Society? Are you an example to them in loyalty to the Christian ideals you profess? Do you teach them the importance of choosing the best in literature and art; do you encourage them in the choice of wholesome amusements and friendships? Do you help your young people to prepare themselves for assuming their rightful responsiblities in the home, the Meeting, and the community?

■ **Race Relations:** Do you endeavor to reverence personality in every human being regardless of race or creed? Do you encourage efforts to overcome racial prejudice and antagonism and economic, social, and educational discrimination?

■ **War and Peace:** Do you faithfully maintain our testimony against military preparations and all participation in war as inconsistent with the teaching and spirit of Christ? Do you "live in the virtue of that life and power that takes away the occasion of all wars?" Do you seek to take your part in the ministry of reconciliation between individuals, groups, and nations?

■ **The Social Order:** Are you punctual in keeping promises, just in the payment of debts, free from defrauding the public revenue, honorable and truthful in all your dealings? Are you careful to live within your income and to avoid involving yourselves in business beyond your ability to manage? Are you helping to create political, economic, religious, and social institutions which will forward the cause of brotherhood on earth?

Taking Stock—Spending Our Time

Time experts remind us that every person has exactly the same amount of time. Lakein says it well: "The basic resource that each person starts with is his or her lifetime—all the minutes, hours, days, and years that he or she is alive."

An exercise that is helpful in thinking about time management is to look back over how you spent your hours during the past week. Even better, you might find it interesting to keep a log of how you spend your time for a week or so.

Probably you can organize your analysis into a few major categories like working, eating, recreation, sleeping, spending time with your children, religious activities, and so on. A table like the following may be helpful for recording your data.

Activity	Hours / week	% of time
_____	___	___
_____	___	___
_____	___	___
_____	___	___
_____	___	___
_____	___	___
_____	___	___
_____	___	___

"Life is too short..."

Life is too short to ice cakes. Cakes are good without icing.

Life is too short to read all the church periodicals.

Life is too short not to write regularly to your parents.

Life is too short to eat factory-baked bread.

Life is too short to keep all your floors shiny.

It's too short to let a day pass without hugging your spouse and each of your children.

Life is too short to nurse grudges and hurt feelings.

It's too short to worry about getting ready for Christmas. Just let Christmas come.

Life is too short to spend much money on neckties and earrings.

It's too short for questions like, "How do you like your new pastor?" or, if there has been a death, "How's he taking it?"

It's too short to be gone from home more than a few nights a week.

It's too short not to take a nap when you need one.

It's to short to give importance to whether purses match shoes or towels match bathrooms.

It's too short to stay indoors when trees turn color in fall, when it snows, or when the spring blossoms come out.

Life is too short to miss the call to worship on a Sunday morning.

It's too short for bedspreads that are too fancy to sleep under.

Life is too short to work in a room without windows.

Life is too short to put off Bible study.

It's too short to put off improving relationships with the people that we live with.

—Doris Janzen Longacre,
from an unfinished manuscript;
in *Living Simply* (1981)

Making Small Decisions

Oh, not enough flour! I've got to take the car and run to the store. No, I'll walk....I need the exercise...it's only a mile. But I need the flour now. The bread must start rising or it won't be done in time. Look, why am I always in a hurry? I've got to slow down, take more time to think, see the clouds, listen to Ann...and walking saves gasoline, energy. Everybody jumping into a car for simple errands is one reason we get that statistic...what is it...six percent of the world's population uses forty per cent of the resources. That way of living makes other people poor.

But the flour. I need it. Now if the bike were here...but Bill took it to work. The flour! If my neighbor were home, I could borrow it...but she never has whole-grain flour. We want to eat more whole grains.... I've got to take the car. No way out.

Wait. I don't have to make bread today. That can wait until I shop for the week,...there's enough flour here for that good muffin recipe. And, lucky me,...I don't have to start that until five o'clock. Ann and I can take a walk.

When you have completed the first two columns of the table, compute the percentages by dividing the hours spent on each activity by the total number of hours recorded.

As a final step you might want to ask yourself, "What conclusions would an outsider, who didn't know me, draw about my personal goals and their relative priority from looking at the way I allocate my time?"

It might also be interesting to carry out this exercise with a close friend or a member of your family.

The point is not to get agreement or to change one another's minds. But it is worthwhile for us to think about how we can have a society that will accommodate as diverse a range of values as possible.

In addition, we need to ask ourselves how we can be sure that our society will be sustainable; that is, that it will persist for a long time or indefinitely.

One of the important personal goals of many of the contributors to *Making It Happen* is trying to find answers to these questions (and, in some cases, to convince others that certain answers are right). I hope their thinking will be helpful to you in dealing with these questions in your own life.

Commentary

The ethics of most Americans have been strongly influenced by the Judeo-Christian tradition. It seemed appropriate, for this reason, to ask a member of the U.S. Association for The Club of Rome, the Venerable John J. Weaver, to address some of the issues raised in this book from the perspective of religion.

His conclusions should not surprise us. Divine revelation, as embodied in the writings of the Hebrew prophets and the life of Jesus, emphasizes, above all:

> justice,
> love,
> charity,
> equality.

The values and behavior most universally condemned are materialism, acquisitiveness, greed, and exploitation.

Biblical Imperatives

By the Very Rev. John J. Weaver

Revelation is to religion what evolution is to biology. Religious documents are, among other things, records of the history of revelation, for religious documents are generally concerned with the insights we gain from all our relationships.

Such writings grow out of our innermost relationships with a power we call by many names—numinous, the holy, the Other. These writings deal with ethical imperatives about our relationships not only with God but with one another and with life itself. The examples I cite here are drawn from Judeo-Christian doctrine. But similar views may be found in many other religious traditions.

Justice: In the Old Testament, it is clear that God was known to be deeply involved on behalf of justice. God did things to make the world a more just place.

God sent Moses into Egypt where his people were in slavery, and Moses—in what came to be called the Exodus—was to "set my people free."

In Psalm 146, the Lord "sets the prisoner free," "opens the eyes of the blind," "lifts those who are bowed down," "watches over the sojourner (i.e., migrant or landless person)," and "upholds the widow and the fatherless (i.e., the powerless without a protector)."

The message of Jesus echoes these Old Testament concerns about justice. Consider the Sermon on the Mount (Matthew 5-7) and Jesus' first sermon (Luke 4:16 ff.). Jesus' message also expressed great hope about a new age that was bursting in upon the world.

In teaching about God's dominion in this coming kingdom, Jesus frequently compared it to a great feast or banquet to which all are invited and at which all have a place (see Mark 2:19, Luke 14:15-24, Matthew 22:1-13, Matthew 25:1-13, et al.). The great eschatological feast was to be an occasion at which the least favored ("last") would be favored ("first") (see also Luke 14:17-21).

In the Matthew 25 account of the final judgment day, the rich, the secure, the well-entrenched, and the powerful are condemned to eternal punishment, while Jesus directs the hungry and thirsty and naked and sick and those in prison to enter into God's kingdom.

David L. Ames

MAKING IT HAPPEN:

How should injustice be set right?

In Proverbs 22, an ethic of charity is urged: "The godly man shares his bounty." But the message of the prophets in the Old Testament in the 8th century B.C. was more far-reaching. Their main ethical principle was the redistribution of wealth. Amos inveighed against those who "trample the needy" and "bring the poor of the land to an end" and "buy the poor for silver and the needy for a pair of shoes" (Amos 2:6-7). Isaiah proclaimed that the fast or abstinence that God prefers is not a matter of simple ritual but a call to "loose the bonds of wickedness," "undo the thongs of the yoke," "let the oppressed go free," and "share your bread with the hungry, and bring the homeless poor into the house" (Isaiah 58:6-7). A year of massive redistribution every fifty years—a Jubilee Year—is proclaimed in Leviticus 25.

Equality: Equality and a kind of voluntary communalism in which all property was held in common characterized the early Christian church. The Apostle Paul extended charity beyond gifts to achieve equality. Writing to Corinth, he said "As a matter of *equality,* your abundance at the present time should supply their lack, so that their abundance may supply your lack, that there may be equality" (2 Corinthians 8:14).

For centuries justice, equality, and hope have been ethical imperatives woven in and through the fabric of societies. At certain times, the ethical teachings, moral imperatives, and religious hopes of prophets, shamans, and religious leaders have been—in part—enacted into law. The income tax, social security, old-age pensions, and food stamps are examples close to home that come immediately to mind. The dynamic for this was in part Jewish-Christian *prolepsis,* or anticipation of a future reality in a concrete pre-actualization of it.

Neighbors: The traditional ethical imperative of Jesus was that we should not only seek justice but "love our neighbor." **The ecological imperative reminds us anew who our neighbors are. Ecology tells me that my neighbor is the life that touches my life or comes close to my life. The trees have life. Grass has**

Who am I? John J. Weaver

I'm a carpenter's son and the father of five daughters, all of whom live within one hundred miles of my home. Two daughters are dance therapists, one is about to become a registered nurse, the fourth is at the University of California at Davis studying nutrition, and the fifth is in high school.

When I retired as Archdeacon and Ombudsman of the Episcopal Diocese of California, I became Chaplain of the Burlingame Police Department. Some say it was a shotgun marriage—a liberal priest and the Burlingame Police. For years I had called at jails and prisons, but now I ride patrol twelve hours each week.

On my second swing-shift ride, I was in a shoot-out: one armed robber was killed not twenty feet from me and the other escaped. Within forty-eight hours I realized that to get into a police car is to take your life in your hands. Police officers see the seamy, tragic, violent side of life.

I've been in the priesthood over forty years, in the U.S. Army over four years (during World War 2), and have been at the bedside of many a dying person, but on the streets you see death close at hand. If you ride with police officers, you live where the rubber hits the road; you witness stroke victims not after they have been washed and clothed in white gowns, but when it happens; you are involved in family fights not two days after the event, but when neighbors and relatives call for help because they're afraid someone will be killed. Nearly twenty-five percent of all police officers who are killed on duty, die at the scene of family quarrels.

And so I carry on my nurturing ministry in homes, city streets, and parks. All this, I presume, is a symbol of the world. The earth has been dealt body blows by men who rape the forest and land; nature is having a stroke because of poisons injected into the air streams and arteries of Mother Earth. Poverty is rampant because greed comes ahead of need. The whole of creation groans and travails awaiting the manifestation of the Son of God.

While trying to prevent violence, curb terrorism, and improve the lot of humankind locally, I pray galactically and work with The Club of Rome globally. I see an actualization of this creative energy all over the world. I'm nearly seventy years of age and I'm thrilled to be involved in the symbiotic relationship between law and order and feeding the poor, clothing the naked, housing the unfortunate, and providing medical care—and hope—for all humankind. □

life. The flowers have lives. The animals have lives. Even earthworms have lives. So all these are my neighbors. We have mistakenly thought that all nature was made for our use, our "dominion." But it was not.

The overarching ethical imperative today extends the Old Testament and New Testament sense of justice and understanding that we are all of a piece and interdependent—neighbors, a family, or a people. We are that and more. As man and woman, as humans in community and society, we are also part and parcel of nature. We must live symbolically "in" nature, not "above" or "apart" from it. **We are not the rich and the rest of nature somehow the poor.**

We are interdependent populations that share the same community of life. In this community of life, the ethical imperative is to live justly, lift the yoke of oppression, and to love one another in the ways we have been loved and cared for so abundantly.

The ethical imperatives of the Bible are one ready source of guidance in shaping a better future, and in the process we may find that we have shaped a better present.

VALUES

Commentary

Personal Ethics and Personal Power

Fundamental questions of personal ethics can be stated simply:

> What is the right thing to do, and how can I know that it is right?

> How can I do what is right?

And then there is the mirror image of those questions:

> What things are wrong, and how can I know that they are wrong?

> How can I avoid doing what is wrong?

Peter Henriot argues that our ethics are inadequate to cope with the transition to a more humane and sustainable society. The values that dominate our society are:

- **individualistic, not societal;**

- **nationalistic, not global;**

- **partial, not wholistic.**

Henriot is saying that the boundaries within which we make ethical judgements are too narrow. We must broaden our ethical horizons in space and in time.

What we think of as ethical conduct must take into account the power we have to inflict harm on human beings who live far distant from us, and whom we have never seen and perhaps will never see. Also, we must recognize that we have the power to harm our children and our children's children.

> We also have the power to help. And our power to help or harm may be greater than we think.

Thinking about Values:

Are Ethics Adequate?

By Peter Henriot, S.J.

Who am I? Peter Henriot, S.J.

I am a political scientist, Jesuit priest, and resident of Washington, D.C.

Living in inner-city Washington has made me aware that "development" is not simply a problem of other countries, but is a matter of serious human choices for the industrialized countries as well.

Working at the Center of Concern has opened to me national and international contacts that challenge my hopes for a future of peace and justice.

Being in pastoral service to many different people has deepened my faith and strengthened my commitment to make sisterhood and brotherhood a reality.

My professional training (University of Chicago and Harvard, political science; University of California at Berkeley, theology) has been augmented by participation in international conferences sponsored by the United Nations and the church (in Bucharest, Vienna, New York, and Rome) and a year of living in a squatters' barrio in Colombia. In particular, the latter experience keeps the names and faces behind the development debate ever in my mind and heart.

Dialogue about ethics and what to do: It was the summer of 1974, and I was offering testimony before a committee of the House of Representatives on the interrelationships between food and population. I was urging a "social justice approach" to stabilizing population, taking into account the fact that children, for poor people, are riches.

Unless we address the basic problem of their poverty, to ask poor people to have fewer children is to ask them to be poorer. When I finished my testimony, the senior member of the committee asked me very pointedly what I had meant by the phrase "social justice." I briefly explained an ethical position rooted in the dignity of the human individual, emphasizing the linkage between human rights and basic needs that is so powerfully articulated in the Universal Declaration on Human Rights. The Representative cut me short with the rejoinder, "If by social justice you mean socialism, then I'm not for it!" He then lectured me for twenty minutes on the evils of "share-the-wealth" schemes and the pointlessness of trying to change the way things are ("The poor you have always with you, you know!").

I tell this story because it exemplifies for me the most serious obstacle to creating a more humane and sustainable future: our inadequate ethics to cope with the transition. I am convinced that the task of creating a better future is at its root an ethical task.

The basic decisions to be made in a world threatened by nuclear holocaust, ecological disintegration, exhaustion of resources, population pressures, and revolt against oppressive structures, are *value* decisions. The global society of the future will depend on more than physical rearrangements, institutional adaptations, and technological breakthroughs. Basically, it will depend upon a system of ethics—the shared assumptions we call values—to hold it all together.

Commentary

Deep inside ourselves, I think we know what is right and wrong.

> But we often do what is wrong. Why?

Because we feel powerless:

> ...Everyone else does it, so I will too.
> ...Nobody else does it, so why should I?
> ...You can't fight the system.
> ...It's always been that way.

Because we are afraid:

> ...You must fight fire with fire.
> ...An eye for an eye and a tooth for a tooth.
> ...I was just following orders.
> ...I worked for what I've got; no one is going to take it away from me.

Because we haven't thought through what really matters:

> ...I don't have time.
> ...I'm too tired.
> ...It's too hard.
> ...I'll get around to it next week.

Doing what is right has always mattered. Today it matters even more.

> We are tied together more closely.
> We come in contact with more people.
> What we do affects more people.
> We can help more people, or hurt them.

We are powerful, whether we like it or not.

VALUES

Inadequate Ethics

Discussions of values and ethics have come up in very specific policy situations in recent years. The crises of hunger, unemployment, pollution, energy, etc.—multiple crises, or the "crisis of crises"—have focused these value discussions.

There also have been elaborate academic debates over values and ethics. John Rawls and Robert Nozick, to cite two outstanding examples, have fascinated many of us with their intricate theories of justice.

But I have doubts as to whether greater clarity of vision or decisiveness of action have been stimulated by these theoretical discussions. I do not mean to speak critically of theory or analysis in itself. But I am critical of theory or analysis that is heavily abstract and naively ahistorical.

Three inadequate ethical stances: To make the point clear, let me describe three examples of current ethical stances that I feel are inadequate to guide a transition toward a more humane and sustainable future.

■ **Individualistic, not societal:** It is enormously difficult for many of us in the United States to move beyond an individual—indeed, privatistic—ethic in our evaluation of people, situations, and decisions.

We tend to view ethics as a guide to individual actions, and not as something that touches on all the structures of society around us— political, economic, social, and cultural

I recall a conversation with an executive of a large multinational firm. The executive assured me that business ethics were a prime concern for his corporation. He cited to the "Code of Conduct" they had recently adopted which forbade the taking or offering of bribes, required honest reporting of any conflict of interest, instructed employees to be courteous and respectful of cultural differences, and so on.

But nothing was said about the ethical questions that inevitably arise simply from a corporation's presence and practices in another country, such as those related to employment policies or pollution effects. Nor was there any questioning of the corporation's stance toward development as in its acceptance of a capital-intensive strategy, and its belief in the "trickle down" theory of the existence of a group getting richer somehow helps the the poor in a society. These were considered "structural" issues and outside the purview of an ethics conceived in individualistic terms.

When I mentioned "corporate social responsibility," the executive cited the playing fields that the firm had constructed for its employees—again an approach centered on benefits to a few individuals. However laudable the provision of playing fields might be in a given situation, "corporate social responsibility" in terms of deeper societal questions of pricing policies, hiring of women and minorities, impact on social structure, etc., went unaddressed.

The religious community in the United States has contributed to this by its long-standing emphasis upon personal morality. Private probity— often interpreted mainly in terms of sexual "good behavior"—has been preached regularly from pulpits. But only recently has social responsibility been posed in religious terms as an ethical issue, and the results have admittedly been mixed.

Underlying this individualistic ethics there is often a belief that individuals acting morally in their own private affairs will together constitute a social system that is righteous, just, equitable, peaceable, and otherwise praiseworthy in moral terms.

This is a variation of Adam Smith's argument in the economic sphere that an "invisible hand" will assure that things work out harmoniously for the common good so long as each individual pursues own private self-interest. Adam Smith's economic views seem increasingly inapplicable to a world of sharper scarcity and closer interdependence, and so also the related position of individualistic ethics seems increasingly inadequate.

■ **Nationalistic, not global:** In our ethical vision we frequently accept the national boundaries of our own country as our exclusive frame of reference.

It is not that Americans are unaware of suffering in the Third World, for in countless instances we have responded urgently and generously. But the assumption underlying our ethical stance is often a "we/they" dichotomy—a desire to separate or "distance" ourselves from those in need—which both narrows our sense of involvement in global problems and greatly limits the range of responses we consider appropriate.

Americans are often the first to send emergency supplies and assistance to cope with sudden natural disasters—an earthquake, or flood. Yet we are reluctant to accept any role or responsibility in the slowly developing human disasters that threaten many peoples of the world.

I have heard repeated discussions about what "they" in the developing countries should do to improve their well-being. These discussions sometimes sound as if "their" problems were unrelated to the historical past we have shared. It is as if "they" were not involved with us in global systems related to national sovereignty, international trade, and monetary policy. It is as if the actions of transnational corporations affecting "them" were not intimately linked to our own economic system, to our own U.S. politics, and our own daily lives as workers and consumers.

At the World Population Conference in Bucharest in 1974 I found that many U.S. citizens and public officials saw the "population problem" as "their" problem, the problem of the poor peoples in the Third World.

It was difficult—if not impossible— for these citizens and officials to comprehend an alternative ethical interpretation that singled out "over-consumption per person in the rich countries" as being at least as serious a threat to global ecological sustainability as "too many people in the poor countries."

Our unquestioned assumption was that people in the Third World had to change, not us. But to create a sustainable future, we all may have to

MAKING IT HAPPEN:

change. Our ethical position must leave room for that possibility.

More than a "nation"—a composite of diverse social forces, classes, groups: A nationalistic ethic also is inadequate as a guide to understanding the complexity of our own society at home. It is true that we are one "nation." But we are also a composite of many diverse social forces, classes and groups.

These social forces, classes and groups are defined by race, ethnic origin, gender, religion, political belief, and economic status—and are not all in harmony. Our life as a nation is the result of the lively, constant, dynamic interplay and tension among these often competing forces.

The "national interest"? A policy that is said to be in the "national interest" of the United States—for example, free trade—may not in fact be in the interest of many of our citizens, such as investors in less competitive industries or displaced workers.

Similarly, a policy in the "national interest" of a developing country—for example, industrialization along capital- and technology-intensive lines—may be of greatest benefit only to a powerful minority elite.

To speak of nations without paying attention to the range and diversity of interests within them is misleading. To do so is to blur significant conflicts *within* each country, and to ignore significant linkages *among* countries.

■ **Partial, not Wholistic:** We in the United States are a very practical people, and we find it congenial to approach issues one at a time, often on an ad hoc basis. We have been remarkably successful with a "mission impossible" mindset which focuses in sequence on individual aspects of a whole situation and designs an immediate solution for each crisis in turn.

We have been less successful as a nation in grasping the sense of the whole, including its many complex interrelationships. Witness, for example, our recurrent foreign policy difficulties, or the failures of many urban programs.

This pragmatic, piece-by-piece and crisis-by-crisis approach has important consequences for the ethics that guide us.

Focusing on individual issues apart from an integrating framework results in a fragmented ethics. It is a piecemeal ethics that offers no assurance that the pieces ever will add up to a meaningful whole.

For example, an ethical approach concentrating on individual value issues inherent in the energy crisis—such as differential impacts of gasoline shortages, or inequities caused by higher fuel oil prices—may fail completely to deal with the fact that these issues pose fundamental questions about the broader working of our present economic system.

The difficulty with taking a more wholistic approach is, quite frankly, that it forces us to go to the roots of the issues and problems. It forces us to examine interrelationships, linkages, and cause-effect connections. That may be frightening to many people because overall solutions often appear "radical."

How ready are we in the United States to accept public discourse that responsibly challenges basic and widely held economic beliefs such as, for example the importance of freedom of opportunity?

Our reluctance to be ethically wholistic is a very significant obstacle to progress in the societal transition to a durable and sustainable society.

At times we appear to be fearful not simply of being called "radical" but of being called something far worse in America—"unrealistic" or "naive." This fear can keep us from probing old boundaries or imagining new approaches.

Toward a More Adequate Ethic

What alternatives do I suggest, if I feel that many of the ethical stances that guide us today are inadequate for shaping a better future?

Let me briefly sketch the outlines of more adequate ethics. The influence of my religious background will be evident, at least implicitly.

■ **The ethics of community:** The "human community" is an abstraction. Brothers and sisters with names and faces are specific, real persons. As such, they are the bases for an ethics that can help us build a better future.

Looking at individuals, we understand that they share very unequally in the advantages and disadvantages of changes that are occurring in the community. To pay adequate attention to community, then, one must take account of the existence of different groupings and classes within society.

There have always been divisions on the basis of race, sex, religion, ethnic background, socio-economic status, geography, and so. These have always existed and, in some form, will probably always exist, as will "dominant" and "subordinate" relationships among classes and groups.

Who's deciding what for whom? A simple "class analysis," designed to assist in the ethical evaluation of any important decision, should pose three questions: (1) Who makes the decision? (2) Who benefits from the decision? and (3) Who bears the burden of the decision?

Certainly one of the prime guidelines of an ethics of community must be the principle that the less powerful—women, children, and aged, the poor, single parents, blacks, Hispanics, native Americans—must *not* be asked to bear most of the burden and disadvantage during the transition to a sustainable society.

When economic growth slows, especially in the industrialized world,

VALUES

the powerful are often able to shield themselves from the effects upon employment, services, expenses, taxes, and so forth. They can accommodate to higher prices for fuel, for example, by conserving energy.

But the less powerful may have to go without because they have less flexibility to rearrange their lives so as to live well while using less.

New systems of incentives and penalties: Movement to new patterns of ecological sanity will require new systems of incentives and penalties. Market subsidies offer no guarantee that the economic and social costs of necessary steps will be borne equitably by all sectors of the global and national community.

An ethics of community is therefore important to help all of us pay particular attention to the weak and poor. Historically, the powerless have paid the major costs of such major societal transformations as the Industrial Revolution. Any contemporary transformation that promised to repeat this sordid pattern would be ethically unacceptable.

Community in Space and Time: An ethics of community also involves dimensions of both space and time. The space dimension of community stresses that no geographic limit can be put on our concern for fulfilling human rights and basic needs.

In a global village, all are our sisters and brothers; on spaceship earth, there can be no first- and second-class passengers. To ignore the rights and needs of some human beings simply because they live far away is not only immoral, it is also foolish and shortsighted in an interdependent world. It ignores the reality of a global community.

The time dimension of community means that each generation evaluates its actions at least partially in terms of their impact upon the human rights and basic needs of future generations.

I recall a popular article two or three years ago that asked in its title, "What has posterity ever done for me?" **An ethics of community would answer that the quality of present civilization is highly influenced by the character of our commitment to the future.**

If human responsibility is constrained by time limits—"Who cares what happens after I'm gone?"—then it becomes so weakened as to lose its legitimacy and effective force even in the present.

Center for Concern, Washington, DC

Proportionate Response: Emphasis on the dimensions of space and time in community does not deny a principle of "proportionate response," by which an individual may be expected to be proportionately more sensitive and responsive to those who are closer geographically and nearer in time. We do not ignore our neighbor today; but neither is our responsible concern limited solely to the here and now.

■ **The ethics of accountability:** Closely linked to the concept of community is that of accountability. A prominent feature of our time, and one that will certainly affect the shape of our future, is a lack of accountability by the major figures taking action in politics and economics. They are not accountable to communities of ordinary people who are deeply affected by the actions of the powerful.

Technology—To whom is it accountable? Technology, for example, has a great and immediate impact on the lives and environment of all people. But to whom is technology responsible? To whom is it accountable?

In the field of energy, the decision to lock a community into the path of large-scale, centrally controlled production and distribution of electricity is frequently presented as inevitable. The nuclear reactor, the LNG supertanker, and the petroleum refinery are then seen as the logical outcome of social and economic choices already made. ◦

Is any particular "future" inevitable? An ethics of accountability would challenge whether any such future is "inevitable" and "logical"? This is done by simply asking basic questions. Who made the decisions? Who benefits from them? Who is placed at risk, and to what extent? Who is to be held accountable for both the good and bad consequences, and who will pay the eventual costs?

Accountability for the uses to which financial capital is put: In a time when financial capital is scarce, to whom are the owners and managers of capital accountable?

Do communities of ordinary people have any say in decisions on capital allocation that forcefully affect their lives? The closing of steel mills in Youngstown, Ohio, and the bail-outs of Lockheed and Chrysler come quickly to mind as examples in which the community of workers, merchants, neighbors, and local leaders had little voice in major decisions determining their livelihood.

The principal controllers of capital—large banks, large corporations, large government—often have an overriding effect on people's lives, yet they cannot be regarded as ethically neutral entities, nor are their actions necessarily right and just.

Power Relationships: An ethics of accountability also takes power very seriously. Amid the repeated calls we hear for restructuring the national and international orders, very little is said about the power needed to bring about such changes.

We need ethical analyses of power relationships. Who holds power now and how is it being used? To achieve progress, what political alliances are necessary? With what groups? For what trade-offs? Where are the principal institutional obstacles to change?

To speak of accountability, however, is to become controversial. Such an approach takes us into the realm of

MAKING IT HAPPEN:

Agency for International Development

thoughts and explore innovative solutions. A utopian vision can stimulate the social imagination in ways that break the old patterns of response—so well summed up as "We've always done it this way"—and enable us to formulate new approaches based on creative thinking and acceptance of risk.

Global equality? For instance, global equality of opportunity is not enough. As Denis Goulet has perceptively noted, this would do little in practice to assure the economic rights of less privileged groups. Rather, the goal we must strive for is equality of results to provide the essential guarantee of socio-economic rights.

Absolute egalitarianism may be neither feasible nor desirable. But I would propose as a realistic ethical guideline that "A floor demands a ceiling."

To fulfill the essential human needs of the world's population, a minimal "floor"—of food, shelter, education, medical care, etc.—is necessary. But in order to achieve that, a maximal "ceiling" on consumption must also be imposed.

The minimum/maximum argument is not an argument for absolute egalitarianism. A distinct distance must always remain between the floor and the ceiling. But that gap in a humane and sustainable society would not be as great as it is today in our world, in which hundreds of millions of people suffer malnutrition and deprivation while millions of others live in societies based on conspicuous waste and affluent consumption.

Utopian ethics inevitably have religious overtones. And today we see a resurgence of religious feelings around the world—with consequences sometimes advantageous to the human prospect and sometimes not.

The Islamic revival, for example, has reminded us forcefully that there can be both advantages and disadvantages. Nevertheless, these manifestations of what I would call the "resilience of tradition" can be a powerful force in promoting utopian visions that enable us to draw upon the deepest of our myths and symbols for guidance as we move forward.

political economy, and sharpens our focus on the power relationships within and among the accepted institutions of our society.

This goes to the roots of our social and economic system. As such it will inevitably stir opposition. But an ethics of accountability is critically necessary if we are to move effectively and expeditiously toward a sustainable future.

■ **The ethics of utopia:** These themes are often challenged as a "utopian." Critics intend that as a put-down, but we desperately need positive visions today.

In a resource-scarce, finite, over-crowded, and interdependent world the future presents us with challenges that are simply without precedent. We have no tested models, ready-made answers, or scientific certitudes with which to face these challenges.

Our visions therefore must be utopian. We must dare to think new

A POSITIVE GUIDE TO THE FUTURE

VALUES

The "Value" of Ethics

Just what is the value of ethics in reaching the hard decisions necessary for a transition to a better future?

Does it really make any difference whether we are guided by what I have referred to here as an "inadequate" or "adequate" system of ethics? I believe that it does.

■ **The forcing function of ethics:** An ethics based on the more desirable concepts of community, accountability, and utopia can provide a "forcing function" in our thinking and action.

It can help enlarge our perceptions and expand our commitments. By going beyond immediate problems, and purely technical considerations, such an ethics imposes a more profound and more humane consideration of the choices that confront us and their implications for the future.

■ **Enlarging the scope of public discourse:** Introducing an ethical base into public discourse creates an atmosphere in which major human questions can be openly debated.

Our personal values are then perceived as directly related to our actions. Values are recognized as central to the meaning of a situation, rather than being peripheral or incidental.

Focus on ethical issues may prevent us from asking, only as an afterthought, what really is happening to the people in the transitions we so often speak about.

■ **Counterbalance to too-small dreams:** An ethics such as I have described can provide a counterbalance to the kind of "neo-conservatism" that dismisses community as unfeasible, challenges accountability as dangerous, and criticizes all utopias as unrealistic.

In contrast to these values, some neo-conservatives seem to offer nothing more than an approach based on the greatest benefit for the individual, and to see a transition to a sustainable future only as a threat to the liberty of the individual.

In many ways today, our progress is being blocked by our inadequate ethical understanding. We make change more difficult and painful by failing to consider the value implications of current decisions. A new system of ethics ultimately can compel us to take a hard look at ourselves, our values, and our willingness to meet the challenges of the future seriously and humanely. □

New Goals and Values

Commentary

For well over a decade, Aurelio Peccei, the principal founder of The Club of Rome, has devoted his life to developing and promoting a kind of new thinking which, in his view, must inform all societies and governments in order to cope successfully with the problems of the future.

This selection of comments on goals and values suggests the outline of a new ethical system, with which readers may agree or disagree. The comments are excerpted from Dr. Peccei's opening address to a conference of The Club of Rome in West Berlin in October, 1979.

By Aurelio Peccei

About World Population

■ *Procreation,* although the supreme expression of the human personality, must be subject to a stern social ethic.

■ *National population policies* must be responsive to and compatible with global conditions.

■ *Quality of population* is more important than quantity, and alone can offset the consequences of the population explosion.

■ *People must become problem-solvers* at least to the same extent that they are problem-raisers.

■ *Human beings should not be equated with their basic needs* (however important these are); we are spiritual, artistic, dreaming, inventive, and fun-loving creatures as well.

About the common heritage of humankind

■ *Earth-keeping* is a primary necessity for the assurance of quality of life and human survival.

■ *Preservation of diverse cultural heritages* throughout the world is equally essential to the quality of human life.

■ Universal are *the right to share—within reason—the use of, and the duty to conserve, the world's natural resources,* irrespective of their geographic location.

■ The same universal principle applies to *the use of information, knowledge, and technical know-how* required for human progress and welfare, irrespective of proprietary rights.

■ *Each generation* should strive to bequeath a better world to the next.

MAKING IT HAPPEN:

About Human Rights and Duties

■ Only the *acceptance of human duties and responsibilities* can provide a context for the declaration of human rights.

■ *Obligations to our successors and to other forms of life* on earth are increasing rather than decreasing.

■ *Consciousness of the human species* must now come first, over and above individual, class, and national consciousness.

■ *Reasonable "social minima"* are the citizen's right and society's obligation, but these entail reciprocal obligations of the citizen and rights of society.

■ *"Social maxima"* are a natural correlative of "social minima."

■ *New "social contracts"* must incorporate these and other covenants between the individual and society.

■ A "new world order" must provide for *equitable regulation of reciprocal rights and duties of all countries or communities* (particularly between the haves and the have-nots) in an interdependent world.

About the Human System

■ *The principle of territorial sovereignty* has become the paramount impediment to peace and progress and must be gradually reformed, eventually abandoned (with the stronger nations setting a positive example for others).

■ *Supranational, subnational, transnational, and anational alternatives* must be explored as building blocks of a new global polity.

■ *Regional unions or communities, complemented by increased local autonomy,* can represent a useful intermediate step.

■ *Security is a primary human goal* that cannot be attained by armaments (the demential way) but only by sociopolitical maturity (the cultural way).

■ *Social justice and human equity are preconditions* for stronger, more viable societies.

■ *Integrated development of the poorer nations* through self-reliance and international cooperation is essential for the good of the entire world community.

■ *Optimal, rather than maximal, use of capital* is urgent in view of the relative scarcity of capital and the need for harmonious global development.

■ *The "growth ethic,"* accountable not only for affluence but for grave societal and economic distortions, must be replaced, and the value of austerity rather than consumption encouraged.

■ *The goal of sustainable dynamic equilibrium*—at a level set by each society—should supersede that of growth.

■ Recognition of *the interdependence of economy and ecology* is indispensable.

■ *New forms of medium- and long-term planning* must be devised to combine global coherence with a maximum of regional and local autonomy.

■ *The growing size and complexity of the human system* demand excellent management at every level, from local to global.

■ In planning, the respective *roles of private enterprise and public initiative must be reconceived* and more closely coordinated.

■ *Technical and scientific enterprise must be reoriented* to serve all humankind over time rather than narrow, immediate interests.

About Human Development

■ *Human development must become proactive and anticipatory,* not simply reactive and adaptive like genetic evolution.

■ *Development of unused human potential* must be given high priority.

■ In times of continuous and complex change, *continuous learning* is indispensable.

■ *Non-material values (spiritual, ethical, moral, socio-political, and cultural)* rank at least as high as material values in defining the quality of human life.

■ *Varied allocation of time for work, education, recreation, and rest during a lifespan* is necessary for the self-realization of the individual and the benefit of society.

■ *New forms and contents of learning* are necessary to foster the spirit of participation, anticipation, human solidarity, and global interdependence. □

David L. Ames

What Do We Have To Work With

National Aeronautics and Space Administration

Commentary _____

When Experts Disagree

"**Just the facts, ma'am.**" Being clear about *values* is only the first step on the path to creating the future we want. We must also be clear about the *resources available* to serve our purposes and the *physical and biological laws* governing what we do.

In short, we must grasp the realities of the world that we all inhabit.

"Reality" sounds like something concrete and measurable, about which there should be little disagreement. But this is not the case.

Experts do not always agree on what the facts are, how one establishes what the facts are, or how one should interpret their meaning. There is no consensus about how the physical and biological laws that we think we understand should be applied to assess the long-term physical and environmental consequences of what we do. There is disagreement about the consequences of current demographic, environmental, and economic trends and even about what the relevant trends are.

Expertise and Ideology. Indeed, "expert opinion" on the future often seems to be in part a function of ideology. If there is something a business executive or political leader wants to do, he or she will probably be able to find a reputable expert who will predict a beneficial outcome.

Opponents will be able to enlist the services of other experts who will predict the opposite. Ironically, it sometimes seems that there is more agreement about basic values and purposes than about what the facts are.

Here are some examples of fundamental questions about which there is no agreement.

Some Ways Experts Disagree

How many people can the planet support at a comfortable, or adequate, standard of living?

One point of view:
We can comfortably support twice the present global population and more. People are a precious resource and human ingenuity is essential to creating the kind of future we want. Population will stabilize naturally at an appropriate level as the benefits of material progress are more widely shared throughout the world.

An Opposing View:
There are already too many people. We are in the middle of a population explosion with potentially catastrophic consequences. Global life-support systems are being threatened. Policies designed to stabilize and then reduce the level of population in all countries, including the United States, must be initiated now to avert disaster for future generations.

Will stocks of nonrenewable resources—such as oil and minerals used in industry—continue to be available to support current and improving material standards of living?

One point of view:
Current stocks are sufficient for the foreseeable future. Where there are shortages, as in the case of oil, a principal cause has been government regulation and insufficient funds devoted to exploration. If the stock of a given resource is shrinking, the functioning of the price mechanism in a free market and the advance of technology will provide acceptable substitutes. There are sufficient resources on the planet to support vast improvement in the material standard of living of all the world's people.

An opposing view:
Stocks of resources are limited and we are running out of things already. Fossil fuels are a good example. Using up our stocks of nonrenewable resources is like living off capital rather than income. The industrialized nations must strongly emphasize conservation, use nonrenewable resources frugally, and develop production and energy systems based on renewable resources. Similar programs must be initiated in developing countries.

How resilient are the life-support systems of air, water, plant-life upon which the survival of the human race ultimately depends?

One point of view:
Natural systems are resilient and not seriously threatened by our present systems of agriculture and industrial production. While we do need to be alert to ecological warning signals, no major problems beyond our control are apparent in the foreseeable future. Should such problems appear, there will be ample time to alter our practices and develop the appropriate technology to deal with them.

An opposing view:
We do not know all that we need to know about these life-supporting systems. Dangers from acid rains, clearing of the tropical rain forests, loss of topsoil, and destruction of biological species are threatening problems already. We cannot control nature, and are not now living in harmony with our natural environment. We must learn to do so, or condemn future generations to life on an impoverished planet.

Is our present style of life and material standard of living in the United States sustainable for the foreseeable future?

One point of view:
Yes. Present ways in the United States are sustainable for the foreseeable future. No fundamental changes are necessary. Moreover, through continued economic growth and technological progress, this standard of living can gradually be made available to the rest of the world.

An opposing view:
No. If present patterns and trends continue without fundamental change, we will do irremediable damage to our life-support systems before the end of the twenty-first century. The result will be a severe reduction in our own standard of living, and the denial to other peoples of the opportunity for material progress.

PLANET

The views of three concerned experts, all of them members of the U.S. Association for The Club of Rome, are presented here. They tell of the ecological, demographic, and physical realities we confront, as well the social consequences as they see them. Note that—other than in this section—there has been no effort to include alternative views. This section you have just been reading is a reminder, however, that alternative views do of course exist.

Experts not speaking with a single voice on fundamental questions of fact affecting our future may be perplexing. But it should also heighten our sense of individual responsibility. We cannot leave the judgment of facts solely to the experts. After listening to alternative points of view, we have the obligation to draw conclusions for ourselves.

Biological realities within us: One way to understand biophysical realities and their relevance is to think about our own bodies. As human beings, we differ in many respects. We have different goals, values, beliefs, and customs. We speak different languages. Our skins are different colors. We have different skills and aptitudes. All of these differences contribute to the fact that the "reality" each one of us sees, feels, and understands is also a little bit different.

Biologically, however, human beings are quite similar. All of us require air, water, food, and space to survive. Our body temperatures remain constant at about 98.6 degrees Fahrenheit. Our hearts beat at rates within the same approximate range. Our bodies respond to exercise, stress, chemicals, bacteria, and inputs of nutrients (or lack therof) in a relatively similar and predictable manner. If our bodies, viewed as biological organisms, were not alike, and therefore predictable, there would be no basis for the sciences of biology and medicine.

These biological realities underlie and also shape our capabilities as economic, ethical, technologial, and political beings. A technical or cultural advance is sometimes referred to as *overcoming* biological limits. But *adapting* to biological limits would be more accurate.

When we heat our homes, amplify our physical capabilities with machines, or heighten our mental capacities with computers—to cite common examples—we have not altered basic biological laws. We can choose to turn up the thermostat if we are cold (assuming there is oil in the tank), but not to lower our body temperature to a more desirable equilibrium with our environment.

If food is scarce, we can sometimes use our intelligence to grow more, but we cannot adjust our metabolism so that 500 calories per day, rather than about 2,500, is sufficient for long-term survival.

We have certainly been able to expand our range of choice but these examples remind us that there are also aspects of our biological existence that are not subject to our control. The only alternatives to living within these constraints are illness and, ultimately, death.

Biological Laws and Individual Choices: Many of the biological laws governing our bodies are easy to grasp because they relate to things that affect us directly and immediately. If I were to stop breathing, I would begin to get signals within a very few seconds that something was wrong. Quite soon, other biological processes would probably intervene to halt this—highly undesirable—pattern of behavior.

If I stopped eating or drinking or if, on a winter day, I neglected to keep feeding wood into the stove that heats my workroom, I also would begin to get signals that something was wrong. In these cases, the process would take a bit longer, the demand would be less urgent, and the choice of response would be more varied.

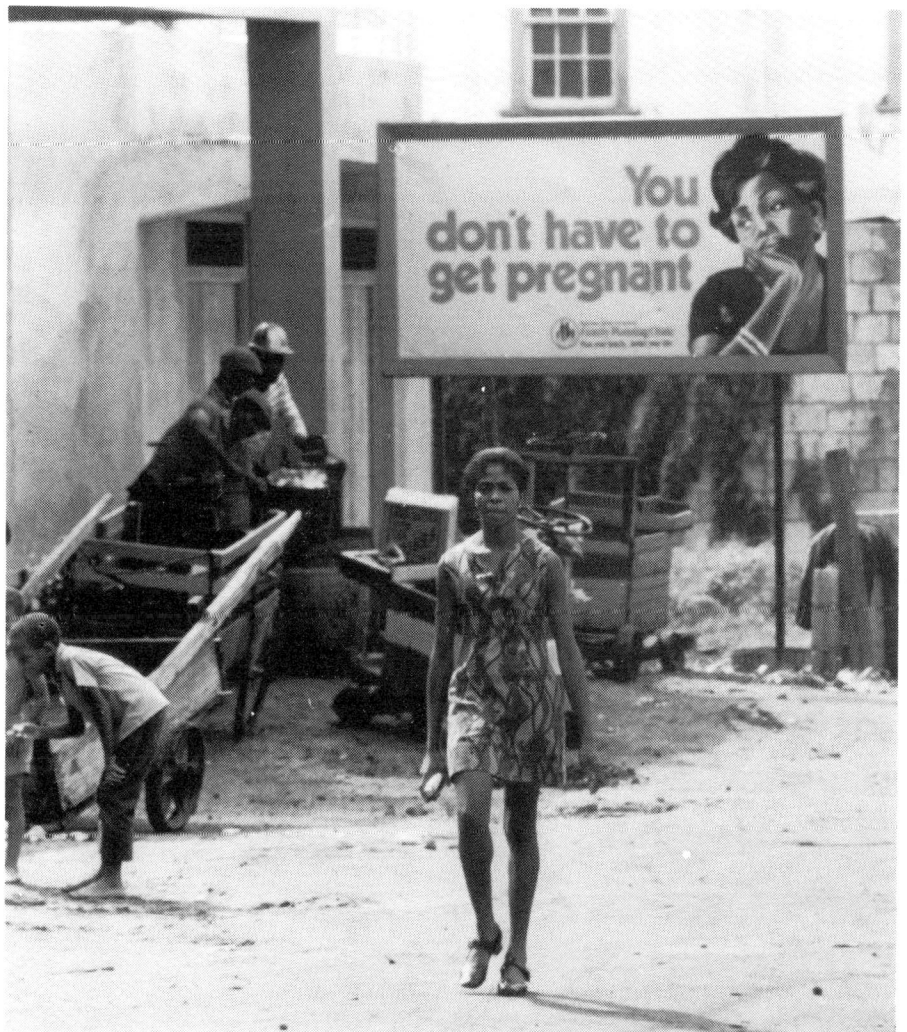

World Bank

As I type these lines, I am puffing on my pipe. I do this because I find writing an often nerve-racking and frustrating activity; puffing and chewing on a pipe seems to help keep my frustration within tolerable levels. I realize well enough that this activity will leave a bad taste in my mouth tomorrow morning, will affect my wind, and may, in the long run, contribute to an earlier and more painful death.

But the prospect of death is—or seems to be—far in the future. The frustration and pressure to complete the manuscript are immediate. If the signals were stronger, and the potential negative results more immediate, I would probably stop. When I have a cold, or my throat really gets raw, I do. If I thought that an early and painful death was highly probable, this probably would lead me to stop as well.

But, in this case, the decision would be conscious, not—as in the case of holding my breath—a virtually uncontrollable physiological response. In the case of my pipe smoking, I can choose to ignore the potentially adverse consequences and the early warnings of danger, up to a point.

Ecological Laws... Ecologists are concerned with the behavior, not of individuals, but of populations and species of biological organisms.

Populations of people, deer, and fruitflies are significantly different in many respects. However ecologists point out there are also important similarities between these admittedly diverse populations—and, they urge, there are some important things for us to learn from that fact.

For example, every population depends upon its environment for both nutrients and energy. And the maximum size of population that a given environment can support depends on the amount of resources and energy available.

Another very important consideration in the study of ecology is the relationship between the growth rate of a population and the size it is likely to attain—and sustain—over a given period of time. Populations tend to grow geometrically like money invested at a compound interest in a savings account. If the population of the world is four and one-half billion (which it is, roughly) and the growth rate is two percent (which it is, roughly), that means that, unless something changes, we will have an additional four billion or so more people living on the planet in about thirty-five years. Seventeen years after that, at a constant rate of growth, we would have added another four billion.

In populations of deer, or fruitflies, this is called an "outbreak." The usual consequence of an "outbreak" is that the demands of the population exceed the resources of its environment; as a result, there are sufficient deaths from malnutrition and starvation to restore the size of the population to a state of equilibrium or balance with its environment. For most of humanity's existence, our numbers have also been governed by these biological laws.

...and Individual Choices. Human beings have a greater ability than fruitflies or deer to figure out what is happening to them now and what may happen in the future. Also, we know that humans make judgments about how we think things ought to be and we shape the future in accordance with those judgments.

In short, we can understand and adapt to the ecological laws that describe the realities of our species' relationship to its environment. But we can also choose to ignore those laws, deny their validity, or even attempt to change the realities upon which they are based. But those choices may be perilous.   □

David L. Ames

MAKING IT HAPPEN:

The Living Earth:

Ecological Imperatives

By Anitra Thorhaug

The living earth as we know it today is a delicately balanced and interrelated system of hundreds of thousands of types of animals and plants. These species live in populations. And these populations, when they exist together at one time and in one place, form ecological communities.

These ecological communities are highly diverse, each having evolved over millennia to take advantage of some special combination of the world's physical, chemical, geological, and biological conditions.

Many more species are extinct than are living today; failure to adjust to changing conditions led inevitably to the elimination of those that have disappeared. The range of conditions to which species have adapted, however, is very wide, extending from the arctic (very cold, with little sunshine in winter) to the tropical (very warm, with sunshine for twelve hours each day year-round), and from the highest mountains to the deepest seas.

Our Place As Humans in the Global Ecosystem: Human beings are but one of the many species inhabiting this planet. Like many other species, we have a remarkably small range of habitats that can provide our requirements for water, air, food, and other basic elements.

We are more adaptable than some species, less so than others. Our technologies assist us appreciably. For example, without an artificial oxygen supply system we are unable to spend more than a few minutes in the largest realm on earth, the watery places that cover 75 percent of the earth's surface. We are similarly dependent on artificial support if we venture above 15,000 feet in the earth's atmosphere, or attempt to remain for long in the earth's extensive desert areas.

Vegetation: Each community of living organisms is built upon vegetation. Plants are the primary producers of energy for all of life. Only plants can directly use the sun's energy and produce the oxygen all animals need to breathe.

Plants use the energy of the sun to assemble complex energy-storing molecules made from carbon and hydrogen atoms, which are the "food" from which animals of all kinds obtain their energy. Animals are thus totally dependent on plants for their survival.

Human beings are not "masters" or "lords" of the earth. Like other animals, we must rely on plants to meet our needs. We would do better to think of ourselves as the biblical Noah, who shared a journey of survival on the Ark. We are only one among many travelers on spaceship Earth, who together are riding a vast—but delicate, fragile, and limited—craft.

Our survival is utterly dependent upon the integrity and survival of the whole system. None of us are passengers—all are crew, and each species has one or more specific functions that contribute to life on spaceship Earth.

This view of ourselves, however, involves nothing less than a revolution in thought. No longer can we expect the natural ("outer") world continually to bend and adapt to human ("inner") needs and realities.

We now are beginning to see that it is we and our "inner" world of thought, society, politics, values, and institutions that must adjust to the constraints of "outer" reality.

We are coming to appreciate that water, food, air, and the sun's energy are continually passing through us—and through all that is alive. Everything is interconnected, so that our own vitality and well-being are intimately linked to the health and resilience of the many plant and animal populations that share in this community of life on earth.

The Requirements of Life

There are certain clear ecological conclusions that follow from understanding that we humans are part of the community of all living things. They are facts we cannot ignore.

■ **Biological realities:** These have to do with the things we need to sustain a stable population of the human species over a long period of time. We require, above all, food, air, and water.

We must understand the biological processes that provide us with these essentials. And we must ensure that they continue without interruption.

We must think carefully about the quantities of these basic elements that are available in relation to the size of population of our own species we wish to sustain, as well as to the population of other plant and animal species upon whose survival and well-being our own lives depend.

■ **Physical-chemical Realities:** These derive not from living systems but from the larger non-living systems of the earth's biosphere. These physical-chemical imperatives involve such earthwide systems as the atmosphere, the nitrogen cycle, the oxygen cycle, and the role of certain pollutants in interfering with these cycles.

■ **Geological Realities:** These grow out of the one-time-only character of the events that formed the earth's crust.

Apollo 17 Astronaut, Eugene Cernan

Ores containing deposits of metals and minerals were long ago concentrated geologically in veins or lodes. Once mined, these metals and minerals are a precious resource that must not be squandered; once used and dispersed, they become inaccessible and unavailable for further human benefit, except at very great cost in energy and other resources.

Awareness of these realities should make us more cautious about actions that might have perilous consequences not for individuals but for entire civilizations or all of human life.

We must be aware of the danger of air unfit to breathe. Or an atmosphere too warm because of the "greenhouse effect" caused by accumulation of carbon dioxide released through burning of fossil fuels. Or water sources (or soils) depleted by unwise or extravagant use. Or minerals and metals no longer available for certain critical technological uses.

We must be aware of ecosystems (or body systems of humans) overwhelmed at critical points by accumulating contaminants. Or entire regional or global systems overwhelmed by human populations of a size that cannot be sustained. Or a globe overwhelmed by the destruction caused by human aggressive responses escalated to the level of nuclear (or conventional) wars.

It is not necessary to list all potential disasters in order to direct attention to these ecological realities. What they bespeak is nothing less than the requirements of life itself.

Biological Imperatives

The Biological Imperatives: We are now making extinct one species of plant or animal life each day. It has been estimated (by Myers, 1979) that by the year 2000 we will be destroying one species per hour. Does the world need more people and fewer plants and animals?

Why are decisions being made by humans to increase the numbers of our species and of the domesticated crops

and animals we need, and to decrease the numbers of "natural" plants and animals in both species and in abundance? Let me cite important instances in which precisely this is happening.

As tropical rainforests are cut down, or as coastal estuaries are dredged or polluted, we are ignoring the long evolutionary heritages of the species that have adapted to living in these environments. Species adapt very slowly, over hundreds of generations. Today's populations of plants and animals have become what they are in part because of their rigorous adaptation to the complex set of physical and chemical conditions in which they live.

Disturb or remove these conditions quickly, and you destroy the entire habitat (natural setting) upon which large numbers of plant and animal species depend. In addition, the earth loses an important part of the richness and diversity of its genetic heritage. Modern agriculture and our pharmaceutical industries, for example, are built on the foundation of this broad and complex genetic heritage. What may be lost is a critical link in some system that is essential to biological life.

The seasonal patterns of the world's temperatures in different locations is founded on the forests of our tropical and temperate zones. Much more heat can be absorbed or reflected by a forest than by bare ground or by a cornfield.

Leveling tropical rainforests, as we are now doing, also alters patterns of rainfall. It alters cloud cover. And, of course, it alters the conditions that define which species of plants and animals can inhabit an area. Many of these species would probably not survive if sufficient vegetation is removed over the earth to change our total climate by just a few degrees centigrade.

In the tropics, 90 percent of the nurseries where fish are spawned are in the shallow waters immediately adjacent to shore, even though the adult fish crop is frequently found far out to sea. The natural production of seafood in these coastal areas is a very efficient and relatively cheap source of protein.

Yet coastal zones throughout the world are the regions in which human

populations are expanding at a very rapid rate, and where dumping and other destructive activities such as dredging and filling are occurring without heed to the effect on precious fisheries resources.

In a similar way, we are losing prime agricultural land to other uses. We must stop thinking of agricultural land as cheap, and begin to recognize that good topsoil is one of our most precious nonrenewable resources. Paving the land for shopping centers, highways, and creeping suburbs must halt. Our cities must expand upward, not outward. The land is not only vital for food production but for maintenance of a viable global ecosystem of water, air, soil, and soil minerals, on which we and our companion species depend.

In contrast to the days of the pioneers, there are no more large stretches of unused prime agricultural land into which we can expand. In the past, we fed our increasing human population in two ways: (1) by widening the cultivated agricultural area, and (2) by raising agricultural productivity through irrigation and such energy-consumptive devices as tractors, fertilizers, and pesticides.

As our human population continues to grow, however, it will have to be sustained by food production costing a great deal more in inputs of energy and without substantial additions of agricultural land. What is in fact happening is that each year large quantities of agricultural land are being lost to other competing uses. This whole vicious circle endangers natural ecological systems over the long term.

Physical-Chemical Imperatives

Physical-Chemical Realities: Human activities today intrude not only upon other forms of life, but upon the great non-living systems of the biosphere whose functioning make life possible.

■ Water as the transportation system of life: Water moves through a complex hydrological cycle that includes not only evaporation, precipitation, rivers, and oceans but also the liquid intake of humans and the flushing of our kidneys and the blood that brings food and oxygen to our various organs, tissues, and cells. Essential chemicals are moved by water not only flowing in our blood but in our rivers and streams and soils.

When water is viewed as the transportation system of life, there is nothing rational about the present pattern in which the single largest consumption of water in the United States is for domestic uses and sewers. Per-person water use in the U.S. averaged 20 gallons per day in 1900. In 1972, 180 gallons. And in San Diego, California, an average of 580 gallons!

Industrial use of water to dispose of toxic chemicals is also irrational from an ecological point of view, for it makes the water unfit for other purposes for undefined periods of time. Water for irrigation is being withdrawn from important natural underground reservoirs (called aquifers) in many important agricultural areas of the United States. The rates of withdrawal are often unsustainable. In some cases we are withdrawing "fossil water," water that will not be replaced by natural processes. In those cases we are "mining our water."

Physical-chemical realities must become as important as political and economic realities in determining national and regional water-use policies. Clean water is not an infinite resource on the planet; it is limited and must be used prudently.

■ Air and atmosphere: We must also heed the realities of air quality as well. Air is essential for human life and for all other life on earth as we now know it. Air circulation patterns are global rather than national, so that air can truly be called a global resource.

Our air problems center upon three factors: (1) the changing balance between oxygen and carbon dioxide owing to the release of contaminants from burning fossil fuels and from industrial processes; (2) the effect of acid-rain fallout (from industrial contamination) onto soils and crops,

WORLD BANK PHOTO by Tomas Sennett, 1977

forests, lakes, rivers, streams, and the fish they contain; and (3) the diminution of the ozone-layer function of shielding all plant and animal species from levels of ultra-violet radiation to which they are not adapted and thus cannot tolerate.

■ Trace Metals: A natural biogeochemical cycling results from the gradual weathering of rock. Industrial uses are now adding sizable quantities of heavy metals to the environment, which now move with the products of the natural biogeochemical cycling through terrestrial to aquatic to estuarine to oceanic ecosystems.

Agricultural practices and industrial pollution are having increasingly important impacts upon the processes by which trace metals pass through natural systems. Heavy metals accumulate as contaminants in fish and animal tissues, which are then consumed by other species including ourselves. These contaminants become further concentrated as they pass along through the food chain.

In short, whole groups of substances are contaminating our physical-chemical environment, often at a rate that is accelerating over time. The most insidious of these are the heavy metals and those which are non-natural (such as DDT or PCB) and do not biodegrade.

Geological Imperatives

Geological Realities: Minerals will never be as abundant or as cheap as they have been in the past. We must learn to use and conserve them more wisely.

Of the twelve most common elements in the earth's crust, five are useful metals widely used in industrial technology: iron, aluminum, magnesium, potassium, and manganese. After this group, however, elements occur in the crust at extremely low concentrations except for geologically concentrated veins or lodes.

Much of what we extract today derives from veins or lodes of minerals that are 100 to 1000 times as concentrated as in the rest of the earth's crust. Due to advances in geologic knowledge during past decades, we are becoming increasingly adept at predicting the location of such veins or lodes, and a great deal of highly targeted geological exploration and exploitation has occurred. Thus, it seems to many geologists that the chances do not seem good that we will be able to find mineral lodes in exponentially increasing numbers to satisfy the future needs of a growing human population.

Biological, physical-chemical, and geological realities lead directly to heightened concern for the ecology of life as it exists today. They also must lead us toward more prudent living patterns and levels of consumption, if we wish to continue to sustain human life as we have known and enjoyed it into the indefinite future.

Who am I?
Anitra Thorhaug & Jack Attias

We are married and live near Miami, Florida. We both formerly worked full-time for large institutions, Anitra for a university and Jack for a law firm. We went to work between 8 and 9 in the morning and came home between 5 and 7 in the evening, worked 5 or 6 days a week, drew regular salaries, spent several hours each day commuting, and used evenings and weekends for leisure activities.

We were "normal Americans," and were frustrated, overweight, under-exercised, tense, toxified, chemical-ized, and feeling that we were on a treadmill getting no place fast. We decided to change our lives.

After seven years in our "new life style," we feel much healthier, happier, and are able to maintain our desired weight; we feel rested and much more personally fulfilled. We feel that we have a richer and more productive life. This is how we did it.

The first step, over a period of months, was to question the assumptions that we had taken for granted. Some of these we had received from society; others from friends and peers; others just from the general culture in which we live. We began with the timetable of our lives.

How much sleep did we really need? Did we need to go to work at 8 or 9? Did we need to stop working at 5, 6, or 7? Did we need to rest 7 or 8 hours? Then we tried to decide which of our personal habits were really fulfilling. Did we need to eat three meals each day at 8:00 A.M., 12:00 noon, and 6:00 P.M.? Did we each need to have a large, gas-burning car, an office, an employer, a regular payroll check? Did we need to drive to work? These and many other assumptions we questioned

The next step was to experiment with different patterns. We started working at different times. Anitra had always liked to work early in the morning, so she began getting up at 5:30 or 6:00 A.M. and working at home on her writing before leaving for the office. We also began working intensely on certain days and relaxing on others.

The big switch came when we decided to sell our suburban home and move to an island off the mainland of Florida, where we bought a large condominium and converted three of the bedrooms into offices. We each opened our own small business, in addition to commuting to our regular jobs, and our businesses began to grow and to make a difference in our lives. Each of us by now has disengaged wholly or in part from the larger organizations of which we were members, in order to concentrate on our own enterprises.

We began waking earlier and earlier and doing our most productive work in the early morning hours. We began eating less and less and started exercising several times a day, especially at the noon break. From this experimentation, we gradually found patterns that fit and seemed right, happy, and sustainable.

We found that eating no evening meal was a far better pattern for us than the usual large dinner. This opened up time for recreation and enjoyment in the evening, instead of structuring our time around cooking, eating, cleaning up, washing dishes, and resultant exhaustion.

The last thing we did was begin to fit the various parts together so that they all flowed and fit: the work, the play, the maintenance, the chores, the consumption patterns, all began to fall into place. We started to have an integrated life in which work contributed meaningfully to our lives and play was as important as work.

One of our goals is to help create a sustainable world, and the way in which we do that is to try to organize our own lives into sustainable patterns. Love is important in our lives: for ourselves, for one another, and for those people with whom we come into contact. Our health is maintained by vigorous daily exercise, eating lower on the food chain, and minimizing stress. We have given up red meat altogether and eat fowl only on occasion. Otherwise, we enjoy lots of raw vegetables, raw grains, and fresh fish.

We devote a good deal of time to personal growth and nourishment because we find this fulfilling. We accumulate our stored energy not in terms of the usual consumer goods, but in land and other long-term investments so that the energy is available for future use. □

World Bank by Thomas Sennet

Why Limit Population?

The Pressure of Human Numbers

By Anne H. Ehrlich

To design a better future than the world now faces, we have to understand the role that the size and growth of the human population have played in shaping our present dilemma. We must also understand the limitations that the momentum of still-growing populations places upon all our attempted solutions.

Resource Consumption by the Rich: An important aspect of population pressure on both resources and environment worldwide is the resource consumption of the rich. That the gap between the living standards of the rich and the poor is widening, not narrowing constitutes a scandal of global proportions.

This living-standard gap is also a threat. Poverty and the related resentments and political polarization are already major factors complicating other world problems. And as the pressures of both rich and poor populations on global life-support systems increase, the task of establishing a sustainable society becomes ever more difficult.

Population Momentum: The human population was small throughout most of its long history of at least two million years. With the development of agriculture, people first gained some control over their food supply. Before then, there had probably been no more than five million human beings on earth at any one time.

Under the impetus of agriculture the global population gradually expanded over the ensuing 8000 years to perhaps 250 million by the time of Christ. By 1650 it had doubled to 500 million, and it redoubled within another 200 years to

MAKING IT HAPPEN:

PLANET

Anne Ehrlich and her husband Paul were among the first to call attention to the potentially catastrophic consequences of global demographic trends, what they called "the population bomb."

Anne Ehrlich's analysis underlines the fact that stringent family planning measures are needed now. Many Americans view such measures as an infringement of personal freedom. If abortion is one of the family-planning measures under consideration, their views are even stronger. Many believe that abortion is murder.

Those who oppose family planning feel as strongly about their point of view as do its proponents. Unfortunately, more time is spent in controversy about means than in trying to reach consensus about ends. When faced with highly charged issues like this, it helps to:
■ establish better communication;
■ define areas of agreement (and disagreement);
■ seek consensus about overall objectives;
■ think positively and constructively; and
■ find out what the facts really are.

Here are some issues and questions that may be helpful in moving the discussion forward:

■ If human life is sacred, then death from poverty, starvation, or war must be as much a perversion of God's will as death from abortion. **How can we focus our attention on the best ways to eliminate all preventable deaths?** To serve this objective, how can scarce resources be most effectively allocated?
■ Laws governing adoption reflect society's judgments about the need for children to be raised in a humane, safe, and nurturing environment. These laws are strict and properly so. Not infrequently, it is impossible to place children in the home of a childless couple who wants them because of the exacting standards that have been established.

Do "natural" children have any less need to be raised in a humane, safe, and nurturing environment? Shouldn't there be a better relationship between the standards set for adoptive decisions and those set for reproductive decisions?
■ The belief that sexual relationships outside of marriage are immoral has been linked historically to opposition to wider dissemination of birth control information and devices. Making birth control information available, in this view, would promote immorality by eliminating a powerful restraint on sexual activity, namely, the fear of

unwanted pregnancy. In an earlier era, arguments against providing treatment of venereal disease were quite similar.

History has shown repeatedly that sexual drives can be more powerful than governmental regulation or religious law. The argument that unborn—or unwanted—children should be burdened with enforcing society's moral standards seems inconsistent with a belief in the sanctity of human life and the need of every child to be raised in a humane, safe, and nurturing environment.
■ There are few rights more important to Americans than the right to exercise informed choice. And, among the choices we make in our lives, there are few, if any, that are more important—both individually and globally—than the choice to create a new life.

As a patriotic American who believes in individual freedom, I reject the argument that any moral imperative should be sustained by the enforced ignorance of those who are expected to follow it. To be truly free, individuals must know the consequences of their decisions and be able to take responsibility for them. They must be capable of meaningful choice, including choice about moral issues.   □

one billion by 1850.

This accelerating growth continued for the next one hundred years until, during the 1960s, the world's human population was increasing with a momentum that would lead to a doubling about every 35 years. There are now some 4.5 billion human beings on earth.

Since 1970, growth has continued but a slight slackening in the rate of increase has occurred. By 1980, population was increasing at a rate that would lead to another doubling in about 40 years instead of 35 years. The slowdown is mainly attributable to reduced birthrates in several regions of the world notably most industrialized countries, the People's Republic of China, and several other less developed countries (LDCs).

This slight decline in the rate of world population increase is a hopeful sign for other reasons. The rapidity of the change offers some hope that the other social changes essential for a successful transition to a sustainable society could be made with similar swiftness.

A five-year increase in the doubling time of the world's population should not, however, be viewed as a solution to the problem of the "population explosion." An end to population growth in most of the developing world is still a distant hope. Because of the rapid growth in LDCs in recent decades, their populations contain a very large proportion of young people—future parents. From 40 to 50 percent of most LDC populations are under 15 years old, and there are relatively few people in the older age

groups subject to higher death rates. Because of the built-in momentum represented by so many pre-reproductive individuals and the apparent resistance of people in traditional societies to limiting family size for many reasons, ending population growth in LDCs will be an enormous task.

So even though the worldwide rate of increase in human numbers may have slowed somewhat, population momentum will almost certainly carry the global population past the six billion mark before the turn of the century.

The maximum population is now projected to reach at least nine billion (assuming birthrates continue to drop and death rates do not rise significantly) before an actual decline in population size can begin a century or more from now. More likely, though still

FOR EACH U.S. CITIZEN ANNUALLY

8000 LBS. STONE

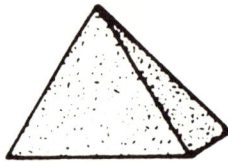

8000 LBS. SAND AND GRAVEL

660 LBS. CEMENT

450 LBS. CLAYS

430 LBS. SALT

1400 LBS. OTHER NONMETALS

1000 LBS. IRON AND STEEL

46 LBS. ALUMINUM

16 LBS. COPPER

14 LBS. ZINC

11 LBS. LEAD

31 LBS. OTHER METALS

PLUS

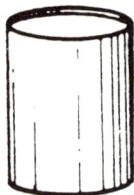

7650 LBS. PETROLEUM

5200 LBS. COAL

4200 LBS. NATURAL GAS

1/7 LB. URANIUM

TO GENERATE:

ENERGY EQUIVALENT TO 300 PERSONS WORKING AROUND-THE-CLOCK FOR EACH U.S. CITIZEN

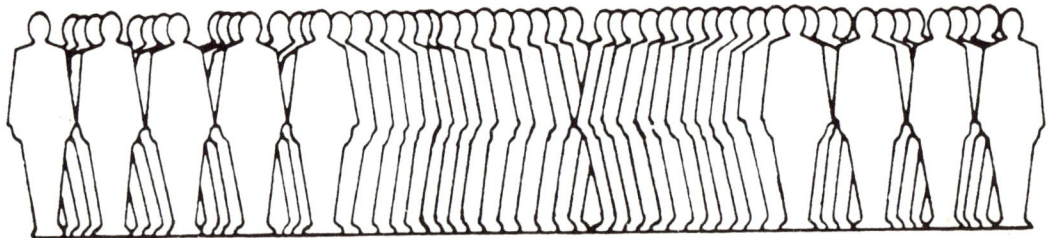

U.S. TOTAL USE OF NEW MINERAL SUPPLIES IN 1975 WAS ABOUT
4 BILLION TONS!

U.S. Bureau of Mines, "Status of the Mined Industries," 1976

---

optimistic, projections have put the ultimate population peak at about 12 billion.

Such a huge human population—nine to 12 billion persons—clearly cannot be sustained by the earth's present life-support systems, certainly not for any great length of time or at an acceptable standard of living for the vast majority.

Population Pressures—Food: In recent decades food production has fairly steadily outpaced population growth. But the improvements in food supply per person have largely been in the already well-fed rich countries. The poorest quarter of the world's population has seen little or no improvement, and some regions have experienced declines in per capita food supplies, especially since 1970.

Over a half billion people today are seriously and constantly undernourished. The proportion of hungry people in the world may have remained more or less the same, but it must be remembered that their absolute numbers have doubled since 1940.

In many poor countries, particularly in South Asia and tropical Africa, projections for food production show harvests over the next decade or two

MAKING IT HAPPEN:

The People's Republic of China

China has reduced fertility in just over a decade to a rate approaching the replacement level—a demographic transition that took close to 150 years in Europe. But, despite the opening of China to outside observers in the past few years, information about population programs is still fragmentary.

China represents more than one-fifth of the world's total population. Its demographic trends thus have greater significance for world population growth than those of any other country....

The Chinese have pushed population planning further and faster than any other developing country and have achieved striking fertility declines almost unique in the annals of demographic history. Most observers are particularly anxious to identify those specific components of China's program which could, in fact, be transferred to other countries. Here are the program components which appear to make up China's success story according to a *Draper Fund Report:*

■ Reliance on a network of paramedics or barefoot doctors to provide most family planning services through a primary health care system which reaches people where they work and live, and makes cost-effective use of traditional medicine;

■ A wide array of contraceptive methods, including sterilization and abortion and some methods unknown outside of China, all provided free of charge;

■ An intensive campaign of propaganda and of community peer pressure, in some cases extending to the actual allocation of a planned number of births among eligible couples;

■ A single-purpose administrative structure in the form of "Leading Groups on Birth Planning" with representation from all relevant sectors and enormous political clout;

■ Major improvements in the health, education levels, and living conditions of the average Chinese family and in the status of women, which have helped change traditional values favoring large family size; and

■ A well-enforced code of conduct involving very late marriage, abstinence from premarital sex, and the sublimation of energies into work, sports, and study.

Despite the success of the program, the 1979 target of one percent growth apparently was not reached and the growth rate may even have climbed. This would help explain several tough new anti-natalist measures, including a system of very persuasive incentives and disincentives.

Behind these tough measures are some serious social and economic problems, among them the thin margin between hard-won increases in agricultural production and escalating demand for food; continued pressure on urban housing and unemployment; and a serious shortage of educational facilities. Chinese leaders are justly proud of the development gains and fertility declines achieved so far; but at the same time they are concerned that these fall short of the mark.

China's official goal is population stabilization by the year 2000 but, for this to happen, fertility rates will have to fall below replacement level in order to counter the effects of an increasing base of reproductive age couples. Hence, the newly announced campaign for one-child families.

How the Chinese Leadership Sees It: (The following is an excerpt from an article in *The People's Daily,* August 11, 1979, by Vice Premier Chen Muhua, Director, Birth Planning Leading Group of the State Council.)

National economic development must observe the law of planned and proportionate development. Thus, the planned control of population increase in our nation is not a subjective and arbitrary decision; rather, it is dictated and demanded by the socialist mode of production.

It is necessary to admit that under the concrete conditions existing in our country, our efforts to develop the national economy, improve the people's standard of living, and create jobs have been rendered more difficult by rapid population increase....

Too rapid an increase in population is detrimental to the acceleration of capital accumulation.... The accumulated total cost... of raising the 600 million persons born since liberation has been more than 100 billion yuan—or about thirty percent

---

continuing to fall behind population growth. Huge increases in food imports by LDCs are expected—a trend that was under way throughout the 1970s as many countries lost ground in food production per person.

It is highly questionable whether food-exporting developed countries such as the United States can continue increasing agricultural production and exports without endangering their own future productivity. The technology of high-yield agriculture has already been widely applied. No new technologies currently being developed or on the horizon promise improvements in crop yields comparable to those achieved in the 1950s or 1960s.

A massive famine has so far been averted—by luck more than design. But the world food picture is no brighter today than it was a decade or two ago. In some respects, it is even dimmer.

LDC Food Potential: Tropical soils often have proved to be much less fertile and productive than once believed; hence the potential for increasing yields in tropical agriculture is lower than expected, while susceptibility to environmental damage is higher. The potential does exist in LDCs, however, for substantial increases in yields through better cultivation methods and especially through introduction of higher-yielding crop strains.

A POSITIVE GUIDE TO THE FUTURE

of the accumulated total national income over these years. If there had been fewer births since liberation... the state's capital accumulation would have been much larger, without creating any shortage of labor supply.

Rapid population increase hinders our efforts to quickly raise the scientific and cultural level of the whole nation.... We must build a vast army of workers, peasants, and intellectuals who are capable of grasping modern scientific and technical knowledge and managing modern production....But the number of persons to be trained...is not counted in millions or tens of millions, it is rather several hundred million....Among the important factors responsible for the backwardness of our educational enterprise and for unemployment are our large population size and the rapid growth of population, especially the population of adolescents and youths.

Rapid increase in population is detrimental to the improvement of the people's standard of living: Between 1953 and 1978, consumer income increased by 180 percent, an increase of no small magnitude. But the population increased by 66.7 percent. Consequently, per capita consumption increased by only one-third. Fifty-eight percent of the annual increase in consumption funds had to be expended to meet the needs of the newly added population, leaving only 42 percent of the increase to improve the living standard of the base population....

...We are in the process of drawing up a series of socio-economic measures aimed at encouraging couples to have one child. The first type of measure consists of a material reward, such as the provision of child health care fees, extra workpoints, extra pensions for the old and retired. A second type of measure is an institutional guaranteed reward: in

allocating jobs and housing in urban areas and private plots and housing lots in rural villages, priority will be given to couples who have only one child. As for those who insist on having several children in spite of patient attempts at persuasion and education, we will impose a multi-child tax on them....

...The land area of our country is roughly equal to that of the United States. But our arable land is only half that of the United States. Because of rapid population increase, the per capita arable land area has become smaller and smaller.

...If the population continues to increase rapidly and massively, the per capita arable land area will shrink further....In view of the plenitude of people and the scarcity of arable land characteristic of our country, combined with our inability vastly to raise the per-unit yield in the short run, it is incorrect to claim that "a large population is not something to be afraid of."

From *Birth Planning in China*, The Draper Fund Report Number 8, March 1980. Reprinted with permission by the Draper Fund.

However, efforts to introduce a technological package based on high-yield varieties—known as the "green revolution"—have met with less than overwhelming success. The "green revolution" package was transferred more or less directly from developed countries with temperate climates to LDCs in the tropics and subtropics, where the techniques were often inappropriate to local conditions.

The "green revolution" also has created a host of social and economic problems. There are serious obstacles to establishing the new technology among small, poor farmers—those who grow most of the food consumed in LDCs and who most need help. But even if these social and economic problems were overcome and the "green revolution" technology, as presently conceived, were universally adopted, the environmental effects would be severe, and most LDCs are poorly equipped to deal with them. Moreover, harvests of the higher-yielding strains tend to be less dependable than those of traditional varieties because high-yield

crops planted as monocultures are comparatively vulnerable to unfavorable weather, water and fertilizer shortages, and pests.

Doubling or Tripling LDC Food Production?

Doubling or tripling food production in LDCs over the next 40 years will not be easily accomplished—even though the momentum of population growth guarantees that the hungry mouths will be there to feed. And this increase is the minimum required. Far greater production increases as well as vastly improved distribution of food would be required to meet expanding demands of the relatively affluent while improving the hopelessly inadequate diets of the poorest third of most LDCs' populations.

The need is enormous, and the problems are many. Meanwhile, the fertility of productive land in wide areas is being undermined by land abuse (deforestation, overcultivation, overgrazing, improper irrigation, lack of soil protection, etc.) and poor management. Consequently, generating needed increases in food production will require reversing the trends toward desertification and land degradation—putting agriculture on a sustainable footing—as well as raising yields. And both goals must be met without inflicting any more environmental damage than necessary. Successfully achieving all this will require the application of huge amounts of capital, energy, and materials, not to mention human ingenuity and hard work.

To repeat: the realization is dawning that doubling or tripling food production in LDCs over the next 40 years will not be easily accomplished, even though the momentum of population growth guarantees that the hungry mouths will be there.

MAKING IT HAPPEN:

Family Planning in Singapore

The small Southeast Asian country of Singapore has made great strides since its independence following World War 2. One important aspect of Singapore's planning for the future has been its policies for the control of population growth.

Singapore has a large ethnic Chinese population, and has had to work against the traditional Chinese value of large families. The rate of population increase in Singapore has been reduced to 1.43 percent.

This population stabilization campaign utilized advertising, propaganda, and economic policy. The economic penalties credited with a major role in decreasing birth rates include:

■ no paid maternity leave for any child after the second;
■ increasing delivery fees with each child in a family;
■ no income tax relief after the third child;
■ no priority rating for primary school admission after the third child; and
■ no priority in allocation by the Housing and Development Board of flats for large families.

The government of Singapore has even considered a positive tax, which would be imposed on parents of more than three children because of the increased burden they place upon the community.

Other institutional changes that have contributed to the decreased birth rate are:

■ education of women to allow them to escape the process of endless motherhood;
■ support of legal abortion and voluntary sterilization; and
■ expanded availability of contraception information and devices through 27 full-time and 10 part-time clinics.

The government believes that, the more highly educated the parents are, the fewer children they will produce. Official policy therefore openly encourages education. Immigration to Singapore is restricted to highly-educated individuals.

Ecosystems Being Destroyed

Accelerating destruction of ecological systems everywhere: This is the aspect of environmental deterioration that most threatens humanity's future. It is also the least widely perceived and understood consequence of the overall environmental deterioration.

Natural ecosystems provide many essential services for human society. Society can neither do without these nor adequately replace them. These free services include:

■ maintenance of the quality of the atmosphere;
■ production and preservation of soils;
■ cycling of nutrients essential for all life, including agricultural productivity;
■ maintenance of natural watersheds to control floods, moderate droughts, and stabilize weather;
■ control of the vast majority of potential crop pests and vectors of disease;
■ disposal of wastes; and
■ operation of a vast genetic reservoir of potentially useful plants, animals, and microorganisms.

The systems that provide these vital environmental services are being assaulted and undermined at a continually rising rate around the world. And the species that are part of

Wind erosion in the south end of the San Joaquin Valley. Before the storm, all the land was grassland; overgrazing is the cause of the soil erosion visible on the land to the right of the fence.

J.K. Nakata, U.S. Geological Survey-Stanford University

these systems are being heedlessly decimated far more rapidly than evolutionary processes can possibly replace them.

All this is happening with no regard for the many plant and animal species' actual or potential value to humanity as sources of food, drugs, fibers, or other useful substances. Still less is the regard for their value as working parts of vital ecosystems.

Healthy, natural ecosystems are utterly indispensable to the support of civilization. Without them, society would quickly choke, smother, and be poisoned by its own wastes. Climates would become harsher, and there could be no successful agriculture.

It is strange that many people think society has been freed from dependence on nature just when exploding human numbers make civilization more dependent than ever on natural environmental systems and more vulnerable than ever to the effects of their disruption.

Unless the destruction of natural ecosystems is halted and a serious effort made to preserve, protect, and—where possible—regenerate them, there is no hope whatever of establishing a genuinely sustainable civilization.

Bills Incurred

Bills now coming due: Assessment of our present situation must include an accounting of consequences that have not yet caught up with us.

Many forms of environmental abuse, such as deforestation, soil erosion, or introduction of toxic chemicals into the biosphere have effects that may be delayed for years. Far from being in total control of the environment, we are only beginning to understand the scope of damage that we and our predecessors have inflicted.

Similarly, the high proportion of young people in the world population guarantees substantially increased resource consumption, even if population growth were miraculously halted overnight. Even with no increase in affluence, as children grow and mature they need more food and materials.

Yet the revolution of rising expectations is continuing worldwide. What will be the costs of meeting the material demands already considered essential by nearly everyone in rich countries and by rapidly growing numbers of people in poor countries? No one seems to have counted up the total cost or attempted to analyze in detail the interrelated consequences— environmental, social, economic.

Demographic Conclusion: Given a human population recently grown to four and a half billion that already shows signs of overstraining the earth's carrying capacity, with a large portion of that population inadequately supported, one demographic conclusion becomes inescapable. *Global population growth must be ended as soon as humanely and politically possible, and a reduction in size must follow.*

The eventual size of a sustainable population is impossible to predict now. The present carrying capacity of the earth is unknown. It is probably well below even the present 4.5 billion except at a very low average living standard. Moreover, the level at which human culture can be sustained indefinitely may well be substantially reduced, at least for a long time, by the stress of supporting even temporarily a far larger population.

Now is the time to contemplate the size of a sustainable population on a country-by-country basis. Many populations will double within a generation, but most of the resources available to support them—arable land, water, minerals, energy, living space— will not. The urgent task now is to put the brakes on growth, to hold the population peak as low as possible, and to move past it to stability or reduction as soon as possible.

Wind erosion: exposed root systems indicate an 11.7 inch loss of loosely consolidated sand and soil.

J.K. Nakata, U.S. Geological Survey-Stanford University

MAKING IT HAPPEN:

What U.S. Role?

Somebody else's problem? The United States, if it chose, could, by its example, play a crucial role in guiding civilization through the difficult demographic transition now in progress and that must be accelerated.

Our nation is, of course, an economic and military superpower; we are the leading proponent of what has become the dominant world culture. We are also per capita the leading consumer—and waster—of the world's resources. Even in the United States, our lifestyle is not sustainable on any long-term basis. Certainly our standards of material consumption cannot serve as a model for the rest of the world.

In many less developed countries, the United States has actively supported family planning programs. But we have yet to establish a domestic population policy of our own. Our policy should be to stabilize and ultimately reduce our domestic population.

Simply by declaring our intention and embarking on a path of natural decrease in our own population within the next three decades, the United States could do much to ensure a brighter future for coming generations. Doing this would also enhance our credibility abroad.

The advantages of ending population growth can be explained through the media and public education. The goal of ending growth can be reinforced by various policies. And the one-child family can be promoted as the norm. Incentives can be created and penalties imposed through taxes, government jobs, and government services. Early marriage and child-bearing can be strongly discouraged. Emphasis can be placed on the *quality* of child care.

Migratory Pressures: Immigration policies can changed to be more realistic and humane but also to conform to the goal of ending population growth in the United States. One way to reduce the present flow of people from LDCs to the United States would be to help poorer countries to improve the lives of their people.

Worldwide migratory pressures will ultimately subside only when the huge differences in affluence and opportunity between rich and poor regions and nations have been largely eliminated, and when the pressures of rapid population growth have been reduced. Poverty, lack of unemployment opportunities, and displacement from the land are major factors in the migration of people to the rich countries.

PLANET

A sustainable world is in our future. We can reach it the hard, unpleasant way by pursuing policies of the past unchanged until we collide with some natural limit. Or we can be leaders in planning and creating a sustainable future that everyone can enjoy.

We can either rise to meet the challenges of population control, human equity (including intergenerational equity), and planetary management—or we can shrink from them until disaster overtakes us. The choice is ours. □

Who am I? Anne H. Ehrlich

I suppose the most obvious fact about my life—and the context in which I am most often seen—is that I am married to Paul Ehrlich. But my interest in population and resource problems began in my college days in the early 1950s before I met Paul. Population growth and pressure on natural resources (particularly land and soil) were subjects of Fairfield Osborne's *Our Plundered Planet* (1948), which I read for Western Civ a quarter-century ago. The message was reemphasized in a course of geography that same year.

Later when I met Paul, we found these concerns to be among our many mutual interests. By then I had also developed some interest and background in biology. After we were married, I took more courses and began working part-time as a technician, at first utilizing my skills as an illustrator.

As our daughter grew up, I worked full-time, doing microscope work that dovetailed nicely with Paul's field work in biology. I accompanied Paul (as did our daughter until she went to college) literally around the world with my microscope. I gained not only valuable experience as a biologist, but also firsthand views of the interrelated problems in developing and developed countries on every continent. And, as a working biologist associating with other professional biologists around the world, I became increasingly familiar with the environmental component of the population-resource-environment dilemma.

During the 1960s Paul increasingly became involved in policy aspects—especially the "population explosion" with which he is most closely identified by the public. I accompanied him there, too. For a long time, I confined my activities to writing and managing the information files (no small task, and vital to our work). I still do both of these but in recent years I have become more "public" myself, giving speeches, teaching, consulting, and actively participating in public-interest groups such as Friends of the Earth and the U.S. Association for The Club of Rome.

The Sustainable Society:

Economic Realities— and Ethical Choices

By Herman E. Daly

Two things are necessary for a sustainable economy. First, there must be a renewable resource base. And second, there must be a scale of population and of per capita consumption that is within the sustainable yield of that renewable resource base.

The resource base: Human beings are the only species that does not live entirely on the budget of solar energy income. All other forms of life live off the produce of the surface of the earth where current sunshine is captured by plants.

Until the advent of industrialization some two hundred years ago, human beings lived almost entirely on a resource base of forests, fisheries, grasslands, and croplands. We are still dependent on these natural systems, but we have increased their short-run productivity through subsidies of nonrenewable fossil fuels and minerals.

There is good evidence that, even with the aid of such large subsidies, the global per capita productivity of each of the four natural systems that sustain us has peaked and is now declining. Forest productivity, as measured by cubic meters per capita per year, peaked in

1967 (at 0.67 cubic meters). Fisheries productivity, as measured by kilograms of fish caught per year per capita, peaked in 1970 (at 19.5 kilograms). For grasslands, we use the measure of annual per capita output of wool, mutton, and beef. Wool peaked in 1960 (at 0.86 kilograms); mutton in 1972 (at 1.92 kilograms); and beef in 1976 (at 342 kilograms).

Of course, trend is not destiny. It is conceivable that some of these peaks will be surpassed, especially the most recent ones. Also, the numbers reflect substitution as well as natural limits: plastics for wood, artificial fibers for wool.

But it is very sobering to remember that these levels of productivity were attained in the first place only with the aid of large fossil fuel and mineral subsidies to mechanization, irrigation, fertilizers, insecticides, and transport. Furthermore, many substitutes (plastics and artificial fibers) are themselves petroleum derivatives.

It is difficult to believe that existing levels of output per person can be

MAKING IT HAPPEN:

Economics—"the dismal science"?

The allocation of scarce resources among competing goals has always been the subject matter of economics. Because this discipline reminds us that our desires often seem greater than the resources available to satisfy those desires, economics has been termed "the dismal science."

However, when one moves out from the individual to the global context, it appears that economics should be labeled "the optimistic science." According to many economists, we need not concern ourselves on a global scale with the issues of choice in the face of scarcity that perplex individuals, localities, and nations. We can live off our global capital indefinitely, these economists suggest, and we need not worry about balancing our global budgets.

Thus, traditional economic analysis has little to say about sustainability or about absolute resource constraints on growth and productivity. Economists also argue that individual allocation decisions will inevitably lead to beneficial social outcomes. They believe, along with Adam Smith, in the operation of a beneficent "invisible hand."

Herman Daly is one of the small but growing number of economists who takes exception to these views. He does not reject economic analysis. Rather, he believes that its precepts must be applied to the globe as well as the individual, community, and nation.

According to Daly, a realistic view of human history, combining economic and ecological perspectives, points to the existence of what he calls a *long-term aggregate biophysical budget constraint*. If one accepts this argument, it follows that *the total number of industrially developed person-years available is limited.* The existence of this limited resource is a fundamental economic reality.

Economic analysis can be of great value in illuminating the choices open to us. But, like most forms of analysis, it cannot decide for us what we ought to do. Rather, it can emphasize our practical options, so that our decisions can combine idealism with realism.

It is clear that attainment of a humane and sustainable future will require us to deal more effectively with problems of scarcity than we have heretofore. Economic analysis is essential. But analysis that begins with the premise that for the earth as a whole the essentially infinite wants and needs of an expanding human population can for the foreseeable future be met may not only be wrong, but dangerous.

---

maintained, much less surpassed, as we deplete the global stock of easily available petroleum and as world population continues to grow.

As nonrenewable resources run out... The danger is that, as we run out of nonrenewable resources, we will try to maintain the existing scale and rate of growth.

We would try to do this by overexploiting our renewable resource base, thereby reducing its carrying capacity and, consequently, the total quantity and/or quality of life ever to be lived on earth.

There are two ways in which the too-rapid depletion of nonrenewable resources contributes directly to the destruction of renewables. First, high rates of depletion result in high rates of pollution of air and water, which directly threaten biological resources. Second, and more importantly, rapid use of nonrenewables has allowed us to reach and sustain temporarily a combined scale of population and per capita consumption that cannot be sustained indefinitely by renewable resources alone.

To the extent that we overexploit natural systems and reduce their capacity to trap the energy of sunlight, we are, in effect, consuming tomorrow's sunshine as well as today's and yesterday's.

The question of how fast: I would not draw the conclusion that all minerals should be left in the ground. Or that we should renounce industrialization.

But I think we must conclude that there are limits to how fast such exhaustible resources should be used. I think we must conclude that we are in danger of reducing the carrying capacity of the earth because we have used mineral wealth too rapidly and built up too large a scale of population and per capita consumption to be sustained by our renewable resource base.

If we persist in trying to maintain the present scale (or worse, the present rate of growth of scale) on the basis of renewable resources alone as our minerals subsidy is depleted, then we will be permanently diminishing global carrying capacity and future life. Even this neglects the problem of past differences in accumulation between rich and poor that must be made up.

Diminishing returns: It also neglects diminishing returns, for we will be forced to use poorer grade ores from less accessible places, and to dispose of ever larger quantities of waste. The gross throughput will increase much faster than the net product, and it is the gross throughput that affects the environment.

This pushes us toward recognizing that there is a long-run aggregate biophysical budget constraint. One way to pose this constraint in graphic terms is to state that the total number of person-years of industrially developed living is limited. It is limited by the pattern of geologic concentrations of minerals in the earth's crust. It is limited by the capacity of complex ecosystems to absorb either large quantities or exotic qualities of waste materials or heat.

Recognizing this limit of the long-run aggregate biophysical budget is the basic economic imperative. Equally imperative is developing the social and

---

PLANET

political institutions and discipline to keep the scale of population and per capita consumption within the biophysical budget. Once we recognize this condition, then a number of important and difficult ethical questions arise.

Ethical Questions

How will the limited number of person-years of developed living be apportioned among nations? Among social classes within nations? Among generations? Among species? To what extent should present luxury be limited to permit more lives in the future?

To what extent should non-human life be sacrificed in exchange for more person-years of developed living? If a man or woman is worth many sparrows, then we must take it for granted that a sparrow's worth is not zero. How many sparrow-years are worth one person-year? How many sparrow-years are worth the difference between one person-year of luxurious living and one person-year of frugal living?

Should the burden of scarcity be made to fall more heavily on the present or the future? On the standard of consumption or on numbers of people?

Varying answers have already implicitly been given at UN conferences in Stockholm, Budapest, and Rome. The leaders of overdeveloped countries seem to be saying that the burden of scarcity should fall more heavily on numbers, especially of the poor. Let the poor limit their populations.

The leaders of the underdeveloped countries seem to be saying that the burden should fall on the high consumption of the rich. Let the rich limit their per capita consumption.

Both sides seem willing to pass as much of the burden as possible on to the future and on to non-human life. Let the future have fewer people, reduced per capita consumption, and fewer non-human species.

To the extent that we refrain from exploiting the future, we sharpen the conflict between classes within the present generation. The old Marxist class conflict between capital and labor has been softened by rapid economic growth.

Ethical questions of fair distribution within one generation must now be considered simultaneously with questions of equity between generations. In this three-way struggle, the future has the great disadvantage of not yet existing.

An important step toward getting the concept of sustainability into economics would be to recognize a long-run aggregate biophysical budget constraint—something like the ecologists' notion of permanent carrying capacity. It would refer to that level of throughput which the ecosystems of a country could continue to supply to the economy on a sustainable-yield basis, and the waste products of which could be absorbed by the ecosystems in a sustainable way.

In technical terms, the supply of both low entropy (i.e., usable) matter-energy inputs and the assimilation of high entropy (i.e., less usable, or waste) outputs must be restricted to a level sustainable by the global ecosystem.

A monument to acid rain and air pollution—"Cleopatra's Needle," sent from Egypt to New York City in the 1890s. The inscription on the east face (*left*) is still legible; the inscription on the west face (*right*) has been erased by chemicals in the city's air, driven by the prevailing westerly winds. Ninety years in New York has done more damage to the stone than 3,500 years in Egypt. (*UN photo*)

MAKING IT HAPPEN:

Institutional Imperatives

The long-run aggregate biophysical budget provides the supply side of the throughput equation. The demand side consists of per capita resource consumption times population.

$$\text{(Supply Side)} \quad B = \frac{B}{P} \times P \quad \text{(Demand Side)}$$

There is clearly a trade-off on the demand side; a larger per capita consumption implies a smaller population and vice versa.

Sufficiency is already built into the economy of non-human species: the standard of consumption is given by nature. But human populations have variable standards of per capita consumption, and the size of human populations must be as much determined by standard of consumption as by aggregate resources.

From this we can see that there are three kinds of interdependent limits that it is imperative to institutionalize.

■ **The real biophysical budget must be recognized and given a financial counterpart in the money economy.** I have suggested a depletion quota auction or a national ad valorem severance tax. Either of these would be an effective and efficient means of limiting the thoughput flow to some ecologically determined (not market determined) level.

■ **The need to limit population has long been apparent and many schemes have been suggested.**

■ **An institution for limiting the range of inequality in per capita resource consumption is needed.** The ratio R/P in the budget equation refers to "average" per capita resource consumption. But there are of course those above and those below that average. Simple minimum and maximum limits on individual income would restrict inequality without implying a jealous quest for flat equality.

Standard growth economics, of course, denies that the long-run aggregate biophysical budget is

Aztec Ruins in New Mexico

National Park Service, U.S. Department of Interior

constrained. The traditional answer of economists, and politicians, is to balance the equation by continually raising B, the supply side of the equation. But the ecological necessity of limiting economic growth at some level is irrefutable, and the evidence that current levels are already unsustainable is persuasive.

Technology: Throughout, I have spoken of per capita resource consumption rather than standard of living or quality of life. Limiting resource consumption certainly does not foreclose all possibility of improving the standard of living. It merely directs our efforts toward improving efficiency and away from increasing the scale of resource throughput. Efficiency cannot increase forever, but we still have a long way to go in that direction.

If, however, one wants to evade the obvious conclusion that economic and demographic growth must be limited, then one must put faith in technological miracles. Even if one believes that such miracles will be possible in the future, does not common sense require that we limit the growth of scale while waiting for the second coming of Prometheus?

Who am I?   **Herman E. Daly**

Herman E. Daly is Professor of Economics at Louisiana State University and holds a B.A. from Rice University and a Ph.D. from Vanderbilt University. He has served as a Ford Foundation Visiting Professor at the University of Ceara, Brazil; as a Research Associate at Yale University; and as a Visiting Fellow at the Australian National University. He was a member of the Committee on Mineral Resources and the Environment of the National Academy of Sciences, and recipient of Louisiana State University's Distinguished Research Master Award. He has served on the boards of advisors of numerous environmental organizations, including Friends of the Earth. His interest in economic development, resources, environment, and population has resulted in numerous articles in professional journals as well as several books, including *Steady-State Economics* (1977) and *Economics, Ecology, and Ethics* (1980).

OBRIAN

"In Larchmont! Well, really!"

In his environmental message of May 1977, President Jimmy Carter directed the Council on Environmental Quality and the Department of State "to make a one-year study of the probable changes in the world's population, natural resources, and environment through the end of the century" to serve as a "foundation for longer-term planning."

Thirteen U.S. departments or agencies participated in this unique study, the results of which, under the title *The Global 2000 Report to the President,* were published in three volumes in July 1980. The following is a brief summary of the major findings and conclusions contained in the report.

The Global 2000
Report to the President:

A Reconnaissance of the Year 2000

It is important to understand that (1) these findings are not predictions of future events, but projections based on the best available information within the U.S. Government on current trends; and (2) that the study proceeded on the basic assumptions that national policies regarding population stability, resource conservation, and environmental protection would remain essentially unchanged through the end of the century; that present rates of technological advance would continue; and that wars or other major global catastrophes would not occur. This overview of global conditions in the year 2000 may therefore be seen as the likely outcome of maintaining a policy of "business as usual" for another two decades.

Perhaps equally as arresting as these findings, *The Global 2000 Report* concluded that the present "foundation for longer-term planning" in the U.S. Government is decidedly shaky. Owing to "serious inconsistencies in the methods and assumptions" used by various agencies, inadequate or incomplete data, and "serious gaps and contradictions" in the U.S. Government's analytic capability, the results of the study may, in fact, present a more optimistic view of global trends than warranted by current realities. For a nation that considers itself a leader among the technically advanced, affluent, industrial societies of the world, it is difficult to find reassurance in this assessment from the study:

"To put it more simply, the analysis shows that the executive agencies of the U.S. Government are not now capable of presenting the President with internally consistent projections of world trends in population, resources, and environment for the next two decades." (*The Global 2000 Report to the President,* Vol. 2, p. 454.)

■ **Population:** World population will grow from 4.5 billion today to more than 6 billion in 2000. Although the annual percentage rate of growth will slow marginally, population will actually be growing faster, in terms of numbers of people, in 2000 than it is today. Most of the 100 million people added to the world's population each year will live in the poorest countries, which will contain about four-fifths of

the human race by the end of the century.

■ **Income:** The income gap between rich and poor nations will widen, and the per capita gross national product of the less developed countries will remain at generally low levels. For example, gross national product in the populous nations of South Asia—India, Bangladesh, and Pakistan—will still be less than $200 per capita (in 1975 dollars) by 2000, despite considerable increases in production and national income. Some 800 million people now live in absolute poverty; if current policies remain unchanged, their number could grow to more than one billion by the end of the century.

■ **Energy:** The increases in world food production projected by the study are based on continued improvements in crop yields per acre—improvements which depend heavily on energy-intensive technologies like fertilizer, pesticides, fuel for tractors, and power for irrigation. Yet the study's projections show no early relief from the world's tight energy situation. World oil production is expected to level off by the 1990s.

Many Less Developed Countries will have difficulty meeting their energy needs because of rapidly increasing prices. Projected needs for wood for fuel will exceed available supplies by about 25 percent before the turn of the century.

"A rapid escalation of fossil fuel prices or a sudden interruption of supply," the report says, "could severely disturb world agricultural production, raise food prices, and deprive large numbers of people of adequate food."

■ **Forest:** The conversion of forested land to agricultural use and the demand for fuelwood and forest products will continue to deplete the world's forests, which are now disappearing at the rate of 18-20 million hectares—an area half the size of California—a year. As much as 40 percent of the remaining forests in poor countries may be gone by 2000. Most of the loss will be in tropical and subtropical areas, rather than in temperate zone countries where forest management regimes are better established.

PLANET

■ **Genetic Resources:** The loss of tropical forests, along with the impact of pollution and other pressures on habitats, will cause massive destruction of the planet's genetic resource base. Between 500,000 and two million plant and animal species—15 to 20 percent of all species on earth—could be extinguished by 2000. One-half to two-thirds of the extinctions will result from the clearing or degradation of tropical forests.

■ **Water Resources:** Deforestation will also contribute to severe regional water shortages and deterioration of water quality. Deforestation destabilizes water supplies, aggravates water shortages in dry seasons, and intensifies flooding, soil erosion, and siltation of rivers and reservoirs in rainy reasons. Population growth alone will cause demands for water to at least double from 1971 levels; still greater increases would be needed to improve standards of living. Competition for water resources will also exacerbate international tensions.

The report notes that 148 of the world's major river basins are shared by two countries and 52 are shared by three to ten countries. "Long-standing conflicts over shared rivers...could easily intensify," the report says.

■ **Air Quality:** Industrial growth · is also likely to worsen air quality. Air pollution in some cities in less developed countries is already far above levels considered safe by the World Health Organization. Increasing burning of fossil fuels, especially coal, may contribute to acid rain damage to lakes, plants, and building materials and to the increasing concentration of carbon dioxide in the earth's atmosphere, possibly leading to climatic changes that could have highly disruptive effects on world agriculture. Depletion of the stratospheric ozone layer, attributed partly to chlorofluorocarbon emissions from aerosol cans and refrigeration equipment, could also have an adverse effect on food crops and human health.

■ **Food:** While total world food production will increase by 90 percent in the 30 years from 1970 to 2000, a global per capita increase of less than 15 percent is projected over the same period. Most of the increase will go to countries that are already comparatively well-fed. In South Asia, the Middle East, and the poorer countries of Africa, per capita food consumption will increase marginally at best and in some areas may actually decline below present inadequate levels. Real prices of food are expected to double during the same 30-year period.

■ **Cropland:** The land on which food is grown will become less productive in many parts of the world. The spread of desert-like conditions now claims an area the size of Maine each year. Croplands are lost to production as soils deteriorate because of erosion, compaction, and waterlogging and salinization on irrigated lands. Meanwhile, cropland in the United States and other industrialized countries is being converted rapidly to other uses—residential development, highways, shopping centers, and reservoirs. In poorer countries as well, villages and cities are expanding at the expense of productive cropland.

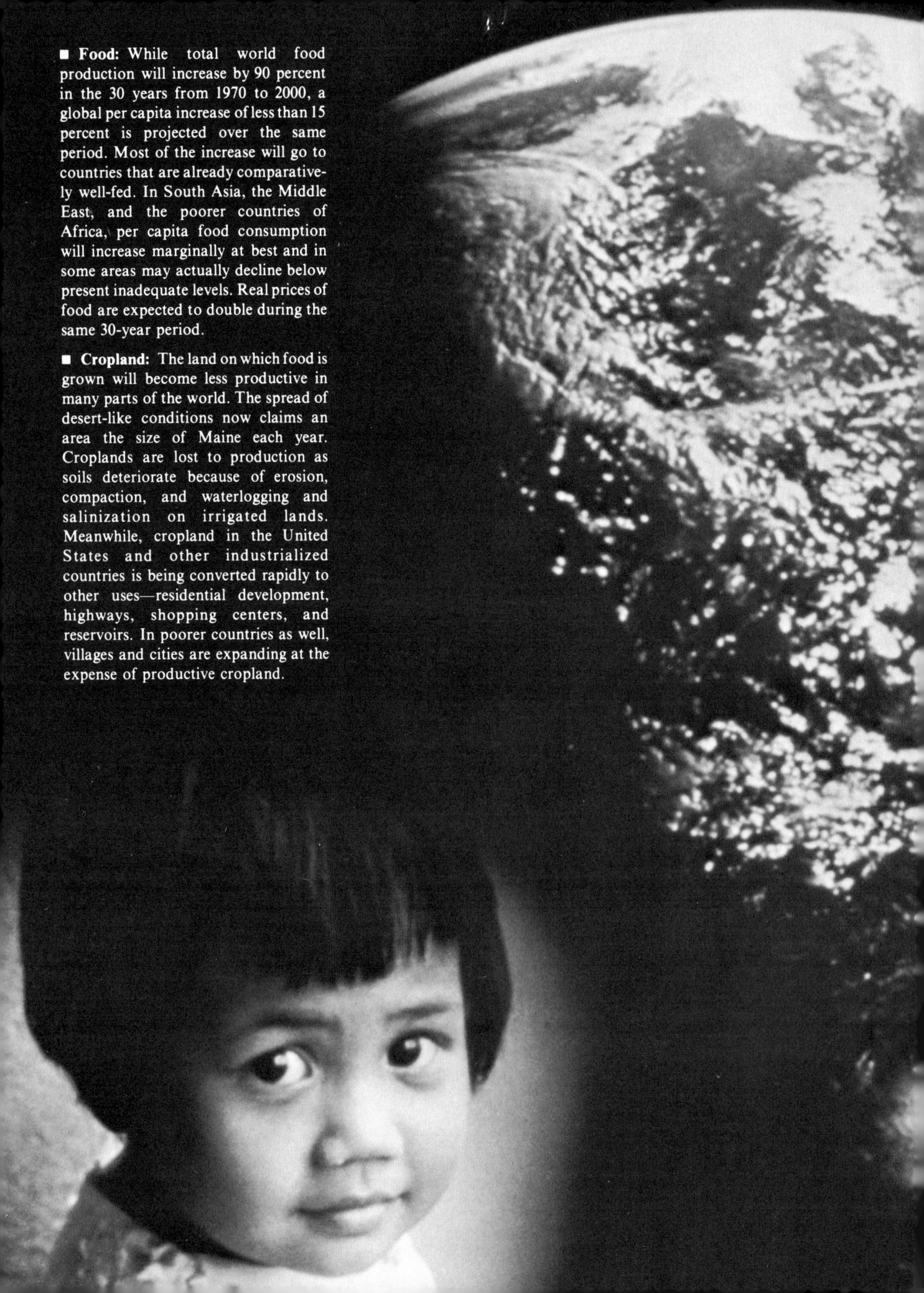

NASA/Carol Christensen

U.S. Air Force, Department of Defense

Rollout ceremony for the Lockhed TR-1, 15 July, 1981 at Palmdale, California.

New Visions—1.

Security for What?

Commentary

There are broad national goals on which most Americans could probably agree, even though our personal goals for the future may differ. Here are some of the most important.

■ **National security.** We would like to be able to live at peace with other nations of the world, and to be secure from the danger that other nations might impose their will upon us and take from us what we have.

■ **Economic security and enhanced quality of life.** We would like to have a healthy economic system in which we have the opportunity to pursue our personal goals without fear, and on an equal basis with others. We would like to look forward with confidence to a better future, economically, for ourselves and our children. We would like our fellow citizens, especially the poor and disadvantaged, to have a fairer share in the benefits of the economic system, preferably without risk or sacrifice on our part.

■ **Efficiency and productivity of industry.** We would like our nation's industrial plant to be modern, efficient, and productive. It should offer the largest possible number of people secure and meaningful employment, and should provide desirable goods and services of high quality at prices we can afford.

■ **Preservation of the private enterprise system.** We would like these goals to be attained in an atmosphere of economic freedom and independence, in which economic choices and business decisions can be made in every sector of the economy with maximum discretion. Every American should have the opportunity to try to "make it" on their own.

We do not appear to have made much progress as a nation toward these goals during the past two decades. In fact, many observers and a substantial number of the American people believe that things are getting worse, not better. There are also predictions of less national security, less economic security, reduced quality of life, less industrial productivity, and less freedom of enterprise in the future than in the past.

Why have things gone less well than we hoped? And why do many see little prospect of improvement in the future?

Our problem is more fundamental than most of us have imagined. It is rooted in a set of beliefs about how things happen in our world—beliefs about cause-and-effect relationships—which we have taken pretty much for granted.

If our mental model were in this respect to be inaccurate or incomplete, or rooted in understandings of life that are erroneous or outmoded, then questions about the merits of any particular program or policy may be completely irrelevant. It would be as if a two-dimensional being were attempting to accomplish things in a three-dimensional world.

Here are some examples of widely accepted views upon which programs and policies have been based, along with possible alternative views of how the world behaves.

The Widely Accepted View:

National Security depends principally on military might. If our national security appears to be threatened, we must respond by increasing our military capabilities.

An Alternative View:

The long-accepted relationship between military strength and national secuirty has been fundamentally altered. Diplomacy and military power may be largely irrelevant to dealing with longer range threats to our security.

The Widely Accepted View:

Economic security, enhanced quality of life, and the general economic health of our nation depend on high rates of economic growth and increased production of material goods.

An Alternative View:

The quality of the economic growth rather than the sheer quantity of it is what matters. Continued emphasis on purely quantitative growth will, in fact, be self-defeating.

The Widely Accepted View:

Economic growth is essential if we are to deal with social and economic inequities in our own society and assist other nations in attaining higher standards of living.

An Alternative View:

Economic growth tends to conceal rather than correct social and economic inequities. Progress and development involve a complex mixture of human factors. The provision of more material goods and services is but one of these.

The Widely Accepted View:

Excessive government regulation is a principal cause of declining productivity and inflation.

An Alternative View:

The present scale of regulation is an inevitable consequence of large-scale of industrial production, and has only minor effects on either inflation or industrial productivity.

The Widely Accepted View:

In order to reduce inflation, we must accept higher levels of unemployment.

An Alternative View:

There is no clear cause-and-effect relationship between inflation and unemployment. We can have high levels of both or low levels of both.

The Widely Accepted View:

Reliance on traditional government budget and fiscal policies can rapidly restore the vitality and momentum of the American economy.

An Alternative View:

The problems affecting the American economy in many cases will not respond to changes in government budget and fiscal policy. They reflect national and global trends that demand new responses.

Self-fulfilling Prophecies? Most people today do not believe we can really create the future we want. It is easy to talk about the need to look at the world in an entirely new way, but extremely hard to do it. Our view of how things happen is a product of lifelong training and experience in our culture. Our view of our world is deeply rooted within our subconscious. We are attached to it emotionally. We are accustomed to it; it is a habit of mind and we unconsciously assume it.

Our model of the world includes the belief that we have no real power to change things. Unless that belief changes, we will never make anything happen. And the predictions of those who foresee a gloomy future ahead will become self-fulfilling prophecies.

The first step in breaking out of this vicious and self-defeating circle is to open our minds to seeing the world in new ways. The following sections deal with some familiar issues from alternative perspectives. Their purpose is to suggest why it is that so many well-intentioned policies have proved to be ineffective. □

Flatland

The characters...are assorted geometric shapes living in an exclusively two-dimensional world.

As the story opens, the narrator, a middle-aged Square, has a disturbing dream in which he visits a one-dimensional realm, Lineland, whose inhabitants can move only from point to point. With mounting frustration he attempts to explain himself—that he is a Line of Lines, from a domain where you can move not only from point to point but also from side to side. The angry Linelanders are about to attack him when he awakens.

Later that same day, he attempts to help his grandson, a Little Hexagon, with his studies. The grandson suggests the possibility of a Third Dimension—a realm with up and down as well as side to side. The Square proclaims this notion foolish and unimaginable.

That very night the Square has an extraordinary, life-changing encounter; a visit from an inhabitant of Spaceland, the realm of Three Dimensions.

At first, the Square is merely puzzled by his visitor, a peculiar circle who seems to change in size, even disappear. The visitor explains that he is a Sphere. He only seemed to change size and disappear because he was moving toward the Square in space and descending at the same time.

Realizing that argument alone will not convince the Square of the Third Dimension, the exasperated Sphere creates for him the experience of depth.

The Square is badly shaken. There was a dizzy, sickening sensation of sight that was not like seeing; I saw a Line that was no Line, Space that was not Space, I was myself and not myself. When I could find voice, I shrieked aloud in agony, "Either this is madness or it is Hell."

"It is neither," calmly replied the voice of the Sphere. "It is Knowledge; it is Three Dimensions. Open your eyes once again and try to look steadily."

Having had an insight into another dimension, the Square becomes an evangelist, attempting to convince his fellow Flatlanders that Space is more than just a wild notion of mathematicians.

Because of his insistence, he is finally imprisoned, for the public good. Every year thereafter the high priest of Flatland, the Chief Circle, checks with him to see if he has regained his senses, but the stubborn Square continues to insist that there is a third dimension. He cannot forget it, he cannot explain it.

—from *Flatland: A Romance of Many Dimensions*, by Edwin A. Abbott [1884] (NY: Dover Publications, 1952) as retold by Marilyn Ferguson, *The Aquarian Conspiracy* (1979).

From *The Aquarian Conspiracy*, by Marilyn Ferguson. Copyright © 1980 by Marilyn Ferguson.

Commentary

In the U.S. Congress, it is almost always easy to find votes to increase the budget for "national defense"—that is, armaments—and to cut the budget for foreign assistance, especially non-military assistance. The Congress here reflects the popularly held view that the first priority of government is "national security"—the survival of our nation and its capacity to live in a peaceful world.

But suppose... What if the greatest threats to our national security are not military?

Suppose, for example, that the most effective way of maintaining national security were to devote our resources to the eradication of hunger and malnutrition in the world?—rather than the purchase and development of greater numbers of sophisticated weapons?

To reach such a conclusion would require that we look at the world in an entirely different way. Thomas W. Wilson, Jr., argues here that *to reduce hunger is to increase security.*

Wilson is a Washington-based writer and consultant. He has studied and written about international problems as a journalist, government official, program director and international civil servant.

Hunger, Politics and National Security:

The Changing Agenda

By Thomas W. Wilson

The point is not merely that spreading hunger could lead to dangerous social unrest and violence—or even that everything is connected to everything else in this interdependent world.

The unfamiliar but straightforward point is that for us to reduce hunger is to increase our national security. There are many places to start this story—and one of them is Stockholm in 1972.

New perceptions of the human environment: Something happened on the way to the United Nations Conference on the Human Environment in Stockholm in 1972, and what happened has profound implications for the behavior of states, for the security of nations, and for the well-being of peoples in the years ahead.

The industrialized nations came to Stockholm wanting to talk about some newly perceived problems in the natural environment—pollution of air and water, depletion of nonrenewable resources, and the like.

But the newly developing countries were only interested in talking about what they considered to be their environment—hunger, poverty, and the deprivations of underdevelopment. And a stalemate developed.

Then, in a rare flash of political genius, the two sides agreed, quietly and unofficially, that the "human environment" necessarily embraces both natural systems and man-made systems—the biosphere and the technosphere and, inescapably, their interrelationships.

MAKING IT HAPPEN:

It was at the same time obvious and a stunning insight, for the concept of an indivisible human environment completely bypasses traditional interstate ("inter-national") affairs. And it embraces matters that are inherently transnational, outside of political-military tradition, and incompatible with all of the prevailing concepts of international relations.

What this perspective implied was nothing less than new ways of looking at the world and fresh outlooks on the human prospect.

Threats to National Security

Yet the security risk of not pursuing this agenda more forcefully is only now becoming evident. What is becoming more and more clear is that a dangerously narrow concept of national defense constitutes a major obstacle to action on global issues. And—surprisingly at first glance—it constitutes also an additional security burden in and by itself.

Security and the threat of military violence: Everyone knows this is a dangerous world. A fragile peace is under constant threat of being ruptured by military adventure and armed violence. Ancient feuds persist. New conflicts arise. By one count, there have been 119 wars since the end of World War 2. And always in the background is the brooding presence of The Bomb.

Meanwhile, a compulsive search for superiority over presumed enemies still drives most military planners. Geopolitical doctrines formulated by European statesmen and warriors in the 18th and 19th centuries still determine the behavior of most governments most of the time. And the "mad momentum" of more sophisticated military technology goes on and on.

No one in their right mind would argue against the need for military protection from military dangers—which explains, of course, the obsessive preoccupation of governments with national defense.

A governmental ho-hum: Certainly governments have not rushed to embrace this integrative view of the human predicament. No governments are known to be building national policies around perceptions of transnational affairs. Responsibility for management of the global agenda remains largely unassigned in national capitals. And political leaders are occupied overwhelmingly with what they perceive to be more urgent aspects of world politics.

But it also means that governmental concerns for security are focused almost exclusively on arms, armed forces, and military facilities; and no one with their wits about them can believe any more that military might alone can guarantee national security.

"National security": Even in a military context, "national security" is a concept as imprecise and many-sided as "balance of power" or "vital interests." What is more, the presumed correlation between military power and national safety has become a tenuous one if the most powerful weapon systems in the world cannot be used in practice—as was the case in Korea and Vietnam.

Indeed, the power to institute a general strike was the major weapon in bringing down a regime in Iran that held all the cards of conventional power. If an armed expeditionary force still has punitive power, so now does OPEC as an international cartel; if a naval task force is an instrument of coercion, so today is a disciplined band of terrorists or kidnappers.

New threats to national security: In addition to the above, a new and profoundly different range of threats to the security of life on earth has emerged in very recent years. These dangers call for strategic concepts that can take account of the intricate ways in which once-disparate areas of thought and action—like security, politics, and hunger—now interact in ways that defy conventional wisdom and the political-military tradition.

At the root of all this is a radical expansion in the number of problems with a global reach.

A Radical Expansion of the Number of Problems

Problems beyond the reach of national governments: These problems with a global reach are not new. The International Postal Union was established in the last century for the simple reason that an internationally agreed system was needed to assure that mail sent from one country would be delivered in another.

Common rules were needed also for maritime navigation to prevent collisions at sea. As needs have arisen, other international agreements and institutions have come into being to cope with problems beyond the control of single nations. Allocations of radio frequencies, international air traffic regulations, weather reporting, and communications by satellite are familiar examples.

Since the end of World War 2, the steady expansion of international organizations and agreements and regulations for dealing with a lengthening list of transnational problems has been a distinguishing feature of international life. The whole system of United Nations Specialized Agencies stands in evidence—as does a dramatic growth in non-governmental organizations and the inauguration of major scientific research projects like the International Geophysical Year.

Most of these activities have been treated by the traditional major powers as technical appendages to the main body of international political relations—located somewhere on the outer periphery of day-to-day diplomacy. The perceived mainstream of interstate relations has remained the traditional political-military questions, plus the pursuit of other national interests, mainly economic, as these interests were defined—usually in competitive terms—in national capitals.

New Sorts of Security Issues

The emergent global agenda: In the 1970s there was an explosive expansion of the agenda of global issues. Suddenly governments were seized at the international political level with an extraordinary range of pressing problems that they were accustomed to think of as domestic issues and as matters for "experts" to cope with.

It can now be seen that the emergent global agenda is made up of two extremely broad, fundamental, and interacting classes of problems:

■ **Issues bearing upon the state of the planet:** During the 1970s governments met at the plenipotentiary level to consider man-made stresses on the environmental systems, global water resources, desert encroachment, and management of the vast ocean systems that cover most of the planet.

■ **Issues bearing upon the human condition:** During the same period governments gathered to contemplate problems of world population growth, world food supplies, the human habitat, the changing roles of women, global employment, basic health-delivery systems, and the use of science and technology to ease the burdens of poverty.

Manifestly, there are no global "solutions" to such world problems. Indeed, major progress surely will require greater degrees of self-reliance at regional, national, and lower levels.

But the fact remains that these issues have been internationalized and politicized within the UN system during the past decade. And while the focus of action for the relief of poverty necessarily must be on the local level, success will depend heavily on ready access to knowledge, techniques, expertise, and managerial know-how that will require new levels of international consultation, analysis, organization, and collaboration.

In brief, a new agenda of issues bearing upon the state of the planet and the human condition has entered the mainstream of world affairs. The very nature and content of day-to-day international politics have been transformed.

Non-military threats to security: There is a dawning awareness of a security component in humankind's rising capacity to bring about disasters analagous to major natural calamities—or, for that matter, conventional wars.

We can begin now to understand that the burning of fossil fuels might trigger a change in the global climate with an impact on the United States comparable to a major military defeat.

We can comprehend that man-made damage to the ozone layer might cause more damage than drought, flood, or crop failure. We can view with alarm the potential consequences of headlong destruction of tropical forests—or the steady deterioration of environmentally crucial coastal zones. And we can hear voices from the scientific community warning of potential threats to human survival implicit in the rapid disappearance of animal species and the accelerating loss of genetic diversity in the world of plants that provide energy for life on earth.

Armed conflict clearly is not the only security risk we face.

Protection from clear and present dangers? What can national security possibly mean for the inhabitants of a living planet whose basic biological systems—croplands, pastures, forests, fisheries—are deteriorating steadily under human pressures?

Certainly no level of exertion under present concepts of national defense can offer protection from clear and present dangers to the security of planet Earth. Notions of "vital national interest" need a drastic revision. Protection of the earth's basic systems must become an integral part of any modern concept of security.

The Slide Downhill

Governments appear virtually oblivious to the security implications of a failure to cope with the new global agenda.

"Defense" issues are still kept in one compartment of policy, analysis and thought—while "hunger," "topsoil," and "nutrition," for example, remain in their own segregated realms of perception, expertise, and action.

This, after all, is how we have been taught to organize and to think about our affairs. The problem now is that this way of thinking about things has itself become a threat to our security.

An extended failure to undertake positive political action on global problems can only contribute to a breakdown of that minimal state of order essential to the peaceful conduct of human affairs—and hence to the security of nations and peoples.

The prevailing obsession with the military dimension of national security imperils that security on three counts:

■ It is limited to perceptions, policies, and modes of behavior that have led, during this century, to two world wars, a nuclear balance of terror, the survival of traditional warfare, unheard-of levels of armament and a conceptual trap from which there seems to be no escape and no outcome save war or the tyranny of massive armaments for the indefinite future.

■ It withholds resources—material and human—from urgent tasks in defense of the security of the planet as a whole, a security without which the very meaning of national security is called into serious question.

■ Near-exclusive concern with the military aspect of security contributes to political paralysis with regard to the emerging global agenda and leads to neglect of those disintegrative forces that are pushing the world toward the unmarked threshold between peace and war.

Manifestly, the only way out of political paralysis is through political action. Positive action on global issues—necessarily cooperative because of the inherent nature of these problems—is not an alternative to national defense. It is an essential component of a security doctrine that takes with utter seriousness contemporary political realities.

The Inability to Act

Political paralysis: There is another, more subtle, and insidious threat to enduring security in the world today— and it joins the new global agenda directly to the issue of world peace and security.

This new menace is political paralysis. It is greatly compounded by the advent of world-level problems. And it is a much more credible threat than instant disaster from either military or non-military sources.

The reality of this danger is cited over and again by respectable and responsible citizens in and out of government. Authors of major economic and technical studies, for example, repeatedly insist that resolution of contemporary problems depends less on physical, economic, or technical factors than upon social, political, and institutional factors. On one subject after another, panels of distinguished experts present their complex and quantified evaluations with the now familiar caveat that their conclusions mean little or nothing in the absence of "political will." Yet the point is left hanging in mid-air.

A general failure in our ability to govern a world? It requires no gift of prophecy to imagine that, in the years just ahead, governments in the industrial world might fail to adapt soon enough to the evident end of an era of cheap and abundant energy, . . . might not come to grips with their problems of inflation, stagnation and unemployment, . . . might fall into divisive internal conflict between "developers" and "environmentalists," . . . might yield to protectionist and isolationist pressures, . . . might find themselves simply unable to meet the combined, inflated costs of military establishments, sophisticated technologies, infrastructure maintenance, welfare programs, decontamination of toxic wastes, and conversion of the economy to sustainable patterns of production and consumption—with the result that policymaking machinery remains paralyzed while once-manageable problems degenerate into unmanageable crises.

It is not difficult, either, to imagine that governments in the developing world might fall short in their efforts to contain the population explosion, . . . might fail to absorb the floodtides of young people now entering the labor market, . . . might be forced to default on foreign debts, lose access to capital markets and see their development

programs grind to a stop, . . . might fail to resolve internal conflicts between forces of modernization and forces of traditionalism, . . . might not invest enough resources in rural sectors to prevent a continuing spread of the deep poverty symbolized by chronic hunger—with the probable result that political and social institutions would become increasingly vulnerable to collapse and overthrow in an atmosphere of endemic violence.

Squandering vital resources? Nor is it difficult to envision, in the world arena, that nations large and small might continue to dissipate massive resources on military arsenals; . . . that developing countries might fail to translate their demands for international reforms into specific, negotiable proposals; . . . that the industrial societies, sorely tried by their own problems and weary of being blamed for all of history's ills, might dig in their heels against reform of the world economy; . . . that UN proceedings might become characterized by extreme rhetoric, political arrogance, double standards, and a diminishing capacity to act or even generate consensus; . . . that the North-South dialogue might remain

---

Summing up: The thesis presented here can be summarized as follows:

■ **Military strength and national security:** There has been a traditional correlation between these.

But this correlation has been lessened over the past several decades by an exponential growth in the destructiveness of strategic weapons, a spread of modern military capabilities to many nations, the heightened vulnerability of essential services in an interdependent world, a rise in the incidence of violence and terrorism, and the emergence of new sources of power and influence such as the OPEC cartel in international affairs.

■ **Sudden emergence of world-level problems unknown to traditional diplomacy:** Demographic, economic, political, and environmental world trends have combined in recent years to create a qualitatively distinct class of unavoidable world-level problems that are virtually unknown to traditional diplomacy. These are problems that are beyond the reach of national governments and cannot be fitted into received theories of competitive

interstate behavior. These problems are coming increasingly to dominate world affairs, cannot be wished away, and are indifferent to military force.

■ **The unfamiliarity of the dangers:** The emergence of these issues has brought, on the one hand, physical threats to planetary systems that support all life, and, on the other, dangers of an irreversible slide into anarchy, tyranny, violence, and even war, through a political paralysis induced largely by preoccupation with traditional military concepts of national security.

■ **Far-reaching implications of world-level problems:** A draft agenda of some of these global problems was identified during the 1970s. But the far-reaching implications of world-level problems for peace, security, and the conduct of international relations has not yet been recognized by national governments.

Serious political efforts to address the most pressing global problems would assist in the national security of all countries by diminishing the threat of political paralysis in the face of shared needs for world action.

might remain paralyzed by stalemate—with the result that international relations would degenerate further into competitive struggles over maldistributed resources while natural systems continue to deteriorate at accelerating rates.

The likely price of political paralysis: There will likely not be a quantifiable catastrophe or a sudden collapse, but rather deepening darkness, degradation, and nameless danger—through drift and delay, standoff and stalemate, indecision, inertia, and a bankruptcy of political innovation as structure crumbles, order unravels, violence is more and more taken for granted—and opportunities proliferate for totalitarian scavengers of domestic or foreign origin.

Belfast, Beirut, Teheran, Phnom Penh, and Kabul may or may not be models of things to come. But evidence of a failing capacity to cope with modern problems—to make policy, to take decisions, to act in time—is to be found on all sides and at all levels.

And perhaps the greatest danger is that the agenda of global issues identified in the 1970s could become the neglected agenda of the 1980s, neglected through failure to perceive the connection between the state of the planet, the human condition, and world security.

Needed—a Turnaround of Global Proportions

What is needed now is a visible, universally accepted point of departure for breaking out of a vicious circle that is degrading the human condition.

As things stand now, population growth, hunger, poverty, and unemployment operate to amplify one another and reinforce negative trends, compounding the general predicament.

Needed—a way to turn the tide: The plain purpose of political action on global issues is to reverse the underlying trends that have produced the present predicament. The point is to reverse the dynamics by setting in motion a positive synergistic process in which progress in one area facilitates progress in related ones.

In principle there are many ways to go about this. Some existing activities could be cited as evidence that a number of starts have already been made in population, environmental protection, health care, and many other areas.

However, the most promising for this purpose seems to be a serious and systematic world program to contain, reduce, and ultimately eliminate hunger and chronic malnutrition everywhere.

This is not suggested as a cure for all aspects of the human predicament, but rather as a way to begin turning the tide.

The moral, humanitarian, technical, and economic arguments for eliminating human hunger are well known and need be mentioned only in passing:

■ Relief of hunger has the automatic sanction of religious and philosophical belief systems and is immune to political attack on ideological grounds.

■ Access to a health-sustaining diet is near the top of all lists of human rights and of basic human needs as well.

■ Experts have testified again and again that existing knowledge and technologies are adequate to the task, and several nations have, in fact, turned the tide against rampant malnutrition in recent decades.

■ To improve nutrition is to strike directly at the roots of poverty—a strategy now considered essential to a successful economic development process in the very poor countries—and to go straight to the desperate needs of the most disadvantaged of all, women and children.

To these familiar propositions, one should now add two important political points:

First, North-South relations are structured essentially around economic development to relieve hunger and other burdens of poverty, and a cooperative attack on malnutrition could help to break the deadlock in these relations.

MAKING IT HAPPEN:

Agency for International Development

Second, a world food system providing greater self-reliance for major countries and areas will require structural changes that would be visible steps toward a more viable international economic system, thus easing political strains over the issue of reforming the system.

In point of fact, the goal of eliminating world hunger already has been adopted by unanimous consent of the World Food Conference of 1974. A broad strategy for stimulating agri-cultural output from small farms in food-short countries was adopted by consensus at that time. New funds have been raised internationally for invest-ment in support of the agreed strategy. International institutions in the agricultural field have since been strengthened. And some of the developing countries already are allocating increased resources to the agricultural sector in their development plans.

Perceptions, priorities and political will: Students of the world food problem are agreed on one fundamental point: the greatest single obstacle to ending world hunger is the lack of political commitment to get on with the job.

Political will has to do, among other things, with perceptions and priorities.

Until fairly recently, the hunger problem was perceived largely as a matter of providing emergency aid to the victims of floods, droughts, and other natural disasters. At the 1974 World Food Conference, the problem was viewed essentially in terms of total world food supply, and hence a matter of agricultural output and productivity.

At the same time, there has been a growing awareness that the day-to-day problem of hunger at the village and neighborhood level is a disease called chronic malnutrition. This is a poverty-rooted problem that has to do with employment, education, the status of women, clean water, and cultural taboos, for example—as well as with land, water, seeds, and fertilizer.

What is finally emerging is an expanded perception of hunger as a political problem on the agenda of global issues that defines the contemporary world predicament. Hunger is near the center of that set of issues that bear on the human condition.

But it also relates to state-of-the-planet issues—for assured food supplies manifestly require the sustained security of those basic natural systems that provide the possibility of agriculture in the first place.

Agency for International Development

The Politics of the World Predicament

The politics of the world predicament: Both common sense and basic morality have long held that the world cannot long endure half fed and half starved. But the case for rolling back the advance of chronic malnutrition goes beyond morality, ethics, justice, compassion—beyond development strategy and technical feasibility—to the politics of the world predicament and to the world's capacity to live in peace by coping with its highest priority problems.

As things stand now, both sides in the North-South dialogue face dilemmas. The developing countries can agree easily that they want to participate in economic decisions that affect their interests. But they cannot agree on just how the system should be redesigned. Nor can they agree just where to take hold of the problem.

Their cohesiveness as a group they perceive to be their only source of bargaining strength. In order to maintain that cohesiveness, these countries have kept their demands extremely general—thus precluding serious negotiations and limiting debate to sweeping abstraction.

The market-economy industrialized nations complain that the New International Economic Order demanded by developing countries is a slogan without recognizable substance. Furthermore, they say that, whatever it means, economic reform is not an event to be declared by majority resolution, but rather a process of adaptation to be negotiated on a technical basis over a period of time.

In this defensive posture, most of the developed countries have managed to appear as stand-pat defenders of an international economic system that no

MAKING IT HAPPEN:

Who am I?   Thomas W. Wilson

Agency for International Development

longer works in the interests of either rich or poor. The socialist countries, for their own reasons, have elected to remain bystanders.

So, in effect, nothing happens: This is the anatomy of political paralysis. It poisons an international political environment already polluted by ancient feuds, strategic conflicts, and recurrent violence. It accelerates the drift into a general crisis in the world's capacity to handle contemporary problems. It reinforces disintegrative tendencies already undermining world peace.

This is the context in which political paralysis can most clearly be seen as a dangerous threat to national security. It is a threat every bit as "real" as military hardware in the hands of unfriendly nation-states.

The relevance of world hunger, then, is the opportunity it offers for political action—visible and positive political action—to enhance the world's capacity to live in peace by resolving contemporary world problems.

Underlying this relationship between hunger and national peace and security is an historic convergence of two sets of interests with dramatic potential for human affairs: *Political action to relieve global problems simultaneously serves both the interests of national security and the interests of people—collectively and individually.*

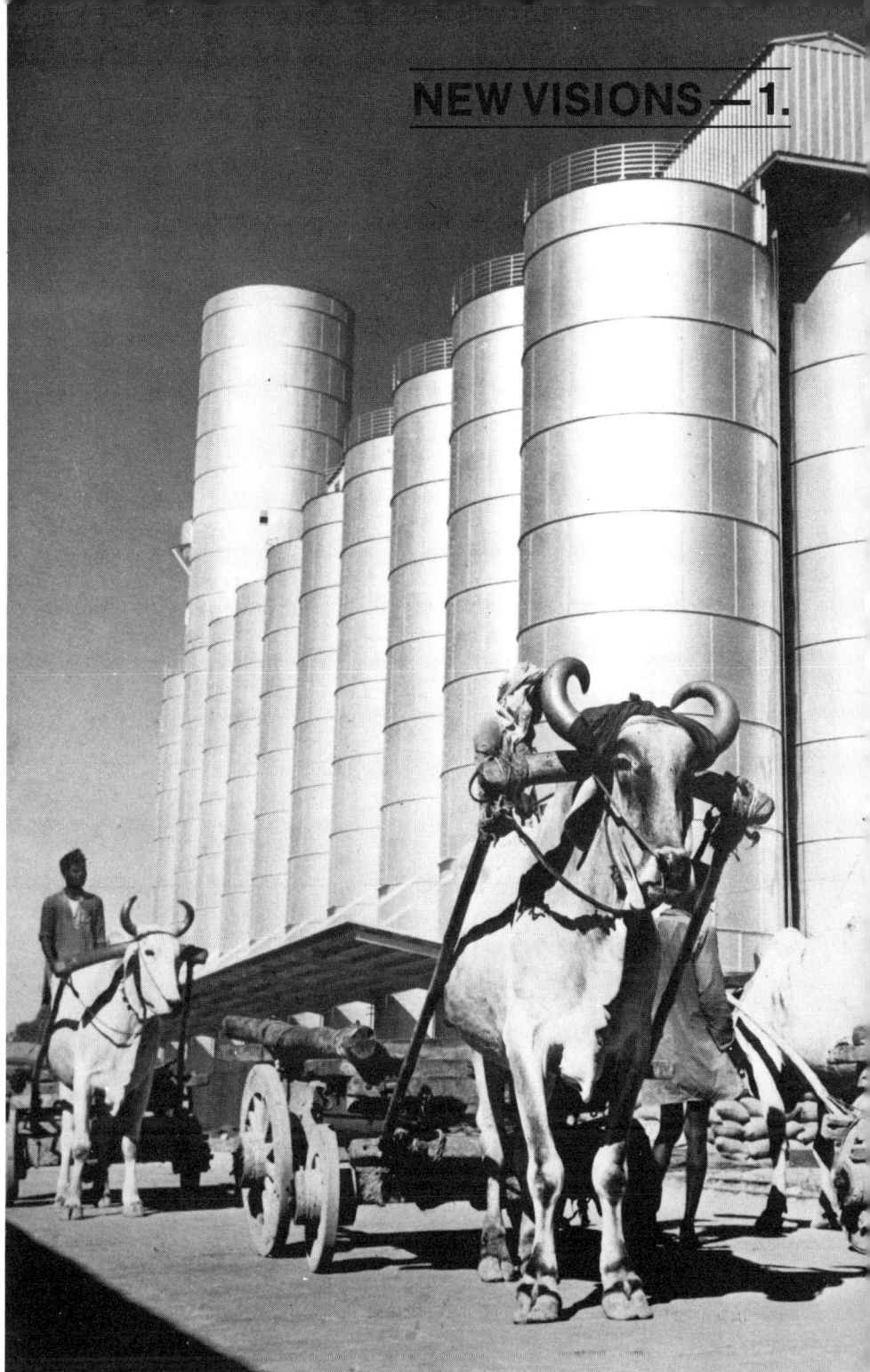

A modern concept of security must embrace not only
■ defense of national borders.
It must include as well
■ the safety of planetary systems, and
■ freedom from the tyranny of political paralysis.

The public perception of the direct connection between world hunger and national security could become the wellspring for that extra measure of political will which is going to be needed to overcome hunger and get on with the rest of the global agenda as well. □

Adapted from a paper originally prepared for the Presidential Commission on World Hunger, May 1980.

Armaments and Human Misery

By Robert Cory

Nearly $500 billion is the annual price tag of the world's expenditure on military activities, more than the total income of the poorest third of the world's people. Beyond the immense consumption of resources that investment represents, there is an impact on human quality of life that is difficult to measure.

Taxpayers support the training and maintenance of approximately 60 million persons directly employed in military activities. Nations devote to military research and development one-third of their skilled scientists and engineers. Many communities are dependent on defense, relying on employment and income from military activities for their prosperity. In the United States as in many other countries, group activities, youth organizations, veterans' associations, and patriotic clubs help sustain attitudes of trust and belief in the value of military institutions. In many societies, weapons represent the highest level of technological achievement. Each year the sophistication—and the cost—of weapons increases.

Arms races, both regional and global, thus have deep roots in global social and economic structures, and directly affect most of the world's peoples.

Armament and development: What does this mean for the relationships between the wealthy peoples and the poorest peoples of the world? In more precise political terms, what is the relationship between global armament and development?

In moral terms, what are the ethics of a world in which guns and bombs proliferate but resources are lacking for a war on the scourges of hunger, disease, and illiteracy?

The outbreak of war cuts dramat-ically through all such theoretical questions: people die, homes are destroyed, land is laid waste, and means of production are crippled. In a vision of the utopia to come at war's end, swords are beaten into plowshares and despite their suffering and oppression the poor ultimately attain freedom. In the real world, however, transfers of wealth and power often involve the use of arms, create ever more complex political problems, and leave a legacy of human pain.

In all nations the process of arms escalation is generally swift and politically easy. The process of arms deescalation, on the other hand, is slow and politically difficult, involving changes of attitude as well as social and economic disruption. Escalation decisions are usually made by nations unilaterally; deescalation decisions usually come only—if at all—through laborious multilateral negotiation.

Nations receiving arms not only pay the price of dependence for training and for replacement of parts, they also pay social and economic costs. These costs may vary, depending on the particular crises a nation faces.

■ **The relatively poor peoples** make the greatest proportional sacrifice in order to acquire a well-equipped, modern military establishment.

Relatively poor nations must use skills and resources that might otherwise be devoted to efforts to meet basic human needs. Foreign exchange and domestic resources tend to move disproportionately to the benefit of a military caste. In the case of dictatorship, the military often serves in addition as an internal police force to help fortify the existing regime against popular uprisings.

Moreover, transfer of sophisticated weapons technology often brings with it "Westernized" patterns of consumption, with the effect of further widening the domestic gap between the rich and the poor.

In a few cases, of course, it can be argued that the stability and mobilization of resources made possible by militarization have laid the foundation for a leap into the modern age. Some maintain this is the case in Taiwan and South Korea. Military aid may indeed be followed by overseas investment, and various forms of payment may be received by a developing country for the use of military bases by a larger power.

How to estimate the comprehensive impact of this type of arms dependence over time, however, is a question of complexity and controversy among students of development. Nevertheless, it is clear that poverty also increases in most of the militarized low-income nations.

■ A second kind of effect is that felt by **the newly oil-rich states,** of which Saudi Arabia and, until recently, Iran are examples.

There, oil-hungry industrial nations compete to sell quantities of sophisticated weapons and send both private and public training teams to help those as yet unskilled in military technology operate and maintain those weapons.

Oil income may thus serve as the primary promoter of social change, for such nations often can afford increased development and social services as well as imports of weapons. But the investment in weaponry may increase both inflation and political corruption, even while giving greater military security.

■ A third effect may be felt by **nations involved in military confrontation:** Israel, one of the world's foremost importers of arms, is an example of a vigorous and potentially prosperous nation making heavy sacrifices for military security. A series of regional wars have been fought since World War 2 in the Middle East. The weapons have been imported predominantly from the arms factories of the Soviet Union, United States, and industrially advanced European countries. Foregone investments, rampant inflation, and social tensions are among the costs.

The peace conversion benefit: The armament traffic of the world has resulted in a transfer of technology and resources unprecedented in world history. While the political demands for a "New International Economic Order" go essentially unheeded, what some have labeled a "New International Military Order" has been taking place.

A committee of experts under U.N. auspices, led by the vigorous Swedish disarmament diplomat Inga Thorssen, has been established to study and report

MAKING IT HAPPEN:

on the possibilities of converting the military resources of both the industrial nations and developing nations to instruments for meeting urgent human needs. In other words, what is being explored is ways to achieve development through disarmament.

How can developing nations use their own disarmament-released resources for meeting basic human needs? There would be an immediate short-term loss of jobs and domestic markets in dismantling the military sector of a nation's economy. Creating supplemental economic and political structures to ease the transition requires not only political will but planning and investment as great as—or even greater than—that previously devoted to the military.

The result in the long run could be a positive reconversion of both economy and society. A large-scale military demobilization would require comparable civil mobilization. This could involve basic social changes such as land reform, extension of medical care, broadening of educational opportunity, and assurance of equitable political participation, thus accelerating the productivity of human capital as well as financial capital. Otherwise, many of the potential benefits of disarmament would be lost.

In industrial nations: How can the industrial nations direct their military demobilization toward the relief of poverty and suffering in the poorer nations?

In the short run, demobilization would bring loss of industrial jobs and considerable economic dislocation even in the developed countries. However, the "peace dividend" would in the longer run bring benefits that also could be shared with poorer nations, provided there were the political will to pursue basic attitudinal and structural changes.

How best to accomplish that sharing is another problem. Development in the poorer nations cannot be assured by the transfer of money alone. Experience in economic assistance programs, both multilateral and bilateral, seems to teach that progress depends, rather, on a multitude of factors such as population control, land reform, health care, management training, education, political skill, strength of morale, and—not least—indigenous hope and aspiration.

Many critics judge present foreign aid programs to be counterproductive. Yet others with long experience in and deep concern for the development process believe such aid is essential. Robert S. McNamara, former president of The World Bank, believes it is possible

NEW VISIONS—1.

within this century to reduce substantially, if not to elimi nate, starvation, epidemic disease, and illiteracy.

That level of achievement can never be attained, however, without a great increase in global investment in development. One great potential source of such investment could be the diversion of resources, technology, and human energy from armaments.

Disarmament has its own justification. The reduction of violence and avoidance of mass destruction. And development, of course, has its own justification: the alleviation of human misery.

If, however, it were possible to pursue both disarmament and development with the same ingenuity, skill, and political will that is now devoted to militarism, a new spiritual, moral, and economic frontier could be opened.

That frontier may seem distant today, and the threat of mass destruction continues to loom. But finding an alternative to the arms race poses a challenge of the highest importance to human ingenuity. It holds the promise of an immense breakthrough in meeting human needs and advancing global development.

Can people be helped to find an alternative to this suicidal arms race?

I write on my return to Washington after a time of retreat on the shores of a mountain lake in Maine (without telephone or television). The beauty of nature is life-affirming. I come back from a family reunion with my children and grandchildren. The joy of celebrating together in many little ways gives me a sense of reality. And then, in this Capital of the nation, I meet again with many people who are wrestling with courage and skill against injustice and against war-threatening policies.

At Hiroshima in 1973, I was gripped by a sense of the world's insanity. I realized that the great-power arsenals already held the

Who am I?   Robert Cory

equivalent of a million Hiroshima bombs!

I am fortunate in being free to work on a frontier, a frontier of hope and reason in the struggle for a world without war, a world of compassion and life-affirmation.

That freedom came to me in 1961 when I put behind me the rituals of college teaching—texts, lectures, and grades. First at the United Nations and then on Capitol Hill, I began trying to open doors to understanding for students of all ages. As a planner of informal dialogues and seminars, I observe people venturing in self-education: experiencing the confusion, complexity, and challenge of political reality.

At a time when many people in positions of power seem willing to sacrifice humane values on the altar of national military security, my work on behalf of the Religious Society of Friends (Quakers) has helped me to hold to a vision of peace.

"Mr. Semple, who wants to stimulate the economy, help the cities, and clean up the environment, I'd like you to meet Mr. Hobart, who wants to let the economy, the cities, and the environment take care of themselves. I'm sure you two will have a lot to talk about."

Drawing by Stan Hunt ©1976 The New Yorker Magazine

New Visions—2.

Growth Toward What?

Robert Hamrin is an economist by training. He writes about the influence of economists on present policies and the need he sees for further evolution in traditional economic views. The present structure of the economics discipline makes it very hard for economists to deal with Hamrin's idea of emphasizing *qualitative* growth in goods and services GNP (rather than growth in their sheer quantity).

Philosophers of science call the particular view of reality associated with an academic discipline such as economics a *paradigm*. The dangerous thing about paradigms is that we often forget we have them. We assume that what we perceive is reality, instead of only one facet of it. Even worse, we often react with hostility to those who don't see the world our way. Part of Hamrin's analysis suggests the outline of a new paradigm for the economics of the future.

The Challenge: Growth with Quality

By Robert D. Hamrin

What we've taken for granted since World War 2: A principal goal of U.S. national economic policy in the decades since World War 2 has been undifferentiated quantitative growth in Gross National Product. We have taken it for granted that:

■ *growth of both the economy and the population is good;*

■ *industrialization, having brought us material abundance, is good;*

■ *raw materials necessary for industrial production are, and always will be, available (if not domestically, then easily through imports);*

■ *the environment is a convenient, free, receptacle for our wastes; and*

■ *we control the behavior of our economy, in large degree, through aggregate domestic economic policies (involving such things as tax rates, the size of government expenditures and budget deficits, interest rates, and rate of increase in the money supply).*

Assumptions like these are often not stated explicitly. Instead, they are implicitly accepted on the basis of a generalized body of experience about what has "worked" in the past.

Psychologists tell us that such bodies of experience influence not only how we act, but even what we see. There is a strong tendency to focus on things that reinforce our assumptions and to neglect those that do not.

When our assumptions about the way the world works are threatened, the goals and values that depend on those assumptions are threatened as well. We therefore often react to new information challenging our world view with resentment and anger. We would rather pretend not to see the new realities, or deny their validity, than abandon goals and values that we have long cherished.

The influence of economists: The world view of U.S. national leaders in both government and industry has been strongly influenced by economists. The economic theories and tools developed to combat the depression of the 1930s and subsequent recessions have been widely accepted.

For example, it is almost an article of faith that tax cuts and public spending programs that stimulate demand are effective means of coping with economic recession.

Economists have also been instrumental in deciding what sorts of data we should collect to measure progress or identify problem areas. Acceptance of such standard measurement concepts as "gross national product," "national income," "capital," "labor productivity," and the like, has made it possible for developed, industrialized nations to collect relatively consistent and comparable information about how their economies behave over time. The world depicted by this information has become, for all intents and purposes, the reality of economic policy making.

How views of the world undergo change: However much we would like to preserve our view of the world, we cannot do so indefinitely if it proves to be distorted or incomplete.

Frequently, the process of change begins with a vague feeling of anxiety and uncertainty; a sense that things are not working out as they should. In the United States, the rise of the environmental movement, culminating in Earth Day 1970, provided a first indication of such concern. Another indication was the intensity and acrimony of the debate triggered in 1972 by publication of *The Limits to Growth.*

The national trauma suffered as a result of the Vietnam war, while certainly going far beyond economic issues, contributed to popular uncertainty and suspicion about the quality of U.S. policy choices. By the close of the decade, in a widely televised speech, President Carter spoke of a "crisis of confidence" and a "fundamental malaise."

The American people and their leaders seemed confused and anxious. Doubts grew about the past vision of America's special destiny and the widely accepted belief that it could be realized, as before, by the pursuit of growth through hard work and the application of greater resources and new technologies. The economic policies and institutions stemming from this belief were increasingly called into question.

Needed—a new focus for American economic policy: Much of the malaise afflicting Americans arises from a

perception that the United States is walking backwards into the future. Like the change of scenes in a motion picture, the old image has begun to fade from the screen but no new one has yet clearly appeared.

Without a vision of what America could or should be like in the future, the nation drifts in uncertainty like a ship without a compass or even a clear destination. It is little wonder that Americans today are apprehensive about "whither we are tending," and uncertain about the prescriptions of government leaders.

What is needed is at least a partial view of a new focus for American economic policy. We must continue to grow, but our growth must be more qualitative than quantitative. Qualitative growth may be defined as sustainable, directed toward desirable human ends, and guided by sound environmental, physical, and moral principles.

A Profound Transformation Already Underway

To grasp the importance of this vision of the future, we must begin with a better understanding of the present. The United States is currently in the midst of a profound transformation of its underlying economic structure, accompanied by an historic shift in values, attitudes, and priorities. At the same time, a changing international economy imposes a new role on the United States.

These developments are defining a new and different reality. In this "new world," total allegiance to the goal of undifferentiated quantitative economic growth is unlikely to provide effective policy options. Greater emphasis on qualitative growth appears to be an attractive, viable alternative.

Sources of economic growth since World War 2: The principal sources of our economic growth during the post-

World War 2 period have been growth in the labor force, rising labor productivity, and rising productivity of capital. All of these indicators have shown reduced growth rates or, in the case of capital productivity, actual declines during the 1970s.

The trend lines contrast markedly with those of the 1950s and 1960s. Many of the same trends are being experienced by other industrialized nations, and they too will witness slower growth. A study by the Organization for Economic Cooperation and Development [an organization sponsored by the industrialized free-market nations] concluded that, even under favorable assumptions, output growth rates would not return to those of the 1960s, while unemployment levels and inflation rates would remain on average higher than in the 1960s.

The heart of the current transformation: Important as those changes are, the United States is experiencing the effects of three much more fundamental, long-term trends. These constitute the heart of the current transformation. These trends are:

■ *transformation of our economy from one based on manufacturing and industry to one based on information, knowledge, and communications;*

■ *change in people's values, attitudes, and priorities regarding growth and material progress, the environment, and work; and*

■ *complete restructuring of the international economy and the emergence of new actors on the world stage, whose considerable power and largely "uncontrollable" behavior have significantly reduced our ability to control U.S. economic activity through purely domestic policies.*

Computer tapes stored at the Census Bureau Headquarters, Suitland, Maryland

The Information Economy

As early as 1955, information workers had surpassed industrial workers as the largest group in the U.S. labor force. Currently, more than half of U.S. workers are primarily engaged in generating, processing, distributing, analyzing, or otherwise handling information.

Today, total information activity accounts for more than half of our gross national product.

Investment and jobs: A major study by Marc Porat of the Office of Telecommunication in the Department of Commerce looked at 2,500 corporations in 37 industries in 1977. Porat found that less and less investment is going to basic industries such as steel, chemicals, paper, oil, and automobiles.

The government and organized labor are properly concerned about this long-term downward trend, since these industries account for almost one-third of the jobs and value added by manufacture in the U.S. economy. But it is inconceivable that basic industry will be restored to its former preeminent role. We must prepare for a fundamentally new economic structure.

Chips—the most radical change ever: At the heart of the information revolution is the microprocessor, or computer on a silicon chip. This single invention is said to have created the most radical change ever in U.S. industry.

Eventually, the microprocessor will become as basic to industry as steel. Microprocessors can vatly increase

work efficiency, and it is little wonder that shipments of microprocessors have risen from 2.3 million in 1976 to an estimated (and astounding) 100 million in 1980. Moreover, the phenomenonal growth of computer use is expected to continue.

Through 1985, the installed population of computers and terminals in the U.S. is projected to more than double every three years. Taking account of technological advances, it is probable that the information processing capability of the U.S. economy will increase in the near future at a compound annual rate greater than 100 percent!

Parallels with the industrial revolution: Clearly the social and economic changes that flow from the information revolution will be as far-reaching and profound as those produced by the industrial revolution.

But there are significant differences. Whereas the industrial revolution made available and employed vast amounts of mechanical energy, the information-electronics revolution is extremely sparing of energy and materials. Much of the industrial revolution technology was crude, with only a modest scientific or theoretical base. The information revolution is the product of the most advanced science, technology, and management, and represents one of the greatest intellectual achievements of humankind.

Impacts: The impact of the shift to an information economy will be pervasive. It will affect how and what we produce, how we transact business, how we pay bills, how news is gathered and spread, where we work and what kind of work we do, and how we communicate.

The changes will not be restricted to the computer or communications industries. At a minimum there will be significant changes in banking, insurance, government, the military, transportation, health, education, communications, entertainment, and manufacturing.

A major issue yet to be resolved is the impact on employment. Over the long run, according to most government economists and computer industry executives, the information revolution will not reduce total employment. Expanding opportunities in information-related activities will, in this view, more than offset jobs lost to more productive electronic equipment.

But what about the employment growth potential of the information industry? If the information work force becomes saturated, this will have profound impact on employment prospects in the 1980s. If not only agriculture and manufacturing but also the information sector are no longer providing dynamic growth in employment opportunities, then where will new jobs be generated?

International context of this phenomenon: Competition, especially from the Japanese, poses a profound challenge. Presently, the U.S. is ahead in terms of technical sophistication and the manufacturing distribution base of our telecommunications industry. But the stakes are high, and growing. It has been estimated that $1.6 trillion will be invested in telecommunications outside the U.S. by the year 2000.

Japan has recognized the comparative advantage of developed nations in this field, and its powerful Ministry of International Trade and Industry [MITI] has declared information the strategic industry of the future. The U.S. government does not engage in such long-range analysis and planning, and maintains a much more adversarial relationship with industry in the telecommunications field. This should

be changed, and government in the U.S. should begin to consider positive initiatives that would help American industry retain both its technological leadership in the computer and information areas and its commanding share of the export market.

New Values and Questions

The second aspect of the great transformation currently underway in the United States involves deep and fundamental changes in what we value, what seems important to us, what seems worth working to achieve. Historical experience demonstrates the significance and impact of fundamental changes in values.

The rise of the Protestant ethic out of the Protestant Reformation was a primary force behind the remarkable expansion of commerce and advances in technology which, together, contributed to the growing dominance of Europe and America, beginning in the 1700s.

The Protestant ethic was far more than a religious doctrine. It encompassed new views on human dominion over the natural environment, the purpose of work, and the virtues of material progress. These views were fundamentally different from those of the medieval era that had preceded it, and provided fertile ground for development of the institutions of capitalism and the industrial revolution.

It is precisely in these three areas—the environment, work, and material progress—that values in the U.S. today are undergoing the most serious change.

The origin of these changes lies in the civil rights movement, the women's movement, the environmental movement, and the anti-Vietnam-War movement of the 1960s. All these shook people out of complacency, causing us to question previous "givens." Such questioning and related activities have

Studies by the University of Michigan's Survey Research Center have documented major changes in American's priorities during the last 10 years. To the average family, the following factors have gained in importance at the expense of an increase in the level of consumption:
■ *job security;*
■ *continuous income even in case of sickness, disability, and old age;*
■ *appropriate opportunities for job and career;*
■ *safety in the home and on the street;*
■ *neighborhoods that are comfortable, attractive, and stable.*

Researchers at the Center concluded: "These new desires are more than a passing fad. They compete with the pursuit of traditional ways of progress and growth. Much thinking and debate will be required to strike a balance between an expansion of production that ignores the new priorities and an attempt to create a humane economy regardless of its consequences for production."

Geoge Katona and
Burkhard Strumpel
A New Economic Era (1978)

been the source of many recent U.S. policy shifts in the areas of minority rights, the status of women, and consumer and environmental protection.

■ **The questioning of material progress and technological development:** A significant turnabout in U.S. values and lifestyles has taken place. Changes in lifestyles and the evidence of recent public attitude surveys testify to this change.

It appears that the American people are increasingly skeptical about the nation's capacity for unlimited economic growth. They are wary of the benefits such economic growth is alleged to bring, and they are beginning to assign higher priority to improving human and social relationshps than to raising the material standard of living.

Progress as double-edged sword: There is also growing recognition that scientific and technological advance can be a double-edged sword, threatening human life and the environment at the same time that it is offering the tempting promise of a better future.

Perhaps the most dramatic examples of how public attitudes toward technology have changed were the national decisions in the early 1970s to halt production of the antiballistic missle system and the supersonic transport [SST]. Current apprehension about the ultimate physical and social consequences of major reliance on nuclear power may retard a development that until recently was expected to yield a cornucopia of benefits. Similarly, research involving genetic manipulation has aroused deep new reservations about the independence of science.

■ **New attitudes toward work:** Attitudes toward the content of the job in the workplace—and also how the job fits into one's life—are also beginning to change radically.

In a 1973 survey of U.S. college students regarding major influences on their choice of a job or career, "challenge of the job" was cited by 77 percent, "ability to express yourself" by 79 percent. The general adult population responded similarly in Detroit Area Surveys.

When respondents were asked in 1971 what they would most prefer in a job, the top two choices were "the work is important and gives a feeling of accomplishment" and "chances for advancement."

Yet not enough challenging, meaningful jobs are being created to match the rapidly growing demand. The result is increasing job dissatisfaction.

The Michigan Survey Research Center found an appreciable drop in overall job satisfaction between 1973 and 1977, affecting virtually all demographic and occupational classes tested. Rising job dissatisfaction among the highly educated holds considerable potential for increasing social malaise.

In 1979, total pollution control expenditures due to federal regulations were $37 billion. The President's Council on Environmental Quality has estimated that such expenditures will total $519 billion over the decade from 1979-1988.

One might expect to see the public backing away from strong support for environmental protection, given the prospect of such heavy costs during a period of high inflation and general economic difficulties. Yet this public backing away has not occurred.

Resources, a publication of the Washington think-tank Resources for the Future, reported on a comprehensive national environmental survey conducted in late 1978 by Robert Cameron Mitchell. Mitchell found that more than half the people consider protecting the environment so important that "continuing improvements must be made regardless of cost."

Black support for this view (55 percent) was virtually identical to that of whites (54 percent), and 49 percent of those with very low incomes (under $6,000) also chose this option. This evidence goes against earlier expectations that environmental concerns were to be found mainly among the upper-middle class.

By three to one, respondents favored the option of paying higher prices to protect the environment over the alternative of paying lower prices and accepting worsened air and water pollution in order to create more jobs.

Robert Cameron Mitchell,
"The Public Speaks Again: A New Environmental Survey,"
Resources, Sept.-Nov. 1978

On the positive side, however, it may stimulate new efforts to reconstitute jobs and the work environment to enhance employee satisfaction.

There has also been a major change in attitude regarding the role of women in the workforce, reflecting the dramatic entry of women into the labor market since the 1950s. The great increase in the particitation rate of women in the U.S. labor force (from 33 percent in 1950 to over 50 percent in 1977) has had an exceptional and very influential effect on the economy as well as many other aspects of American life. In particular, there has been increasing acceptance of the fact that a mother can work without being uncaring or irresponsible in regard to her children. Clearly, the large-scale entry of women into the labor force has also been a major factor in the movement toward more flexible, fulfilling, and non-discriminatory employment in the United States.

New Global Economic Realities

The international economy at the beginning of the 1980s is entirely different in character from that of 1970 and would have been undreamed of in 1960.

All nations have become highly interdependent, but this has affected the United States more than most because of its relative isolation from the world economy in the past.

Historically, foreign trade has accounted for a very small proportion of the U.S. gross national product. Americans became vividly aware of their new interdependence in 1972, however, when bad weather in the Ukraine led to higher bread prices at home, and again in 1973-74 when the actions of a small group of OPEC countries caused a quadrupling of oil prices in the United States over a period of a few months.

This interdependency is best understood through examination of four new forces that exerted growing influence over world events during the 1970s. *Each of these forces is largely "uncontrollable"—that is, no single national economic institution or policy can substantially alter their actions or effects.*

As a result, there has been a significant reduction in the effectiveness within each country of purely domestic policies in controlling economic activity. This amounts to an erosion of each nation's sovereignty—including that of the United States—over its own economy.

■ **Energy dependency: The OPEC cartel:** The impact of interdependence has been and will continue to be felt primarily in the energy arena. The Organization of Petroleum Exporting Countries (OPEC) is the dominant actor.

OPEC's 1973-74 quadrupling of oil prices triggered three fundamental changes:
■ a sharp slowdown in world economic growth,
■ a decline in the rate of growth of world trade, and
■ an increase in the productivity of labor relative to capital.
One effect of the latter change has been to strengthen the economies of the more advanced developing countries.

Two basic lessons have been learned from this experience. The first is that the energy crisis at present is essentially an oil crisis. Virtually all recent studies conclude that the global production of liquid hydrocarbons will peak in the last two decades of this century.

The second basic lesson is that economic factors have less influence on the international flow of oil than political realities—which encompass questions of ego and institutional power, as well as conflict and cooperation among nations.

The degree to which the United States will be able to exercise sovereignty over its domestic economy by the year 2000 is still uncertain. The answer depends, in particular, on the intervening rate of resource depletion, the speed of technological progress, and the impact of the information revolution.

The most pessimistic expectation is for rising real costs for mineral resources, in combination with increasing dependency on foreign nations for a number of critical minerals.

On the other hand, exploitation of our comparative advantage in information technology, coupled with conservation programs and possible but still unforeseen technological breakthroughs could lead to a more favorable future.

■ **Third World demands for a New International Economic Order:** OPEC actions have been at the cutting edge of Third World efforts to engineer a New International Economic Order.

Developing countries recognize the enormous disparity between their own per capita incomes and rates of growth and those of the developed countries. They are determined to see the gap closed.

They want a fairer share of the world's economic growth, technology, wealth, status, and power. Their argument basically runs as follows.
■ The advanced nations have begun to exhaust their own supplies of many of the most important natural resources needed for an industrialized society.
■ What advanced countries now are facing is sharper competition for the remaining supplies of those resources in Third World countries.
■ Continually increasing consumption in the industrial nations, which shortens supplies and raises prices, has begun to impinge upon growth possibilities for the developing countries.
In short, the poor nations are arguing that, apart from their remaining natural resources, the rich nations hold all of the cards in the present international specialization of functions, and it is impossible for developing countries to catch up with the industrial world unless a dramatic transformation of the international economy takes place.

■ **Multinational Corporations** will have an important role in deciding these matters. In the first half of the 1970s, the multinationals grew at an annual rate of 10 percent, twice that of the world economies taken as a whole. In 1980, their sales constituted approximately 16 percent of the gross world product.

NEW VISIONS—2.

Large size, by itself, however, is not their most significant characteristic. The multinationals enjoy a freedom of action denied to smaller companies bound by the laws of a single nation:
■ They can juggle their profits by arbitrary pricing arrangements that magnify the profitability of operations in low-tax areas and minimize it in high-tax areas.
■ Multinationals can escape a given country's labor standards by transferring production to plants located where wages or health and safety requirements are lower.
■ They can wreak havoc with pollution control by transferring "dirty" production to countries without such standards.
■ They can ally their economic power with the political or military power of the host government, as in the case of IT&T in Chile.
■ Or, contarywise, they can deploy their considerable economic power in ways that are contrary to the political (or economic, or monetary) designs of their host countries, or of the country of their own origin.

Yet the multinationals hold the key to stabilizing the global economy, for they have considerable potential for raising or lowering living standards, enhancing global progress and understanding—or for concentrating solely on maximizing their own markets, power and profits.

■ **The new realities of international finance:**

■ *Floating exchange rates:* The collapse in 1973 of fixed monetary exchange rates significantly altered the face of the world economy.

The previous system of fixed rates of exchange-value among national currencies was succeeded by a system of "floating" rates, in which the relationships among currencies are continually changing and transient. One has only to consider the headlong decline in the value of the U.S. dollar in 1977 and 1978 to understand that no nation can escape the great uncertainties that floating exchange rates have wrought.

■ *The massive Eurocurrency pool—* estimated at around $550 billion on 1980—is another of the new forces in the international economy that is beyond the control of any single nation. Some 80 percent of this pool is in U.S. dollars—so-called Eurodollars—deposited with banks or branches overseas.

The Eurocurrency pool has swollen faster in the 1970s than anyone's ability to understand, contain, or manage it. It currently is 10 times larger than a decade ago and four times bigger than it was as recently as 1972.

Lying outside of increasingly tough national exchange controls, the Eurocurrency pool constitutes an autonomous credit system that is available to anyone for trade or investment. Primary borrowers are governments and businesses, while the principal investors are the Arab oil countries and the treasurers of multinational corporations seeking to turn a profit on their idle cash.

International commerce has become totally dependent on this market and its associated supranational banking system. Multinational corporations could not operate in the world of floating exchange rates without it. The new banking order tremendously increases the efficiency of moving cash around the globe.

But the rapid movement of currencies from one country to another may stimulate inflation in one country, undermine the stability of the local currency in another, and generate much more volatile shifts in exchange rates than otherwise could be anticipated. At times, such exchange rate movements are on a scale that cannot be justified by any accepted economic criteria.

Each nation has its central bank, comparable in its function to the Federal Reserve Sytem in the U.S. It falls to these central bankers to, among other things, stabilize within some desired range their country's currency exchange rate in relation to other currencies. These central bankers (who in 1977 could draw on only $220 billion in reserves) have been described in their attempts to control the gyrations of this half-trillion-dollar fund, as being in the "untenable position of chasing an elephant with butterfly nets."

"Gosh, how I envy you the future, son. Almost my whole has been lived in a Keynesian context."

The Need to Rethink Economics

Present economic theories provide an incomplete and often misleading basis for making both public and corporate policy. But this would not be critical, were it not for the fact that economists are a very important source of information for policy makers as to how the economy works. Furthermore, economists are a very important source of recommendations as to what ought to be done to make the economy work better.

Economic advisers serve at the highest levels of government and industry. For non-specialists in high positions in government and in industry, it is often the economist's expertise that defines what reality is. With the exception of lawyers, no other group in our society has remotely comparable influence over the way in which national policy issues are posed for decision.

The fact that current economic theory and resulting policy prescriptions (1) are inadequate to deal with new global economic realities and emerging economic problems, and (2) do not complement progress toward the goal of qualitative growth, is therefore a matter of much more than academic interest.

New economic theory and practice must be wholistic—which means that the scope of economic analysis must be expanded in data, time, and space. Consideration is going to have to be given to many non-economic factors and trends and to the development of better tools for long-range analysis. The new economics will have to incorporate explicitly the workings of the global economy and subnational economies into domestic, national considerations.

The broad dimensions of needed change are direct and simple to understand, yet revolutionary in their significance. They demand nothing less than reconceptualizing the entire nature of economics—a most difficult task.

Economics and "equity": Among the non-economic factors and trends that economics as a discipline must incorporate, those from political science and the physical sciences are the most critical. Economics must become more firmly grounded in people's values, needs, and aspirations in all their diversity, and then consider the most effective and equitable means to achieve them.

The word "equitable" is key, for the practical world of politics is centered very much on equity while economists talk in terms of efficiency, costs, and benefits—a very different world.

Equity and efficiency often conflict, or at least appear to do so. Neither is a free good, and at least in the short run emphasis on one tends to "cost" in terms of the other.

Such considerations will become increasingly important as the United States moves into the anticipated period of slower growth in the 1980s, for slower growth will force much more explicit attention to questions of equity. Periods of high growth help diffuse the equity issue since even those on the lower rungs of the ladder are able to climb a bit higher. If growth slows or stops, however, the people on the ladder all become increasingly aware of their relative positions.

Economics can no longer assume that resources are given or infinite. Economic policy alternatives must be evaluated not only in terms of short-run efficiency but long-run ecological balance.

In the 1980s, for example, economic policies must be judged not only with respect to their impact on such variables as investment, prices, employment, and income, but also upon the rate of resource depletion and environmental deterioration. This would reduce the risk of potentially disastrous damage to the earth's systems of life support.

Incorporation of ecological values in economic thought would lead to basic redefinitions of output, income, wealth, productivity, cost, and profit.

Economic analysis also must become more explicitly normative, if economics is to serve as a guide in the pursuit of qualitative growth. The word "explicitly" is used purposefully. Most economists would shudder at the suggestion that their discipline will or should consider norms.

But economics has always been implicitly normative. As far back as the

"invisible hand" of Adam Smith, economics has assumed a normative model of how *Homo economicus* acts and ought to act. Based on this view, economists for 200 years have avoided making economic decisions directly on the basis of moral considerations of the larger social good. As a result, we have economists who (in the words of Oscar Wilde) know the price of everything and the value of nothing.

The Challenge of Qualitative Growth

A three-to-one majority in a Harris Poll endorsed the statement "The trouble with most leaders is that they don't understand people want better quality of almost everything they have rather than more quantity."

This and other evidences of serious questioning about the value of growth, along with the increasing expression of diverse quality-of-life concerns, suggest we are on the threshold of a redefinition of goals in our national economic life.

In place of the previous goal of quantitative, undifferentiated economic growth, a new goal for America in the 1980s could be achieving qualitative, selective growth.

This will involve asking new questions about purposes: Growth for whom? Growth for what? Growth must come to be seen as a means and not an end in itself. The goal of an expanded GNP must not be applauded until we have asked how such growth will be achieved, at what cost, and to what end.

What might it mean in practical terms to pursue the goal of qualitative growth? What specific actions and policies would be required?

Obviously, these cannot be spelled out in detail here. But one can identify at least two broad principles to help guide our thinking about new policies and programs.

■ *Conservation of physical resources:* Corporations and governments—as well as individuals—should commit themselves to use the minimum amount of physical resources necessary to carry out an activity or produce a product with the fewest possible undesirable side effects.

■ *Total employment of human resources:* The goal of corporations and government should be not only to enhance material well-being but to provide satisfying and meaningful employment to everyone who desires it.

The Role of Market Forces and the Corporation

Many corporate activities, driven by market forces, will help significantly to foster qualitative growth in the 1980s. The last two decades of this century will certainly be characterized by increasing resource scarcity and rising real costs, so the current transformation to an information economy is fortuitous. The United States would have found it very difficult to generate a substantial share of its GNP from traditional, heavy industries and to remain competitive in those industrial products in world markets.

Furthermore, the information revolution is so sparing of energy and materials that its impact is likely to be enduring and environmentally benign. Qualitative growth will thus be given substantial impetus by this transformation in the U.S. economic base.

■ **Corporate social responsibility:** Corporations tend to be rather passive participants in such broad historical market changes as the one from quantitative to qualitative growth. The question remains: Should they have a more active role, perhaps even a responsibility, in helping to shape a future of qualitative growth?

The traditional view of the corporation's social responsibility has been succinctly stated by Milton Friedman: "There is one and only one social responsibility of business—to use its resources and engage in activities to increase its profits."

An opposing view gained strength during the 1970s. In this view, corporations are creatures of the state, and have an explicit responsibility to conform to and support broad societal goals. This position has been endorsed not only by outside critics of business but by an increasing number of corporate leaders.

The late Louis Lundborg, former chairman of the board of the Bank of America, argued strongly that corporate leadership should be responsive to environmental and social concerns: "Those in corporate life are going to be expected to do things for the good of society just to earn their franchise, their corporate right to exist."

According to Lundborg, debating the issue of corporate social responsibility is nonsense: "Environmental and other social problems should get at least as much corporate attention as production, sales, and finance. The quality of life in its total meaning is, in the final reckoning, the only justification for any corporate activity."

■ **Profits vs. conservation?** There is widespread belief that socially beneficial goals such as conservation of resources and energy can be pursued only at the expense of corporate profits.

The results of corporate conservation activities during the past decade contradict this view. It is true that, in many instances, environmental regulations have forced companies to engage in wholesale rethinking of their manufacturing processes and product design. But that rethinking has often resulted in beneficial—and profitable—innovations.

Recycling, for example, is a practice that can yield a number of benefits: it contributes to the supply of materials; it reduces the volume of waste; and it usually generates savings in terms of energy consumption, environmental protection, and process efficiency.

The contributions to material supply and waste reduction are inherent in recycling; they are benefits that always accrue (at least in principle) and are the main arguments for recycling. The savings in the energy, environmental, and process areas are contingent on the efficiency of the recycling operation.

Corporations have also learned the advantages of energy conservation. U.S. industry officials reported in 1978 that energy conservation was one of the most profitable uses of their capital. This led companies to invest hundreds of millions of dollars in that area.

Rapidly rising spending on energy conservation, which is currently adding to total capital outlays, will be increasingly important in the next few years. Dow Chemical, for instance, foresees over $200 million of energy-saving investment opportunities in its Texas and Louisiana facilities alone, with each project offering a pre-tax return of over 50 percent on investment.

Significant resource savings have also been achieved through materials substitution. In many cases this has been a byproduct of developing new technologies.

The principal instance of this has been communications, where research and development have reduced materials requirements significantly through introduction of solid-state electronics, more widespread use of microwave transmission, and commercial satellites.

This process has been referred to as functional or system substitution of a component or system. The transistor, for example, requires perhaps one-millionth of the material needed to

make the vacuum tube it replaces.

The establishment of waste bourses (exchanges) in at least 14 states is another example of recent corporate resource conservation efforts resulting solely from market forces. Basically, the bourse brings one company producing an industrial waste into contact with another company that can profitably utilize that waste. Wastes that might otherwise pose a real financial liability because of high disposal costs or possible damage to the environment can thus be made doubly profitable. The seller realizes additional income and the buyer gains a cheaper source of raw material.

The corporation of the future will have to recognize the profit in getting more from less, and then have the wit and the will to do so. U.S. corporations are becoming aware of the almost unlimited potential for and benefit from recyling, energy conservation, and process change for pollution control purposes.

In the future, greater emphasis will be placed on the development of production methods, technologies, and products that extend the life of renewable resources and maximize their sustainable yield, reduce energy and resource consumption per unit of output, eliminate or cut down on waste generation, allow for recycling, provide for greater longevity and durability of products, and do not overburden the natural environment. This is an overall strategy of corporate stewardship that is compatible with the coming age of global resource scarcity and, happily, also consistent with long-term profitability.

The Role of Government in National Growth Policy

Our country has a critical need to develop a new policy framework capable of dealing not only with immediate and isolated problems but interrelated and long-range issues. We must create better means of understanding the interrelationships among problems and of anticipating future dangers and opportunities.

Policy formulation of that kind cannot succeed, however, until clear national goals and priorities have been established, by which policies can be directed and progress measured.

If we want government to exercise effective control over the forces influencing long-term growth, we will need a national growth policy capable of fulfilling three functions:

■ *establishing national priorities and goals and measuring progress toward their achievement;*

■ *conducting comprehensive analysis of long-range trends in the socio-economic system, and anticipating likely future problems; and*

■ *guiding the coordination and integration of policies.*

■ **Long-range analysis and definition of goals** would be at the heart of the process of setting national growth policy. The process would involve a sequence of steps:
■ specify broad, long-term national objectives;
■ consider alternative policies;
■ establish priorities among policies;
■ lay out alternative plans;
■ evaluate the consequences of those alternatives;
■ coordinate the study; and
■ disseminate the results.

These steps would lay the foundation for planning and decision-making throughout government and in the private sector. The United States would then have moved closer to the ideal stated by Winston Churchill: "Those who are possessed of a definite body of doctrine and of deeply rooted convictions based upon it will be in a much better position to deal with the shifts and surprises of daily affairs than those who are merely taking short views, and indulging their natural impulses as they are evoked by what they read from day to day."

The key to the success of a national growth policy would be its comprehensiveness. Such a policy would provide a framework and mechanisms for harmonizing the conflicts that inevitably arise among our broad social, environmental, and economic, objectives.

Economic efficiency itself will have to be judged by new and more comprehensive criteria. We will have to aim for efficiency in overall economic performance, measured by how well we apply our resources and capabilities to the solution of national problems and attainment of national goals such as ecological balance and improved quality of life.

A comprehensive national growth policy would also need to take account of regional and state concerns. This could be accomplished in a number of ways: by designating those regional and state policies that need not be dealt with at the federal level and incorporating others into the national process; creating stable mechanisms and procedures to resolve conflicts between levels of government; explicitly recognizing unique growth requirements or impacts on regions or states; and anticipating trends and problems that might emerge in regional, state, and local contexts as obstacles to achieving national growth and development objectives.

Finally, the growth policy process could not operate in domestic isolation from the larger world. The hard reality of interdependence demands that there be closer international coordination and cooperation in economic policies.

We live in a world in which shrinking energy supplies, volatile Eurodollars, and abuses by multinational corporations pose problems beyond the capacity of any single nation to solve. At the same time, inflation, worker migration, environmental pollution, and scores of other issues have taken on transnational dimensions. Past government "drift" or attempts to "go it alone" must be replaced by purposive coordination of policies with our neighbors, allies, and even adversaries.

Granted, the process of developing a national growth policy that is integrative, anticipatory, and goal-oriented is at present far more of an art form than a science. Some, on that basis, may question its validity.

To them, I would gently suggest, as did Lord Keynes: "There will be no harm in making mild preparations for our destiny."

There should be no illusion that a national growth policy would solve all current problems or prevent others from arising in the future. It would, however, help us in the United States to regain confidence in our ability to manage our affairs, to deal with our problems, and take charge of our future. Most importantly, it would help generate a renewed sense of national unity and purpose. □

Who am I? Robert D. Hamrin

Any personal description of who I am must begin with a fact of life that has dominated not only many of my waking hours in recent months but also, alas, my "sleeping hours"—I am the father of twin baby girls and a three-year-old boy! Some of my economist friends have suggested that my wife and I have gone beyond the call of duty to help alleviate the long-run productivity decline.

Briefly, I am a political-institutional economist with the perspective of a futurist—a rare breed, indeed. I am also a bit of an iconoclast.

I got into the "long-run growth game" in 1975 when the late Senator Hubert H. Humphrey, then Chairman of the Joint Economic Committee [JEC], asked me to "look into this growth question" as a follow-on to the tumultuous limits-to-growth debate of the previous three years. For the next three years, I had the tremendously exciting task of serving as the Director of the JEC study series entitled U.S. Economic Growth for 1976-1986: Prospects, Problems, and Patterns.

This was a unique effort involving a host of non-economists among the 41 authors, as well as a liberal sprinkling of "challengers of the conventional wisdom." In the course of this project, I came to know many of the founding members of the U.S. Association for The Club of Rome.

I had been granted considerable flexibility throughout the study series and in the writing of the final report, but I wanted the complete freedom of expression that only a one-author book allows, and, with the kind support of the Rockefeller Foundation, I spent most of April through October 1978 on my patio writing the book *Managing Growth in the 1980s: Toward a New Economics,* which was published in early 1980. A "positive externality" for me during this time was being at home with my 9- to 16-month-old son.

Finding a "long-range analysis home" in the Executive Branch was not as easy as I expected. Most of the mainstream economic agencies did not have such positions. Senior officials at the Environmental Protection Agency [EPA] were looking for a broad-gauge economist, however, so I joined them as Senior Policy Economist in late 1978.

During the following summer, I wrote five research papers for the EPA on various aspects of the interrelationships between economics and environmental principles and performance. The unique part was that I did the writing in Peking, where my wife had been stationed in the American Embassy by the State Department. Suffice it to say that our time in China was a fascinating interlude in our lives.

During 1980, I served on the staff of the President's Commission for a National Agenda for the Eighties. Ostensibly, this was to be the comprehensive, innovative foresight activity in the Executive Branch that I had long yearned for. It proved to be relatively comprehensive, but alas within the boundaries of conventional wisdom—which by definition means that it did not produce the innovative look into the future I had hoped for.

This bold, creative look, I am convinced, is conveyed nowhere better than between the covers of this book.

"Closing averages on the human scene were mixed today. Brotherly love was down two points, while enlightened self-interest gained a half. Vanity showed no movement, and guarded optimism slipped a point in sluggish trading. Over all, the status quo remained unchanged."

MAKING IT HAPPEN:

"I have before me, gentlemen, some figures that may shock you, as they did me."

Counting the Bads with the Goods:

The Inadequacy of Economics

By Hazel Henderson

Hazel Henderson has a name for the world view that underlines many of today's economic policies. She calls it the "Golden Goose model." But this golden goose, in her view, lays rotten eggs.

The rotten eggs are the "bads" that inevitably accompany the "goods" in economic production. It is far easier to count the "goods," and we are only beginning to take the "bads" into account fully. Even now, many of the social costs of remedies for pollution, disease, and social disruption are counted as additions to—rather than subtractions from—the gross national product.

Our nation faces a paradoxical situation today. There is broad agreement about the ultimate goals of economic and public policy. There is consensus about the major economic problems we face. And yet we cling to outmoded practices and policies in both the public and private sector that certainly are not making things better. Indeed, we often seem to be creating new problems rather than solving the old ones.

Many of our practices and policies derive from traditional economics, and this is a principal source of our current difficulties. Economics, like most disciplines, is based on a particular model or representation of the way our industrial society works. Associated with the model are some conventional, and usually unexamined, assumptions about the goals of economic policy.

The economists' model may have served at one time as a reasonable and useful approximation of reality. That time, however, has passed. Today, the economists' model is too limited. It no longer is adequate to represent the complex interactions of our society, which go far beyond the abstraction called "the economy."

As a consequence, many or most of our present economic policies are confused, and often make our problems worse rather than better. For example, efforts by the Federal Reserve System to reduce inflation by rationing credit by price (i.e., by imposing high interest rates) simply increase inflation. Their further detriment is that they create more unemployment and bankrupt some small businesses, while leaving speculators untouched.

To devise better policies, we must

first replace our outdated, inaccurate models with more realistic ones. These must specifically recognize that economists are dealing only with that half of economic activity conducted in cash in the competitive marketplace and measured by the official GNP, while ignoring the other half—the informal, voluntary, local household and community sectors, where activity is based on cooperation, reciprocity, barter, and use-value production.

Paradoxes of Current Economic Policy

■ **Controlling Inflation:** The limits of present economic policies are perhaps best seen in our attempts to control inflation. You may have heard political leaders or academics speak of the need to "accept a certain level of unemployment if we wish to reduce inflation."

The intellectual basis of this view is a statistical relationship called the Phillips Curve, which asserts that there is a constant trade-off between unemployment and inflation. But, as everyone knows, we now have had *both* unemployment *and* inflation for a protracted period of time, and each recession has been more inflationary than the last.

Wage costs are, of course, an important factor in prices. But in today's industrial societies wage costs are by no means the only or even the dominant factor influencing rising prices.

The new causes of inflation involve a host of new conditions. Among these are:
■ the global interlinkages among national economies;
■ the effects of releasing a tidal wave of U.S. dollars on world markets through military expenditures in Vietnam and elsewhere;
■ the persistent imbalance of U.S. exports and imports due to oil imports;
■ the rise in oil prices by the OPEC cartel in its effort, among other things, to keep abreast of inflating U.S. dollars;
■ the vagaries of climate and rainfall, as they affect food prices;
■ the power of large corporations to control the selling prices of what they make and to anticipate subsequent inflation in setting those prices; and

■ the mounting social and environmental costs, which economists traditionally ignore.

■ **"Gnawing on the bone":** In my view, another important cause of inflation is that the industrial economies are now "gnawing on the bone" of their natural resources and must divert more and more of their wealth to the process of extracting energy and raw materials from lower-grade and ever more inaccessible deposits.

It is worth remembering that in many areas fifty years ago, one had only to drill a hole and stick a pipe in the ground to get a gusher. By contrast, an investment of more than nine billion dollars has been required to provide us with the oil currently coming out of the North Slope of Alaska (oil which, incidentally, does not come close to meeting our present energy deficits).

■ **Growing and increasingly unmanageable levels of complexity:** In our society, and the unanticipated social costs they are generating, constitute still another basic and often overlooked source of inflation.

It has long been assumed that "bigger means cheaper" because of benefits derived from economies of large-scale production and merchandising. Consequently, we have had a seemingly irreversible trend towards centralization and bigness in industry, business and government.

It is clear now that we are encountering serious management problems and social *dis*economies of scale. Coordination costs, social costs, and transaction costs, of big, centralized enterprises are soaring. Such costs of

bigness are still counted as positive contributions to GNP, but that fact should not obscure the reality that such enterprises are inefficient.

The cost of trying to manage very large organizations, whether in industry, business or government, makes a real "contribution" only to inflation.

■ **Deregulation and inflation:** We have been told recently that the cause of inflation and declining productivity in the United States is excessive government regulation. To turn things around, we are told, all we need do is return to the "free market." This view is ill-informed and naive.

Our technical and economic systems continually evolve and change in structure, and there is no possibility of turning back the clock to the simple, atomistic world of small producers in full and open competition.

The current debate about deregulation is therefore unrealistic. Each order of magnitude of technological mastery and managerial scope inevitably dictates an equivalent order of magnitude of government coordination and control.

Deregulation can only be feasible if we are willing to simplify our large institutions and decentralize our technologies, so that their effects would be less interlinked and pervasive. This course seems unlikely, even though many excessively centralized technologies can be uncoupled, and probably should be.

Without regulatory bodies such as the Securities Exchange Commission and the Federal Reserve Board, for example, maintenance of orderly capital markets would be impossible. Our goal should not be to repeal regulations across the board, but to follow the less simplistic alternative of making them function more effectively.

■ **Erosion of democracy in a "high-tech" society:** Advancing technological innovation tends systematically to destroy the conditions required for free markets to function and for voters to exercise well-informed choice.

The complexity of nuclear power technology is a good example. Apparently, this is a technology which cannot be fully mastered by even our

94

most senior political leaders, let alone by the average voter.

Such vastly complex technologies become inherently authoritarian. Even worse, their scale requires immense social investment and taxpayer subsidies at the same time that they preclude full public participation and representation in the guidance and control of technological innovation.

Even while we continue to develop ever more complex systems, we have not figured out how to assure public choice in the management of the complexity we already have. This situation be faced squarely before we can proceed with the task of devising better alternatives.

■ **Improvement of productivity and efficiency** are being proposed as central goals of economic policy. Before we adopt them, however, we need to ask hard questions about what, as they are conventionally used, these terms really mean. Productivity and efficiency *of what* and *for whom*?

Our measures of "productivity" usually involve computing output per employee-hour or labor productivity. Yet it appears that declining productivity of energy and capital—not labor— are our major problems. Hence, we need to correct the overemphasis on labor productivity, and curb the related drift toward excessively capital-intensive jobs, a drift which has been accelerated by tax credits for capital investments.

Human and social factors in efficiency: Efficiency is a meaningless concept unless time horizons and efficiency-for-which-system are specified. For example, "efficiency" may be defined as an increase in "productivity." But it cannot be casually assumed that the benefits of such increases in productivity, or the inevitable burdens of costs and dislocations, will be shared fairly on an average per capita basis. In some sectors, greater micro-efficiency in industrial production means less social efficiency and consumer efficiency, a paradox that is leading to widespread social alienation.

■ **Supply-side economics:** Just as we thought that the "trickle down" approach to dealing with poverty and structural employment had been

expunged from our thinking and policies, it has been resurrected by the proponents of "supply-side economics." This self-serving, simplistic, and discredited view of the way our economy works is remarkably resilient, even though the focus has shifted from Keynes' concern with demand to the current stress on supply.

Efforts to "hype" supply and force-feed capital investment can be expected to cannibalize the social fabric and the environment, producing more social and environmental costs and hence more inflation. Persistent structural unemployment will persist, with a significant proportion of our population below the poverty line.

Production in a technologically sophisticated society is such a complex process that the relationship between the input—the factors of capital, land, and labor—and the output cannot be readily established. Therefore, there are no clear economic criteria for judging what constitutes a "fair" distribution of benefits.

Our models, in other words, are not only inadequate for analyzing the relative productivity of various factors of production, but they are no longer useful in determining equitable distribution in incomes, profits, and dividends. Nor are they useful in designing public sector transfer programs, or in assessing technological development and public works projects. Traditional cost/benefit techniques that averaged all costs and benefits across the entire population on a per capita basis simply concealed until later who were going to be "winners" and who "losers."

Structural unemployment and hard-core poverty were first addressed by the President's Commission on Automation, Employment, and Economic Progress in 1966. Little has been accomplished in the intervening years to develop a new point of view that would help us understand and diminish these social inequities.

The Commission recognized in 1966 that automation and the drift toward greater capital intensity contributed to structural unemployment. But their analysis, based on conventional economic thinking, made two erroneous assumptions:
■ essentially "perfect" labor markets would make it possible to redeploy workers with little disruption; and
■ any workers remaining unemployed would be absorbed by a continually growing economy.

We are less sanguine today as we try to address these continuing, chronic problems in the context of the new worldwide "stagflation." In addition, many today are forecasting greatly increased unemployment owing to further automation and widespread use of microprocessors. In 1978 the Organization for Economic Cooperation and Development [OECD] warned that the 1980s would be an "era of virtually jobless economic growth" for most of its member countries.

Killing the Golden Goose

If traditional economic perspectives and policies are parodoxical and confused, we must look more closely at the world view that spawned them. I call this the Golden Goose Model. Unfortunately, the eggs that this goose lays appear to be golden but are often rotten.

The Golden Goose Model assumes that the private sector is the creator of

all real wealth and that some of this wealth is then transferred through taxation to the public sector. There we try to work out a democratically determined menu of public goods and services, and also transfer some of our wealth to so-called "unproductive" uses.

In earlier times, this Golden Goose Model probably was a fair representation of a growing industrial economy of small entrepreneurs, where buyers and sellers met in the marketplace with roughly equal power and information and with a continent of unexploited resources at their disposal.

In today's crowded, polluted society, dominated by corporate giants and large institutions of many kinds, this simple model no longer describes reality. Furthermore, it obscures the extent to which the wealth and profits generated in the private sector are achieved at public cost.

In addition, we notice that the Golden Goose has been on a life-support system since the Full Employment Act of 1946, which established government responsibility to employ Keynesian tools to pump enough adrenalin into the economy to keep the Golden Goose going.

Similarly, the Goose's health seems to be growing ever more delicate: it is always threatening that if the "business climate" isn't just right in one town or state, it will move to the Sun Belt, or take its payroll to some Third World country with a cheaper labor force and fewer environmental restrictions.

Lastly, we find today that the Golden Goose requires an ever-richer diet of tax credits and special incentives, and even asks its customers to provide its investment capital.

into the environment);

■ brown- and black-lung disease;
■ sterility;
■ stress-related diseases.

The list can easily be extended when one takes into account alienation in the workplace and boredom on the job, and the frequent concommitants of alienation and boredom: drug abuse and crime. Similarly, there are definite but indeterminate social costs both for families and communities that are associated with plant closings and relocations either of key employees or entire plants.

■ **Rising public costs of maintaining environmental quality:** Many experts say that our industrial society is creating problems faster than its technological fixes can solve them. It is my contention that the only part of the GNP that is growing is what we are spending to pay the social or public costs to have safe streets, clean air, drinkable water, rivers that aren't sewers, and so on. Expenditures on such things as cleaning up the Three Mile Island nuclear plant after its accident, for example, constitute a public cost of using a complex technology and at the same time maintaining a safe environment for human beings. As Ralph Nader has noted, "Every time there is an automobile accident, the GNP goes *up* by the cost of repair or replacement of the automobile!"

The Need for Reconceptualizing Economics

Economic policy-makers are haggling today across the very narrow spectrum of concepts generated by the Golden Goose. This will continue until there is a complete reconceptualization of the stage that all mature industrial societies have reached.

We must first recognize that mature industrial societies have been shaped for 200 years by the belief that progress can be defined as maximization of GNP. Structural imbalances in distribution of wealth and income haven't been taken into account. And even though GNP continues to increase, heavy social and environmental costs have been incurred, subtracting from the actual quality of life.

Among the social costs that have been neglected or ignored are the following:

■ **Unemployment:** Fewer workers are needed when production is increasingly automated, capital-intensive and energy-intensive.

■ **Increasingly skewed distribution of wealth and income:** Viewing efficiency only as corporate efficiency and productivity only as the productivity of labor lead to technologies that are

larger-scale and more energy-intensive and capital-intensive—as well as to the larger and more complex organizations required to develop and manage these technologies.

Distributing the benefits of increased productivity made possible by new technologies is an unsolved political and social problem. The income transfer systems—unemployment insurance, welfare, and so on—are not regarded by anyone as adequate solutions. Public projects initiated to provide employment are often mismatched with real human needs. Tax cuts, instead of increasing the purchasing power of the poor, have usually favored middle- and upper-income people. Investment tax credits for business often fail to "trickle down" in the form of more jobs, as firms often invest to increase labor productivity (which means fewer workers produce more).

■ **Unanticipated side effects and social costs of high-technology production and consumption:** Examples include:
■ soaring cancer rates (80 percent of cancers are attributed by some experts to cancer-causing substances released

Facing up to Difficult Choices

These rapidly accumulating and increasing social costs are not, as socialists have argued, a problem of who *owns* the means of production. *The means of production themselves are the problem.*

This is a much larger crisis of industrial societies than simply the combined social costs which are being created. This larger crisis is rooted in the technologies we have chosen to develop, and this is a crisis that affects all industrial societies, the centrally planned (socialist or communist) economies as well as the Western market-oriented economies.

The plain fact is that the technologies we have chosen to develop can generate massive costs that never show up in the corporate ledgers or in the cost of products, but which nonetheless must be paid by the public and the environment in terms of impaired health, community well-being, and a deteriorating capacity of the natural environment to support our own and other forms of life.

Today's choices are no longer the simple choices of yesteryear. They involve higher technological stakes and graver human risks than ever before.

These choices are not simply choices between technologies. Yes, we must of course make choices among technol-

ogies—between energy options of coal, solar, or nuclear; and between transportation options of automobiles or mass transit; and also between institutional options of reliance on the public or private sector.

But fundamentally the choices before us involve:

■ *greater (or lesser) specialization and division of labor, and associated social costs (or savings);*

■ *greater capital- and energy-intensity versus greater labor intensity (with a more complex and complete reckoning of costs to the public and the environment, even though these costs may not immediately be costs to the firm);*

■ *greater centralization versus more decentralization of both production and population.*

Who am I? **Hazel Henderson**

I am an independent, self-employed futurist and social critic. I am working actively to create alternative futures for industrial countries in a global context of human interdependence.

I do a good deal of writing—my books include *Creating Alternative Futures* (1978) and *The Politics of the Solar Age* (1981)—and I serve on the editorial boards of *Technological Forecasting and Social Change* and *Journal of Humanistic Psychology*. I also do frequent public speaking, both in the United States and abroad.

One of my greatest satisfactions is helping worthy public-interest groups to get under way, and I serve on the boards of several, among them the Council on Economic Priorities, The Cousteau Society, Worldwatch Institute, and the World Future Studies Federation (Rome). From 1974–80 I was one of the original members of the Advisory Council of the Congressional Office of Technology Assessment.

Right now, I am spending a good deal of my time on citizen networking to promote planetary awareness and a new world order based on justice, equity, and sustainability. I am convinced that more exciting things are happening in the grass-roots settings than in large bureaucracies and institutions. My home is now in Gainesville, Florida, known as the "solar energy capital of the world," where I am an avid tree-crop grower.

Keeping Options Open

■ **Flexibility as a resource:** In making such choices, we must strive to preserve our flexibility and keep our options open.

This requires an entirely new view of finance capital, which constitutes our last stock of cheaply available flexibility. We must learn to consider flexibility as a resource, just like coal or oil. We must seek to conserve flexibility just as we conserve energy, and prefer decisions which do not foreclose other options or preclude major revisions in the light of subsequent experience or the changed needs or preferences of subsequent generations.

The new social and institutional choices that we are called upon to make consciously in this generation are comparable to those made unconsciously by other biological species over eons of evolution. The fundamental issue underlying our choices is how best to adapt to a rapidly changing environment.

■ **The economics of flexibility:** All these evolutionary choices involve the "economics of flexibility," i.e., choosing to spend flexibility now, or to conserve and store flexibility for the future. We can see this clearly in our technological

choices. We can invest now at the risk of programming our future into irreversible paths. Or we can keep our options open and fund a diversity of approaches to test over time.

As in genetic evolution, timing is all. If adaptation to change is *too* rapid, we may find we have hindered our ability to adapt to subsequent changes we must face.

The paradox is that nothing fails quite like success. Success at any one point means being completely adapted to circumstances which are passing from us. We see this in recognizing that we have exhausted the evolutionary potential of industrialization guided by the goal of ever-increasing GNP. The next adaptation will be in a dimension for which new measuring tools have yet to be developed.

America's third century, like the future of all industrial societies, will not just be more of the same. Rather, we must recognize that we are in the process of transition to something new that can be qualitatively better, in which we recognize that the real factors of production are energy, matter, and knowledge, and in which the output is happier, more productive, more satisfied human beings.

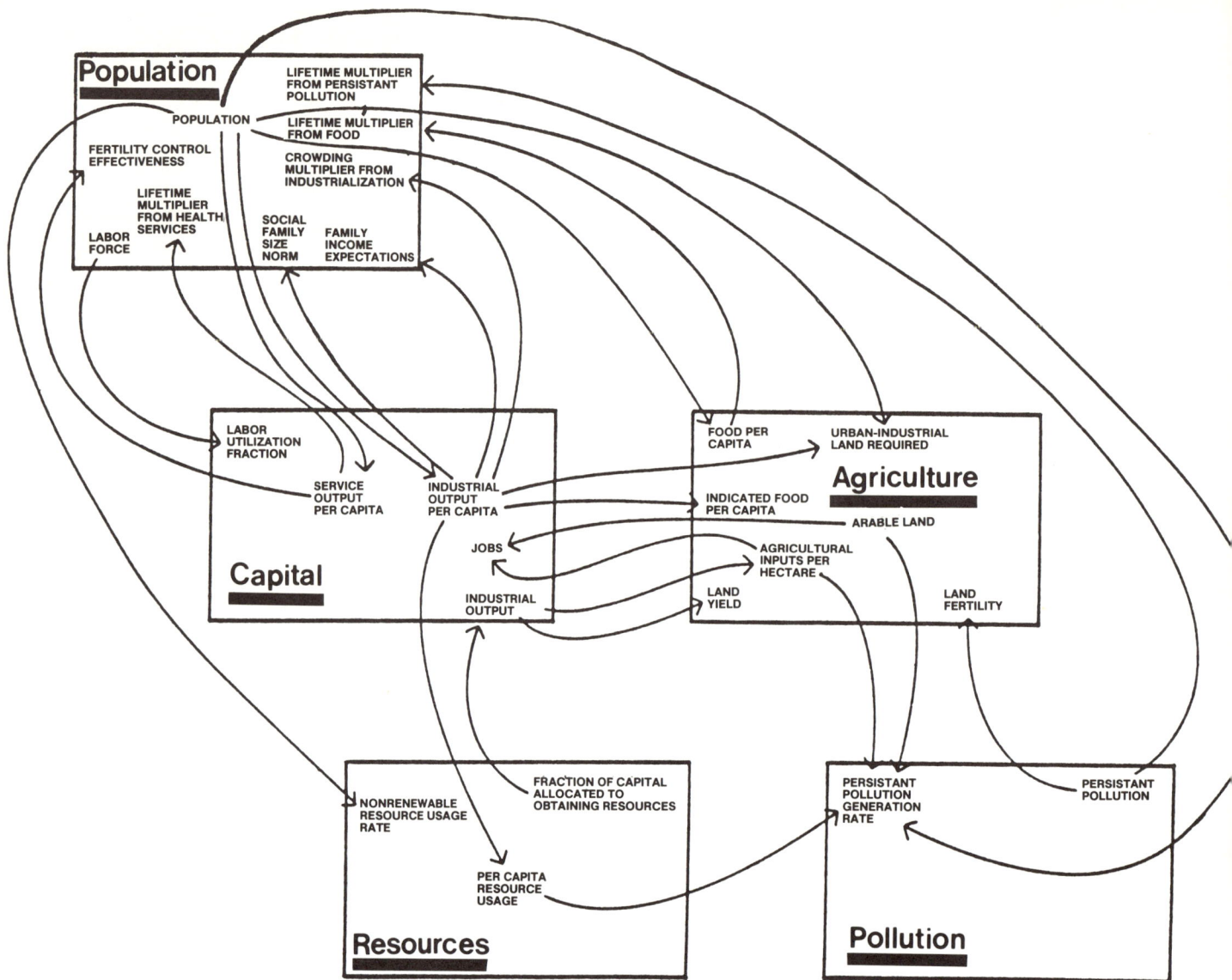

THE FORRESTER/MEADOWS MODEL (World III)

From *Dynamics of Growth in a Finite World*, by Dennis L. Meadows, et al. MIT Press, 1974.

A diagram drawn by the builders of the World III computer simulation model
to show how major features of the world interact with one another as both cause and effect

The U.S.—A Sustainable Society?

Commentary

Sustainability: There is nothing very complicated about the idea of sustainability.

A particular pattern of behavior is sustainable if it can survive, without impairment, for long periods of time.

National security is often viewed as the preeminent goal of governments, but it is really just another word for sustainability. Most Americans would agree that the goal of our government that takes precedence over all others is the preservation of the nation, without impairment.

Sustainability, so characterized, can hardly be viewed as a controversial issue.

Sustainability of present national behavior? The author of the next contribution, Dennis Meadows, is highly controversial. He believes that

MAKING IT HAPPEN:

our present behavior as a nation—emphasizing sustained and even increasing growth in material wealth and in our consumption of resources—is *not sustainable.*

If Meadows is correct, then the growth-emphasizing behavior patterns in our society may be regarded as a significant threat to our national security. Meadows would say that:

■ *A nation whose energy consumption already significantly exceeds its resources, and is still growing, is not sustainable.*

■ *A nation whose consumption of other nonrenewable resources exceeds its supplies, yet is still growing, is not sustainable.*

■ *A nation with a relatively small proportion of the world's population that is responsible for almost half of the annual global consumption of certain resources is probably not sustainable.*

Fears: Most of us recognize that nations, even the United States, are subject to constraints and limitations, just as we are in our personal lives. In the area of energy, where just a decade ago the United States was a net exporter, we are learning about sustainability the hard way.

But, if you familiarize yourself with the debate about indefinite growth versus the steady state, you will find the discussion is often more emotional than rational. Those who refuse to admit that our resources are ultimately limited and that material growth must stop sometime, I believe are afraid. They are afraid that:

■ without growth, we cannot meet basic human needs;

■ without growth, we cannot cure the ills of our society and the globe;

■ without growth, we cannot preserve "the American way of life"; and

■ without growth, our society cannot be sustainable.

The belief that there can be no limits to material growth may also be related to the fear that there are:

■ limits to human potential,

NEW VISIONS—2.

■ limits to American ingenuity, and
■ limits to America's capacity for change.

According to Dennis Meadows, we need not be fearful of a society in which there is no longer a commitment to unlimited material growth. **The things that are of real importance to Americans have not depended on growth and will not depend on it in the future.**

America, he believes, is in a unique position to set an example and carry this message to the world. Because of our world role, both our example at home and what we do abroad can be significant forces for constructive change.

Perhaps more than any other nation, the United States has the capacity, in a foreseeable period of time, to build a truly sustainable society.

Alternatives to Growth:

The Search for Sustainable Futures

By Dennis L. Meadows

The development of a steady-state economy will be the product of an unpredictable but conscious social evolution in which many ideas will be tried out. However, just as the auctioneer must begin by calling out some specific price, so it seems we must begin by calling out some specific notions about a steady-state economy, even though we know that they are no more likely to be the final solution than the auctioneer's initial price is.

HERMAN DALY

Dissenters from perpetual growth: There have always been dissenters who have questioned the notion of perpetual growth, and thus of a limitless improvement in personal welfare, on moral or ecological grounds.

But their protests have been drowned out by those who have praised the progress achieved through the past two centuries of rapid expansion, and by those who have found growth more attractive than the prospect of redistribution.

Whatever its merits, industrialization has been accompanied by environmental deterioration, social disintegration, and the depletion of resources.

Growing awareness of these problems now makes for much greater interest in the question: **How might a modern society be organized to provide a good life for its citizens without requiring ever-increasing population growth, energy resource use, and physical output?**

Not a future need but a present one: The "limits" thesis is by no means universally accepted. Important debates still rage on issues ranging from the purpose of human life to the magnitude of the globe's ultimate carrying capacity.

But many individuals, institutions, and even world regions are already confronted with essentially zero growth in their population, economic output, or use of specific energy, mineral, and land resources. In almost no instances are the resulting problems being dealt with effectively.

■ Some nations, accustomed to the growing use of oil imports to provide more energy, now face bankruptcy if they do not learn how to stabilize their use of fossil fuels or learn to rely on alternative energy sources.

■ Many regions have still not developed institutions and norms that can bring agricultural and industrial emissions under control at environmentally acceptable levels.

Rapidly falling population growth rates in some Western nations already pose daily problems.

■ Industry in those countries must learn how to cope with a constant and aging work force.

■ Schools must develop policies to remain solvent and innovative even though enrollments of new student are constant or declining.

■ National social security schemes must find new ways to avoid bankruptcy while financing the support of a growing proportion of retired citizens.

■ Whole sectors of the economy must develop appropriate responses to saturation in demand for the goods they are equipped to provide.

The Search for Guiding Concepts

If these and many other contemporary problems associated with zero material and demographic growth are to be solved, new goals and procedures must be developed. Alternatives are needed to guide decision-makers who now consider their organization's annual rate of growth to be the preeminent index both of their own personal success and of their potential for coping with future problems.

Anthropologists give us some insights into the role of religion, economics, and population control in traditional, steady-state communities. But those bucolic examples are of little clear relevance to an industrialized, urbanized, mobile, energy-intensive society.

Neither theoretical studies nor practical experience currently offer much assistance to those in Western nations forced to negotiate a transition from growth to a steady state.

"They're bumper to bumper on the B.Q.E. The approaches to the Lincoln and Holland Tunnels are stalled, and there are rubbernecking delays on the Major Deegan."

There do exist, however, texts which chart out paths to the steady state: for example, John Stuart Mill's *Principles of Political Economy,* Harrison Brown's *The Challenge of Man's Future, The Ecologist* magazine's *Blueprint for Survival,* Donella Meadows' *The Limits to Growth,* Dennis Pirages and Paul Ehrlich's *Ark II,* and Herman Daly's *Toward a Steady-State Economy.*

The Steady State

The steady state: Daly's book is one of the most important contributions, and this definition of the steady state is borrowed from him:

By "steady state" is meant a constant stock of physical wealth (capital), and a constant stock of people (population).

Naturally these stocks do not remain constant by themselves. People die, and wealth is physically consumed—that is, worn out, depreciated. Therefore the stocks must be maintained by a rate of inflow (birth, production) equal to the rate of outflow (death, consumption).

But this equality may obtain, and the stocks remain constant, with a high rate of throughput (equal to both the rate of inflow and the rate of outflow), or with a low rate.

Daly clearly states the necessary conditions for a steady state. What he does not specify are the attributes of a sustainable state—that is, what such a society would be like that was both consistent with global limits *and also* acceptable to that broad spectrum of individuals and institutions. After all, their sustained compliance with diverse ethics, laws, and norms is going to be required if such a social system is to work.

Reliance on continuous physical growth certainly makes any system *un*sustainable. But simply attaining a steady state of no further growth doesn't in any way guarantee that such a society is intrinsically worthwhile—or even sustainable over the long run.

The goal of a sustainable steady state forces attention toward ways of making zero material growth consistent with equity, personal liberty, cultural progress, and the satisfaction of basic physical and psychological needs.

Even if levels of population and capital are constant, there are still many degrees of freedom in determining

- the appropriate magnitude of the flow through each physical stock,
- the degree of social equality,
- the rate of innovation,
- the form of the political system,
- the tradeoff between size of population and degree of material well-being,
- and the nature of religion, art, science, recreation, education, commerce, and law.

What "Steady State" Does Not Imply

At present it is easier to specify which attributes of society are not necessary to a steady state than to define which are.

For example, nothing in the definition of a global steady state implies either an equal or an unequal distribution of wealth or income among members of the population. Growth has increased equity in some regions and worsened it in others. It seems likely that zero growth will also be associated with a variety of distributional patterns.

Typically, those who believe that a steady state is mandated by physical or institutional limits also believe that a modern society with great inequities cannot be politically stable over the long term. Thus they argue that the richer areas of the globe should begin now to end their period of material growth, while working internationally to raise consumption levels in the poorer regions.

Neither is there any reason to believe that a steady state must be technologically or culturally primitive. Historians point out that Japan during the Tokugawa period (ca. 1600–1867) enjoyed a high level of scientific and social sophistication, yet had little population or economic growth.

Greatly increased understanding of natural and social processes will be essential in bringing population and resource use into balance with the constraints of the planet.

Fluctuations in a steady state: Some demographers have correctly objected to the goal of a perfectly steady state, because natural fluctuations in biological and physical systems will always prevent attainment of absolutely constant levels in any population or material stock.

The idea of a steady state need not imply a perfectly static system. At the micro level, individuals and institutions will continue to pass through life cycles of growth and decline. At the macro level, it is only necessary that rates of change be significantly lower than those that persist today.

Whether the overall growth in population and material stocks is slightly positive at some times and slightly negative at others is unimportant. It is only essential that the value system of the society direct activities toward attaining a constant level that is believed to be desirable and sustainable, rather than toward achieving a positive growth rate.

No use of nonrenewable resources? It has been pointed out that a true steady state would be one that used no nonrenewable resources, since perfect recycling with no waste at all isn't possible.

Again, such a strict definition is neither intended nor useful. Any foreseeable steady state will include use of nonrenewable resources, but at greatly reduced rates of use, so that pristine materials will remain available to society for many generations, rather than just for a few decades.

Under these circumstances, technological advance and market forces will gradually cause a shift to use of those materials economically available in greatest abundance. Compensation for lower consumption of finite resources will come from greatly increased preferences for activities that require few materials and little energy.

Steady State Political Systems

A steady state does not imply the necessity for any particular form of government. The types of political institutions most appropriate for each region depend much more on that region's cultural heritage than on the rate of change sustained by its population and capital stocks.

It is clear that none of today's governments has the precise institutions required for it to attain a sustainable state. Material growth is still viewed as a cure-all by communist, capitalist, socialist, totalitarian, and democratic states alike. Debate over the nature of changes to be introduced into each region's political institutions will be an enduring, difficult, and exciting part of the effort to conceive of sustainable societies.

Do basic human psychological processes require material growth and change? For most of our existence as humans on this earth we have lived in steady-state societies. Today's dependence on material growth springs not from within the individual human psyche, but from the operations of current political and economic institutions.

A sense of progress probably is essential to our intrinsic well-being. But there are many dimensions of progress perfectly consistent with a material steady state. Indeed, it is these activities—music, art, learning, athletics and spiritual development, for example—that most distinguish human beings from other species.

Loss of variety? Finally, attainment of a steady-state system would not imply a loss of variety. To be sustainable over long periods, any social system must be consistent with local environmental conditions and with the ethics, norms, and institutions of its members. The challenge is not to conceive of the steady-state society, but of many steady-state options.

It is neither likely nor desirable that all societies would choose the same goals or the same timing to guide their transition policies. There is no fundamental reason why an individual, family, corporation, community, or region could not begin shifting to a steady-state existence while it remained interdependent in important ways with others that continued to pursue growth.

Characteristics of Sustainable Societies

While no specific social or technological trait must characterize all possible sustainable societies, there will be common themes.

■ **Contact with natural ecosystems:** This relationship is necessary to physical and psychological well-being; there is no artificial substitute. Therefore it is imperative that we protect our natural environment and reestablish our mental and physical linkage with biological processes and cycles.

■ **Social experimentation and learning:** These are exciting processes and are to be encouraged, not avoided. Human kind has many cognitive capacities that have yet to be tapped. More human challenge, innovation, and satisfaction may come from trying to live within limits than from striving to transcend them.

■ **Less emphasis on material goals:** In the richer countries, environmental, psychological, and social amenities are being increasingly eroded in the process of producing more material goods, and the accumulation of wealth is serving as an inferior surrogate for them. This vicious circle can be broken, but not by producing more and more. What is needed is the substitution of more humane goals for current excessively materialistic goals, and sufficient redistribution to guarantee access to necessities for all.

■ **"Richesse oblige":** The wealthy areas of the world, before promoting birth control, conservation, political reform, or value change for other countries, have a special potential, and obligation, to develop steady-state policies within their own borders.

■ **Decentralization:** It is detrimental to the global system's long-term viability to continue the progressive centralization of economic power, political influence, and scientific expertise.

Such centralization deprives individuals and local communities of more and more power over the vital functions required to ensure their own humane and secure existence. The total society is also robbed of the full measure of its innovative potential and resilience.

Smaller communities should resume more control over local norms and services and should strive for greater self-reliance. Technological development should be redirected toward the production of machines and procedures that are diverse and matched to the needs of small communities rather than the opportunities offered by international markets.

■ **Short-term sacrifice for long-term goals:** A sustainable society requires economic and political decision-making processes capable of making significant short-term sacrifices in the pursuit of longer-term goals. Expressed in other terms, current decisions must be based much more on consideration for their distant consequences.

■ **Humane technologies:** Few significant problems have purely technological solutions. Technologies must be designed in concert with changes in social values, goals, laws, and institutions. Because human institutions will always be prone to human error, society requires technological systems that can safely fail rather than those that must be fail-safe.

■ **Economic inducements for conservation:** Market-determined prices and the desire for financial profit will remain important in the process of resource allocation in the Western economies. But the market system must be extended and augmented to accord intrinsic merit to the conservation of nonrenewable resources and to ensure greater equity.

■ **Guiding image of a global system:** Changes in one component of society at a time, enacted on the margin, rarely solve important problems and often exacerbate them.

There are no universal, quick, or easy solutions to the problems that make the current system unsustainable. A long, slow process of thorough revision lies ahead, guided by an image of a viable global system that can only be achieved in the distant future.

■ **Individual effort:** A sustainable state can only be attained by *individual* initiative and change. A large number of personal decisions—each of them individually insignificant but each influenced by shared, feasible images of the long-term future—can begin a process of change that will reinforce itself, gather momentum, and gradually produce a sustainable system that meets humankind's basic needs.

It is easy to label these shared notions as naive or utopian. Yet they seem far less naive than proposals that global problems can be solved by intensifying the very policies that have produced the difficulties in the first place.

They are also less utopian than the belief that current physical growth rates can be maintained for another generation.

The concept of zero material growth need not be a source of anxiety; instead it can be the stimulus leading to identification of new personal and social goals both more feasible and more attractive than those currently pursued. The analyses presented thus far also justify hope that the paths to a sustainable society remain obscure not because they are impossible to find, but because so little effort has been devoted to searching them out.

Who am I?

Dennis & Donella Meadows

NEW VISIONS—2.

Someone visiting our farm awhile ago remarked that he had never before been in a room with a woodstove burning, three spinning wheels, and a new IBM word processor. Maybe that sums up who we are. We're the sort of people who own our own sheep and spin our own wool in between sessions of working with computers.

We were both chemistry majors at Carleton College in Minnesota. We married and went to Massachusetts, where Dana got a Ph.D in biophysics from Harvard and Dennis got a Ph.D in management from MIT. Right after finishing our Ph.D theses, we left for a year in Asia, driving a Land Rover from England to Sri Lanka and back, climbing mountains and kayaking whitewater rivers along the way.

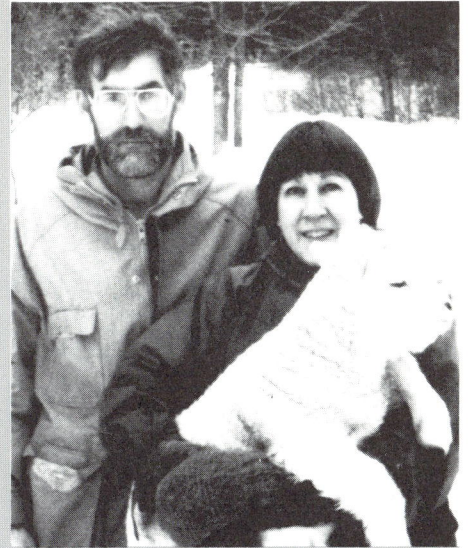

We had considered the trip recreational, a pure lark after five hard years of study. But it was immensely educational, and we came back with two resolutions: (1) we wanted to work together, and (2) we wanted to work on the problems that had become very real to us on our

Designs for a Sustainable Society

To stimulate discussion: In 1974, George Mitchell, a Texas business-man, resolved to encourage a more positive, rigorous, and comprehensive discussion of the constraints on and alternatives to growth.

He brought together businessmen, educators, and futurists with similar concerns, and challenged them to help design a ten-year program to define needed new social options. To guide their efforts, the group adopted five principles:

■ The program should not attempt to prove or disprove the limits-to-growth thesis. Instead, it should search for the policy implications of a societal transition to a steady state, a transition away from continuing growth of population, materials use, and energy consumption.

■ Directors of the effort should seek out and encourage the participation of the best minds from a large variety of cultural, disciplinary and ideological perspectives.

■ The emphasis should be on long-term issues, those that will confront humankind over the next 30 years or more.

■ The investigation should emphasize the use of sound empirical data and rigorous analysis to provide viable images of the future.

■ The analysis must acknowledge global interdependencies, but the specific goal of the program should be to stimulate development of new information useful to policymakers in the industrialized West, as they work to decide what must be done *by them, now,* and *within their own countries.*

The Mitchell Prize competitions and the Woodlands Conferences: From this charter, there emerged a plan for a series of five international essay competitions to be conducted once every two years for a decade. At a series of five conferences, each coinciding with the end of one prize competition, the best essays on the transition from growth to a steady state were to receive an award called the Mitchell Prize.

Over 300 papers were submitted to the first contest, and the first four Mitchell Prize winners—along with more than 500 other participants from around the world—attended the first Alternatives to Growth Conference in Houston, Texas, in October 1975. *Alternatives to Growth—1.,* the first of five volumes to accompany each biennial competition, contains the four papers entered in the contest or presented at the conference.

The second competition, which culminated in 1977, drew more than 2,400 inquiries and led to the award of five $10,000 prizes. In the third competition, which concluded in the fall of 1979, awards totalling $100,000 were divided between competing papers and a special group of commissioned papers.

The fourth competition, in the fall of 1982, emphasizes the role of the private sector in creating a sustainable society.

A POSITIVE GUIDE TO THE FUTURE

journey—the problems of poverty and injustice, hunger, population growth, erosion, polution.

Within two months after our return, we were launched on the study for The Club of Rome that resulted in *The Limits to Growth,* several other books, and what has become our professional and personal commitment.

We had spent two years working with the world's statistics, simulating its systems, and talking to scientists, planners, and politicians from North, South, East, and West. And we were convinced that many of the practices of industrial societies are unsustainable and also undesireable.

We had also found from our analysis, much to our surprise, that there is a wonderful world possible, one in which each person's needs are met, amply, elegantly, and sustainably. We wanted to bring that better world into being, as soon as possible, for ourselves and anyone else who wanted it.

Our way of doing that was to move to Dartmouth College in New Hampshire, where we created interdisciplinary undergraduate and graduate programs that teach and explore the principles of a sustainable, equitable society. We bought a small and exhausted hill farm, with a crumbling house and barn, and gradually turned it into a thriving organic homestead, shared with many other people. We continued computer simulation studies of resource systems, particularly energy systems, and we also began to learn about the philosophical, psychological, and spiritual sides of social systems.

We didn't know in advance how to do any of these things. We learned as we went and are still learning. We have made many mistakes, and yet slowly we have progressed farther than we evr suspected we could. We have done a lot of work and had a lot of fun.

We are always mindful in all the decisions we make of the conditions in which our friends in Asia are living, and of the strong, wonderful, and yet vulnerable ecosystem that sustains us.

Without any particular plan, our way of living has changed considerably, easily, and naturally, as a result of that mindfulness. We live with a jumble of old and new technologies, ancient wisdom and modern science, local self-sufficiency and global interconnections.

Our way of life is still changing. It is adapted to our personalities, needs, New England climate, and cold clay soils. And yet its general outline and principles could probably be adopted by everyone in the world, without overstressing any resource base, or exploiting anyone.

Some people, hearing about our life, think we have "given up" a lot. Probably our per capita consumption of energy, food, materials, and cash is rather low, at least by American standards. We are vegetarians, we heat our house and water with wood we cut and split ourselves, we grow much of our food, make many of our clothes, we have no TV, and a big night on the town for us is a contra dance at Cornish Flat.

However, we have a new rototiller, a root cellar full of vegetables and preserves, 100 pounds of wool, an FM radio, a car and a farm truck. We feel immensely and increasingly privileged, and most people who visit us sense not deprivation but a material and communal abundance.

We have also progressed from near-hopelessness about the future to excited anticipation. We have our eyes on that world of sufficiency for all and sustainability for the long term. We see that world forming already, in small pockets everywhere, in the middle of all the bad news. We have had a hand in small demonstrations of it, and we know that it is feasible, and that the process of creating it is challenging and joyful.

Our own next steps along the way will be to work to end hunger permanently on the planet before the end of this century; improve the soil of our sheep pasture this year; build a model usable for managing the total resource bases of five regions of the world within the next three years; and build a solar greenhouse by 1983.

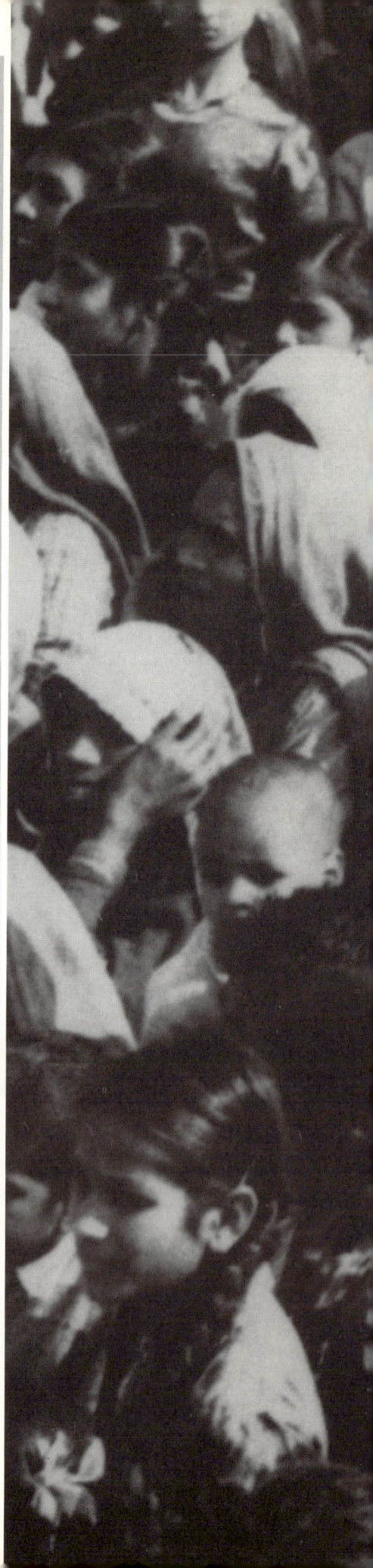

Our Partners:
The Invisible People

Passing Through

We travel through life
as one speeds on a freeway
through the heart of an inner city.

Below the steel and concrete roadway
human beings are born and die
amid the brick and concrete structures,
behind the filth encrusted glass
of a million windows.

The storefronts are barred
or shuttered
or shattered;
the refuse,
the desolation.

Human beings are there
like you, like me:
breathing, eating, sweating, urinating, defecating;
shouting, whispering, screaming;
talking, sobbing, laughing;
hearing, sometimes even listening;
loving and being loved,
hating and being hated.

There is ugliness, cruelty, veniality,
killing, stealing, beating, hurting;
disease and suffering;
fear and sadness.

Human beings are there
like you, like me.
There is compassion and caring,
warmth and concern,
dreams and aspirations,
beautiful things,
wonderful things,
and truth.
Wherever there are human beings
like you, like me,
there are these good things too.

But to those on the freeway,
the inner city
is just an indistinct blur
on the way from somewhere to somewhere.

Let's turn our flashers on.
Let's step on the brakes and pull over.
(The traffic can get by.)
We could get out of the car, you and I,
and breathe the air of the inner city.
We could look and listen.

We could step over the guardrail,
jump down to the cement and asphalt terrain
of a new world

and walk among the invisible people.

National Park Service, U.S. Department of the Interior

MAKING IT HAPPEN:

Creating the Future:

As If Children Mattered

By Page Huidekoper Wilson

The crucial link: There are two givens about the world's children:

- *The future of the planet is in their hands.*

- *Of all our fellow human beings, they are the most fragile.*

It should follow that concern for children would be high on the list of the world's priorities. The fact is, pious platitudes to the contrary, most societies around the world ignore the basic needs of their children and trample on their human rights. The condition of millions of the world's children is wretched.

This situation is intolerable both from a humanitarian and practical standpoint. Care of children is a moral imperative in its own right. At the same time, the child is the crucial link for breaking out of the vicious circle of overpopulation, unemployment, poverty, diminishing resources, hunger, and other human-made problems that beset the world—both in the northern hemisphere and in the South.

Tides of change that can be turned: The grim realities of the present cannot be denied, but what of the future?

Fortunately, there are tides of change in the world that I believe can be turned to the advantage of children. Everywhere there are revolutions—in different stages and degrees of intensity—against what various societies perceive as exploitation and materialism. These revolutions are forcing a deemphasis of economic goals alone; they demand greater attention to human, social, and cultural considerations.

This offers an unprecedented opportunity to see the child in a new dimension, and to recognize that the cause of the child and the cause of development—in its broadest sense—are one and the same.

The new message is that if we care about equity and justice, if we care about the fulfillment of human rights and the delivery of basic needs, if we care about the future, then we must start by caring for the child.

This shift in attitudes which prizes

PARTNERS

people above things obviously will not progress in an unbroken line. There will be zigs and zags which will carry it temporarily off course. The cooling toward human rights and the priority of business interests over all else in President Reagan's administration are examples of those zigs and zags.

Children in America

For the children of America, everything should be coming up roses. It isn't. Far from it.

Of all the so-called developed countries, the United States has the shabbiest record of solicitude for its children. Children pay most dearly for the excesses of the counter-reformation of the Reagan administration. The budget ax falls most heavily on them.

Too short to reach the lever: Cornell University's child expert Urie Bronfenbrenner points out that the United States alone of the modern industrialized countries does not insure health care for every family with young children, does not guarantee a minimum income level for every family with young children, and has not established nationwide programs of child care services for children of working parents.

There is no overall government policy

Seeing the Invisible People

By Elizabeth Dodson Gray

Individual human beings are often hidden from our view, concealed by mathematical and conceptual language. This full humanness of people is often invisible in our discussions, just as women are invisible in male generic language that speaks about "mankind" and "man's future."

When we think of population trends, forecasts of problems, and other projections from present statistical evidence, there are people behind all those numbers, trends, and projections, people who are male and female, young and old, rich and poor, living in skins of different hues and in villages and homes in many different locations.

Concealed in abstractions: The scene is a dormitory room at Deerfield Academy, a private preparatory school in Massachusetts. A group of male students is lounging about late at night, having a discussion about politics. Someone is saying, "All those lazy people on welfare! They won't work, so we're supposed to support them. It's disgraceful!"

My son told us later that he'd burst out, "Have you ever really known anyone on welfare?"

None of them had.

"I have a friend, Tony," our son continued, "who comes to visit us every summer. He's black and lives in

East Harlem in New York City.

"He's one of nine children, including a brother who is retarded. There's no father, and ever since I first met Tony when we were both five the whole family has survived because of welfare.

"Sure, he's black, and his father didn't go to Deerfield and make lots of money for them. Tony's a lot like me except for where we were born."

Our son went on. "You guys—when you say 'people on welfare,' you don't have any idea of the real people you're talking about."

Our son might have been talking to those of us who write and read books like this one. When we talk of the needy of the world, do we see the real human beings we are talking about?

on families, despite the fact that the family has always been seen as the vital center of our society. Nor is there any comprehensive U.S. policy for children.

Responsibility for childrens' programs is fragmented and fractured—scattered in an impenetrable thicket throughout Congress and the federal, state, and local bureaucracy. There are gaps and overlaps; some programs are in conflict with others, and there is, of course, rivalry over "turf" in the children's field as in all others in Washington.

The reason why children in our society don't count for very much is simple: they aren't tall enough to reach the lever in the voting booth. And it is, of course, the children of the poor who are the shortest of all.

Twenty percent divides up 5 percent: The poorest fifth of the U.S. population doesn't get a much larger chunk of U.S. wealth than the poorest fifth in the world gets of the world's wealth.

The poorest fifth of the world's people gets 2 percent of all the wealth the world generates. In the United States, the poorest fifth gets only a little over 5 percent of the country's income. Obviously, the standard of living in the United States is far higher than that of any developing country and there are some compensating amenities for poor American families, but they still get a skinny slice of the economic apple pie.

Indeed, of the industrialized countries, only Spain and France have a more skewed income distribution than the United States.

The price children pay: Children pay a dear price by being so low on the totem pole:

■ Seventeen and a half million American children under the age of 18 live in families below the poverty level. The Food Stamp Program has had a major impact on the lives of the poor, but millions of American children are still malnourished. Three-fourths of all retarded children come from impoverished families.

■ A lot of American children get off to a bad start in life. One in every five births in the United States is unwanted. Yet a full third of our people, mostly rural, do not have any family planning services.

American teenage and pre-teenage childbearing rates are among the highest in the world. More than 600,000 babies are born to that group each year.

■ Despite the pitiful picture of babies having babies, only six states and the District of Columbia require sex education in the schools. There is only one school-based contraceptive clinic in the entire United States.

■ In the United States, the infant mortality rate (18 per thousand) isn't bad, compared to developing countries where the worst rate soars to 200.

But there are 17 developed countries that do better than the United States. Furthermore, there is a vast discrepancy between the mortality rates of white and non-white infants within the United States. In a ranking of mortality rates with other countries, white American infants are eighth; non-white American

infants rank 31st.

■ Health delivery services for poor children in the United States are spotty, to say the least. Until very recently, more than 20 million children had not been inoculated against childhood diseases that have been wiped out in other developed countries. Some three million school children with visual defects requiring correction do not have eyeglasses, and thousands more need hearing aids. Over eight million children need help for various psychological disorders.

Young people are starting to drink earlier than ever before, and over one million preteens and teenagers in this country have serious drinking problems. The misuse of drugs has reached epidemic proportions.

■ Some states pay less for care of a foster child than kennels charge to board a dog. A special commission reported in the spring of 1979 that foster care in the United States actually damages large numbers of the half million children under its wing. The commission report cites instances in which some children changed foster homes 18 times, with obviously dire consequences. These are the children who never find a life of their own, and end up in prison or in a mental institution. They are, a children's rights lawyer has said, "flushed down the institutional drain."

Banishment: Children are "warehoused" in institutions of all kinds, and some thousands not even in their home states. This system, known as "banish-

Street child in Accra: Page Huidekoper Wilson gives us this vignette of a street child in Accra, Ghana, telling about himself.

"My name is Kweku," he says. "I am nine years old. A lot of people call me small boy. But I live on my own. My work is that I sell chewing gum around the Orion Circle at cinema time. Plenty boys and girls come buy it before they see cinema.

"I don't go to school. I don't go because I have no money. My mother died before they born me. My father nobody knows. Some woman give me milk when I am a little baby, now I am old so I work. I sleep in the far

night. I have no sleeping house. I sleep at lorry petrol station."

He ends his little story for the interviewer by requesting that no pictures be taken of him. "I don't want white man see me dirty," he says.

Seeing behind the numbers: In what we write and read and think, we need to see behind the words, behind the numbers, behind the abstractions, to the human faces of boys as different as these at Deerfield, in East Harlem, and in Accra. We must see the diversity and reality of the human beings who are ones being active today and in our future.

Are these actors men? Are they women? Children? What are their needs, aspirations, fears? What blockages do they face? What are they thinking? Feeling?

We cannot see the future until we open our eyes to see what it means to be human now, and see the full humanity of those whose present actions are shaping that future.

We cannot create our future until we really see the other human beings who will be part of it. We cannot see the future until we open our eyes to see what it means to be human now.

David L. Ames

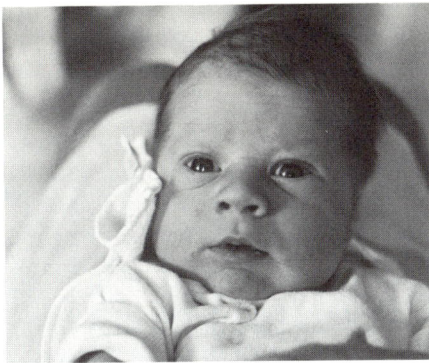

ment," is broadly practiced in the United States. Banished children include the physically handicapped, retarded, neglected, juvenile delinquents, and those adjudged in need of supervision because their parents cannot handle them. Virginia, for instance, sent more than 560 children in 1976 to institutions in at least 29 other states, with little or no monitoring by Virginia officials.

■ Children in the United States of America are still routinely committed to mental institutions by their parents, without any representation by counsel.
■ The juvenile justice system is often "simply used as a dumping ground for children," according to former Senator John C. Culver, who chaired the Subcommittee to Investigate Juvenile Delinquency. A substantial number of children who go through this system "suffer social, economic, and psychological change."
■ Prostitution and incest: There are other kinds of child abuse in the United States than those commonly described. It is estimated that nearly a million children from six to sixteen are involved in prostitution. It is not confined to girls. Young boys are exploited by "chicken hawks" and other sex mongers. Also, one out of every four female children will be sexually abused before the age of 18, according to a report from a conference on Violence Against Women, held in Boston in 1980.

Children "Included-Out": There have been sweeping changes in adult work patterns and in family structures in the last decade. This has resulted in a vast increase in the number of working mothers with young children, and that number is rising rapidly. A recent study predicts that by 1984 over half of all California children under six will have working mothers.

Commentary

Do you remember how you felt
and what you thought
when you first saw
your first child?

My daughter is eighteen years
old
and beautiful (I think)
She rides horses,
Doesn't pick up her room,
Is entering college,
Leaves dirty pans in the sink,
Works hard (when she wants to),
Doesn't (when she wants to),
Often, we don't communicate
very well.
I love her very much.

When I first saw her
at four A.M. in Honolulu
She was nineteen inches long,
Weighed five pounds,
Had big eyes, which looked at me
(I thought),
And a receding chin.
(Being a practical sort,
I thought, I'll bet she'll need braces.)

I also thought about
times we might spend together
how happy I was
growing up,
college,
what she might become,
and how I would do
anything to make it happen.

(How lucky I was, because
things have turned out, so far,
even better than I could have
imagined.)
Here are some things that I didn't
think about.

Will she be one that starves
to death?
How can I cope with this
new mouth to feed?
What will I do with this
unwanted child?

PARTNERS

How can we survive?
Should I abandon her?
Should I kill her?
Can you imagine what it
would
be like
to have a child—or
to be a child—
who was thought about like
that?

Can you imagine what it would
be like
to live in a world
in which *millions* of children
were thought about like that?
You do.

These are the children Page Wilson
writes about.
And they don't all live
in the "developing world."
Some of them live within five miles
of where you live.

It's true that you didn't decide that
these children would be born.
But neither did they.
Any more than my daughter decided
that she would be born.

It is easy to say
I don't know about these
things.
I won't see them.
I won't think about them.
There is nothing I should do
Or can do.

It is hard to say
I must learn about these
things.
I will see them.
I will think about them,
and I will see what I can do
and do it.
But at least we have a choice.

The number of female-headed families in the United States has risen by a whopping 43 percent in the last decade. This rise reflects a global pattern. The staggering fact is that today, throughout the world, one family in three is headed by a woman. And many of them—in the United States and elsewhere—are poor.

There are more than one and a half million mothers under 25 in the United States who have one or more children under the age of six and who limp along on a median yearly income of $2,800. And yet there is a huge shortfall of the day care facilities essential for mothers to be able to take jobs.

There are day care centers and family day care homes for only 1.25 million American children. As a result, millions of young American children look after themselves while their parents work. It is estimated that there are more than two million latch-key children between the ages of 7 and 13; further thousands of preschool children under age 6 are left alone while parents work.

As if they didn't exist: Some of the children "included-out" are simply treated as if they didn't exist. High on the list of the groups about whom few give a damn are the children of America's migrant workers. These children are "suffering from heat prostration in the field, drowning in irrigation ditches, or being run over by machinery," according to a 1976 Denver *Post* article. And these tragedies are not a rarity. "They are an almost common occurrence to field-working families," the Denver *Post* states.

Sometimes the exclusion of children is deliberate. There's a new version of "redlining." "Adults only" housing policies are spreading through the country. A man who owns more than 5,000 apartment units in Houston, all of which ban children, put it succinctly: "More people prefer to live in a child-free environment."

We really let children know how we feel about them. In some cases, children are zoned out of entire communities. The Board of Supervisors in Riverside County in southern California has passed an ordinance permitting cities to ban residents younger than 18.

Hopeful signs: American attitudes are going through a transformation of mammoth proportions, just beginning to be noticed by political leaders and media pundits. Old assumptions and certainties are being challenged and new concepts and values are emerging. There is hope that this melancholy picture for millions of America's children is changing.

One reason why the overall change taking place has been so little recognized is that there is a whole series of what appear to be unrelated movements and few see the cumulative effect. Each change is like a single wave in the ocean, but when they combine they form a giant tide.

■ **Public-attitude survey results:** Recent polls testify to changes. One study found three themes running through American society: the desire to live on a human scale, to devote time to interpersonal relationships, and to improve existing facilities rather than to break new ground. Other polls confirm that quantum changes in public attitudes are taking place.

■ **The rise of "rights" movements in the past decades:** The most compelling evidence of the American commitment to non-material values is the political movements in the last few decades that centered on aspects of human rights: the struggle for civil rights; for protection of the human environment, including the anti-nuclear protest; the peace movement; the movement for women's rights; for homosexual rights; and for the rights of the elderly.

Now the movement for human rights in the United States has found a new frontier: the human rights and needs of the child. The movement is only barely under way and it has taken a long time to come this far.

The counter reformation will slow the momentum, but it won't be able to stop it. The nation was nearly two hundred years old before children were considered "persons" under the protective scope of the Constitution. It wasn't until 1967—in a landmark decision, the Gault case—that the Supreme Court decided, among other things, that a juvenile has the right to an attorney, to cross-examine a witness, and to refuse to testify in a self-incriminating way.

Child Advocacy Groups

■ Among the most effective of advocacy groups is the *Children's Defense Fund,* headed by lawyer Marian Wright Edelman in Washington, D.C. The Fund litigates, publishes, and monitors on behalf of children and their families. It has brought successful class action suits that have rescued children from institutions in various parts of the country and returned them to their home states. Its main concerns and the subjects of its legislative agenda are children in foster care; child health assessment programs; Head Start, day care, and the child development centers of the Appalachian Regional Commission; and improved laws and programs for disadvantaged children.

■ *The American Civil Liberties Union* is trying to establish the broad principle that children should have all the legal and constitutional protections currently afforded adults.

■ Other organizations working to restructure our laws and institutions dealing with children include: the *National Council of Jewish Women,* the *American Parents Committee;* the Washington division of the *Child Welfare League of America*, the *Legal Rights Information and Training Program*, the *Coalition for Children's Justice,* the *American Public Welfare Association*, and the *Association of Junior Leagues.*

■ Development of a core of experts with a professional focus on children has been a major factor in raising the national consciousness about the problems of American children. Among the more prominent are psychiatrist Robert Coles, consulting economist Mary Dublin Keyserling; MIT human development professor Kenneth Keniston; former New York Judge Justin Wise Polier; C. Henry Kempe, head of the National Center for Prevention and Treatment of Child Abuse and Neglect; and the aforementioned Urie Bronfenbrenner and Marian Wright Edelman.

■ *The American Bar Association* recently called for sweeping reforms in juvenile courts.

■ A growing number of organizations are concerned with special aspects of children's issues. Among these are *ACT (Action for Children's Television)*; the *Coalition of Labor Women,* which is pressing the government to help finance the construction of high-standard day care centers for the children of an estimated 14.4 million working mothers; and the *Children's Foundation.*

Uwe Rau, *Development and Cooperation, German Foundation for International Development.*

A State of Quiet Emergency

What of the children in the developing world? Are changes taking place that will improve their condition? First, let's look at the conditions in which they live.

We are not addressing ourselves here to the tragic fate of children caught in episodic disaster, such as war, flood, or earthquake. The pictures of such children have been flashed around the world and are emblazoned on our hearts forever. Americans respond with their usual generosity to the plight of these children.

A continuous state of quiet emergency: We are talking here of the millions of the world's children who exist in a continuous state of relentless,

quiet emergency that rarely hits the headlines.

These millions of the world's children exist in crushing poverty, mainly in the rural areas of Africa, Asia, and Latin America. Every day there are over three hundred thousand new babies; 85 percent of them are born in the developing world, and by far the majority to the poorest families in the poorest countries.

To comprehend the tyranny of the poverty in which these children live, bear in mind that the poorest 20 percent of the world's people ends up with only 2 percent of all the income that the world generates, so that today nearly one billion souls subsist on an income of

less than $75 a year per person. Brutal as it is for the adults, it is the children—especially in the rural areas and especially the little girls —who suffer most and who end up most often with the empty bowl.

Odds are stacked against girls in many areas of the developing world by the simple fact of having been born female. Discrimination often starts in the cradle, especially in the countries where there is no bride price, which means the baby girl is looked upon as a liability.

In any case, no matter where she lives, a daughter is seen as a transitory member of the household, for she will be married off as soon as possible; there rarely is any other alternative in life for her.

The sooner she is married the better, for then there is greater likelihood that she will have retained her virginity, a commodity both highly prized and highly endangered. In many societies there will have to be tangible proof of her chastity on her wedding night—"Tokens of the damsel's virginity," as the Old Testament puts it.

It may be illegal to marry the girl off when she is young, because during the past 30 years some fifty-odd countries have passed laws setting minimum ages of marriage for girls. But in many developing countries these laws are more honored in the breach than in practice.

A worker in a slum section of Dacca writes of the child-mothers there (but it could apply to countless other communities around the developing world): "Usually girls are married at very young ages, say 12 or 13 years old. By the time they are 25, they have already had five or six sickly babies."

For most women the route to social acceptance is their fecundity, and there are great pressures for them to start on that route early in life. . .and stay there until menopause. The average rural woman in a developing country will have had eleven pregnancies in the course of her life.

In some societies, women are thought of as mothers rather than as individuals. For example, in some highly traditional Moslem communities, a woman is called by the name of her son, that is, Ali's mother or Mahmoud's mother. The number of children, and especially the number of sons, determines a woman's social status.

Miseropoli: And these babies are born to that sizable part of humankind that must spend 80 percent of its low income on food. The doubling of the price of wheat and rice in recent years has been a cruel blow to already meager diets for millions of those families. As Indian poet Dom Moraes puts it, "Every ninety seconds an Indian baby left the dark secrecy of the womb and came weeping into a world that could not afford it."

It isn't just numbers alone that create the population problem. The age structure is a crucial element. The dependent population—those under 15

years old—is huge, more than 45 percent of the population of the developing world. For example, in Algeria with its high birthrates, every 100 persons of working age in 1970 had to support 98 children under the age of 15. By contrast, in Sweden, with its low birthrate, every 100 persons of working age had to support only 32 children under 15.

Statistics tell the woeful tale

■ Eighty million children under five in the developing world suffer from the world's most widespread disease: chronic malnutrition. Girls are more likely to be afflicted than boys because, as nutrition expert Jean Mayer points out, "Throughout the world there tends to be discrimination in nutrition in favor of boys."
■ On top of that eighty million, another ten million under the age of five are severely malnourished. This generally means irreversible damage to the brain as well as to the body.
■ Only five percent of the children born in the developing world have been vaccinated against polio and other diseases such as diphtheria, measles, and tetanus.
■ Only 15 percent of the rural children throughout the developing world have access to an adequate supply of safe water for drinking, cooking, or bathing. In fact, in the tropical world where most of the developing countries lie, filthy water and lack of sanitary facilities are the first links in a chain that often ends in death.
■ And death comes early to millions: nearly 30 percent of the children born in the developing world will not even live to see their fifth birthdays.

Further, the world must brace itself for yet another explosion—that of the labor force. Yesterday's children will converge on tomorrow's job market at an estimated rate of 300,000 each week, which means that between now and the year 2000 some 900 million more people will be looking for work. . .in a world where unemployment is already pervasive.

There are not enough jobs because there are too many people, and neither private enterprises nor the governments have the financial capacity to invest enough in job-producing endeavors. Thus the cycle of poverty and overpopulation tightens, each reinforcing the other.

Streams of people continue to leave the economically stagnant countryside searching for jobs in the big cities and provincial capitals of the developing world. Over 25 million people a year in the poor countries leave rural areas and move to what an Indonesian journalist calls the "miseropoli."

This rapid urbanization in large parts of the globe is having a devastating impact on children. They already make up half the population of the slums and shantytowns. At current rates of growth, the numbers of children living in the poorest sections of cities and towns will double by 1990.

On top of the 25 million people who will migrate into the cities this year, another 25 million babies will be born there in the teeming deprived areas of the developing world's towns and cities.

Women's goals: Surveys show that women would prefer to have smaller families, and that they would like to bear only the number of children they feel they can take care of. The steps women take to reach that goal prove their commitment.

If scientific methods of contraception are not available—and they are not available to an astounding 70 percent of the 500 million women of childbearing age around the world—women will try traditional methods to prevent an unwanted pregnancy.

Journalist Perdita Huston writes in *Message from the Village* that some village women use a sort of aspirin in the vagina to prevent conception. "Sri Lankans sometimes rely on charmed coconuts and other talismans. In Egypt women place cotton, saturated with oil, in the vagina prior to have sexual relations—a centuries-old contraceptive method."

She continues, "Some told of swallowing mothballs and then laughed at their foolishness. One Tunisian woman, now using a modern contraceptive, referred to the making of a contraceptive consisting of the dried umbilical cord from the last-born child, ground meal, and cows' urine.

Of course, if a pregnancy cannot be prevented, an unwanted birth can be averted by abortion. It is estimated that some 30 to 55 million abortions take place annually. Indeed, whether abortion is legal or not, the World Bank estimates that one out of every three or four pregnancies worldwide ends in abortion. In Latin America, where abortion is generally illegal, the abortion rates matches that of the United States. In many Latin American countries, botched abortions contribute to the high maternal mortality rate.

Millions of women resort to other "solutions." If they can't get rid of an unwanted pregnancy, they find ways of getting rid of an unwanted child. Recent studies indicate a noticeable increase in "child-riddance" patterns, through infanticide or abandonment or sale.

It is, of course, impossible to get figures on infanticide—direct or masked—but recent stories about "abandonados" in Mexico and Brazil and "gamines" in Colombia, as well as abandoned children in Asia and Africa, suggest the numbers may run into many millions.

These tragic children were either unwanted or have become too great a burden for their families to sustain. They are sad proof that runaway population pressure actually means a small demographic explosion in the limited and personal universe of the couple.

It is there—at the family level—where all the major problems (not confined to population, of course, but including poverty, diminishing resources, unemployment, and the like) come home to roost. And, as we have seen, the children always pay the dearest price of all.

The Arithmetic of Poverty

Decide, mother,
who goes without.
Is it Rama, the strongest,
or Baca, the weakest
who may not need it much longer,
or perhaps Sita?
Who may be expendable.
Decide, mother,
kill a part
of yourself
as you resolve the dilemma.
Decide, mother,
decide....

APPADURA (India)

Hopeful Signs

Hopeful signs: Fortunately, there are some signs of progress for the child in developing countries. Three major trends are under way today that have direct bearing on the state of the child in the Third World, and therefore on the future of the planet.

■ The growing concern for equity and justice which is already triggering massive changes in political, economic, and social institutions. Development theory, for example, has turned completely around.

The hope that the benefits of economic development would trickle down from the privileged upper class to the poor masses was never realized. So concentration on economic growth alone is giving way to a broader concept of human and social growth. The goal is to improve life for the poorest of the poor, to assure them greater equity and justice.

■ The needs of poor men, of course, are still considered first. Women's needs are beginning to be addressed—and the children's turn comes next. An obvious aberration in this trend was the U.S. vote against a code on overaggressive selling of infant formula to poor, illiterate women in the developing world. This vote—the only negative one cast—was made under instruction from the White House against the advice of the heads of UNICEF, the World Health Organization [WHO], many concerned U.S. officials and countless other experts on women's issues and child nutrition.

From *Third World Women Speak Out: Interviews in Six Countries on Change, Development, and Basic Needs*, by Perdita Huston (New York: Praeger Publishers in cooperation with the Overseas Development Council, 1979). Reprinted by permission.

PARTNERS

Lucia

...Lucia [was] fifty-five years old, and extremely poor. The town in which she lives is in the rich El Bahio region of central Mexico. The town is surrounded by huge farms owned by corporate firms. The men of the region find only seasonal work here because the farms are highly mechanized.

Throughout this region, production of export crops has displaced farming for domestic consumption, and the nutritional problems of the area are acute. A young doctor told me that 90 percent of the population suffers from nutritional deficiencies. Anemia is very common among women.

Lucia is landless and has no remunerable skills. She was dressed in ragged clothes and broken plastic sandals. Her eyes were those of a person who expects nothing but hardship in the years still ahead. Her skin was dark, and she covered her head and shoulders with a worn, green shawl.

"I am fifty-five years old, and those years have not been good. I didn't even have shoes or many clothes. I was very, very poor. Every night I had to wash my clothes and then put them on again in the morning. I didn't have anything at all, just the fifteen children.

"But only seven of my children are still living. The other eight died when they were babies. I think it was because of the hunger. I was very weak while nursing them because we never had enough to eat. All we had was beans, beans, and more beans. Yes, it was the hunger that took the babies.

"My husband was a laborer, but my mother-in-law kept the money. My husband was cruel with me. He beat me and screamed at me. He did many, many bad things. When he died, I sent the children to work as cattle herders. The owner of the cattle gives us some food. They eat better now."

Perdita Huston, *Third World Women Speak Out*

■ **More "wanted" babies:** The second development is a phenomenon of extraordinary importance for children, although little viewed in that context.

Somewhere between the mid-sixties and the present, the rate of world population growth began to slow down. This decline has justifiably been seen as an extraordinary demographic achievement. But its implication from the human point of view has scarcely been noted: it means that in millions of cases only wanted babies were born. . . babies that their parents felt they could adequately care for.

This surely is a major step toward assuring the rights of a child: that he or she be born as a result of an intentional, planned, mindful decision on the part of both the man and the woman. This could mean that each birth would be a celebration, instead of being a burden. This could mean that the joy and love of children would be given full rein. It could mean a new reverence for life.

■ **Basic services for children:** The third trend offers by far the most promising way to bring in the Third World fundamental and permanent improvement in the lot of children and, as a

Stephen C. Beuby

consequence, to the life of the entire community.

UNICEF and WHO have devised a development strategy called Basic Services for Children, which breaks with traditional approaches by tapping the largest unused resource of all in the developing countries: the people themselves. This reflects the growing belief that no substantial development will take place unless the local people are involved in both the planning and implementation of programs.

The strategy is also unconventional in that it starts at the grass roots whereas past development assistance came from above, from the provincial capital or the national government—or from abroad. Instead of "trickle down," the new strategy is, in effect, "trickle up."

The new approach works like this. Local communities—rural and urban—identify the most pressing needs of their children and select their own development workers from among themselves. Those selected are given intensive training with other workers similarly chosen from nearby villages and neighborhoods, after which they return to their respective communities to share their newly acquired information with their neighbors, to help them meet their basic needs.

The Basic Services Strategy for Children includes such areas as health services, maternal and child care, and family planning; safe water supply and waste disposal; in foods, local production, conservation, storage, and consumption of better-quality foods; functional literacy, elementary education, and the introduction of simple

technologies, especially those to lighten the daily tasks of women and girls.

The strategy is both conceived and delivered at the grass roots, but to be effective it requires consistent linkages to and support from the central government, with connecting links in between. It also presumes initial support from the international community. The recurring costs of maintaining such services are expected to be sufficiently low for governments and communities to sustain them from their own resources within a reasonable period of time.

Bite-sized morsels: Among the advantages of Basic Services for Children is that it breaks the problems into bite-sized morsels. To supply children all over the world with adequate nutrition, for example, sounds like a Herculean task. The problems loom so large and

---

A Mother's Pride

No madonna and child could touch that picture of a mother's tenderness for a son she soon would have to forget.

The air was heavy with odors of diarrhea,

of unwashed children with washed-out ribs and dried up bottoms, struggling in labored steps behind blown empty bellies.

Most mothers there had long ceased to care, but not this one; she held a ghost smile between her teeth, and in her eye the ghost of a mother's pride, as she combed the rust-colored hair left on his skull and then—singing in her eyes—began carefully to part it. . . .

In another life this must have been a little daily act of no consequence before his breakfast and school; now she did it like putting flowers on a tiny grave.

Cinua Achebe, *Refugee Mother and Child*

Several years ago, in a Saharan oasis, I witnessed a scene I will never forget. A group of children ranging in ages from two to five or six were walking together holding hands. Their eyes were encrusted with secretion and flies. Each led another in a collective attempt to find their way in blindness. The scene is not uncommon; nor is blindness from trachoma or other diseases. But such suffering could be avoided at little cost: one person trained in hygiene—working with mothers of that oasis—might have prevented the children's blindness.

PERDITA HUSTON, *Third World Women Speak Out*

MAKING IT HAPPEN:

are so bewilderingly complex that societies are frozen into inaction.

But otherwise massive and seemingly insuperable problems, if disaggregated as this new strategy advocates, can be reduced from staggering to solvable.

Julia

Every morning before six Julia went to the nearby government CEIMSA store to queue up for the milk sold there at half-price. Rumor said it was diluted with water and vegetable fat, but Julia paid no attention to that for she needed four quarts a day to feed the many people who depended upon her.

She went early to be sure the milk would not be sold out and to queue up twice, since she could obtain only two quarts at a time. She was late this morning and hurried, clutching her shawl around her against the cold. She had bronchitis and her chest hurt, but if she did not go for the milk no one else would and her stepchildren and grandchildren would have to go without.

Julia felt put upon: she thought her married daughter, Yolanda, or her stepdaughter, Lola, should properly go for the milk when she herself was ill. But Yolanda, who lived two doors down in No. 7, was lazy and besides had recently given birth to her fifth child. Lola was only fourteen and was not permitted by her father to go out so early. Panchita, the wife of Julia's son, Maclovio, who lived in No. 9, could not be expected to go because she worked and her husband paid Julia fifty pesos a month to cook for them and their two children.

The only other woman available was Julia's mother, Rufelia, who lived in a tiny room in a nearby *vecindad*, but she was old and no longer in her right mind. No matter how Julia fumed and complained about her heavy responsibilities, she continued to provide food for these people, sixteen in all, because she knew that they depended upon her. Julia had been the eldest of twelve children and was accustomed to assuming the burdens of others.

OSCAR LEWIS, *Five Families*

Consider, for example, a village-scale community of 1,000. There might be 6 children severely malnourished and some 35 moderately malnourished. The villager who has received simple nutrition and health training can help parents treat the moderately malnourished and see that the severely malnourished are taken to the closest clinic or hospital. Further, and of primary importance, the village worker can teach other villagers how to prevent malnutrition and other diseases, a fundamental element of the Basic Services approach.

Many low-cost, local technologies can be introduced by the trained village worker. Simple new technologies can fight the "grain drain." It is estimated that 25 to 40 percent of each year's grain crop in developing countries is spoiled or otherwise lost after harvest, more than the total annual food aid sent to the developing world. Simple improved grain handling and storage techniques can be taught to other villagers by the trained village worker.

There is no single blueprint for the Basic Services Strategy. To reduce the likelihood of a collision between modernization and traditional ways, each program will develop within the cultural framework of the individual country or region and thus build on existing customs.

Basic Services has countless other advantages. It can be an effective stimulant to other forms of local development. Involving villagers in organizing their own essential services can be the starting point for revitalizing the entire countryside.

The Basic Services Strategy is labor-intensive and thus mobilizes the resource most abundantly available. And, most important, as retiring UNICEF executive director Henry Labouisse put it, "Basic Services focuses on children—on the society's future."

So compelling is the idea of the Basic Services Strategy for Children that three recent United Nations General Assembly resolutions have urged the international development community and developing countries to incorporate the approach in all development plans and strategies. □

Who am I? Page Huidekoper Wilson

A million years ago, in the spring of 1942 when I was a reporter on the old Washington *Times Herald*, the city editor beckoned to me. "You, lucky creature," he said, "as the newest person on the paper, are presented with the opportunity of taking care of that lady." He pointed to an old woman emerging from the elevator.

As I approached her, she drew out of the beat-up old sack she was carrying a huge drawing of lobster. The drawing was executed in thick black lines. Next to the lobster a great pot of water steamed away. Down one side of the crustacean visage flowed several huge teardrops.

The woman wanted me to use my influence to see that the drawing was carried in the *Times Herald*, along with an editorial that she had written, calling for an end to cruelty to lobsters. The battle for Guadalcanal, in the southern Solomon Islands, was taking place at the time, with a heartrending toll of American lives. So I told the Lobster Woman as gently as possible that I didn't think the moment was propitious. It wasn't, I said, that I could be considered anti-lobster—I really was concerned for them, but....

I escorted her to the elevator, muttering to myself that maybe someday there'd be no more wars; poverty would be wiped off the face of the earth; nobody would be hungry or cold; justice would reign. Then I, too, would work for Lobster Heaven.

Well, that was a million years ago, as I've said, in the spring of 1942. We—you and I—go on working for human rights, civil rights, women's rights, and children's rights, even if Lobster Heaven still seems a long way off.

Unique Perspective,

Unique Potential:

Women and Global Society

By Elizabeth Dodson Gray

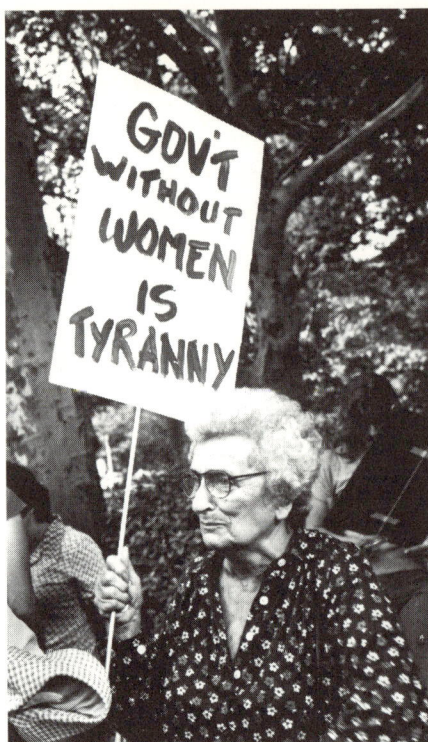

Freda Leinwand

Most of the time when we think of the present or the future, we are thinking of the world of men. Industry, government, business, finance, academia—all are mainly populated by men. Problems are discussed in such terms as "man" and the environment, or the future of "man" or "mankind."

But concealed in this male vocabulary and this world of male actors is the fact that half of the world's population and half of the actors on the real stage of life are female.

For example, the problem of meeting "basic human needs," has been cast in terms of development, technology, industrialization, monetary flows, and the large-scale distribution of aid. The language, concepts, actors, and structures are all reflections of male perceptions and institutions.

Yet around the world it is women who are the basic care-givers of life. It is women who have defined their total existence in terms of meeting basic human needs. It is women in many societies who actually grow the food

that is eaten. It is almost invariably women who are cooking that food, serving it, and cleaning the dirty dishes after it is eaten.

And it is women who are bearing and caring for the children, keeping the homes clean and doing the laundry, in addition to nursing the sick and caring for the dying. In culture after culture, women are charged with providing for many, often most, of the basic needs of the human beings around them.

Like seeing with one eye closed: Time after time the unique perspective and potential of women is ignored or disregarded. To do so is to proceed into the future still wearing the curious one-gender blinders we have worn in the past. Like driving a car or bus down the highway with one eye held firmly closed, or listening to music with one ear completely blocked, this is curious behavior. For a two-gender human species interested in survival, it seems curiously self-destructive.

Western development programs provide vivid examples of one-gender

MAKING IT HAPPEN:

When I asked whether she talked about these things with other women, she replied:

"That's all we talk about—family planning, women's freedom. We talk about all the subjects that concern women. In my day, because we were not educated, we lived like beasts. We didn't know anything. It is obvious that we were always bypassed by men."

I asked her if she thought men were happy to see women taking advantage of these changes.

"In any case, it's none of their business," she replied. "We are equal. The President says so—it's all thanks to him. So even if the husbands are not happy about all these changes, they can't do anything about them. Now women can go to buy things by themselves; they have the choice to come and go. Their husbands can't forbid it anymore. It is much better. But still there are problems for all the women of the world anyway. Not just Tunisian women. All women are reaching out to learn, to go out, to listen. Not only us. All the women of the world."

World Bank

orientation and the problems it can cause. In Third World countries, these programs have promoted technology and new jobs for men. Men reared in Western culture assumed that all farmers are men. It seemed logical to them that if men anywhere got jobs paying cash, they would assume the traditional responsibilities of being breadwinner for their families as in the West, and that the entire family would have a better life.

Imagine our surprise to discover belatedly that in many countries of the world most of the food is raised by women. Giving tools and instruction to men accomplished little for family nutrition and food supplies.

Imagine our surprise, too, to discover that in many other cultures there is no male role as breadwinner, and that women are responsible for feeding the family. Increases in a man's income in such cultures do not go home to bring a better life to his family but are viewed as personal discretionary funds, to be invested in a bicycle or transistor radio, or to be spent on Coca-Cola, entertainment, or other pleasures.

Thus, as a culture follows the Western development model and moves into a cash economy, village males earn more money. But women and children get less food because women's traditional ways of getting food are displaced, and both women and men have greater need for cash incomes.

All this is documented in recent studies of how Western technologies have displaced women's traditional jobs, increased the work still expected from women, and resulted in greater malnutrition among women and children at the same time that national income levels and GNP are increasing.

Development with one eye closed does not work: That face should have been obvious to us, had we been good systems thinkers. If we wish to maximize the health and well-being of an entire system, then all the parts of that system must participate, all the variables be considered, all the actors be taken seriously and given significant roles. To do less is not to understand the nature of systems, and not understanding systems in today's very interconnected world may be fatal to our own future well-being.

Commentary

Thinking about Women (from the perspective of a white American male): Elsewhere in this book it has been suggested that creating the future requires that we look at things in a fundamentally new and different way, which is hard to do. Elizabeth Dodson Gray is suggesting that many women *already* look at the world in a different way. Hers is one of the most hopeful messages in this book.

This casts an entirely new light on the movement for women's rights. The rationale for this movement has been, for the most part, moral and ethical: women should have equal rights because such rights are fundamental and inalienable

Elizabeth Dodson Gray is saying something quite different. She is saying that a world in which women participated fully in decision processes would be different from the one we now have, in which decision processes are dominated by men. And it might be a better world.

My own views on these matters are the result of twenty years of marriage to a woman who simply would not accept the role that was traditional for those of her generation. I was not at all prepared for this—I did not see the world in the way she saw it.

Changing my mind took 15 years of struggle and heartache for both of us. Changing how one sees things, especially if it involves relinquishing a belief in one's innate superiority, is almost always a wrenching emotional experience.

But the benefits of that experience may be:
■ a relationship based upon equality rather than dominance (Is a loving relationship really possible without that?);
■ the gift of access to fine minds and points of view you didn't dream existed;
■ an awareness of feelings and an ability to communicate that most men, so far as I can see, never experience; and
■ a better chance to achieve a humane and sustainable world.

A POSITIVE GUIDE TO THE FUTURE

What The Other Eye Sees

As we hurtle into the future, what might the human race see if it were to try to open its "female eye"? What unique perspectives and sensitivities do women bring to the thought and action of our species?

■ **Awareness of systems:** The domestic world constitutes much of women's experience. This experience teaches women to be intimately concerned not only about their own well-being but the well-being of the systems of which they are a part.

By contrast, the organizations men have made and managed so successfully in the larger world beyond the home have often focused on maximizing some part or factor, "suboptimizing" for efficiency, power, profit, or market share, for example.

In suboptimizing for one factor while ignoring the larger system, the complex and resilient social or environmental fabric can be stretched until it is distorted or even torn. In this way much that has been accomplished by suboptimization can be destroyed.

In dealing with her family, a woman has learned that she lives in a dynamic and complex system of interacting people, each with his or her own needs, goals, dignity, and feelings. Her family is a constantly changing system: the children grow up; experiences mature and age adults; accidents, illnesses, and death intrude from time to time. Operating within such systems, women know intuitively that you cannot consistently rob Peter to pay Paul, and that it is best to find ways to optimize the health, happiness, and long-term well-being of everyone within the system.

■ **Dealing with feelings:** Strength and rationality, control and mastery, linear thinking and quantification—these are the traditional currency of the male world of thought and action. The traditional domain of the woman has involved living with weakness and emotion, vulnerability and helplessness, responsiveness and attention to the needs of others—in short, nurturing

"*Your wife's on the phone. The azaleas are out.*"

Drawing by Ross; © 1976 *The New Yorker Magazine, Inc.*

and caring for the world of children, the aged, and the home.

Thus, many of the more elusive and intangible aspects of our human life together have been delegated—or relegated—to women.

What are we to do when projects based upon traditional quantification and rationality will not work because factors seen to be "soft," uncertain, and unmeasurable—and therefore regarded as unimportant—in fact have proved to be very important?:

■ What are we to do when "mastering the earth" is finally perceived to be

I was told that modern, Western-style housing does not in most cases serve traditional family communication patterns. In Tunisia and Egypt the government has recognized this problem and has begun the construction of homes whose design takes into account the roles of all family members, old and young. These "new traditional" homes provide for the needs of animals, the storage of crops, and child care. I was told that the involvement of women in the design of housing projects might help to alleviate problems of alienation and anxiety that are at present intensified in most urban housing programs.

PERDITA HUSTON, *Third World Women Speak Out*

causing our own destruction, since we ourselves are part of that earth and need it to sustain life?

■ What are we to do when it appears we must do less mastering and controlling, and become more sensitive to what often seems "soft," unquantifiable, and emotional?

■ How do we go about becoming more responsive and caring about our total situation, more attentive to consequences of our human activities, more nurturing of the world's total life-system?

Will men still strive to "rule" such a world by their old strategies? Will men place their hope in evolution and in time for the males of the species to become more responsive, more attentive, more nurturing?

Or will they find in themselves the humility—as well as the survival instinct—to draw on the other half of human experience and allow women to give leadership and use the nurturing skills that life as a woman has taught them?

Women as tenders of the emotional fabric of life in the home have learned with practice ways of dealing with realities that are soft and elusive, real though intangible. Can we let women bring those skills into the male world? Or must men do it all themselves? Are men able to do it all themselves?

Living with Uncertainity

The transitional years ahead will involve shifts in perspectives, organizational structures, and in the mental models or paradigms we use to understand and organize our thoughts and experiences. It will be a time of heightened uncertainty for all of us.

To such a time women bring unique experiences and unique potential, for in their own life-cycle women have experienced—and are experiencing—similarly comprehensive transformations of their own identities and circumstances.

Consider the psychic flexibility demanded by the traditional American woman's life. As an adolescent a traditional American woman formed her identity as a single, independent individual.

Then, if she married (and she almost always did), she adjusted to living with another person in a society that expected her to take his name and to focus her identity and life around him and around the task of maintaining his home. She was uprooted and moved whenever and wherever it suited his career needs.

As her children were born, she became the hub of an expanding family. Each successive child became a spoke dependent on her centering care. It was

the woman's lot to sustain and balance the family's life amid the diverse needs and activities of everyone in the family system. Men, of course, had families, too. But in the traditional marriage, men were not expected to focus their identities or adult lives upon their families but upon their work, their "careers." Men had careers; women had marriages and children.

Then slowly but with the inexorability of the calendar, the children grew up and left home. The woman's identity as mother faded in prominence. Her outlets for nurturing diminished within the family. In midlife she had to find a new identity and purpose for living to replace that of mothering.

She soon was back to life in a twosome, and she lived with the expectation that her husband would die before she did. She would then have to shape yet another identity as a widow, alone.

The traditional woman's life has been one of constant change. Just as she figured out how to balance life with two adults and one child, she had two children. Just as she had finally learned how to "safeguard without discouraging" an exploring toddler, she was confronted with a "terrible two" whose only word seemed to be "No!" She had

no sooner figured out how to detour around the turbulent emotions of a two-and-a-half-year-old than her child was an angelic three whose major problem was one of diffidence.

Yesterday's strategies, born of last month's desperation, became quickly irrelevant to today's child and growing psyche. She constantly was devising new strategies to keep herself upright on the tightrope that was her life.

In this domestic life of the traditional American woman, there was always uncertainty. Nothing was sure. Nothing was quantified. All was elusive, emotional, responsive, intuitive. She was constantly monitoring her entire system for small feedback "signals" so that her behavior could adapt to changed needs.

She developed a tolerance for ambiguity, for moving through and riding with the waves and turbulence in her life. Those had a difficult time who were perfectionists or control-oriented in their personalities; adaptability and flexibility became the modes for successful coping and living.

The transition under way in global society involves heightened uncertainty for all of us. Donald Michael has pointed out that living and coping most effectively with the uncertainties of this societal transition requires that leaders and organizations acknowledge their

First in the minds of the women who wanted training to enable them to earn cash was the welfare of their children. In Maskeliya, Sri Lanka, a thirty-nine-year-old housewife and mother of six children was one of the many women I spoke with who daily struggle to make ends met and to assure the education of their children. She told me she knew how to read a little because she had attended school until she was ten years old. Her husband finds occasional work in a local hotel, she said, but his intermittent earnings are not enough to provide for eight people.

"We don't have enough to eat—

and it is because we have such a large family. But somehow I manage. My father earns a bit of cash, and an uncle works in a laundry and gives me a little money each month. This way I am able to buy schoolbooks for my children. I may be having a lot of troubles now, but I am determined to give my children an education so they don't be in the same kind of situation I am in. My life is not very easy."

...Nearly every woman with whom I spoke wanted her children to go as far in school as possible—expecting that an education would assure their ability to earn a decent living: "I will do anything to get an education for my children."

...Maria Luisa, the semiliterate

Zapotec Indian woman with whom I talked in southern Mexico, had a totally unambiguous opinion on this subject As she rolled tortillas near the open hearth fire of her home, we talked at length about her family, the changes taking place around her, and the future.

When I asked her if she thought boys and girls should be educated equally, she turned toward me with a look of amazement. Almost aggressively, she declared:

"I would educate women more than men. Women bear and raise the children—so women prepare the future. How can the future be good if women are ignorant?

PERDITA HUSTON, *Third World Women Speak Out*

own lack of sureness about what they are doing and their own sense of vulnerability in these circumstances.

Insofar as acknowledging uncertainty and vulnerability is beyond the masculine mystique, our society will need to turn to women in this transition. Women can acknowledge their vulnerability and their lack of certainty without feeling their identity and femininity are threatened. Women are already accustomed to riding the uncertain waves of family life and can help lead us—if we will allow them to—in the "white-water living" of our future.

■ **Orientation toward the longer term:** The daily involvement of women with their children teaches them to look to the future. The chores that go with tending a two-year-old are not just for today. They are done in anticipation of the adult that child will grow up to be. Women's experiences of caring for their children inevitably expand their time horizons to include the world of their children's future.

This long-term orientation is badly needed in our present culture, in which the value of the future is often discounted. A dollar of expense (or income) a generation hence becomes almost invisible, as though hidden by a foreshortened time horizon.

How could men ever create an economic system that does this to the future? It cannot be accidental. It must be somehow related to the fact that in the world of men the next generation of children has never been at the center of men's attention, efforts, and hours.

What is there in the reproductive experience of the male that might cause him to feel involved in future generations? The male's one function of providing semen is overwhelmed by the sensation of orgasm, a sexual satisfaction he seeks innumerable times, in many contexts, and often with little reference to human reproduction.

Women, by contrast, experience nine intimate months of each child's gestation and then intense labor during birth. All this is often followed by long months of being on call for breast feeding the child. Don't ask that woman to accept a world view that ignores the life of the next generation!

There is still another subtle form of biological programming toward the long-term future that women have in common. Women during puberty become aware of the potential long-term consequences of their sexual encounters. In every sexual situation, they must balance the short-term pleasure of making love with the potential long-term costs of bearing and rearing a child.

If women do not immediately understand the long-term parameters of every sexual meeting, they alone pay the price for their lack of comprehension. Even in our day of ready access to means of birth control, it is usually the woman who must take the responsibility of making sure that some form of contraception is used. If she does not, the most extreme consequences—whether birth or an abortion—affect her body alone. Men are biologically able to walk away from the consequences of every sexual encounter.

No biological imperative conditions men to be sensitive to long-term consequences. But women's consciousness—which is so beautifully, albeit painfully, programmed to consider the longer term—has rarely been allowed into the boardrooms where decisions are made on corporate or public policy.

Yet our survival as a culture and perhaps as a species may depend upon our ability to adapt our dangerously

MAKING IT HAPPEN:

foreshortened time horizons to longer ones with greater survival value. Policy made while devaluing the future is policy made with the female eye closed and with the female voice stilled, or ignored.

■ **Parenting children and technologies:** Women have learned in love and pain how to parent their biological children. Have they gained thereby a capacity to parent the technologies we create?

To parent a technology means to give thought and care to its place within the sphere of human relationships, so as to make sure that it is based on positive values and that it fits into human life in a positive way.

It has been women's special task to rear children so they can fit into human life in a positive way. Men have conceived children and then left them to women to parent. In a similar way, men have also tended to "conceive" their technological "children"—their inventions, their machines, their technological systems—and then handed them on to society as creations that were fundamentally amoral, saying to society, "You determine whether this brainchild of mine will be used for good or evil!"

This is like leaving a baby in a basket on the doorstep. Society is left the task of parenting these technologies and finding for them a positive identity and role. Whether men recognize the implications of their attitude toward these brainchildren or not, it is a refusal on their part to parent what they have conceived. Mary Wollstonecraft made this point in her novel about Dr. Frankenstein's refusal to take responsibility for the life he had created. Langdon Winner builds upon this point in his important book *Autonomous Technology.*

If we are to deal responsibly with the future—its promise as well as risk—we must learn not only to use technology, but also to parent that technology. Technologies must be parented until they are used only for human benefit and not for profit, war, and the obliteration of ecological systems. If this is to happen, then skills at parenting such as women acquire in child-rearing must be incorporated into societal decision-making about our technologies. And men must spend more of their own time and energy parenting their children, so that men also gain these essential and deeply human skills.

■ **Understanding cultural oppression:** There is one final skill women can bring to our future, this time to our diplomacy. There is a rapidly increasing sensitivity in the Third World to what is perceived as dependence upon First World technology, finance, and know-how.

■ Third World nations have called for a New International Economic Order [NIEO] that would change the terms of exchange and the trade relationships between the First and Third Worlds. North-South discussions about NIEO have bogged down, because, among other things, First World diplomats seem unable to comprehend the Third World's analysis of the dependency they perceive to have been an invisible cost of aid, development, technology transfers, and previous international financial arrangements.

PARTNERS

■ In July 1979 at MIT Third World delegates to a meeting sponsored by the World Council of Churches presented this analysis of the oppressive aspects of dependency. It led there to bloc voting by Third World delegates on behalf of a moratorium on extending civil uses of nuclear power.

■ A similar analysis can be found in *No Limits to Learning*, a report to The Club of Rome. Third World educators there cite "cultural imperialism" and "cultural aggression" as problems inherited in their educational systems from their countries' colonial past.

■ A North-South split stalled the United Nations Conference on Science and Technology for Development in 1979. First World white males again found it difficult to comprehend Third World sensitivity to being dependent and subject to cultural invasion.

First World white men have not had the experience of being "mythed upon" by a more powerful culture and ideology that told them who they really were, how they felt, and specified their status and place. In the Western world, white males are the dominant culture; they are the norm by which all else is judged.

It is difficult for men with such a background to be sensitive to the ways in which language and mythology, nuance and assumption, become vehicles of dominance and oppression. They lack the breadth and depth and intensity of experience out of which such sensitivities arise.

First World women (as well as blacks and other minorities) understand all too well the identity problems experienced by those labeled as inferior. In his capacity as U.S. Ambassador to the United Nations, Andrew Young drew upon his experience as a black person in America to build an important bridge for understanding and exchange between the United States and African and Third World countries. There is a possibility that women's bitter experience of similar cultural oppression might yet bear sweet fruit in helping us all understand that we are "one humanity in one ecosystem."

Unique Perspective, Unique Potential

This analysis does not lead to the conclusion that men are devils and women are angels. That it is neither said nor intended.

The point is that everyone's consciousness bears the indelible marks of biology and life experience. Male consciousness has many strengths. It is also limited by the biological experiences and socialization of growing up male. Women's consciousness is equally unique.

Women's biological experiences and socialization as females provide women with unique strengths as well as characteristic limitations. But it has also been women's fate to live in what feminists now label a "patriarchal" society. Rules governing women's role and place have kept almost all women from access to the male world of decision-making. As a consequence, the world and those decisions have not incorporated the unique perspectives and strengths of women.

We may be fortunate. Through the pressure of the feminist movement, this moment in history has opened many doors to women. It may also be the moment in history when we realize our need of the unique perspective of women in order that we survive into the future.

If, so that we can overcome the "population crisis," women must find something else to do rather than simply bear children; if we collectively must nurture the planet and parent our technologies; if those who have experienced cultural oppression must mediate for those who have not; if we must begin to live with greater uncertainty, vulnerability, and sensitivity to emotional intangibles; if all these things are so—then it may well be that women hold the key to a successful adaptation of the human species to the problems of today and the promise of tomorrow. Let us hope that one-gender thinking left over from our past will not prohibit the human species from using this unique key to unlock the door of the future. □

Quality of life is a term often used by defenders of the natural environment. But, to us, quality of life describes the lifestyle my husband and I have chosen. What we are defending is us—our personhood our own use and enjoyment of our lives, our creativity, our sense of life's meaning and fulfillment.

Working at Home: For years, we were in parish ministry and had a lifestyle that was similar to that of most other people. Parish ministry helped us develop many of the skills, sensitivities, and concerns that are still very much a part of our work and life today. We were working with the life-cycle needs of people as we sought to help a parish grow in its understanding of the Bible, of the meaning in life, and of justice among people and groups.

In those parish years, we arose at 6 A.M. to the shrill command of the alarm clock and scurried through an

---

The warmth, sincerity, and openness of the women I interviewed were often overwhelming. Nearly all of them expressed curiosity and concern about women in other parts of the world.

They wanted to know more about the lives of women because, they said, they cared about them. This "caring" was particularly evident in an experience I had in central Kenya.

A cold winter drizzle was falling on Nyeri when I arrived late one morning. A meeting with a group of fifty older women had been arranged in the unheated town hall. The women were poor and illiterate, but anxious to learn new skills by attending a town-sponsored education group to which I had been invited. I told them (as I did each group with which I met) that I had come to collect their words—that the United Nations had sent me there to listen to them so that they could help me write a book.

The book, I explained, would be about women's lives and about the changes, needs, and aspirations of those lives. I would take their words back home, where they would be published so that women and men around the world would better understand the lives and needs of women like themselves.

After an hour of group discussion, I asked if anyone would like to talk with me further, to tell her own story in private. I chose four women from among the volunteers, thanked the group for their participation, and spent the next three hours interviewing in a small office-like room adjoining the hall.

When, much later, I emerged from the building with the last interviewee, all the women with whom I had met hours before were still there, standing in the rain, without shoes or coats, shivering in the winter cold.

I was distressed and embarrassed: I had no idea they were waiting for me. I thought they had gone home once the group discussions ended. It seemed they had warmed to my mission. As I moved toward the group, they began to sing and dance. The interpreter explained that they wanted to make me an honorary member of their tribe and give me a tribal name.

In the midst of the ceremony, a seventy-year-old woman—toothless, shoeless, and in rags—rushed out of the crowd and took me by the arm. Grinning and shaking her finger in my face, she said, with authority: "Now you go back and tell the women in your place that the women in Nyeri care about them."

Perdita Huston, *Third World Women Speak Out*

early morning routine of driving our children to school 20 miles away before David began work about 9 A.M. David had his office at home, where he wrote sermons each week and mimeographed the weekly parish newsletter from our basement in late-evening hours.

It seemed natural when we left the parish ministry for an issue-centered ministry that we continued working from our home. Later, when we took over leadership of the Bolton Institute for a Sustainable Future, and wondered how we would find money every month to pay for office space, it again seemed natural to combine home and institute. We found there are tax benefits in sharing costs of home and work, and it is easier to save on rent money than to raise it. But, most of all, there are the quality-of-life benefits, and they are why we have persisted in this pattern.

The Daily Round: Visualize a small duplex townhouse 3 minutes walk from markets and commuter train, 5 minutes from shops, bank, and post office, and 20 minutes from a college library with facilities for inexpensive photocopying. Then picture in your mind's eye a combined living room and dining room that is also an office. There are three large glass sliding doors opening onto our own fenced-in patio. The sun is pouring in now, mottled by the shade of birch trees in summer. In winter, when the leaves have fallen, one of the first things we do upon coming downstairs in the morning is to throw open the long heavy insulating curtains to start harvesting the solar heat and light that will warm us at our work until we draw the curtains late in the afternoon.

David's electric typewriter is tucked in one corner of the room by his upright desk near the fireplace. Running the length of the room is a teak dining table where we eat and also entertain guests for lunch. The table also doubles as Liz's desk, and is of a clever Swedish design that can be expanded to nearly twice its

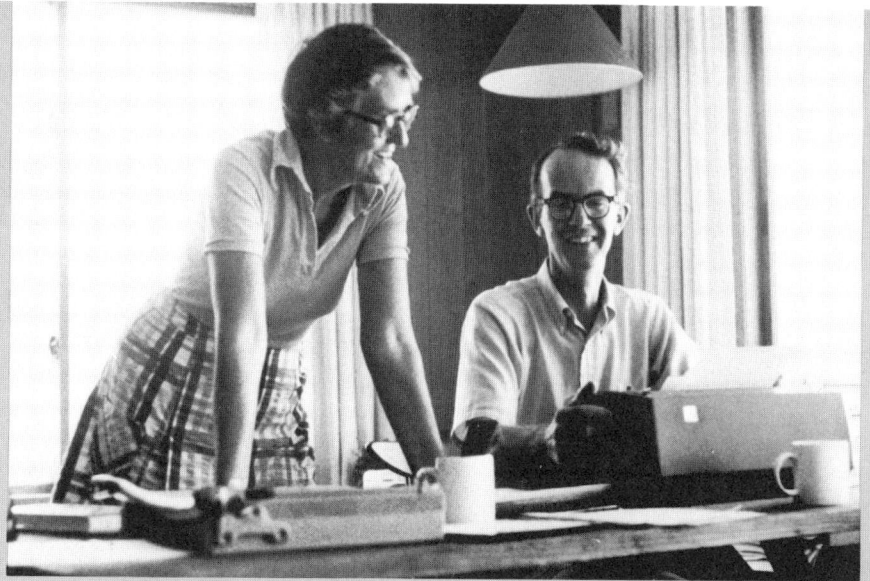

normal length when a task requires spreading out a lot of material.

Because we work at home (and our children are now grown and away), we no longer rise to the command of an alarm clock. In warmer seasons, sometimes the first sound we hear is the song of birds. Or the gentle sweeping of an older neighbor's broom. Our evenings are often our most productive times, and we may keep working until late. Then we can sleep until 9 the next morning and be wakened by our first phone call. Our working day then begins with the rest of the world, but we have not had to arise and spend our first two hours preparing for and getting to a place of business "downtown." When we so choose, we can sleep until the world comes to us by phone.

We often have breakfast and start our working day while in bathrobes—or in swimsuits during the summer. Our suburban patio, whether it is covered with snow, or bright with springtime crocuses and tulips, or in the full flower of summertime, is never far from our awareness. When the weather is right, Liz suns as she writes papers or jots off the handwritten part of our correspondence.

In late afternoon, we often walk to the post office with the day's output of mail, stopping to do errands and food shopping on the way home. Depending upon the day, the TV schedule, and what most urgently needs doing, we may have a very

productive, quiet evening of writing. Or we may have a prolonged session of "cottage-craft with television" in which we fold, staple, and sort some communication for bulk mailing. The rainbow logo we use on our Bolton Institute mailings is hand-drawn in evenings of this sort.

Moving with the rhythms of our days: Because our living and working space flows visually out-of-doors so much, we feel in tune with the gentle change of seasons and the quiet rhythms of sun and rain. As we work, we watch the flowers and the sky and the trees—and find it easy to care and write about preserving the earth.

Because we work at home, we can eat and sleep, work and play, take a spot of tea or a walk, or lie down on the couch. Liz often turns to playing the piano when she's organizing her thoughts and getting into a new piece of writing.

We like working together. We enjoy the companionship and the chance to play ideas off one another, mutually energizing and criticizing our insights. We find it much easier to be creative when we are in dialogue together. Our talents overlap in some ways, and in other ways they are very different. Liz is into consciousness-raising and women's issues, David into business and numbers and money-flows. Both are into ethics. David writes, edits, types, typesets, designs. Liz outlines, writes many of our first drafts, and critiques. Liz cooks and plans and sets day-to-day priorities and is in charge of aesthetics. David makes travel arrangements, handles finances, and "cleans it up if it is dirty," whether it is clothing or dishes or the house or writing.

Because we work in the privacy of our home, we can touch during the working day. What a contrast this is to the sensual desert of most workplaces, where working colleagues labor encased in personal space no one is supposed to violate by touching.

Third Wave? You can construe our work and life in a number of different ways. You may see an issue-centered ministry where biblical concerns about justice and life's meaning are set in a broader cultural context of how we deal with energy, resources, value change, and our care of the earth and the future. We feel we are now ministering not to a single parish but to a whole culture as it passes through a mid-life transition to a different life with different values.

You may also look here and see Alvin Toffler's "electronic cottage," where high-technology information flows are making it possible for people to communicate from decentralized locations while being home amid family living.

Or you may look at us and see an "alternative" small business. We fund ourselves by publishing books, by our speaking and writing and consulting, and by sponsoring an annual conference for professional women. The Bolton Institute funds its lectures, film purchases, and mailings by tax-deductible contributions and film rentals. As in ecological systems, diversity here is a means of achieving stability.

In 1972, when we left the security of being on someone else's payroll, we had to learn to cope with the anxiety of the entrepreneur. That psychic cost is offset, however, by the excitement of projecting ahead our various enterprises and by the nourishment we find in the intimacy of our shared lives. □

Thinking About Power

The power to disrupt and destroy, especially in the hands of those with nothing to lose, is real and it must be taken seriously.

The power of the hitherto powerless majority on the globe is growing—at least their power to disrupt and destroy. This power is being enhanced by the growing complexity, interdependence, and consequent vulnerability of the developed world.

Problems of giving up power: Robert Browne has witnessed—and experienced—oppression. As Director of the Black Economic Research Center in New York City's Harlem, and as a member of a special U.S. Mission to the Union of South Africa, he has also had the opportunity to reflect on the problems of giving up power.

His conclusion is that power is only relinquished in the face of self-interest, fear, or force.

In the United States, the history of the trade union movement tends to bear out that conclusion. Browne argues, in fact, that there are virtually no examples in recorded history in which power has been given up voluntarily.

The hazard of misperceptions by the powerful: The world may face no greater danger than the misperception by the powerful of their ability to maintain an inherently vulnerable and unstable status quo.

All too often, the last vestige of declining real power is devoted to supporting delusions of a reality that no longer exists. Hitler, isolated in his bunker in 1945, continued to issue orders to imaginary armies and to demand the execution of those who tried to tell him the truth.

A most important objective for the future should be to ensure that the powerful—those with the power to create, or to control, or to oppress, *or to disrupt and destroy*—are, at all times, fully aware of both the realities and limits of their power.

Monstrously strange bedfellows
Kenneth Boulding, in the conclusion of his book *Conflict and Defense*, writes about the problem of making the transition to a more humane and peaceful world in the face of our present vulnerabilities and capacities for self-destruction.

His words could have been written for those we have called "the powerful":

"There is no defense, no isolation, no protection from the awful task of living together with monstrously strange bedfellows.

"As long as we had defense, we could simplify the task of living together by only loving the like and the lovable and by keeping away the unlike and the unlovable. Now we find ourselves all cooped up together on this little ball of a spaceship and forced to live together in peace for fear of wrecking it.

"The problem is part of a still larger one, and we may have to think about the larger one before we can solve the smaller.

"The technical revolution in warfare that has made peace a necessity is part of a larger change in the knowledge, skills, and abilities of mankind through which we are now passing, which began to get noticeably under way in the seventeenth century and has been accelerating ever since. It is carrying mankind to a state of affairs so different from that of the civilized societies out of which it developed that it has been called postcivilization.

"We are still in the era of rapid transition and are not within sight of the final equilibrium state. An equilibrium state there must be, however, or at least a state that is not merely transition, for every transition must lead toward something.

"We only see very dimly what this high level equilibrium might be like....There is no way back to Eden, to innocence or ignorance;

having eaten of the fruit of the tree of knowledge, it is Zion or nothing.

"I was recently sitting in an airplane waiting to take off. It was spring and a little bird was trying to build her nest in a little hole at the end of the wing. She flew busily in and out carrying bits of straw and twigs as the plane sat on the ground waiting for the signal to take off, and then the plane roared away and left her far behind.

"I could not help seeing in this a parable of our day.

"We are all going about our various tasks, each trying to build for himself a little shelter from the inclement world, a little defense against want or hardship or loneliness, and we are all building on the wing of a great sweeping process of change that may soon roar away with out little efforts, we know not where or how.

"There were men in the cockpit, however, and not sparrows. We do have the gift of understanding, even of the systems that we create ourselves. It is not too much to hope, therefore, that man can learn to fly the great engine of change that he has made and that it may carry us not to destruction but to that great goal for which the world was made." □

What Future Role?

The Powerful Minority

By Robert S. Browne

We can look back on the International Year of the Child and the Decade of Women. But do we ever stop to wonder why the United Nations has declared no year of the man, no decade for whites? Is it because every year is the year of the man, every decade lived for the benefit of whites?

One of the more unsettling current statistical projections is that, while 20 percent of the world's population lives in developed countries today, by the year 2000 that figure will have shrunk dramatically.

Presumably, the basis for this startling conclusion is a mathematical extrapolation of present demographic trends, coupled with some rather pessimistic assumptions about the expected pace of development in the Third World.

But what of the faces behind the statistics? Are they male, or female? Which are black, which white? Which are those with power and affluence?

PARTNERS

Who is the powerful minority? One of the most durable realities is that the global population consists of a relatively impoverished majority and a relatively well-off minority.

In contemporary formulations, there are two possible ways of perceiving this affluent minority: (1) as the inhabitants of the 35 or so countries whose per capita GNP exceeds $2,000 (or some other arbitrarily chosen, four-digit number), or (2) as those persons in any country whose income, or wealth, places them within the upper 5 percent, or perhaps the upper 1 percent, of their nation's population.

Obviously, these are two differing conceptualizations of the powerful minority, with one characteristic in common: they define power in economic terms. But the two conceptualizations lead us in vastly different directions and focus our attention on two rather different sets of individuals and institutions, despite the fact that they do overlap in some significant ways.

The conceptualization along national lines defines a "powerful minority" of roughly 1 billion persons, about 25 percent of the globe's 4.5 billion inhabitants. These are the people of the industrialized economies, of the Westernized nations, of the white countries (Japan and the sparsely populated, oil-rich Arab states being the exceptions).

In current parlance, these nations are termed, with a certain disrespect for accuracy, the "North," while the remaining 75 percent of the world's population is labeled, with equal inaccuracy, the "South."

The alternative conceptualization along individual or, one might say, "class" lines is more difficult to measure with any degree of precision.

If, however, one mechanically applies the suggested "upper 1 percent" criterion to a global population of 4.5 billion, the result delimits a "powerful minority" of some 45 million people.

Of course, the 1 percent figure has no scientific basis, but the pyramidal distribution of wealth and income prevalent in countries where such data is readily available suggests that the pattern of a small group of super-rich persons atop a mass of much poorer people characterizes most countries irrespective of their stage of industrial development. In the United States, for example, it is reported that the wealthiest 1 percent of the population owns more than one-third of the private wealth.

The fact that the rich/poor dichotomy is both inter-national as well as intra-national greatly complicates the task of alleviating poverty on a global scale. For the purposes of this analysis, let us lay aside the second, or intra-national conceptualization, and focus only on the North/South dichotomy.

Relationship of the weak majority to the powerful minority: Viewed through the inter-national prism, the North—this powerful minority encompassing one quarter of the world's population—is arrogating to itself a vastly disproportionate share of the world's output.

The North consumes far more food than needed, both because its caloric intake is excessive and because it prefers to consume its protein principally in the form of meat, especially beef, which is a notoriously inefficient and expensive way to obtain protein.

In terms of consumption of the earth's natural resources, this favored 25 percent of the world's population probably consumes more than 75 percent of the total goods and services. Indeed, through the sullen eyes of the world's deprived majority, the powerful minority's entire lifestyle can only be perceived as profligate. Our wasteful patterns of energy usage in the United States and our widespread practice of overtaxing the environment and occasionally of despoiling it for frivolous reasons, are perceived as both senseless and selfish by those in the poor nations.

> The evening arrived; the boys took their places. The master, in his cook's uniform stationed himself at the copper.... the gruel was served out, and a long grace was said over the short commons. The gruel disappeared, the boys whispered to each other, and winked at Oliver.
>
> ...Child as he was, he was desperate with hunger and reckless with misery. He rose from the table, and advancing to the master, basin and spoon in hand said, somewhat alarmed at his own temerity:
>
> "Please, sir, I want some more."
>
> The master was a fat, healthy man, but he turned very pale. He gazed in stupefied astonishment on the small rebel for some seconds, and then clung for support to the copper....
>
> "What?" said the master at length, in a faint voice.
>
> "Please, sir," replied Oliver, "I want some more."
>
> The master aimed a blow at Oliver's head with the ladle, pinioned him in his arms, and shrieked aloud for the beadle.
>
> The board were sitting in solemn conclave when Mr. Bumble rushed into the room in great excitement, and addressing the gentleman in the high chair, said:
>
> "Mr. Limbkins, I beg your pardon, sir! Oliver Twist has asked for more."
>
> CHARLES DICKENS, *Oliver Twist*

The poor nations not only face inadequate supplies of basic food, shelter, and energy but are told that they need not aspire to a "Northern" standard of living because there simply are not enough resources in the world to permit universal imitation of present levels of industrial affluence.

Differing perspectives of history: A constructive North/South dialogue around such issues is hindered not only by the barrier of this vast economic disparity but also by the differing perceptions of history that each side brings to any such dialogue.

Many of the developing nations achieved independence within the lifetime of their present adult population, and their people harbor bitter feelings and bear ineradicable scars from the colonial experience and the indignities inflicted upon them by foreign domination.

They may have forgiven or forgotten the worst of the human atrocities that accompanied their national subjugation, but they remain acutely aware of the economic exploitation that characterizes both colonialism and imperialism. They are keenly aware that the unattainable affluence of the life style of most of the North has derived at least in part from their own exploitation.

They are understandably resentful—and their resentment is deepened by the realization that they must now look to their former colonial exploiters for assistance to eradicate the poverty that plagues their nations.

View from the North: Meanwhile, the North contemplates its neighbors of the South with growing uneasiness. Changing moral and ethical standards have cast a retrospective pall over the "glorious" colonial conquests and civilizing missions of the 19th century, which are increasingly seen as racist, barbaric, and exploitative.

Under this growing weight of guilt, the North vacillates between expiation and paranoia. Of these two traits, expiation is certainly the more rational and might indeed provide a useful base on which a North/South dialogue could proceed. Unfortunately, expiation too often collides with other human traits, such as pride and greed. Or it degenerates into an offer of development aid, but only on terms that make the assistance profitable or politically advantageous to the donor.

Incomes in the industrialized nations are no longer rising fast enough to make foreign assistance relatively painless. A host of factors account for this slowdown. Among them are:

■ *Rising costs of raw materials,* occasioned by the demonstration effect of OPEC oil price hikes, progressive exhaustion of the more accessible mineral and petroleum deposits, and greater reluctance of supplier countries to make their nonrenewable resources available to others.

■ *Growing sensitivity to environmental considerations,* leading to a more accurate assessment of total production costs and thus to higher prices.

■ *Aging of the populations of the industrialized nations,* attended by higher social costs (and possibly lowered productivity).

■ *Higher capital (i.e., interest) costs* deriving from the greater uncertainties that characterize a world of sovereign and equal nations, rather than one of a few metropoles and their many colonies.

■ *Diminished work ethic,* stemming from rising worker expectations as regards both work and leisure, leading to higher unit labor costs.

The combined net effect of these impersonal forces is to slow the rate of economic growth (and the rise in living standards) in the industrialized nations. Foreign assistance never reached the targets set during the First and Second Development Decades, and the impact of all this on future levels of is likely to be devastating.

Meanwhile, the evidence mounts that their overall position in relation to the developed countries is not really improving, the less developed countries (LDCs) become increasingly alarmed. Their demands for correction of these gross inequities have taken the form of a call for a New International Economic Order (NIEO).

The demands of the poor nations are specifically for more aid, debt relief, easier access to developed-country markets for their manufactured goods, stabilization of the relationship between

prices of the raw materials LDCs typically export and the manufactured goods they import, and less restrictive access to the technology of the industrial North.

Power shifts between North and South: There should be little surprise that the response of the powerful minority in the North to these demands has not been encouraging. The economies of the developed countries are reeling under the inflationary impact of OPEC price hikes. U.S. economists are resurrecting the largely forgotten Kondratieff cycle of 50-60 years as a possible explanation for continuing U.S. economic stagnation.

Developed countries have virtually lost their domestic constituencies for foreign assistance—and there was never much reason to expect widespread support for other aspects of the NIEO.

These economic deterrents are being reinforced by a gradual shift in political power. Third World nations have felt under less pressure to line up with one or the other of the global superpowers as the Cold War has cooled, and at the same time a stronger group consciousness has come into existence within the Third World.

This has meant that slowly but inexorably the nations of the North have been losing their ability to dominate the South. This shift is perhaps best exemplified by actions of the Group of 77, but it is also felt in numerous unstructured ways as well.

The realization that power is trickling away into the hands of their former vassals is difficult to accept, even if it accords with their egalitarian rhetoric. Northern nations had dominated the

Who am I? Robert S. Browne

I am a black American, an economist by training, and am currently serving as an Executive Director of the African Development Fund—a regional development bank for the continent of Africa. My adult career has been divided among academia, international (Third World) development, and research and activism focused on improving the economic situation of U.S. blacks.

I consider my greatest contribution to society to have been the very considerable efforts I made to alert and inform the American people about what I felt to be an obscene U.S. policy in Vietnam in the years just prior to heavy U.S. military involvement there, and my subsequent anti-war activities. I had lived in Cambodia and Vietnam during the period 1955-61 and observed at first hand, with considerable chagrin, the ill-reported emergence of the American disaster in Indochina.

Eradicating social injustice and easing the pain of those who are suffering have provided the motivating force in my life. I trace the impetus for that force to my early childhood and the barely controlled rage I internalized from ingesting a steady diet (largely from the black press) of the humiliations and suffering regularly perpetrated by white people on non-whites, in the United States and in the colonial world. Ideologically, I vacillate between racial integration and racial separation as offering the more promising solution to the racial issue in America.

My professional analysis of the global situation and outlook is highly pessimistic, but in my personal life I remain a perennial optimist, always operating on the assumption that individuals are honest and unselfish, and possess other good qualities which the evidence suggests is not the case. If I were to accept the dreary daily evidence of the baseness of human nature as the whole story, I probably would find life to be untenable. □

A POSITIVE GUIDE TO THE FUTURE

globe in an economic and political hegemony that went virtually unchallenged for five centuries, these successive blows to that traditional hegemony have led to the growth of a siege mentality in some of the industrialized countries.

The fear that this shift in power will be accompanied by a shift in wealth probably causes even greater concern. The prospect of losing cheap and easy access to raw materials that are vital to the maintenance of the Northern life style introduces an air of genuine crisis. When one considers the other attitudes that have long characterized the affluent white nations, such as racism, Christian mission, and cultural ethnocentrism, one can easily understand why the powerful minority may be experiencing serious pangs of paranoia.

The developed nations' minority position has been tenable only because their predominant share of global wealth and power has provided them with vastly superior political, economic, technological and military power. A substantial a shift of that wealth and power toward the formerly-weak majority would upset this balance, with consequences that the developed nations do not like to contemplate.

PARTNERS

Consequently, the South's demands for a NIEO are likely to go unheeded and unmet until such time as the Third World succeeds in fashioning coercive mechanisms to oblige their acceptance.

The powerful minority may be able, in the meantime, to delay a confrontation around this shifting power balance by merely alleviating the worst conditions of poverty among the weak majority. At the heart of this tactic is the question of how the powerful minority can go about meeting essential needs in the Third World without either inflicting unacceptable economic pain on itself or placing the LDCs in a position that would too swiftly erode the economic and political superiority of the donor nations.

There is, to be sure, another body of opinion to the effect that much of what the LDCs are requesting in their demand for a NIEO can be accommodated by the developed countries without cost to themselves.

The reasoning behind this position is, basically, that the weak majority constitutes a vast potential market for the products of the powerful minority, that the exploitation of this market can provide the stimulus that the North's economies so desperately need, and that the only way to realize this potential is to enable the Third World nations to improve their economies to the point at which their present desire for goods and services can become effective market demand.

Development, in this view, could be a game in which there would be no losers.

Self-interest: Whether the latter theory is true or false, its emergence tells us something about the nature of the powerful minority. One way to move that minority to action is to appeal to its self-interest.

This should not be surprising, of course. It is what we generally expect of human institutions and of human beings. An appeal to self-interest is almost always more effective than an appeal to altruism.

The appeal to self-interest would appear to be especially appropriate in the present context, where the donors may perceive (rightly or wrongly) that altruism is a waste of their money, leading to an erosion of their power. A start has been made in this direction, but the tactic has obviously not yet been successful.

Politics Without Revenge

Salisbury, Zimbabwe, April 22, 1980—Journalists are skeptics by profession. But something odd has happened to the large press corps that has watched this country over recent months. The correspondents feel, and express to each other, a sense of awed amazement at what they have seen: the transformation from brutal war to relatively tranquil politics.

I felt it in myself and those around me the night Rhodesia formally became Zimbabwe. Just before midnight, battalions of well-drilled troops marched into the soccer stadium where the ceremonies took place and parade past the reviewing stand: a unit of the regular army, then one of Robert Mugabe's

guerrillas, one of Joshua Nkomo's, finally the air force.

It was incredible: men who a few months before had been shooting, knifing, bombing each other, were snapping to attention and presenting arms at a single command. The crowd roared. The foreign correspondents looked at each other, almost embarrassed at their emotions, their suspensions of disbelief.

The spirit of reconcilation symbolized in those marching battalions is reflected also in the way former enemies have joined in the new Government—not just the politicians in the Cabinet but civil servants. Prime Minister Mugabe emphasizes in every speech the need to forget the hatreds that ravaged

Rhodesia: black against black even more than white against black.

To write such things is to risk seeming credulous. And of course the old bitterness could erupt at any time. There have already been some incidents of violence apparently motivated by black political factionalism. Mugabe and his ministers have begun speaking strongly about law and order. But the difference between the state of the country today and the terror as recently as last fall remains remarkable.

In how many other countries, a few months after a civil or revolutionary war, have the opposing sides joined in the government and the armed forces? In the American Revolutionary War, patriots hounded and abused Tories.

WHAT'S YOUR PROBLEM?

I DON'T WISH TO INTERFERE BUT DO YOU REALISE THAT WORLD POPULATION IS GOING TO INCREASE BY NEARLY 50% IN TWENTY YEARS? WHAT ARE YOU GOING TO DO ABOUT IT?

WHAT'S WRONG WITH PEOPLE? I LIKE PEOPLE.

WELL SO DO I, OF COURSE. BUT YOU SEE THE WORLD'S RESOURCES CAN'T SUPPORT AN EVER-INCREASING POPULATION.

I SEE. SO IT'S A PROBLEM OF RESOURCES AS WELL AS PEOPLE?

YES.

SO THE ANSWER IS RESOURCE CONTROL AS WELL AS BIRTH CONTROL?

YE...ES

WELL THEN, I DON'T WANT TO INTERFERE BUT DO YOU REALISE THAT THE RICH 10% OF THE WORLD CONSUME ABOUT 90% OF THE RESOURCES? WHAT ARE YOU GOING TO DO ABOUT THAT?

It took 100 years after the Civil War for the hatreds of that bloody conflict to drain out of American politics.

Revenge is a legacy of most of the world's racial, religious, and ideological conflicts. Think of Ireland, or the Middle East. Why should it be different here? Some say it is because the dominant African language group in Zimbabwe, the Shonas, are by nature a gentle people: forgiving. Perhaps they really will be able to let the past be past.

Where skepticism is still required is in looking to the future. Will today's peace in Zimbabwe become longer-term stability? Much depends on Robert Mugabe. His words and actions have reassured the whites so far, and covered over at least for the moment the old political divisions among blacks. Most people now say, in hindsight, that it was a good thing his party won an absolute majority in Parliament: he has power to match responsibility. But Mugabe faces daunting problems.

Integrating the armed forces and getting them down to size are the first challenges. The new Government has created a joint command over the old Rhodesian security forces and the two guerrilla armies. But Mugabe says his first priority is to meld the units completely, retraining individual guerrillas and putting them into the security forces. That process has started but has a long way to go....

The economic situation is a big obstacle to reducing the number of soldiers and getting the guns away from those not needed in the forces. Unemployment is high in the towns. And in tribal lands the peasant farming that used to sustain much of the populace has suffered terribly from the war.

Before the war the country had 3 million head of African cattle: the herd is down now to 2 million. Of 1,500 cattle-dip tanks, 1,000 were destroyed. Only 3 of 50 mission doctors remain. More than 1,500 schools are closed. The new Government estimates that it will take $110 million to rebuilt or replace lost facilities: clinics, schools, wells, dams, dip tanks. And beyond the problem of repairing war damage in the countryside there is what people in the new Government call "the crisis of expectations"....

The economic problems are hard, but the possibilities are also good. A British official put it: "This country could take off. It has potential—if Mugabe can hold people together." It is a big if, one with implications not for Zimbabwe alone but for North and South, East and West.

ANTHONY LEWIS, *New York Times,*

Fear: It may well turn out that fear provides the only way of appealing successfully to the powerful minority. The case can be made that the weak majority (with little to lose) can impose—or threaten to impose—severe costs on the powerful minority (which has much to lose), if concrete steps are not taken to narrow the gap globally between rich and poor.

Indeed, the threat to disrupt our tranquility constitutes, in the short run, the only effective weapon that the weak majority has available in its struggle to win a greater measure of equity for itself. The example of OPEC has not gone unnoted.

The obstacles to redressing the international balance between rich and poor, between the powerful minority and the weak majority, appear—from whatever perspective one approaches the issue—to be *not* economic but principally social, political, psychological, and moral. The need for fashioning new human beings with new values has perhaps never been more critical than at this juncture.

The future of humankind may depend on whether there is a voluntary decision by the powerful to redistribute some power and wealth, or whether that decision must be imposed by less desirable and more dangerous means.

There is little basis for optimism. History offers virtually no precedents for the generous surrender of power and privilege. □

Retirement

Our names are as they were.
We look the same.
Our wives are just as kind.
In fact, more thoughtful.
But we don't feel the same, not quite.
The young men do not stand,
    we never felt they should.
Our old friends smile,
    but turn a moment sooner
    to the younger man.
And that is fair.
We're just as good friends as we were,
    but not quite so important
    any more.
Not so important.
No.
But wiser?

Gaylord Freeman,
former Chairman of the Board,
First National Bank of Chicago,
in *American Dreams, Lost and Found,* by Studs Terkel

Agency for International Development

Leadership:

The Public Sector

Official Photograph, The White House

"We are Too Great to Limit Ourselves to Small Dreams..."

By President Ronald H. Reagan (1981 Inaugural, excerpts)

The orderly transfer of authority, as called for in the Constitution, takes place as it has for almost two centuries and few of us stop to think how unique we really are. In the eyes of many in the world, this every-four-year ceremony we accept as normal is nothing less than a miracle....

These United States are confronted with an economic affliction of great proportions.... For decades, we have piled deficit upon deficit, mortgaging our future and our children's future for the temporary convenience of the present. To continue this long trend is to guarantee tremendous social, cultural, political and economic upheavals.

You and I, as individuals, can, by borrowing, live beyond our means, but only for a limited period of time.

Why should we think that, collectively as a nation, we are not bound by that same limitation?

We must act today in order to preserve tomorrow. And let there be no misunderstanding—we are going to begin to act beginning today.

...From time to time, we have been tempted to believe that society has become too complex to be managed by self-rule, that government by an elite group is superior to government for, by, and of the people. But if no one among us is capable of governing himself, then who among us has the capacity to govern someone else?

...As we begin, let us take inventory. We are a nation that has a government—not the other way around. And this makes us special among the nations of the earth. Our government has no power except

that granted it by the people. It is time to check and reverse the growth of government which shows signs of growing beyond the consent of the governed.

Now so there will be no misunderstanding, it is not my intention to do away with government. It is rather to make it work—work with us, not over us; to stand by our side, not ride on our back. Government can and must provide opportunity, not smother it; foster productivity, not stifle it.

...We are too great a nation to limit ourselves to small dreams. We are not, as some would have us believe, doomed to an inevitable decline. I do not believe in a fate that will fall upon us no matter what we do. I do believe in a fate that will fall upon us if we do nothing.

So, with all the creative energy at our command, let us begin an era of national renewal. Let us renew our determination, our courage, and our strength. And let us renew our faith and our hope. We have every right to dream heroic dreams.

Those who say we are in a time when there are no heroes—they just don't know where to look. You can see heroes every day going in and out of factory gates. Others, a handful in number, produce enough food to feed all of us and much of the world beyond.

You meet heroes across a counter—they're on both sides of that counter. There are entrepreneurs with faith in themselves and faith in an idea who create new jobs, new wealth and opportunity. They are individuals and families whose taxes support the government and whose voluntary gifts support church, charity, culture, art, and education. Their patriotism is quiet, but deep. Their values sustain our national life.

I have used the words "they" and "their" in speaking of these heroes. I could say "you" and "your" because I am addressing the heroes of whom I speak—you, the citizens of this blessed land. Your dreams, your hopes, your goals are going to be the dreams, hopes, and goals of this administration, so help me God.

MAKING IT HAPPEN:

We shall reflect the compassion that is so much a part of your makeup. How can we love our country and not love our countrymen? And loving them reach out a hand when they fall, heal them when they are sick, and provide opportunity to make them self sufficient so they will be equal in fact and not just in theory.

Can we solve the problems confronting us? The answer is an unequivocal and emphatic yes.

...On the eve of our struggle for independence, a man who might have been the greatest among the Founding Fathers, Dr. Joseph Warren, president of the Massachusetts Congress, said to his fellow Americans, "Our country is in danger, but not to be despaired of....On you depend the fortunes of America. You are to decide the important question on which rest the happiness and liberty of millions yet unborn. Act worthy of yourselves."

I believe that we, the Americans of today, are ready to act worthy of ourselves, ready to do what must be done to ensure happiness and liberty for ourselves, our children, and our children's children.

And as we renew ourselves here in our own land, we will be seen as having greater strength throughout the world. We will again be the example of freedom and a beacon of hope for those who do not now have freedom.

...Above all, we must realize no arsenal or no weapon in the arsenals of the world is so formidable as the will and moral courage of free men and women. It is a weapon our adversaries in today's world do not have. It is a weapon that we as Americans do have....

The crisis we are facing today... [requires]... our best effort, and our willingness to believe in ourselves and in our capacity to perform great deeds. To believe that, together and with God's help, we can and will resolve the problems which confront us.

And, after all, why shouldn't we believe that?

We are Americans. □

A POSITIVE GUIDE TO THE FUTURE

Political Obstacles to a Global Perspective

By Patsy Takemoto Mink

What the American people really feel and what they really will accept is hard to determine from the perspective of Capitol Hill. But Members of Congress—especially those in the House of Representatives—do their best to be aware of the current concerns and desires of their constituents. They have to. Their political survival depends on their success in doing so. From the perspective of Capitol Hill, it is hard to be optimistic about the prospects for a more globally-oriented economic and foreign policy.

A major educational task ahead: Both elected representatives and the American public need to be made more aware of the fundamentally new and different global order that we face. It poses challenges we must prepare ourselves to respond to in the future. Some Members of Congress and public officials, including myself, have been pressing vigorously for a new point of view for some time. But we have not been very successful so far.

The lack of acceptance of "foreign aid" by the American public and by the Congress is perhaps the best example of the problem. I have concluded that, until the public at large understands foreign aid is necessary for our survival, not much will be done with global issues. That view is scarcely widespread today.

Each year the most difficult program for Congress to enact is the foreign aid bill. When a bill is finally passed, it is usually the wrong bill passed for the wrong reasons. And, in times of economic stringency, the foreign aid budget seems to be the easiest to cut.

Justifying foreign aid: Advocates often begin by casting their arguments in humanitarian terms, but this never succeeds. The usual response is, "We need the money here at home to help our own people, so why give away our hard-earned taxes." Opponents point out, moreover, that governments who have received our aid in the past have looked upon it as a handout, and this attitude is probably inevitable.

We are reduced to justifying foreign aid on the basis that over 80 percent is subsequently spent in the United States and thus creates U.S. jobs and supports U.S. industry. To make sure that this is actually the case, we write into our assistance programs restrictions, which limit their effectiveness and arouse the suspicion and skepticism of recipient nations.

The only exception is foreign military assistance which, like the defense budget, always passes easily. For some reason, it seems far simpler to perceive our "self-interest" in the distribution of weapons and military supplies than in the provision of technical and economic assistance.

Who am I? Patsy Takemoto Mink

For years in the arduous calling of day-to-day political action, Patsy Takemoto Mink has expressed her deep commitment to creating a more humane and sustainable world. She has done this as legislator, Assistant Secretary of State, and, most recently, President of the Americans for Democratic Action.

Participation by an educated and informed citizenry is an integral part of her vision of the future. Present political "realities" do not encourage such participation, and she recognizes that these "realities" are real because we have chosen to make them so.

Other choices are possible. As a nation and government, we still have the time and the opportunity to choose.

Maintaining the Global Status Quo: Recent emphasis on the goal of "meeting basic human needs" is, more than anything, a reflection of domestic political realities—that it is simply not possible to justify direct economic aid to the American public by other means. In essence, we are emphasizing food, public health, housing, water, energy, and population because we cannot propose and implement employment-producing programs that might eventually undercut the position of labor and industry in the United States. Thus, it avoids global problems we are not ready (or able) to solve, for example, trade (imports as well as exports), transfer of technology, and competition from "cheap foreign labor."

The U.S. position in U.N. forums such as the Conference on Law of the Sea and the Conference on Science and Technology for Development involves much the same thinking. Basically, we have allied ourselves with the bloc—even assumed the leadership of the bloc—of those nations that favor, if any, only marginal adjustments to the global status quo.

It is difficult for U.S. politicians to support self-sufficiency for these countries when U.S. multinational corporations are engaged in world trade based upon their need to sell their natural resources. U.S. industries are dependent on these foreign resources, and our government believes it must maintain policies that will keep those supplies available and flowing freely to U.S. businesses.

Thus we seem to place ourselves in opposition to the demands by Third World nations for a New International Economic Order, and even to their developing economic self-sufficiency.

Our "welfare approach" to Third World nations cannot produce what is most needed in developing countries: self-sufficiency and the economic/industrial base to provide jobs for those who need them.

Even if we could supply their people's basic human needs—clean water, food, fuel, housing, and health facilities—how could they pay for these things? It is no solution at all to survive and still be poor and unemployed.

What we must do, clearly, is help the poorest nations of the world to develop "cash" economies through the production of goods and services that we of the industrialized world are willing to buy.

Whether we ever will adopt a policy based on this principle is much less clear. To pose the basic questions to be answered is easy. To find practical, feasible, and politically acceptable answers is much, much harder.

The transfer of technology is a most critical issue. Can we transfer our industrial technology to Third World governments without threatening our own industrial basis? Can we help Third World countries produce goods to sell in world markets without threatening our own access to, and position in, those markets? Will not helping Third World nations develop new forms of production then flood our domestic markets with cheap imports, which in time will shut down our own factories? How, in short, can we help developing countries without hurting ourselves?

The question of money is equally important. Where is the money to come from to help the poorer countries improve their economic conditions? We pay barely $10 million a year to the U.N. Environment Programme, for example. The amounts of money we quibble about are only an infinitesimal portion of what a truly effective program for worldwide economic development would require.

Congressional appropriations are heavily influenced each year by what politicians hear from constituents in their home districts, and U.S. contributions to the United Nations and to a variety of other international and regional bodies are attacked every year.

Is it really a global win/lose situation? When all is said and done, the basic issue is whether we are to continue to view the world as one in which we are playing a zero-sum game—where, if others "win," we must "lose."

Or is there another way to look at things? To the extent that we help others attain more of the "good life," does this mean that we have to learn to do with less? And what is the "good life" anyway?

I believe the American people are ready to view the world from a genuinely global perspective and assume global responsibilities. But first, experts and political leaders need to give the American people better answers to all these questions. And we have to feel that we are not the only ones being called upon to make sacrifices for a better global future.

The national dialogue has been started, but I must be candid about the fact that I, and those who share my views, have not yet been very successful in getting our message across. □

Stephen C. Beuby

MAKING IT HAPPEN:

Creating Our Future:

A View from Capitol Hill

By Senator Claiborne Pell

There may be places where today's problems seem more immediate and pressing than they do on Capitol Hill. But I am not aware of them. Nonetheless, we cannot ignore the future, however great the temptation may be to do so, and however urgent the problems of today and tomorrow may appear.

The heritage of yesterday's decisions: Decisions that were made years—even decades—ago—gave rise to many of the problems we face today. Thousands of day-by-day and year-by-year decisions by individual citizens, business leaders, and our elected government officials at all levels will, in turn, shape the kind of life we live in the future.

Yet too little thought is being given to where our society is heading, and to what kind of society we would like to develop in the future. We tend to be so occupied with the concerns of this day or this year that we seem to have neither time nor incentive to look ahead for twenty or twenty-five years.

There is no more important task than to develop a vision of America's future, a vision that takes account of both our problems and opportunities. In creating a vision and setting a direction to guide these decisions, Members of Congress such as myself must play an important leadership role.

Preoccupation with the short term instead of the long term is understandable. In government, we must act on this year's budget and resolve this year's pressing issues.

Development of a truly comprehensive long-range outlook on our national transportation needs, for example, is thrust aside while we deal with the immediate problem of bankrupt railroads and airlines tottering on the brink of insolvency. Problems such as these abound, and there are always pressures to do something about them now.

The need is for the leaders of our nation strike a better balance between the problems of the moment and those issues which, if neglected, may become severe—even insoluble problems—for future generations of Americans?

Our oceans provide a good example of this necessity to look beyond immediate problems. We currently need to develop a sound, comprehensive law to govern human exploration and use of the oceans, seabeds, and their resources in the long-range future.

When I worked at the San Francisco Conference setting up the United Nations more than thirty years ago, I wrote my first paper on the Law of the Sea. More than ten years ago I introduced in the Senate a draft treaty for a regime of law in ocean space. I hope that we are now on the brink of broad acceptance of an idea that some called visionary, even harebrained, just a few years ago.

The U.N. Conference on Law of the Sea is dealing with an area comprising no less than 70 percent of the earth's surface. There have been no laws here, and anarchy prevails in exploitation of the resources of the oceans and the seabeds. A few years ago, President Lyndon Johnson referred to the resources of the oceans as "the heritage of mankind," and now—unless we act in time—we are in danger of seeing each country race to carve out its chunk, and the devil take the hindmost.

We can be certain of one thing, and that is that the human race will be deriving far more of its food, its protein, its minerals, and even its energy—through ocean wave motion or ocean thermal gradients—from the sea in the year 2000 than we do now.

The choices we face: We in the United States are not unique in having to confront serious issues and tough choices. Many of our most important and difficult problems are worldwide.

Who am I? Senator Claiborne Pell

Claiborne Pell has served as United States Senator from Rhode Island since 1961. He was elected in 1960 and reelected in 1966, 1972, and 1978.

Pell is Rhode Island's senior Senator and ranks 11th in the Senate. He holds influential Senate posts in a number of fields. He is the only member of the Senate to have been a Foreign Service Officer.

Pell has taken the lead in proposals to ensure peaceful uses of the oceans and international cooperation in protection of the environment. Through Senate resolutions and hearings, he spurred negotiation of a treaty prohibiting the emplacement of weapons of mass destruction on the seabed. He also fathered another international treaty to prohibit the use of environmental modification techniques as weapons of war and initiated work on a treaty that would require nations to file environmental assessment statements for projects that might affect the environment of other nations or the global commons (the oceans).

SPLIT LEVEL
OVERLOOK
—
FOMERLY
PLEASANT VALLEY
OVERLOOK

Drawing by H. Martin; © 1975 The New Yorker Magazine, Inc.

• •

Underlying many of them has been growing concern that the unprecedented worldwide growth in production and consumption of material goods during the past 50 years may soon be approaching some natural limits to growth.

There appear to be limits to the natural resources available on this planet earth—limits to food resources, to readily available energy resources, and mineral resources—although I believe technology and recycling processes may continue to push back each of these limits.

My own view is that the ultimate limit, the real obstacle to continuing material expansion, is pollution. *The Global 2000 Report* and other studies have demonstrated that growth of production and consumption are beginning to exert severe stresses on the natural environment that sustains all life. And doubts are beginning to be expressed about whether all that we have proclaimed as economic growth

and progress really adds up to an improved quality of human life.

Alternative views: There are still many who believe we need only apply still more scientific and technical know-how on an ever-larger scale to assure an abundance of energy and a clean environment, as well as new material substitutes to replace depleted resources. But there are others, like the late E.F. Schumacher, who believe the time has come to question the wisdom of unbridled growth and massive reliance on ever more complex technologies.

In his book *Small Is Beautiful,* Schumacher observes that "In the excitement over the unfolding of his scientific and technical powers, modern man has built a system of production that ravishes nature and a type of society that mutilates man." "The cultivation and expansion of needs," Schumacher continues, "is the antithesis of wisdom. It is also the antithesis of

freedom and peace. Every increase of needs tends to increase one's dependence on outside forces over which one cannot have control, and, therefore, increases existential fear. Only by a reduction of needs can one promote a genuine reduction in those tensions which are the ultimate causes of strife and war."

The great Indian leader Mahatma Gandhi eloquently expressed a concern about limits when he said, "Earth provides enough to satisfy every man's needs, but not for every man's greed."

There is enough cause for concern, I believe, to consider whether more of everything will really improve the quality of our lives and our environment, or whether a stronger emphasis on conservation and less emphasis in consumption might be wiser. Isn't it, at least, an option that deserves careful consideration?

I am inclined to believe that the ethic of unrestrained economic growth, which is so keenly ingrained in our

MAKING IT HAPPEN:

American outlook, must be tempered in the future by the realization that not all growth is good and that bigger is not always better. I believe that we must take a close look at our national habit of measuring the quality of our lives by the quantity of our national production.

The responsibility of public officials: As an elected public official, I am very deeply aware that it is easier and much more popular to promise the people that tomorrow will bring more of every good material thing—more economic growth, more production, more things to consume.

I am convinced, however, that responsible public officials today must make clear the disadvantages as well as the advantages of economic growth; that increases in the gross national product can contain elements of both good and bad; that we must not, in advocating quantitative growth and change, neglect the great values of permanence and tradition in the quality of human life. In other words, we must be selective.

This is not only theory, it is very much a part of present-day reality in the United States. We have an unacceptable level of unemployment in our nation today. And to provide jobs for the tens of thousands of young Americans who embark each year on new careers, we must sustain a healthy level of economic activity; with a growing working population, we must have economic growth.

In my view, we can and must provide meaningful work for every American—and we must do this without abandoning a responsibility and concern for the nature and quality of our economic growth. This growth can and should be, in large part, in service industries, in education, in the many areas of human endeavor that are not heavily dependent on the consumption of natural resources, and not abusive of our natural environment. Here I would add that, as long as a single man or woman seeks work and cannot find it, the government has a responsibility to serve as an employer of last resort.

Looking ahead: As I contemplate the future and the huge tasks that lie ahead, I am nevertheless optimistic. I believe that the necessary individual,

social, and political accommodations are possible. I believe we can maintain a standard of material sustenance for all our citizens more than adequate to permit every American to pursue the fullest development of his or her human potential. And I believe it is possible to do so within the limits that nature imposes on our natural resources, and without sacrificing the natural environment that has nourished human life for millions of years.

In looking ahead, I hope that we, as Americans, can work cooperatively to realize our vision of a society that measures progress and growth in human terms and not merely in the dollar value of production and consumption.

If we can do that, if we can begin to agree on what it is that each of us really needs—as an individual, as a member of a family, and as a citizen of society—for a life of quality and fulfillment, then I think we can all look forward very much indeed to the years ahead.

The American People:

Leaders or Followers?

By Donald R. Lesh

The anatomy of leadership: The American people are often characterized as being ahead of their leaders in perceiving current problems and being receptive to new and innovative solutions.

But can the people actually take the lead? Or are we dependent for shaping the future course of our nation on finding skillful and charismatic political leaders?

In short, where are the levers of political change in a representative democracy such as ours? Are the American people leaders?—or followers?

In the short run—over a period of a few months to a few years—and in the absence of some major catalytic event, the institutions of government and society pursue policies that are pretty much beyond the reach of ordinary people and the public at large. Over this short run, the people are able to exert only very limited control over policies affecting their lives.

People can vote, of course, in local, state, and national elections. And they can attempt singly or collectively to influence the decisions of their representatives.

But elected officials by nature tend to judge issues and decide on policies on the basis of lessons learned in the last election, just as military planners assiduously prepare to fight any future war with the strategies and tactics of the last.

Likewise, the inertia of large bureaucracies—in both the private and public sectors—will usually defeat any expectation of rapid response. Bureau-

crats, whether in the public or private sector, are characteristically resistant to new ideas or practices that threaten established procedures and entrenched interests.

I do not exclude the possibility of bringing public influence to bear at a given moment on critical policy decisions through lobbying, demonstrations, strikes, marches, write-in campaigns, oand so on. These forms of public expression have played a significant role in the history of the United States during the last two decades.

But such tactics seem to be effective mainly in urgent situations, and when public opinion and mass participation can also be mobilized around specific issues that are capable of simple expression. You will recall the effectiveness of such recent simple summations as freedom now, stop the war, ban the bomb, hell no—I won't go, free the hostages, and no nukes. Note the preponderance of negative demands in these examples.

Few of the issues posed in this book lend themselves to such simple expression. They demand, instead, a different order of sustained and positive leadership over time, and such leadership must be capable of addressing highly complex and interrelated problems. Such problems, by definition, do not have straight-forward and easy solutions.

In the longer run—over five years and beyond—I believe that the American people can play a true leadership role. This leadership, however, will be in the actual search for and implementation of workable solutions to such problems, rather than in affecting the day-to-day exercise of executive authority in public or private institutions.

The American people contribute to constructive change in the policies of their government and the shape of their society in basicly two sorts of ways:

■ *People can build a new awareness and understanding of basic issues in the local and national community.* Ideas come into common currency in this way and establish a place and priority for themselves on the public agenda. Helping create a climate of public and institutional acceptance of the need for innovative and foresighted decision-making would be an example of such leadership.

■ *Individuals, acting alone and in groups, can discover and demonstrate alternative solutions to social, economic, and technical problems.* This form of leadership is a demonstration that workable future choices can build upon but go beyond the traditions and problems of the past.

Building broader public awareness and understanding of the issues is comparatively easy as an exercise of leadership in the United States. This is readily done working through comfortable and familiar channels. These include schools and universities, communications media of all kinds, churches and related organizations, labor unions, and a wide variety of voluntary and civic groups.

Americans are brought up to be joiners and civic activists. One is expected to become a member of the PTA, support the Boy Scouts and volunteer rescue squad, and cooperate with the local neighborhood improvement program. So the customary

---

Examples of Demonstrative Personal Action

In the 1970s and early 1980s a great many Americans did one or more of the following in response to their new perception of what the times were requiring from them and other Americans:

■ install solar collectors, a wood-burning stove, a windmill, or all three;

■ sell the four-door gasguzzler and buy a small, economical fuel-efficient compact car; sell the compact and buy a moped; sell the moped and buy a bicycle; ride public transport or walk;

■ build a tank to catch rainwater, put in a composting toilet, or lay out a "graywater" system so that household waste water can be used to irrigate a garden; enlarge the garden;

■ take up beekeeping or begin to cultivate fish for food in the backyard;

■ remove existing air conditioning units and plant more trees and shrubs to shade the house;

■ sell the house and join in some communal living arrangement;

■ adopt a form of "voluntary simplicity" in consumption of material goods, diet, living pattern, clothing;

■ work as a volunteer in local conservation and ecological programs; serve as a representative of local views in public hearings;

■ limit the family to one child, at most two, or possibly none;

■ support the care and education of a needy child in a Third World country; adopt such a child;

■ eat less red meat, or no meat; smoke and drink less, or not at all; establish a routine of regular physical exercise for health and pleasure;

■ announce that a company will voluntarily meet or exceed water and air pollution standards, or gas mileage requirements, prior to deadlines mandated by law;

■ specify that the next annual meeting of shareholders will include a report of corporate social and ecological as well as financial performance.

American patterns of life and work are congenial to individuals taking leadership in an essentially educational effort on complex global issues and their often unforeseen interactions.

This form of quiet leadership is absolutely vital in building a constituency for change. The goal of such leadership is to put new ideas into good currency, an essential preliminary step for any eventual legislative and executive action.

Demonstrative personal action implies another kind of leadership with an entirely different range of demand upon the individual. Essentially, the demand is for philosophical and ideological consistency between one's expressed world view and one's personal practices and lifestyle.

Those who lead in this mode live their beliefs. Their actions may also be demonstrably beneficial to both the individual and to society at large. But the governing factor in their leadership is that in some measure they make clear the possibility of an alternative response, a way that departs from prevailing social, economic, or cultural norms.

No one has been in a position to do all of these things, and that is to be expected. But the burgeoning movements in the United States for alternative lifestyles, energy and resource conservation, recycling, appropriate technology, and individual and local self-reliance include many people who have chosen some of the paths cited here. And together they constitute a growing repository of innovation and leadership that will be of increasing value as our society seeks solutions to the problems of the future.

Health and survival in the biological world depend in large part on the preservation of diversity of species, and so too our economic health and social survival may depend on the preservation of alternative lifestyles and diverse adaptations to our environment.

Today, these alternatives may seem curious, unnecessary, even laughable—like the Furbish Lousewort—but tomorrow they may give us confidence in a tested alternative idea, skill, or concept that will be essential to our society.

Polling Public Attitudes about Readiness to Adapt

Cautions about Survey Results

Polling of public attitudes about readiness to adapt the way we live has been undertaken with increasing frequency in recent years. Recognized authorities in the field include The Gallup Organization, Opinion Research Corporation, and Yankelovich, Skelly, and White.

Daniel Yankelovich presented a very complete summary of his organization's work over time on these issues for the Third Biennial Woodlands Conference on Growth Policy held at Woodlands, Texas, in October, 1979.

The current state of mind of the American people in 1979 Yankelovich described as in the middle of a process of "working through" a variety of attitudinal and value shifts.

The shift is away from an earlier unquestioning conviction that material growth was very important and a definition of progress primarily in terms of increasing consumption. The change is toward a new set of beliefs not yet fully defined.

Here are the points Daniel Yankelovich included in his profile of the emerging priorities of the American public at the close of the 1970s:

■ The public wants to *retain the gains it won in the affluent years.* It seems unwilling to sacrifice these in an effort to regenerate the economic machine or to expand vastly the existing system of social supports.

■ The public has little taste for self-denial and austerity for the purpose of adding new consumer products to the market or increasing efficiency. *What sacrifices the public is prepared to make will be directed toward maintaining economic stability and a reliable and fair supply of essentials* (e.g., gasoline), even if the amount is reduced.

■ Americans want to *strike a new balance between hard work and leisure.* They are prepared to slow down their pursuit of luxuries if that gives them the freedom to explore the possibilities of self-fulfillment and allows them a measure of economic stability.

■ Americans appear to *want to halt the expansion of certain government services if this will reduce their taxes and protect their privacy.* They do want, however, to *retain those services that they consider entitlements,* such as social security and pension benefits. And they would like to be protected against the high costs of catastrophic illness.

■ The public has *clearcut priorities about what forms of consumption it is prepared to give up and what it considers essential* to its well-being and freedom. People don't want to give up their family cars, their central heating, their own homes, their washing machines. They are prepared, however, to make modest cutbacks in the use of energy, to keep their old model cars longer, to waste less, to reduce consumption of meat and clothing, and to reduce their use of items that can't be recycled if these involve waste.

■ *A new antiwaste morality* is gaining momentum. The public is unlikely to support any government program that it regards as potentially wasteful, and there is support for regulations that curb wasteful practices by the public itself. This attitude extends to the consumption of products that are in relatively short supply. So the public would go along with such measures as closing gas stations on Sunday to limit consumption and restricting the use of credit cards. It should be pointed out that in the public's mind the rising rate of inflation is fused with wastefulness. The public would support higher taxes on foreign-made "luxury" goods, such as color television sets, in the hope that it would reduce inflation and discourage the purchase of non-essential products.

Americans' values in conflict: The Yankelovich report underlines their conclusion that the American public finds the answers derived from an earlier, easier, and more comfortable period of our history no longer seem to

Survey research on public policy issues provides us with both "snapshots" and "moving pictures." The answers to one question posed at a single point in time have only very limited value, and may be conditioned by many factors, including recent related events. What research at any one point in time provides is a static view—a snapshot—of the attitudes of Americans on that issue at that particular time.

Far more interesting and important is what is happening to those attitudes? In which direction are they moving?

Those all-important answers are developed by Daniel Yankelovich's organization and others by posing the same question periodically to comparable national samples under comparable circumstances. In that way they can attain a dynamic view—a moving picture—of where the attitudes of Americans seem to be headed.

But we must recognize nonetheless the volatility of public attitudes, as well as the occasional over-interpretation of survey results. We must also be realistic in recognizing (1) the limits of survey research as a predictor of *future* behavior, and (2) the existence of other survey data that suggest Americans may not be as ready as we might wish to face up to the realities of a new international order.

So caution is advisable when asserting, on the basis of public attitude survey results, that Americans are ready to accept new challenges. Without doubt, there is definite evidence that in the past decade major changes have been taking place in American perceptions and attitudes, as pointed out by Yankelovich (and others as well). But caution, as well as interested attention, is appropriate.

A POSITIVE GUIDE TO THE FUTURE

apply to the realities of today, and that there is in the American public a yearning to strike in our national life a new balance between the material and the spiritual.

It is too early to state with any assurance when and how that balance may be struck, and under what internal and external influences. Public opinions and values do change, sometimes very quickly, and one cannot assume that the views of the American public will follow a single direction consistently over time.

This is especially the case in a world characterized by high rates of change as well as by increasing interdependence. National and geographic boundaries formerly seemed to guarantee Americans security and isolation from foreign problems. Future events may demonstrate to the American public that this security and isolation has become less than they had become accustomed to.

Trends in Public Attitudes and Behavior

What a more sustainable future means for a particular community or individual is not always clear or simple. Understanding the implications of a commitment to long-term sustainability involves dealing simultaneously with issues that range from scientific and technical to social and political, on to emotional, ethical, and philosophical.

All this needs to blend in the understanding and actions of the individual, so as to motivate appropriate attitudes and responses.

Public attitudes about this cluster of issues: No one research group or survey organization has studied this total cluster of issues systematically over time. However, periodically several such groups have examined parts of that picture. The conclusions here rely on that evidence.

■ **Energy use:** There are clear indications that Americans are on the right track about energy use. Several periods of oil and natural gas shortages, rapid increases in energy costs for autos, home and office heating, and industrial and agricultural production—plus a little nudging by the federal government and a variety of nongovernmental groups—have made Americans far more frugal in energy consumption. Conservation is now seen as not only a virtue but also good economic sense.

■ **Protecting the environment:** Even before the petroleum crunch, protecting the environment had become a national goal to be pursued on at least an equal basis with expanding economic activity and growth.

This has been confirmed by the Harris poll, the Gallup poll, Opinion Research Corporation, and Yankelovich, Skelly and White. There have been many different sponsors of this research, including private research groups such as Potomac Associates and Resources for the Future; local, state and federal governments; business concerns; and a number of newspapers and broadcasting networks.

In September, 1981—in the midst of a major economic recession—this view was again confirmed by a phone survey of Americans conducted jointly by the *New York Times* and CBS News.

Nationally, a full 67 percent of those interviewed agreed that "we need to maintain present environmental laws in order to preserve the environment for future generations." Fewer than one in four said that "we need to relax our environmental laws in order to achieve economic growth."

What this tells us is that enactment of the National Environmental Policy Act [NEPA] in 1970 ratified in law a conclusion already reached by a majority of Americans: conservation and prudent environmental protection are the only sensible long-term policies for our nation—not to be pursued exclusively at the expense of all others, but also not to be abandoned or temporarily set aside for short-term motives.

■ **Global interdependance:** In a world that shares global resources such as the oceans and atmosphere, moving toward long-term sustainability involves more than thinking and acting locally or nationally. What about U.S. public attitudes here?

In 1972, 1974, and 1976 for its *State of the Nation* series, Potomac Associates commissioned the Gallup organization to design and conduct special hour-long surveys to be conducted throughout the country. When appropriate, use was made of comparable survey data going back as far as 1964.

By posing over time the same set of issues in identically worded questions to comparable national samples of Americans, it proved possible to establish trend lines on changing the international outlook of U.S. citizens.

The *State of the Nation* series was designed to highlight the inevitable contrasts and contradictions among the responses. The tensions between international and domestic concerns were prominent among these.

The standard questions used were related to belief in cooperation with the United Nations and associated international agencies; readiness to come to the aid of close allies in Europe or the Far East with military supplies or U.S. troops in the event of Communist-inspired attack; feeling as to whether the United States should frame its foreign policy independently or in collaboration with its allies and friends; desire to preserve the U.S. position as "Number One" in the world; and so on.

State of the Union survey conclusions: Using these indicators, the results led Potomac Associates to the conclusion that there had been a progressive withdrawal from foreign involvement in American attitudes during the 1970s. This development could be variously interpreted as a heightened spirit of nationalism, or an increased desire for unilateralism, or even as a "new isolationism."

Each survey produced a ranking of priorities for federal spending across a wide range of domestic and international programs. Virtually without exception, and without significant deviation among the major demographic categories, Americans ranked international programs last each time.

For example, the 1976 composite scores in this sector of the *State of the Nation* survey placed four programs at the very end of the list of 24 ranked. They were: maintaining U.S. military bases overseas; contributing to the United Nations; providing economic assistance and loans to developing countries; and supplying military aid to our allies.

This is no surprise for those who fought the good fight in the U.S. Congress over the annual foreign assistance bill. In this light, the position adopted by the Reagan Administration for the first global summit meeting at Cancun, Mexico in October, 1981 would appear to have been based on documented U.S. public attitudes.

Emergency appeals for disaster assistance and the like will certainly continue to be met with traditional American generosity and goodwill. But based on these public attitude surveys, longer-term international programs based solely on these values, or on the missionary impulse, seem likely to fail.

It seems more likely that Americans will accept global participation and responsibilities when they perceive that this course of action is in their enlightened self-interest.

To get the people of the U.S. to "think globally" it seems likely that a productive strategy would be to replicate what happened in regard to resource conservation and environmental protection.

Present efforts to move U.S. public opinion are often quite different, and negative in tone. We are warned—probably quite accurately—that we are moving toward a more crowded world, with sharper competition for scarce resources, in a deteriorating global environment. And we are cautioned that the outcome is liable to be a less stable climate of international relations with greater danger of war.

In practical political terms, this argument translates into an assertion that the United States must either do more now to help improve the lot of the world's poor, or risk a widespread shift of allegiance among the peoples of the developing countries to our Communist adversaries, or economic and/or military conflicts that will inevitably involve the superpowers and open the door to nuclear holocaust.

These predictions may or may not be well grounded. But to many Americans, the dangers they portray seem distant or unreal—or the problems appear insoluble in traditional terms. It does not seem irrelevant that the one international area in which Potomac Associates found there has been a significant increase over the past decade in the willingness of Americans to commit federal tax dollars was national defense.

Motivating effective action: Tactics and strategies based on ideology, politics, military force, and diplomacy are increasingly irrelevant to emerging global issues. The true challenge is to have U.S. policies based on our national stake in a world of closer global interdependence.

As a start, we can begin looking at poor countries differently. They are not hordes of potential enemies clamoring at the gates of Fortress America. Instead, they are both potential trading partners and essential allies in coping with great shared problems—in particular, the overarching task of our time, namely, making our shared global environment stable and healthy for all its populations.

An essential characteristic of the great and interlocking problems we now face is that no one nation can solve them in isolation. This is the case no matter how wealthy, powerful, or technically advanced a nation is.

In virtually every case, first steps must be national, or even local and individual. And, to be effective, all actions need to be taken *in coordination* with similar actions in other countries.

No nation can be expected to achieve such action while its people face immediate problems of malnutrition, starvation, disease, unemployment, alienation, and despair. In order for individuals and local communities to do the things needed, there must be economic well-being, social stability,

public understanding, a certain level of technical ability, and a general social commitment of the part of the public.

Where will we get leadership on this issue in the U.S.? It remains to be seen whether the quality of leadership demanded to build a more sustainable future will come from the center or the grass roots in the United States. Ideally, there should be a combination of both.

In the near term, however, it is important that we understand that many of our national and regional political leaders are unprepared or unwilling to exercise leadership in these areas, and often deny the existence of the problems and their relevance to the U.S. and global future. So leadership must come from some other quarter. Our work is cut out for us! □

Who am I? Donald R. Lesh

It was a lot easier to answer that question fifteen years ago than it is today. My children have trouble explaining to their friends what I do for a living, and I understand that.

I used to be a Soviet expert of sorts. I had studied Russian language and Soviet history, first in the Navy and then in graduate school at Harvard, and then I had lived for over three years in the Soviet Union (for an academic year at Moscow State University under the cultural exchange program, and then for over two years on assignment to the American Embassy in Moscow). I was an officer in the U.S. Foreign Service then, and that gave me an easy, comfortable, and traditional way to identify myself... until, after ten years, I resigned.

People often ask why, since I'd had a promising career, timely promotions, good assignments—London, Moscow, the seventh floor of the State Department, and finally the staff of the National Security Council under Henry Kissinger. The answer is complex.

A small part of the answer is that I realized my future chances to serve in the Soviet field were slim, since my tour in Moscow had ended with my being expelled as *persona non grata*. A much larger part of that decision was my growing sense that more important and exciting things were happening at home in U.S. society— it was the late 1960s—than abroad. I also realized that I could never again summon up quite the same commitment to service as a diplomat overseas after what was for me the profoundly subversive experience of learning at first hand in the Nixon White House how U.S. foreign policy is actually made.

My decision was influenced, too, by a moment of personal insight I went through on coming back to the United States in late 1966. I had been abroad for nearly six years. During that time, I had watched (and voted in) two presidential elections from the curious vantage point of Moscow. I had shared vicariously in the trauma of President Kennedy's assassination, the first of the tragic deaths of national leaders. And I had tried—through a steady diet of USIA press summaries—vainly to grasp what was happening in Vietnam— and at home—to my country.

For days after I returned, I couldn't understand why my happiness at being back in the United States should be mixed with feelings of disappointment and frustration. Finally I realized that I had an image in my mind of the country I had been representing abroad, an image based on an amalgam of my Midwestern upbringing, my German and Scots-Irish heritage, my education, experiences, idealism, and naivete. But it was a country that no longer existed, or perhaps had never existed.

I had gone through my own little time warp. The mental portrait I had carried with me for several years no longer corresponded to the reality of America in the 1960s.

Working for a time on Capitol Hill thereafter provided a quick and effective cure and catchup. There are few places in America where the panorama of the nation can so readily be observed. On any given

day on some issue of current national importance, there is a ranking expert in some field testifying before some subcommittee.

I experienced the same panoramic perspective upon America with Potomac Associates, a small, non-profit, policy research group, where I spent the succeeding seven years. I learned here about the application of survey research to public policy decisions, and I stepped tentatively into the world of publishing, and did some editing and writing. That was also where I first encountered The Club of Rome, through sharing in work on the manuscript of *The Limits to Growth*. My life has never been quite the same since.

I feel a bit like a reformed alcoholic giving a testimonial. First it was a little nip of systems modeling now and then to be sociable, then a shot of sustainability theory to get me through the morning....Before I knew it, I was into the hard stuff— paradigm shifts, changing values, learning and planning, patriarchy, finally historical discontinuity, global transformation, and human potential. Only I haven't yet reformed.

In 1976, the U.S. Association for The Club of Rome was founded. I was privileged to help in a small way, and the following year I wound up as the first Executive Director, staying

in that position until the summer of 1981, and for more than two years assisted at the long gestation and birth of *Making It Happen*. I am now Executive Director of a new group, The Global Tomorrow Coalition, a consortium of more than 55 organizations concerned with global trends in resources, population and environment.

If all this has taught me anything, however, it is that I can't answer the question of "Who I am?" by telling what I do.

I'm a concerned father of two teenage children. My wife and I are chronic do-it-yourselfers. We both are learning and enjoying hatha yoga. I'm a Libra who pooh-poohs astrology but always instinctively seeks the middle ground of compromise. I know that my life is riddled with inconsistencies, and I console myself by worrying about them and occasionally correcting a few. I believe strongly in the power of love in human life, and have a suspicion that—beyond most organizational and motivational theory—people do whatever they do, at work and in their personal lives, out of some form of love. I also believe in the role of luck.

Right now, through the U.S. Association for The Club of Rome and The Global Tomorrow Coalition, I'm trying to help a country think through the changes that are taking place in our society and others, and their implications for the future. We want to stimulate other people to do the same, in the hope that together we can figure out how to do a better job of organizing our society and government and world.

I'm sorry, kids—I know this doesn't help much. When people ask about me, just tell them "Dad is a generally serious, sometimes crotchety, basically optimistic, ex-kneejerk liberal who at nearly age 50 is still trying to decide what he really wants to be when he grows up." That ought to hold 'em.

Radar for Government:

What Can Be Done to Improve Foresight?

John M. Richardson, Jr.

In mid-1979, I received a call from the Office of Food and Natural Resources in the U.S. Department of State. This office, along with the Council on Environmental Quality in the Executive Office of the President, shared responsibility for the Global 2000 study. I was asked to prepare a series of recommendations based on the study. The subject was to be "Improving U.S. Government Projection Capabilities."

What's lacking: The Global 2000 study had confirmed that mathematical modeling and forecasting techniques were used quite extensively in government to investigate environmental and resource problems, but it had found that there was little or no coordination of these efforts.

Forecasters in one government agency were unaware of what their compatriots in other agencies were doing. There was minimal sharing of basic data. In many cases, agencies were working on closely related problems but using contrasting or conflicting assumptions about basic factors such as energy supply and price level.

The Global 2000 Report **concluded that the government lacked the capability to provide the President with an overall, integrated assessment of long-term trends in population, resources, and environment.**

My task was to develop recommendations to help correct that situation.

Can we get effective foresight? My report, *Towards Effective Foresight in the U.S. Government,* was completed about a year later, in June 1980. Portions of the report—somewhat revised—are presented in the pages that follow.

The report was written to "identify, analyze, and recommend options for improving U.S. Government capabilities to make projections, both domestically and in concert with other nations." It responds to concerns raised in the Global 2000 study about U.S. Government projection capabilities.

The intended audience was the President, his immediate staff, and other policy-level officials. Unfortunately, in the present structure of the government, there is no single individual or group below the President's Chief of Staff who is responsible for addressing the issues raised in *Global 2000* and in my report.

Writing this report raised serious questions in my mind about looking to the federal government for leadership in foresight. While Americans are natural futurists, our government is not, by its nature, future-oriented.

Perhaps this president or his successor will possess the vision, the leadership, and the will to effect needed changes. But the task of creating our future cannot wait for a president, or any elected public official, to act. This responsibility is not his, or theirs, alone; it is shared by all of us.

Our government does respond—slowly, and sometimes crudely—to the highest priority concerns of its people. I have been told, again and again, that we lack effective foresight because it is something the people of the United States do not understand or do not care about.

A POSITIVE GUIDE TO THE FUTURE

What Do We Mean by Foresight?:

"Foresight": As used here, foresight encompasses capabilities that have been called:

- projection
- forecasting
- prediction
- impact assessment
- long-term planning
- "futurism"

We will be particularly concerned with the capability to exercise foresight about questions that are likely to be of concern to the President and policy-level officials. Such questions—

- *are long-term;*
- *cross departmental lines;*
- *often involve relationships between the public and private sectors;*
- *often involve both domestic and foreign policy;*
- *concern Congress and the public (or should); and*
- *may affect the health and survival of our nation* (and, not inconceivably the survival of the human race as well).

Here are some specific examples:

■ **What effect would an additional doubling of imported energy prices have** on our rate of inflation and balance of payments? What would be the probable impact on U.S. agriculture? On world trade in other commodities? What ecological and political consequences could we (and should we) anticipate? How could we prepare to cope with them?

■ **To what degree is a significant increase in atmospheric CO_2 and "acid rains" likely to result from an increased commitment to fossil fuels for energy production?** What will be the consequences for agricultural productivity? If adverse impacts are anticipated, to what degree will they be international as well as domestic and with what consequences? When are these impacts, if they occur, likely to require political decisions and/or new policies? How can we anticipate and prepare for these eventualities?

■ **What problems and opportunities are posed by the likelihood that the United States will, in the near future, become virtually the sole exporter of grain in the world?** What new policies and political decisions will be required and when will they be required? What can be done now to ensure that our nation derives maximum benefit from its position as a producer of agricultural surpluses? How can our domestic policies—especially land-use policies—be shaped to ensure that, as in the case of energy, we do not fritter away our advantages?

Foresight must be part of the total system of governance. It must incorporate—

- **political judgment,**
- issue relevance,
- technical excellence, and
- effective communication.

Do we need a more effective foresight capability?

Numerous arguments can be found in the relevant literature and in *The Global 2000 Report* to answer this question. Here are five that I find persuasive:

■ Every time the President has appointed a commission or group to study some aspect of the long-term future, the commission or group has recommended, in one form or another, establishment of a better foresight capability.

■ As far as I know, every significant study of the future completed within the past seven years (even the most optimistic) has sounded warnings about probable "discontinuities" in economic, political, and social development during the next few decades.

■ The present foresight capabilities of the U.S. Government are seriously deficient.

■ Very important national decisions have been and are being made using our present, seriously deficient capabilities.

■ In at least two—very visible—areas, transportation and energy, we are now living with the consequences of our failure to develop an effective foresight capability and learn something from using it.

But so long as our political processes remain open and democratic, change can and does come from the "bottom up" as well as from the "top down."

Foresight for what?

The Global 2000 Report *focuses on probable changes in population, resources, and environment through the end of this century.*

But for the President and policy-level officials, probable changes in population, resources, and environment are not intrinsically important.

Such changes may become important if the exercise of foresight indicates a probable or possible impact (especially an adverse impact) on:

- *the national security of the United States;*
- *its military and political influence and power, relative to those of potential enemies;*
- *the health of its economy;*
- *the standard of living, state of health, and, in general, quality of life of its people;*

144

- *the viability and health of its political institutions; and*

- *the popularly perceived "success" of its leaders,* as measured by polls, elections, and other indicators of support.

In a democratic society, popular support is sometimes regarded as an indicator of how well the other objectives, which are more difficult to measure, are being achieved. It is often viewed by political leaders as the most important objective of all, and probably it should be.

These factors are examples of the broad strategic objectives that must occupy policy-level officials, especially when one of these objectives is threatened.

In general, policy-level officials feel they are doing well if they can prevent degradation in the areas defined by these objectives. (A problem is a threatened degradation; it immediately assumes the highest priority.)

In the time left over from "firefighting" activities to prevent things from getting worse, policy-level officials try to make them better. Unfortunately, there doesn't seem to be much time left over.

I believe that a more effective foresight capability could help matters. But this will only begin to happen when credible results of foresight activities are clearly and convincingly linked to the broad objectives.

Drawing by Charles Addams ©The New Yorker Magazine

Obstacles to Effective Foresight

Before developing a set of recommendations, I decided it might be useful to review the history of recent attempts to improve the foresight capability of the U.S. Government. It was a sobering, even depressing, experience.

Almost everything I thought of had already been tried or proposed by somebody else. In many cases, these "somebodies" were experienced, powerful individuals.

History pointed unequivocally to the fact that an improved national foresight capability will probably not emerge from a special study like *The Global 2000 Report,* or from a report like this one. It is not easy to be optimistic about changing our government's capabilities.

Here are ten reasons that others have offered to explain our present deficiencies in foresight and our failure to do something about them.

■ **There is Little or No Top-Level Support for Foresight.**

"...lack of top-level support...has manifested itself not only in decisions concerning initial acquisition of models, but often as a lack of support for ongoing maintenance and use of a model...." (A.D. Little Corp. study of modeling for the Department of State)

■ **The "Best Talent" Has Never Worked on Broad, Long-Term Issues.**

"Because broad, long-term issues have been so low in priority, the best talent in government has never been put to work on them. Bureau chiefs and office directors know that the real payoffs lie elsewhere." (Confidential interview with senior government official)

■ **Bureaucratic Rigidity, Compartmentalization, and Specialization Have Frustrated Attempts to Promote Cooperation Between Departments and To Take a Broad, Long-Term View.**

"Executive agencies tend to feel resentful about information which has not been internally derived and defensive about their own abilities to do long-range policy analysis." (Informal communication from senior government official)

"Even if there were time for long-range planning, most of the real national problems cut across the entire Federal Governmental structure, across disciplines or across departments so that individual department planning is not adequate." (Congressional Research Service, *Long-Range Planning,* 1976)

"Our bureaucratic organizations, divided into regional and functional bureaus and, indeed, our academic tradition of specialization compound the tendency to compartmentalize. American pragmatism produces a penchant for examining issues separately; to solve problems on their merits...." (Henry Kissinger, *The White House Years*)

■ **Time Pressures Restrict Vision to the Short Run.**

"There is little time for leaders to reflect. They are locked in an endless battle in which the urgent constantly gains on the important. The public life of every political figure is a continual struggle to rescue an element of choice from the pressure of circumstance." (Henry Kissinger, *The White House Years*)

"The pressure of short-term tasks often requires the agency's modeling experts to make expeditious simplifications, which are rarely reviewed in depth and which are difficult to revise, once made." (Global 2000, Volume 2, The Technical Report, Chapter 14)

■ **By the Time Models or Forecasts Are Developed, Policy-Level Officials Have Either Moved On or Lost Interest.**

*"The interest of a President or Congress or the public proved to be much greater when a study was started than when it was completed.... Sometimes, the period allowed for a study was too short, as with preparation of **Toward a Social Report**. That study also ran into a frequent timing problem, having been started by one President and submitted either at the end of his term or to his successor."* (Global 2000, Volume 2, The Technical Report, Appendix A)

"Models are often designed and built on the basis of strong support from an individual decision-maker or group of decision-makers who envision use of the model for a specific policy task or set of tasks. When new policies and issues emerge to dominate the scene, or new administrators enter the picture with less personal commitment to a modeling project, models typically languish in disuse. This situation has occurred repeatedly in the Federal Government with all types of policy models." (A.D. Little Corp. study of modeling for the Department of State)

About Costs and Benefits of Foresight

The cost of significantly improving the government's foresight capability will not be insignificant.

But, by almost any standard of measurement, it will be quite modest.

It is possible, however, that:

■ We may fail. (Personally, I believe the chances are quite good that we won't.)

■ We may discover it really wasn't necessary. (I believe this is highly improbable.)

On the other hand, the costs of *not* developing such a capability could be very great indeed.

(Of course, this is the sort of argument that everyone offers up when his or her pet program is being proposed. But that doesn't necessarily make it wrong in this case.)

■ **Policy-Level Officials Lack the Knowledge and Experience to Use Models Properly.**

"Policy-makers have often had unclear ideas about the nature of policy models, the appropriate uses to which they might be put, and the most effective way to integrate the results of a model forecast into the overall policy development process. Lacking knowledge of modeling techniques and often without access to adequate documentation, policy-makers have often been faced with a situation where they had to accept or reject a model on the word of the modelbuilder alone." (A.D. Little Corp. study of modeling for the Department of State)

■ **The Products of Modelers' Efforts are Incomprehensible, or Irrelevant, or Both.**

"Eventually, the model is delivered and the results of the model are presented to the decision-maker. Much to his or her surprise, the decision-maker discovers that not only does he not understand the model, the assumptions embedded in the model are contrary to his view of the world and the results useless for the pressing policy decisions he now faces...." (A.D. Little Corp. study of modeling for the Department of State)

■ **There Is Poor Communication Between Those Who Contract for Models and Forecasts, Those Who Develop Them, and Those Who Are Supposed to Use Them.**

"...There is a basic distrust of forecasting in the bureaucracy and in the Presidency. There is little communication between those in the bureaucracy who let and monitor contracts for the development of forecasting techniques and those who would use the products of these techniques. Among the reasons for this lack of communication may be unfamiliarity with forecaster's jargon, impatience with it, an unwillingness to understand it, or a failure on the part of planners and forecasters to package their message in comprehensible ways." (Congressional Research Service, Long-Range Planning, 1976)

■ **Congress Doesn't Care About the Long-Term Future.**

"The Executive Branch would be strongly influenced by the desires of the Congress in looking at the long-term future. But, with the exception of a very few members, taking a long-term view and improving the government's foresight capability are not matters of high priority." (Confidential interview with senior government offical)

■ **The Public Doesn't Care About the Long-Term Future.**

"People are not much concerned about the long-term future. Everything which has been said in the literature about the time horizon problem is true. However, part of the problem is that people don't have much information about the future upon which to make their judgments or form opinions. They are simply not in a position to examine intelligently the trade-offs between the short and long run." (Confidential interview with senior government official)

Guidelines for Effective Foresight

1. Broad national goals should be clearly defined.

The foundation of effective foresight must be a clear conception of:

■ those characteristics of U.S. culture, political institutions, economic system, and values whose preservation and enhancement must, as a matter of policy, take priority over all other concerns; and

■ the role that our nation visualizes for itself and for its people in the emerging global system of the future.

Earlier, several matters of very high priority for the President and other policy-level officials were identified. It seems to me that, at least implicitly, these comprise our broad national goals. They are defined as such by the *behavior* of the President and policy-level officials. The point here is that:

■ the linkage between foresight activities and the important strategic, long-term goals of the nation should be explicit; and

■ insofar as possible, the process of defining goals and considering trade-offs between them should be self-conscious.

(One reviewer of this report considered it most important that I make one further point. In the past, our implicit goals have been principally *national.* We have grown up in a world in which it was taken for granted that nation-states were the principal actors. But many believe that, in the future, organization of human society must be based on a much higher degree of global interdependence. We must not exclude from our consideration other "models" of the organization of human society than the present one.)

2. The process of defining goals and exercising foresight should be democratic, adaptable, flexible, and humble.

I believe that an effective foresight capability in the U.S. Government must:

■ involve the public in the process and educate them about the results that emerge (in the State of Minnesota, this is being done right now);

■ approach the task with humility, recognizing that we are largely ignorant about the future (although we can know more than we do);

■ recognize that we do not now have an adequate theory of social change, and may never have one;

■ realize that we can learn from other cultures as well as from how we have done things in the past;

■ be flexible and adaptable;

■ be willing to experiment, take risks, make mistakes, and learn from them.

3. A commitment to effective foresight should permeate the entire government.

Foresight capability must not be localized in a single office or bureau (for instance, a centralized "Bureau of Foresight and Planning" in the Executive Office of the President).

Rather, it must permeate the entire decision process.

Making the future part of the present and making current policies "future-responsive" must become a matter of habit throughout the entire government.

This isn't going to happen in a month or a year, no matter what actions are taken by the President. That is all the more reason to get started.

4. The president and policy-level officials must be integrally involved.

The foresight process will not be devoid of technical complexity and will require, to some degree, the services of "specialists" and "experts." But the President and policy-level officials must define the issues, participate in the process by which they are explored, and use the "results." Ultimately, the activities of those exercising foresight and those making policy at high levels should become indistinguishable.

5. The exercise of foresight should evoke competing perspectives and identify real options; choosing among them will always require political judgment.

The goal of a foresight capability should be to raise questions, evoke competing perspectives, and identify real options. There is no one best way to achieve foresight. *The temptation to produce a single "answer" or believe that there is one should be resisted.* Issues of importance must be explored by different individuals, reflecting different biases, using different techniques. We should expect different results and expect to learn from the differences. Resolving differences at the point where policies are formed and decisions are made must be a matter of experience and informed political judgment.

Upon reading these five guidelines, you might conclude that my view of effective foresight strongly emphasizes *attitudes,* in contrast to:

■ techniques
■ doctrines
■ methodologies
■ procedures
■ theories, or
■ organizational arrangements.

You would be right; my view of effective foresight strongly emphasizes attitudes.

Lack of imaginative proposals is not the reason we do not have an effective foresight capability. Rather, it is because of the obstacles that are found in our attitudes and institutions.

The obstacles to improving our foresight capability are, in my view, formidable but not insurmountable.

They permeate the Congress and the Executive Branch of the government. They are present in the scientific-technical community and in the society as a whole. They are institutional and attitudinal. They are mutually reinforcing.

The "state of the art" in foresight is also such that the President is reluctant to make a commitment to building broad public support for a better foresight capability (perhaps properly so).

All these impediments to more effective foresight are complex and pervasive because they are a product of the physical and cultural environment in which our values and our institutions have evolved. For more than 200 years, we have been in the fortunate position of not having to worry much about foresight.

However, now a growing number of individuals (like myself) have come to believe that effective foresight is something we do have to worry about. We feel that building an effective foresight capability should become a matter of high priority.

The very special problem of overload and lack of "slack" in the policy system at the very top: It is easy for a group or individual—or even a president—with a special concern to talk about raising the priority of that concern. Unfortunately, that is not so easy for the President and policy-level officials to do it. The problem is that there is no "slack" in the system. It is already overloaded.

This means that *when you raise the priority of one thing, you must lower the priority of something else.*

Unfortunately, all of the other "somethings" also have concerned supporters and seem to deserve their high priority status. If they didn't, they wouldn't have attained that status in the first place.

Decisions like this require *political judgment.* An outside expert can do no more than argue for his point of view. He has no way of knowing, for sure, what the judgment ought to be.

To Initiate an Effective Foresight Capability

Building an effective foresight capability will require, at the minimum, a consistent high-level commitment over the course of an entire Presidential term. It will require Presidential time (the scarcest resource in government) and the time of other policy-level officials.

Attitudes—the most intractable obstacle: Institutions can be changed by directive or by legislation. But attitudes are the most intractable obstacles to effective foresight. These can only be changed by the passing of time and the unfolding of events. Making our present policies future-responsive is something new. Most people don't think about things that way, and they don't understand those who do.

Five important things to keep in mind as the process of change is initiated, are:

■ **The Timing of Initiatives is Important.**
Poor timing is one of the principal reasons for the failure of previous efforts to improve our foresight capabilities. Typically, studies have been initiated early in a Presidential term. By the time recommendations emerged, most people no longer cared. Those who did care had no time to do anything significant. As noted above, I believe that the ideal time for initiating action to improve the government's foresight capability is at the beginning of the second term of an incumbent President.

■ **Choosing the Right People is Important.**
Careful choice of individuals for key roles will be a critical factor in the success of any new organizations, procedures, policies, or programs. It is hard to set down explicit selection criteria—personal chemistry means so much in these matters—but here are some things I would look for:
■ They should have some political experience and some contacts in Washington.
■ They should be recognized by and familiar with several of the professional communities involved in foresight.
■ They should have credentials and/or recognition in at least two of the academic disciplines that are relevant to foresight.
■ They should be exceptionally effective at communicating technical subjects to non-technical audiences.

■ They should be familiar with several foresight techniques, not just one.
■ They should have a reputation as moderates, not zealots.

■ **Success Breeds Success.**
The value of one or two early successes to create a positive "demonstration effect" (bandwagon effect) should not be underestimated. For this reason, I would recommend the initiation of two or more carefully selected pilot projects, with good prospects for success.

■ **No Matter How Careful the Preparation,**
    Everything Will Not Work Out As Planned.
    Multiple Initiatives Should be Undertaken,
       in Parallel, to Allow for
       Mistakes, Unforeseen Developments, and Failures.
    We Should not "Put All Our Eggs in One Basket."
Today, no government in the world has a really effective foresight capability (although there is something to be learned from experiences in Scandinavia, the Netherlands, France, and several Communist countries). There is no way we can know for sure which approaches and institutional arrangements will work best in the United States. Accordingly, it is important to undertake several initiatives in parallel and watch carefully to see what works and what doesn't. If there is a total commitment to one approach as "the best," there will be an almost irresistible temptation to cover up failure, if it occurs, rather than frankly acknowledging it and learning from the experience.

■ **Every Foresight Activity Should Encourage Approaches to Problems That Are Not Only Parallel, But Competing.**
There is real danger in becoming too attached to one model or approach. The purpose of foresight activity should be to ensure that the President and other policy-level officials are provided with (a) a broad range of options, and (b) good information about their consequences, including differences of opinion. These results are most likely to emerge by comparing perspectives and results from different approaches and learning from the differences. □

MAKING IT HAPPEN:

Specific Next Initiatives

Here are seven specific, interrelated initiatives that I would recommend for consideration:

■ **Appoint a Special Assistant to the President for Foresight.**
This individual would be responsible for coordination of all the new initiatives in the foresight area and would serve as the President's principal advisor on matters pertaining to foresight. Of course, the precise nature of the position, as it evolved, would depend upon the President, the individual appointed, and other circumstances that cannot be foreseen at this time.

■ **Create a New Position in the Executive Office of the President (Possibly Elsewhere) of "Ombudsperson for our Grandchildren."**
This is not an original idea. But the concept of a position with statutory responsibility for the concerns of future generations is an appealing one. Moreover, I think the idea would be politically popular as well. Obviously, the specific details would have to be fully explored, but I would suggest something like a six-year term, not subject to reappointment. Appointment would be made by the President, subject to confirmation by the Senate. Possibly, the Ombudsperson could issue a small, periodic report; however, the principal function of the position would be advice to the President on the very long term consequences of contemplated programs and policies.

■ **Initiate Two Issue-Oriented Pilot Projects Emphasizing Foresight.**
The lead role for these projects should probably be delegated to departments of the Executive Branch, but they would be under the general direction of the Special Assistant for Foresight to ensure breadth of focus. The projects would have two objectives: *first,* to make a real and substantive contribution; *second,* to demonstrate the capabilities of the government if issue-oriented foresight were made a matter of high priority. The issue areas I would choose are:
■ National agricultural and land-use policy and its impact on U.S. foreign policy.
■ The domestic and foreign policy impact of the micro-electronic and computer revolution.

■ **Convene a Meeting of a Small Number of the Presidents of the Most Outstanding Universities in the Nation to Address the Lack of a Foresight Orientation in Our Educational System.**
Propose That They Incorporate Mandatory Topics Relating to Foresight in Their Entrance and Graduation Requirements.
The lack of emphasis on national foresight capability in our educational system at all levels is also a national disgrace. However, as a former university administrator, I know that introducing changes in curricula is a long, arduous task. The standards set by leading universities are, I believe, a powerful point of leverage. If they were to take the lead, both secondary and higher education in general would have to follow. Students (and especially their parents) would demand it.

■ **Establish a "Clearinghouse for Foresight Activities." This Office Would Also Be Responsible for Follow-Up Activities Related to *The Global 2000 Report,* including Additional Periodic Reports.**
The clearinghouse function is one that could and should be undertaken even if the President decides not to make a major commitment to foresight. It also makes sense to commission periodic studies similar to *The Global 2000 Report.*

■ **Form a Task Force to Explore the Possibility of *Greater* Standardization of Regions, of Data Bases, and of the Inputs and Outputs of Models Developed by the Federal Government.**
This sounds like a weak recommendation. However, *complete* standardization could be a very mixed blessing. The present state of the art in the field of foresight is such that, for the next few years, we need to make sure that we do not stifle creativity and experimentation as we move toward greater standardization. We should proceed carefully and seek an appropriate balance between extremes.

■ **Direct the Office of Management and Budget [OMB] to Develop and Enforce, Without Equivocation, the Most Meticulous and Rigorous Documentation Standards for all Models Developed With Public Funds.**
The state of documentation in the field of modeling is a disgrace. Poor documentation wastes money and degrades the field. The present state of affairs can no longer be tolerated. If the enforcement of documentation standards were assigned to the OMB, perhaps documentation would be taken more seriously.

Enterprise:

The Private Sector

A Businessman's View:

Social Systems in Trouble

By Roy R. Anderson

The insurance business as a special window:

■ The insurance business feels immediately the impact of any major event affecting society—whether it be a natural catastrophe such as an earthquake, or an made event of human origin such as a riot or depression.

■ The insurance business is usually one of the first of our institutions to feel the cutting edge of change, whether in lifestyles, in driving practices, or in laws.

■ The problems of the insurance business are closely related to broader and deeper societal issues, so that insurance companies have no choice but to consider the long term.

■ An overview of the problems of the insurance business may help placing larger societal problems in clearer focus and even suggest some solutions.

Decades of Change

The 1970s were unusual years for the insurance business, as for all of our society. It was a period in the insurance business in which serious questions were raised as to whether some of our insurance systems are systemically flawed. Proposals were made that would have produced major, fundamental changes in some of those systems—and, in turn, in the social systems to which insurance is integrally related. In all such proposals, the public interest was deeply involved.

"No-Fault" insurance: As the 1970s began, bills were being considered in Congress for "Federal No-Fault Auto Liability Insurance"—and variations of such plans had already become law in a number of states. The major charge against the traditional system of Auto Liability Insurance was that it was a very inefficient way to provide "compensation" to auto accident victims, and had become much too expensive.

Similar charges then were raised against Medical Malpractice Liability Insurance, and Product Liability Insurance. Although there was a great deal of furor about these issues during the 1970s—and although a good number of state legislatures did take remedial actions—the basic underlying difficulties of these systems persist today.

Health insurance and escalating health-care costs: The 1970s also began with another proposal that had existed in one form or another for about two decades: a system of National Health Insurance [NHI]. By the mid-1970s, it seemed that adoption of some form of NHI had become "inevitable." But in 1976 the costs of medical care increased sharply, and in retrospect it appears that 1975 was the high-water mark with respect to the possibility of enacting a full-scale system of comprehensive National Health Insurance. Since 1976 the rate of increase in the costs of medical care have run substantially ahead of the inflation rate for the rest of the economy.

The major problem of the health care and health insurance systems in recent years has been to "control costs." Because there has come to be general recognition that no effective way has yet been found to control such costs, there has come int being a consensus that the nation could not afford to adopt any of the numerous forms of National Health Insurance that have been proposed.

Insurance as investment: Virtually

all forms of insurance felt the impact of a sharp increase, during the latter half of the 1970s, in the rate of economic inflation—at times at a double-digit rate. Because we cannot foresee an end to continued, severe inflation, this increasingly gives rise to questions as to the viability of certain forms of insurance.

This question may be directed even to as venerable a form of insurance as the Whole Life (or Ordinary Life) insurance policy, but also to other forms of insurance with a substantial "investment" element built into their structure.

Challenge to the classification of risks: Still another challenge arose in the late 1970s and continues in full force in the 1980s. Virtually all forms of insurance—both governmental and private, and property and casualty as well as life and health—have come under great pressure for a major systemic revision with respect to the practice of how groups at risk are categorized, or "classified."

This is a weighty and complex subject. I cite it simply because it is an issue that has emerged as the result of important changes in societal values, such as those relating to privacy; discrimination by age, sex, or marital status; charging premiums by area of residence; and so forth.

Pensions: Difficult though the foregoing problems may be, we may find that during the 1980s the most serious difficulties in the insurance area will be encountered in pensions—both private and governmental.

The current system of private pension plans will come under great strain as inflation increasingly undermines their value and effectiveness. Many state and municipal governments may be unable to fulfill their obligations—either because their plans were unduly liberal in their design, or because the ability to levy taxes has diminished, or because the ability to raise money through the bond market has been drastically curtailed.

I could sail futher on in this "sea of troubles." But I will close with the observation that the Social Security System itself will come under increasing pressure. As it is constructed today, younger generations pay increasing rates of taxation to support the Social Security payments of those of us in older generations.

What will this mean at a time in the future when the productive capacity of our economy may be stabilizing, or decreasing, as energy and resources become scarcer?

Searching for the Fundamental Problems

All of the problems I've just described are, to some degree, "systemic" in nature. But as I analyzed each of them in those terms, I became aware that the real roots of each of them were entwined in a deeper problem. The underlying social systems were themselves in trouble.

For example, the problems of liability insurance arose in large measure due to the fact that the system of tort law was being expanded drastically in scope (with increasing costs to the public). This expansion leads to the basic question whether our entire system of law is now truly serving the interests of justice and equity.

Some of the problems of the health insurance system could be traced, in a similar way, to problems of the underlying health care system, as I will explain in detail later. What was happening was that all lines of insurance were undergoing trauma because of instability in the underlying economic system, and especially because of inflation.

A New Awareness

Two other events had jolted me earlier into an awareness that some deep-rooted problems in our society were beginning to surface.

■ The race riots in the late 1960s in Watts, Detroit, Newark, and other U.S. cities, harshly underscored the messages we were hearing from the protesters of the Vietnam war and the dissidents on the college campus.

■ The "Torrey Canyon" disaster was almost trivial in comparison to the riots, but it had a profound impact upon me. The "Torrey Canyon" was a jumbo oil tanker that broke up off the coast of

Who am I?   **Roy R. Anderson**

Roy Anderson is a Vice President for Strategic Planning for Allstate Insurance Company. By profession he is an actuary, which is in the nature of being an engineer of the systems of insurance. He is a Fellow of the Society of Actuaries, and since the mid-1970s his responsibilities have been with long-range future corporate planning.

Anderson is a member of the Committee on Futurism of the Society of Actuaries, the World Future Society, the Steering Committee of the Trend Analysis Program of the American Life Insurance Association, and a board member of the U.S. Association for The Club of Rome.

Ireland and had fouled the coastal beaches and the sea.

The problem of the "Torrey Canyon" for the insurance business was in determining the amount of liability, a question of dollars and cents.

But for me the "Torrey Canyon" disaster posed a deeper question of whether such an enterprise should ever have been permitted? Had the preoccupation of our society with placing dollar values on almost everything blinded us to the real nature of the risks of some of our commercial and business ventures?

So when I first learned of The Club of Rome and of *The Limits to Growth,* I had already accepted the basic message of that report. Essentially, that message was that the world is confronted with a goodly number of interlocking global problems which, if not recognized and properly addressed, could lead to catastrophe.

In my view, the *Limits* report was not a doomsday message, although it has been commonly so described. The report suggested that we face doom only if we continue on mindlessly with the production/consumption and growth/expansion goals that have been characteristic of industrialized nations, especially during the years since World War 2. This book is, of course, another example of an attempt to help us avoid following that course to destruction.

The end of industrial society: Another part of the "message" of The Club of Rome appears to have been much less widely heard. This is that our civilization has entered a period of transition. After a period of roughly 200 years, Western Industrial Society has ended. And, at some time during the next decade or so, we will begin to see the outlines of a new society with different perceptions, different beliefs, different values, and different institutions.

In my view, this latter concept is of greater importance than the more commonly heard message of the world problematique, or "problem of our interlocking problems." The latter are our problems of population, pollution, consumption of natural resources, etc. These are indeed grave. But I believe it is of even deeper significance that we are now in the process of changing how we see things, what we believe in, and how we value things. *And, entwined in these deeply personal changes, some of the institutions that support our society are in the process of a comprehensive systemic change.*

We have arrived at one of the most difficult and elusive features of the challenges that confront us: the concept that some of our social institutions must, and will, undergo systemic change.

It is exceedingly difficult for anyone to see that an institution they know and rely on may no longer be properly serving the purpose for which it was intended. It is hard to see that such a system can no longer be "repaired," but must undergo a fundamental change (or even be replaced or abandoned). And, for each of us, it is almost impossible to see such a need if the institution happens to be our own.

We may find in the future that our experience in the 1980s will have been summed up by Hans Christian Andersen long ago in his fable of "The Emperor's New Clothes." The Emperor had bought and paid for some magnificent clothes. But they were so magnificent their magnificence was visible only to the wise; they were invisible to fools. Neither the emperor nor the adults around him, for fear of being deemed fools, would say what was obvious—that these magnificent clothes were but a trick. Or perhaps they were mesmerized by their duties in the court and simply assumed that the emperor was clothed.

In Hans Christian Andersen's fable, it was a child who finally said what should have been obvious to all, that the emperor wore no clothes.

"Now then, is there anything else? Shirts? Socks? How about this tie?"

Drawing by Noel Ford ©1980 Punch

MAKING IT HAPPEN:

We face a similar problem with some of our major institutions. They aren't providing the product or the service for which they were designed. Sometimes what has happened is that the product or service is now being provided is actually quite different from that which we conventionally think of it as being.

Like the emperor's new clothes, these too are extremely hard to see. We persist in seeing what we expect to see, or what we want, or even need, to see.

Let me try to illustrate this with a case-study of a system with which I have been involved throughout most of my career: health insurance, and the related health care system of medicine.

Medical Care for What?

Laser test for malignancy

To refer to our system of medicine as "health care" is a serious misnomer. The annual cost of this system is spiralling up towards $200 billion—and virtually all of the care that is provided by doctors and surgeons, by nurses and hospitals, is devoted to the cure of sickness or the avoidance and postponement of death.

When a patient has been dismissed from treatment by this medical care system, his sickness may have been cured—but he will seldom have achieved the state of good health. "Health" is not the calling of medicine.

The expression "health insurance" is doubly a misnomer. It has even less to do with health than does the medical profession. Most of the efforts by doctors which are oriented toward *maintaining* good health (e.g., consultation for better diet or life style) are not covered by an insurance policy. Also, health insurance is not so much insurance as it is a method of pre-paying medical costs—i.e., a system of financing rather than insurance.

So we have an important clue that something may be amiss in the systems of health care and health insurance in the fact that each has so very little to do with health.

More than semantics: What we call a thing helps determine how we think about that thing and how we value it. Calling our system of medicine a

"health care delivery system" has contributed greatly to enthusiastic public support for the growth of that system.

Where fault has been found in the system, it has usually been that some aspect has been deemed inadequate in some way, and the resulting decision has been that the system should be further enlarged. We have regarded the system of medicine itself as an unalloyed blessing.

Partly because of this perception, we have been unsuccessful in devising any effective way of controlling its burgeoning costs.

Costs out of control: Why is it that there can be no effective control of costs under our present interrelated systems of medical care and its financing by "health insurance" (both private and governmental forms)?

A CAT-scan

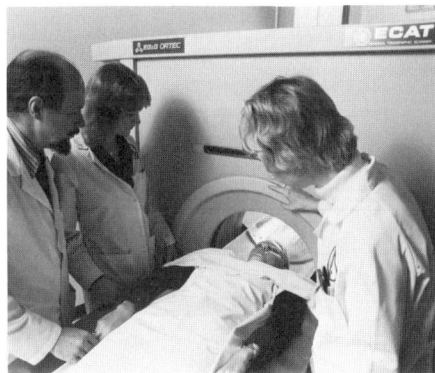

The cause lies at the deepest roots of our medical system, the point at which physicians prescribe care for their sick patient. Especially if the illness is serious, for both patient and physician one issue is paramount: the best possible and most immediate care for the patient.

In the vast majority of cases, the patient has little or no concern as to costs; 90 percent of Americans are adeqately insured in some way for medical care. In recent years another factor has been added to this picture. Doctors have been motivated by the success in the courts of medical malpractice suit when treatment has been unsuccessful, so doctors now, at no financial expense to most patients, can prescribe further tests, additional consultations, and expensive care—all "to be sure."

A trail of dollar bills: One way of tracing the origins of our present system of medicine over the past four decades is to follow the trail of dollar bills.

Hospitalization insurance began in the depression years of the 1930s when a group of hospitals in Texas devised a system of pre-payment under which the public, by payment of regular monthly premiums, could be assured hospital care when required. Thus was Blue Cross born—not, it may be noted, as an insurance service to the public, but as a means for the hospitals to be assured of revenue.

The fact that insurance for medical care had its origins in a system of pre-payment for hospitalization had much to do with the subsequent development of the system of medicine itself. In the 1930s and 1940s, hospitals were regarded as places for the treatment of the seriously ill. In those days, it was intended that health insurance would provide coverage mainly for serious illness—and, thus, in those days, only medical expenses incurred for treatment in a hospital were covered by insurance.

But, gradually and steadily physicians adapted their practice so as to admit their patients to hospital confinement whenever possible so that their medical care would be paid for.

There was nothing wrong with these actions. They were the logical responses of the participants in a system to changes in that system.

Two other developments of a monetary nature played an important role in the years after World War 2 in determining the direction of medical care. The first was the federal Hill-Burton Act, which helped finance the building of hospitals. The second was the growth in research grants that encouraged study of the more serious and catastrophic forms of illness, and thereby fostered further specialization of medicine.

The Role of Private Enterprise

There is no evidence to indicate that the challenge of creating our future can be met by relying totally on the government. On the contrary, we will have to depend upon institutions, organizations and individuals in the private, non-governmental sector also to provide creativity and leadership.

As we become more clear about the purposes of our own lives and think further about a desirable future, we will be led also to do the same sort of thinking about our organizations and institutions.

■ *Our "health care" system,* Roy Anderson points out, is not really designed or operated to promote better health.

■ *The purpose of employment* may not be, principally, to provide income, Glenn Watts and Lou Gerber remind us.

■ *The source of disillusionment with organized religion* may be that the church has so far refused to be what it claimed, according to Episcopalian Bishop of Washington, DC, John Walker.

We must remember that the institutions we have created were intended to be our servants, not our masters. Human institutions, like human beings, can change.

The Pursuit of Health

As a result of the forces I have described, all of an economic origin, we now have a system of medicine in the United States that is highly specialized, technologically oriented, hospital-based, very expensive, and increasing in cost at a higher rate than the rest of our inflating economy.

Systemic problems in controlling costs: There are several very human reasons why we have not been able to place the problem of medical costs in clear perspective.

■ Virtually none of those who are addressing the problem of controlling medical costs are themselves affected by those costs. Members of the medical profession are taken care of through professional courtesy or are well insured. Also insured are the cognizant governmental personnel—politicians and bureaucrats. The same is true of the members of corporations and representatives of labor who are involved in decisions about the medical care system.

In fact, none of those who customarily discuss the problems are

themselves adversely affected by the high costs of medical care. Many are, in some way, beneficiaries of the dollar flow through the medical care system.

Even most of the public is not directly and immediately affected by the increasing cost of medical care. Most are covered by health insurance, either through their employer or by a government agency. Typically, the larger share of group premiums are borne by the employer. And, to make this system even more entrenched and seemingly to the benefit of employees, the premium payments by an employer are not counted as taxable income to the employee.

"Health" is not the objective. I said earlier that the word "health" was really a misnomer when applied to these systems—and that the use of the word had caused us to perceive and think about those systems wrongly.

In the same vein, I suggest we are wrong when we think of health insurance—whether private or governmental—as being primarily a system for protecting the public. Granted, it does

provide such protection.

Nevertheless, I suggest that a more accurate perception of these systems of insurance is that they serve to assure the medical profession of a rich and growing source of income. And both the size of that flow and its direction is largely within the control of the profession itself.

Why most proposed "solutions" will not work: How can we find our way out of this labyrinth we have worked ourselves into over the past four decades or so?

We might hope that the answer could be found in the many proposals that have been offered during the myriad hearings held by Congressional committees. Unfortunately, they would lead us even further into the labyrinth. Some of these proposals have been aimed at controlling costs by imposing artificial limits on hospital costs. Others have offered amazingly complex schemes to control costs by purporting to introduce competition in the medical care "marketplace"—or by adjusting the income-tax structure relating to the treatment of health insurance premiums.

The activities of the medical profession cannot be controlled by manipulating economic factors that are far removed from the doctor/patient relationship, where the critical decisions affecting costs are made. These attempts to do so would seem to represent the ultimate in tunnel vision by economists.

Other proposals would further expand health insurance coverages by mandating coverage for catastrophic illness, while some propose the ultimate solution of a full-scale comprehensive system of National Health Care with the hope that government agencies could control the costs of the medical profession.

None of these proposals would be effective in controlling medical costs. In fact, most could turn an already thoroughly complicated mess into something even worse.

Yet the proposals have been developed by experts with the best of intentions. How can this be?

I believe the answer is that some experts suffer from "economic astigmatism": their vision has been distorted by their preoccupation with viewing systems from a purely economic perspective. Others, however, are simply unable to see that "the emperor wears no clothes"—for example, that their systems have little to do with health.

Where, then, shall we find the solution? I suggest it will be found only by disengaging ourselves from all of the details we have just been considering, and trying to define more accurately the real purposes and goals of our "health care" system.

For myself, this began with an inquiry as to the meaning of "health." One of the best articles I found was a profound paper by Dr. Leon M. Kass, appropriately titled "Regarding the End of Medicine and the Pursuit of Health," in *The Public Interest* magazine (1975). Then for several years I studied health practices and health modalities, many of which may not be considered part of the medical establishment and most of which are not considered appropriate for health insurance.

■ I have learned that health comprises physical health, mental health, and spiritual health—and that these three concepts are intertwined and indivisible.

■ Something else that is equally important is that for each of us, our state of health is our own individual responsibility—and we each have an obligation both to ourselves and to society to conduct ourselves so as to achieve and maintain the state of good health.

One of the most heartwarming developments of recent years is to observe the extent to which the public itself has come to a growing awareness of what health is and how best it can be achieved through individual action.

This has been manifested in many ways: programs of physical fitness, such as jogging, running, tennis, etc.; the increasing interest in better nutrition and the rejection of junk foods; movements aimed at "inner peace"—biofeedback, relaxation response, meditation, etc.; the avoidance of bad health habits, such as smoking; and many others.

National Park Service, U.S. Department of the Interior

R_{X.} for Systems That Are Not Working

My associates in the health insurance business can rightly say that the foregoing observations are both inadequate and uneven. And my friends in the rapidly developing "wholistic health" movement would describe the last few paragraphs as being only a brief beginning of an explanation of the significance of their activities.

However, my purpose here is to put in perspective some things that may be helpful as we address deeper societal issues that are the main subject of this book. I would suggest that the following conclusions may be appropriate:

■ **Much of our difficulty in addressing the problems that confront our society is that we fail to identify the nature of the problems—especially when the "system" is no longer providing a product or service that best meets the needs of the public.**

■ **When a system has become so basically flawed that it can no longer be repaired but must undergo fundamental change, those who are least capable of recognizing the nature of the problem are the experts within that system.**

The reason is that the experts' personal values are deeply enmeshed in the present system. So long as their values remain unchanged, so also will their perception of the role of that system remain unchanged.

■ **Economics** has been the language of Western industrial society. However, the economic perspective that has been meaningful in guiding our society during the past 200 years of expansion and growth now often serves to distort our understanding of how our society functions. Ideas that gave us direction during a bygone era of seemingly abundant cheap energy and limitless natural resources now serve to blind us to a growing reality of scarcity.

■ The combination of the preceding two conclusions leads to the perception that *the economist is the expert who is probably least able to understand the nature of the global problems that now confront society.*

David L. Ames

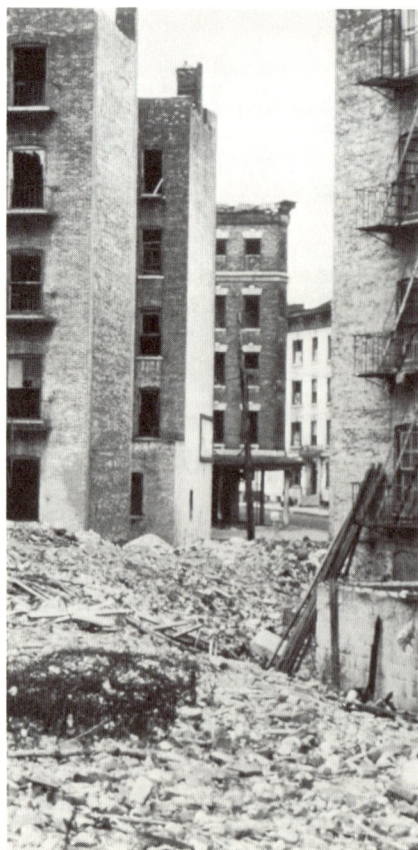

This is not intended as a polemic against economics and economists. Nor the medical profession. Nor my own business of insurance. Rather, my comments are addressed to the reader who is not an economist or a businessman, including my fellow authors in this book.

■ **The message is that the business community is no longer capable of taking on additional obligations in order to meet new needs that someone decides "must" be addressed.**

This is the case whether those needs pertain to segments of our society within the United States or to foreign countries, such as the nations of the Third and Fourth World.

In fact, the challenges for survival for the business community are no less grave than are the challenges for other institutions.

Where does the answer lie to the problems identified by the world problematique? I can only suggest what I have learned from my studies of the insurance business.

I believe we will begin to find answers only when we begin properly to identify the problems. To do this, we must understand that our civilization has begun a period of transformation—a period during which new perceptions of reality, new beliefs, and new values are emerging. My own sense is that we will begin to see things more clearly as we begin to find better and more durable values to supplant those that have undergirded our society and economy for so long.   □

Detroit continues to struggle with the dark reputation that it turns out cars inferior to those made by Japanese or West German manufacturers and that American workers are not sufficiently productive.

But one Big Three plant belies such notoriety. The General Motors factory in Tarrytown, New York, one of the plants where the company assembles its hot-selling front-wheel-drive Chevrolet Citations, has earned the reputation of being perhaps the giant automaker's most efficient assembly facility.

Tarrytown's current renown is more surprising because in the early 1970s the 55-year-old plant was infamous for having one of the worst labor-relations and poorest quality records at GM.

The turnaround at Tarrytown grew out of the realization by local management and union representatives that inefficiencies and industrial strife threatened the plant's continued operation. Automakers sometimes use forced plant closings caused by sluggish auto sales to unload a lemon facility. Ford, for example, decided...to shut the gates of its huge Mahwah, New Jersey, plant largely because it had a poor quality record.

After Tarrytown lost a truck production facility in 1971, bosses and workers became fearful for their jobs and got together to find better ways to build cars. At first hesitantly but later with enthusiasm, they embarked on an unusual joint experiment to improve work and to tap shop-floor expertise for running the factory.

The setting for the initiative could hardly have been more dismal. Some 7 percent of the plant's workers were regularly failing to appear for work, and the number of outstanding employee grievances against management totaled 2,000. The result of the confrontation and conflict was sloppy work, rapidly rising dealer complaints, and an unprecedented number of disciplinary and dismissal notices.

"Workers and bosses were constantly at each other's throats," recalls Gus Beirne, then general superintendent of the plant. Agrees Larry Sheridan, the former United Auto Workers shop chairman at Tarrytown: "It sure as hell was a battleground."

The first significant payoff from the new mood at the plant came at model changeover time in 1971 and then again the following year.

GM management showed workers the proposed changes in the assembly line and invited their comments. Says Beirne: "A lot of good ideas came forward, and we were shown a lot of problems we didn't realize existed. Things we had missed were picked up, and we had time to implement them before the start of the new models."

The cost savings produced by simply sharing information with the shop floor encouraged Tarrytown's executives to move further. In 1972, the plant's supervisors began holding regular meetings with workers on company time to discuss worker complaints and ideas for boosting efficiency.

In order to turn the gripe sessions into something more substantive, both sides agreed to bring in an outside consultant to organize worker-participation projects. They chose Sydney Rubinstein, 52, a former blue-collar tool-and-die worker and white-collar engineer, who had become an expert on worker innovation and productivity.

Rubinstein's first breakthrough came in a trial project with Tarrytown's 30 windshield installers. Half of the workers had been disciplined during the previous six months for poor work.

During discussions it was revealed that each worker selected a different point around the windshield to begin applying the sealant. One worker explained that he started at the spot where the radio antenna wires emerged from the windshield because "you get a little extra adhesive, a puddle, and that stops

leaks." That little trick was new to the other workers, the foreman, and the plant engineers. The method was immediately adopted and resulted in a rapid reduction in the number of dealers' complaints.

Later, the plant's body-shop workers held informal discussions on welding problems. Within a few months, the percentage of bad welds dropped from 35 percent to 1.5 percent. When the small voluntary program of worker participation was expanded to the plant's 3,800 employees, 95 percent of them took part. The plan eventually cost GM $1.5 million.

As a result of these projects, workers say, they now readily inform supervisors that they would rather discuss problems than knock heads. "The evolution that has taken place is terrific," says Ray Calore, president of the local UAW. "There are no longer any hidden-ball tricks. If management has a problem, we sit and discuss it."

No panacea, but lots of benefits: The UAW insists that job-participation programs like those at Tarrytown are neither a panacea to end all labor disputes nor just a management tool to boost output. But giving workers a greater voice in their job can improve productivity by bringing about declines in grievances, absenteeism, and waste.

The benefits...are clear. Since 1976, the Tarrytown plant has turned out high-quality products. There are now only about 30 outstanding worker grievances, while absenteeism has fallen by two-thirds, to 2.5 percent. Disciplinary orders, firings, worker turnover, and breakage all show significant declines. Says Dartmouth Business Administration Professor Robert H. Guest: "Tarrytown represents in microcosm the beginnings of what may become commonplace in the future—a new collaborative approach on the part of management, unions, and workers to improve the quality of life at work in its broadest sense."

TIME Magazine, May 5, 1980

A POSITIVE GUIDE TO THE FUTURE

General Motors production line with robots

Organized Labor:

"Busy Being Born"

By **Glenn E. Watts,** president, Communications Workers of America,
and member, Executive Council, AFL-CIO

and Lou Gerber, registered lobbyist, Government Relations Office, CWA, Washington, DC

A period of reordering our priorities: The United States is entering a new economic epoch, and the American labor movement is alert to that fact. In the decades ahead, mastery over the physical environment will no longer guarantee growth in productivity and in employment.

We are already seeing a heightened interplay between technological development, the availability of vital resources, and changes in human values. The evolving recombination of these forces will form the DNA "building block" that will determine organized labor's role in the United States and in the world.

The traditional image of America has been of a cornucopia endlessly able to satisfy consumer appetites. But because of the transition that is now under way, that image is giving way to a new reality. As a consequence, the United States will now endure a period of painful readjustment, as we seek to cope with natural resources that are shrinking and a slower pace of economic expansion.

As America enters a post-affluent period of reordered priorities, this process of transformation will stand in marked contrast to the unparalleled economic uplift experienced by our nation's wage earners since the end of World War 2. Indeed, as working

people in the decades ahead contend with what Buckminster Fuller has described as "more with less," they will experience a series of austere challenges.

One outcome will be a new ethic, which will significantly alter the landscape of human values. It will extol the virtues of recycling and conservation. It will rein in the impulse that drives us to acquire and consume material goods.

158

Technology and Jobs

As new technologies flourish and others gradually disappear, the jobs of many wage earners are going to be eliminated or radically altered. And our country will confront the perplexing problem of providing these displaced wage earners with employment opportunities and suitable working conditions.

The development of efficient new machines may constitute "progress." But the evolution of useful inanimate devices can also be accompanied by the dark prospects of unemployment, personal alienation, and economic upheaval. It is understandable that workers dread and resist being simply cast aside as social driftwood before the onrush of technology.

Yet without the improved productivity that comes with the development of more efficient machines, America and the world may not be able to meet essential human needs. So, like Solomon, we face a dilemma as we try to balance adverse arguments, a dilemma that will demand our most creative thinking.

The telecommunications industry and its patterns of technological development are a case study of all this. New devices are rapidly coming into use which will significantly transform the composition of the telephone industry's labor force in the coming decades. In fact, massive changes are already altering job content and skill requirements. In particular, efficient electronic switching systems and broad-based computerization of operations are causing a decrease in labor requirements throughout the industry.

Examples of new instrumentalities of telecommunication that are being developed, with portentous potential impact on jobs, are glass fiber cables and a contrivance known as a millimeter wave guide. The glass fiber cables will transmit pulses of light in place of the electrical signals and radio waves now in use. The millimeter wave guide is an underground tube through which radio signals are transmitted.

It is not yet clear which of these evolving systems, waveguide technology or fiber optics, will be the primary telecommunications transmission medium of the future. But what is becoming unmistakably evident is that either or both could profoundly alter the composition of the industry's basic workforce.

■ Telephone operators have already been enormously affected by indoor developments in telecommunications. The switchboard, for example, has been replaced by an electronic console that automates most of the switching and billing tasks on previously operator-assisted and long-distance calls.

■ Intercept operators, who handle calls to disconnected or other nonworking numbers, are being supplanted by a machine that automatically handles such calls. This is done by means of computer-assembled voice response, explaining the cause of the interception and providing new number information.

■ An automatic coin telephone soon to be tried involves a further threat to telephone operators' jobs. This machine can monitor and compute charges on coin phone calls without any operator contact at all.

Jobs traditionally held by women have been adversely affected by these recent innovations and impending changes more than jobs traditionally held by men. Male employees in the industry have been engaged largely in construction, installation, and telephone maintenance occupations. In the future, however, technological change will also affect a wider variety of telecommunications employment, including the highly skilled craft positions that have been dominated by men.

A possible solution to this and similar problems in other American industries would be to require, as a component of technological advancement, careful examination of the implications of proposed industrial advances for job dislocation. Such an examination could be made a mandatory part of an overall assessment of a new product's value to society.

In any case, if the United States and other nations are to avoid creating a large class of dissident unemployed former wage earners, there will need to be a heightened awareness of the job dislocation prospects inherent in technological development. And it will be essential to have available job retraining programs and, if necessary, adjustment assistance to help displaced workers overcome job dislocation.

More generally, when a technological development threatens the well-being of large numbers of workers in any industry, the government should be required to conduct a human dignity or social impact study. This would parallel the requirement under the National Environmental Policy Act of 1969 that an environmental impact statement [EIS] be prepared before major public projects are undertaken.

Just as today the design of proposed bridges or dams must include an EIS about impacts and alternative ways to less endanger the environment, the effect of the implementation of technological changes on human dignity and social well-being should be an integral part of our technological progress and rational economic planning.

Technological change and job-induced stress: The notion of a human dignity impact study would also be relevant in another challenging area, that of the relationship between technological change and job-induced stress. Most research in this area has been centered on the "stress of success," the workaholic pattern among middle and upper-level management in business. In 1979, however, the Communications Workers of America [CWA] conducted a national "job pressures" day to sensitize the public to the stresses that workers are currently experiencing in coping with the modern worksite, impassive supervisors, and mechanization.

In the future, labor will emphasize the need for close scrutiny of the stress of adjusting to changing work roles. Examples of the many facets of this problem are compulsory overtime work in a leisure-oriented society, entrapment in dead-end jobs, and the feeling of many workers that they are treated like "machines" rather than people. Negative feelings arising from such work-related problems directly contribute to job dissatisfaction, absenteeism, and stress-related illnesses.

Technology affects working people not only by reducing the need for their services and by producing job-related stress, but also by changing the patterns of activity at the workplace. To assess the implications of technological change for working people, the Communications Workers of America recently held the first national conference sponsored by an American labor union to focus exclusively on helping workers adjust to new patterns of work.

A theme repeatedly emphasized by union delegates attending this conference was the need for continuing education and retraining to enable employees to keep abreast of new techniques and equipment. This need for the enhancement of old skills and the acquisition of new ones contrasted sharply with the situation in the past, when workers went to school or enrolled in apprenticeship and training programs that were expected to prepare them for lifelong careers.

To analyze further the present awkward relationship between the technology of tomorrow and future employment, the labor movement must continue to monitor all new developments and their potential impact on workers.

Similarly, *the actual number of women in America's workforce leaped in the same period by almost 40 percent, from 31.5 million to 44 million.* The women who have entered the labor force in recent years were not, by and large, "liberated" women in quest of self-fulfillment. Instead, they were bringing home an essential second income necessary to put food on the table, buy shoes for their children, and pay the rent or make a mortgage payment.

As a result of the changing male/female composition of the workforce, only a small percentage of the country's 58 million families today consist of a father who works and a mother who remains at home, the pattern of a generation ago.

■ As a sidelight of this new social situation, one of the most illuminating statistics of our time is the fact that *8.5 million American families are now solely supported by women breadwinners.*

■ Despite the growing number of working women, and the existence of equal pay laws, *female workers earned only 59¢ for every dollar male employees were paid in 1979.* By comparison, 40 years ago, in 1939, wages of female workers comprised 58 percent of male salaries, meaning that despite the recent emphasis on equal rights and affirmative action in the workplace, there has been a change of only one percent in four decades.

The low pay of these workers has resulted largely from the fact that women have been segregated into female job ghettos. For example:
■ 80 percent of women in the workforce are found in the lowest-paying, least-skilled, least-unionized occupations.
■ One-third of all female employees are in clerical occupations, the same proportion as a decade ago.
■ 98.6 percent of all secretary-typists, 97 percent of nurses, 91.5 percent of bank tellers, 90.7 percent of bookkeepers, and 86 percent of file clerks are women.
■ Despite the increases in the number of women in the American workforce, only 6.7 percent of all female wage earners carried a union card as of 1979. Between 1976 and 1978, however, the labor movement gained one-half

The Changing Workforce

Burgeoning technological developments may well revolutionize the way in which Americans live in the future, but human energy and skill will continue to be the United States'—and the world's—most precious resource. The nature of our national workforce is rapidly changing, however, and will soon bear little resemblance to the employment picture we knew as recently as a decade ago.

■ In the coming years, *the rate of growth of the domestic workforce will decline drastically* as a result of the slowing increase in the number of working-age individuals. The Congressional Joint Economic Committee has projected the expansion of the labor force to be only two-fifths as rapid in the next decade as it was in the last one.

■ Moreover, as the post-World War 2 baby-boom generation approaches middle age, *a major transformation will occur in the age of American jobholders.* Persons in the 25–54 age group in the United States constituted 61 percent of the total workforce in the middle of the 1970s, but they will amount to almost 90 percent in 1990. Teenagers and young adults (ages 16–24), who comprised 27 percent of the labor force in 1975, will make up only 18.5 percent by 1990.

■ Despite the slowdown in the rate of growth of the workforce, *the labor movement anticipates more and more young workers of both sexes will choose to benefit from collective representation.* It is especially interesting for the future of the labor movement to note that *the majority of union members today are under 40 years of age, and a substantial part of the majority consists of those under 30. The average age of union members is expected to decrease in the coming years.*

Women in the workforce: *This slowdown in the growth of the labor force will be somewhat offset by a continuing increase in employment participation rates among women.* In 1970, 43 percent of women held jobs. Nine years later, a clear majority, 51.4 percent of women were employed.

An industrial electrician at work

million new female workers. Because of this sudden upsurge, *women now constitute 27.4 percent of all organized American workers.*

■ *Eleven million more women are expected to enter the workforce by 1990.* Many of these new women workers, along with those currently employed, will be motivated to join unions if the deplorable disparity between the pay of female and male wage earners is not corrected.

In the coming period, the labor movement will redouble its efforts to organize women, especially those in clerical, retail, and other traditionally female jobs. Labor unions will seek to raise women's consciousness so that they will become aware that there is no better road to economic equality in the workplace than via a union contract.

A related trend involving female members of the labor force is the goal of "equal pay for comparable work." Recently, with this goal in mind, the Equal Employment Opportunity Commission launched a study to determine whether procedures exist or can be developed to measure and evaluate women's jobs according to their "real worth."

The purpose of the study is to devise a means of ensuring that real progress will be made toward seeing that wages paid all workers reflect skill, effort,

responsibility, and working conditions—without regard to the sex of the jobholder. Promotion of the concept of equal pay for comparable work was urged in a resolution adopted unanimously by the 105 affiliated unions at the AFL-CIO's convention in November, 1979.

College graduates entering the labor force: In addition to women, the number of college graduates entering the labor force will expand in the near future.

■ The National Planning Association projects that, *by 1985, there will be an annual surplus of 700,000 college graduates relative to professional and technical jobs available.* Estimates of the total oversupply of recent degree recipients in comparison to the positions open to them range as high as 6–8 million by 1990.

This gloomy prospect contrasts sharply with the expectations of college students, 68 percent of whom, according to a recent poll, will be seeking jobs in which they can express themselves and 77 percent of whom will be looking for a challenge in their employment.

■ The predictable clash of high hopes with harsh reality may trigger a traumatic reversal of the historical pattern in which successive generations of college graduates have obtained employment in work of a higher status than that in which their parents were engaged. Instead, *many degree holders may be forced to accept jobs of lower status, although they will have received more education.*

Disillusionment from this experience could result in a rise of alienation and the development in the United States of a class of dissident, underutilized intellectuals similar to those who form a chief ingredient in the seething cauldron of frustration that often erupts in emerging nations. A "Coxey's Army" of unemployed college graduates, however, could be avoided through the development of programs similar to the Federal Writers and Artists Projects undertaken in the 1930s.

Continuing shift to a "service economy": An additional prominent feature of the labor force in the years to come will be the continuing shift in the

ENTERPRISE

United States to a "service economy." America first became a service economy in the early 1950s, when more than half of the labor force became employed in non-goods-producing industries. Indeed, during the quarter-century from 1950 through 1974, only a little over one million of 27 million new jobs added were in goods-related industries.

■ Early in the 20th century 3 out of every 10 jobs were in service industries. But by 1970 it was 6 out of 10. And *by the mid-1980s, only 20 percent of the labor force will produce all of our agricultural and manufactured goods, while the remaining workforce will be concentrated in services.*

Workers' Values Changing

As its physical resources dwindle, America is beginning to experience a stunning revival of neglected human values. Reflecting this humanistic reawakening, the range of workers' values is undergoing a rapid transformation.

■ *Employees are placing a growing emphasis on attaining self-fulfillment at the worksite as a basic human need.* As we approach the third millennium, "being rather than having" may become the ultimate value at the workplace as well as in other phases of life.

Because of this development, "self-actualization" may well be the psychological watchword of the future in labor-management relations and in industrial psychology. This term connotes improving one's opportunities for individual development, autonomy, and choice.

■ The United Auto Workers has pioneered in the emerging trend toward emphasis on the *"quality of worklife."* The UAW signed an agreement in 1973 with General Motors, which urged local management and employee groups to cooperate in experiments and projects designed to augment humanization of the workplace.

There are more than 50 such UAW-GM programs under way. They have resulted in improvements in discipline and product quality as well as a diminution of absenteeism and worker turnover. CWA has also been active in the quality-of-worklife movement.

The principal achievements, however, have been the enhancement of human dignity, the strengthening of self-esteem, and the promotion of self-fulfillment at work. These have been the fundamental objectives of the trade union movement since the 19th century, when it was in the forefront of the effort to humanize the workplace by fighting for restrictions on child labor.

■ Another idea that is part of the new thinking on the quality of worklife is a program of *sabbatical educational and advanced training for all members of the workforce.* Under such a program, employees would take leave from their jobs one year out of every seven, to go back to school, acquire new skills, improve existing skills, or pursue public service.

Some companies, in fact, have established a system of "Fulbright Fellowships" for people who want to take a year or two away from their jobs and engage in public service. Expanded implementation of this idea and similar plans would not only assist workers in preparing to develop new skills, but also improve the outlook and performance of those who have grown stale on the job.

Employers themselves would benefit from such a program. Among the rewards reaped by employers would be a reduction in job-hopping and the providing of management with a more stable, interested, and regularly upgraded workforce.

Reappraisal of material success: One of the most interesting examples of the revolution in values taking place in the workforce is the growing conviction among both white-collar and blue-collar employees that the "nose to the grindstone" way of life is too high a price to pay for material success.

This appraisal entails a dilution of the Puritan ethic, with its spartan precepts of hard work, unflinching loyalty to employers, and suppression of desires that conflict with "duty."

The drive to reach the top is being replaced by the need to keep one's life on a satisfying and relatively even keel. Success is defined in relative terms, achieving a rational balance between commitment to making a living and enjoyment of an enriched lifestyle.

■ In a development closely related to this, *young workers especially evidence a preoccupation with finding a way of life that expresses the unique individuality of each wage earner.* Indeed, the compelling appeal of the "human potential" movement is shown in a Yankelovich poll of workers under age 30. According to the survey, young workers—male and female, white and black, white-collar and blue-collar—want jobs that
■ contribute to others or society,
■ are challenging, and
■ offer the opportunity to learn and grow.

Beyond GNP: One of the most striking ideas with regard to worker values is the notion that the gross national product will soon outlive—or may have already outlived—its usefulness as the basic index of America's national progress. To replace GNP, Dr. Preston Cloud of the University of California at Santa Barbara has proposed a new barometer of national well-being which he calls the Enhancement of the Human Condition [EHC]. Other efforts with a similar goal are being pursued elsewhere.

Dr. Cloud's formula for measuring the EHC involves adding together the positive indicators that reflect improvement in the quality of life, such as the number of jobholders, advanced educational degrees, protected land, and other desirable attributes, and subtracting such negative factors as joblessness, crime, poverty, unrecycled waste, and other components of the "misery index" in our society.

Drawing by Whitney Darrow © 1977 The New Yorker Magazine

"Faster!"

MAKING IT HAPPEN:

Work as self-expression: Finally, of special interest to social theorists, the growing emphasis placed on "quality of work" may even compel a sharp modification of the age-old assumption of manpower economists that people work to make money. This, in turn, may result in a redefinition of what we mean by the word "work."

The next generation may come to think of work as an essential human need for self-expression in the spirit reflected by Robert Frost in his poem "The Road Not Taken," in which he explained how he decided to make his avocation his vocation and why "that has made all the difference."

Collective Bargaining Agenda

During the next 20 years, organized labor will expand its collective bargaining agenda to include several pathbreaking trends that are beginning to be evident.

■ One evolving practice provides hope for workers to satisfy their need for personal participation in the shaping of a world of proliferating complexity. This is the process of *codetermination,* the joint labor-management planning of

Glenn E. Watts

a company's future. Already embraced in Western Europe, this concept may take hold in other nations as a means of giving wage earners a greater sense of partnership in guiding a business' destiny.

The Chrysler loan guarantee legislation signed into law by President Carter, for example, contains a provision requiring representation of the United Auto Workers on the board of the auto company. The results of this pioneering development will be closely scrutinized.

■ Akin to codetermination is another idea that gives working people an incentive to achieve prosperity for their employer. This concept involves the *increased use of employee stock ownership plans, intended to give workers a direct stake in their company's financial health.* The goal of these plans is to improve productivity in the workplace. This idea also would benefit business by providing much needed capital, the "mother's milk" of economic expansion in the private sector.

CWA and the American Telephone and Telegraph Company have recognized the rewards that this new idea promises for both management and working people. They have cooperated in the establishment of employee stock ownership plans.

■ Another emerging idea is the policy of *indexing workers' wages in relation to the cost of living.* The indexing concept as a means of fighting inflation has been endorsed by political economists spanning the spectrum from the late English Fabianist John Maynard Keynes to the contemporary University of Chicago conservative Milton Friedman.

Automatic inflation adjustment is a principal feature of the federal government's budget policy. Virtually all federal retirement and disability programs are indexed, as are many welfare benefits, including food stamps, child nutrition assistance, and supplementary security income payments. In the private sector, cost-of-living provisions were included in 26 percent of union contracts negotiated in 1979.

■ Along a different line, *we may see a workweek shortened to 32 hours.* Moreover, *"flextime"* programs, which are found in a number of collective

ENTERPRISE

bargaining contracts in European nations, may become more prevalent. Under "flextime," employees are permitted to select work hours that meet job requirements but also enable them to fulfill their varied life activities more conveniently.

■ Perhaps the most difficult conflict in the collective bargaining arena in the coming years will be the struggle for the *control of workers' pension fund assets.* Indeed, the late Senator Philip Hart (Democrat, of Michigan), who chaired the Senate Antitrust Subcommittee, prophesied that the future battle for control of pension capital will "be the central structural and policy problem of America's economy for years to come."

Pension fund assets—the deferred wages of 50 million American workers—are now the largest source of investment money in the American capitalist system. They are now worth over $600 billion.

The pervasiveness of pension funds is reflected in the fact that they own an estimated 20–25 percent of equity in American corporations and 40 percent of corporate bonds. By way of comparison, the total accumulation of workers' retirement assets in the United States is larger than the *combined* GNP of the United Kingdom and France. Given the present growth rate of pensions, which is about 10 percent a

Lou Gerber

year, these assets will be worth $1.3 trillion by the end of this decade.

While retirement money represents the deferred wages of millions of workers, many large pension funds are not directly controlled by the workers who are their intended beneficiaries. Instead, management in such cases acts as the sole executor of workers' pension money rather than sharing the administration with employee representatives.

To many unions, management's exclusive control of workers' pension capital represents "investment without representation." To the labor movement, this calls to mind the similar slogan of America's founding fathers 200 years ago.

Ironically, the managers of pension funds sometimes invest workers' prospective retirement income in blatantly anti-union companies. In this way, they provide an invigorating transfusion of economic assistance to union-busting employers.

Moreover, such pension fund managers are not attuned to good investments that are also socially valuable. As a result, unions are now reexamining the current policy of management control of pension funds, with an eye toward attaining joint administration of this vast pool of venture capital.

Transnational Unions

Labor unions in the United States have observed with concern the unprecedented growth of U.S. companies with foreign affiliates or subsidiaries. During the last 10 years, such international corporations have grown so fast that their combined sales exceed the gross national product of every industrial country in the world except the United States and the Soviet Union. Several years ago, General Motors alone had annual sales that exceeded Switzerland's gross national product.

Many foreign nations provide a bountiful, cheap labor supply that will work under substandard conditions at less than American wage levels. For example, in Hong Kong alone, 60 percent of the adults work a seven-day week, and 40,000 children aged 14 or younger work at least 14 hours a day.

Taking advantage of these concentrations of low-priced labor, large multinational companies in effect have exported the jobs of millions of American workers. Furthermore, employment of foreign nationals in plants of U.S. companies abroad is predicted to increase at a rate more rapid than the employment of American wage earners at these companies' plants in the United States.

To cope with the problem of runaway plants and other vexing issues, American labor unions may well turn increasingly to existing international organizations, such as the ILO [International Labor Organization] and the 16 international trade secretariats composed of national unions from different countries with members working in related industries or occupations.

These structures may be utilized more in the future than they have been in the past. They can provide the institutional framework for promoting cooperation among unions of many nations seeking to counter the global threat of businesses that exploit employees.

Drawing by H. Martin © 1981 The New Yorker Magazine

"He's an absolute treasure. We got him for four thousand eight hundred and ninety dollars at Radio Shack, batteries not included."

Forging New Coalitions

Organized labor has long been an active participant and an agent for progressive change on our national legislative-political scene. Although the traditional emphasis of labor's thrust was on bread and butter issues, unions are becoming more cognizant of the need to maintain an ecological balance and to preserve the environment from the ravages of pollution. Reflecting this awareness, they are more and more joining forces with other thoughtful groups in pursuit of a sustainable world.

MAKING IT HAPPEN:

To this end, the labor movement worked alongside environmentalists to obtain enactment of a landmark federal law outlawing strip mining. Similarly, environmentalists have joined with labor to defend the Occupational Safety and Health Administration, to demand the removal of carcinogens and other toxic substances from the workplace, and to protest the continued operation of textile plants in which workers have been stricken with brown lung disease.

Along the same line, an organization, Environmentalists for Full Employment, lobbied for the establishment of federal programs to achieve the purposes of the Humphrey-Hawkins Full Employment and Balanced Growth Act.

The emerging resolution of former differences between the labor and environmental movements is a hopeful sign of recognition that the human species is riding a precarious vehicle in its voyage on spaceship Earth, and that the planet's "supply depot" must be carefully utilized.

An Evolving Society

Two hundred years ago the English statesman Edmund Burke wrote that "a nation without means of reform is without means of survival."

While America (plagued by high unemployment in the early 1980s) is not on the verge of becoming an economic paradise, neither does it appear about to fulfill the negative threat of Burke's warning by plunging into a national collapse. Instead, just as President Franklin Delano Roosevelt forecast in the 1930s that his generation of Americans had a "rendezvous with destiny," so the current generation of Americans appears fated to confront a dramatic challenge and a propitious opportunity to build a new and better world.

Organized labor has long perceived the American Revolution not as a finished product or a priceless antique to be polished and admired every July 4th and then placed back on the shelf,

but as a dynamic, ongoing process, involving a never-ending drive toward improving the quality of life. The evolutionary character of our society will require unions to continue to put their shoulders to the wheel of history and provide a more fulfilling life for working people and their families.

Trade unionists are congenital optimists. We firmly believe in our ability to effect change for the better by facing up to the challenges and opportunities as we approach new frontiers of the future. The American labor movement is in step with a sentiment expressed by the contemporary poet Bob Dylan who, in a way

ENTERPRISE

different from that of Robert Frost, is in tune with the temper of his times. Dylan has written that "those who are not busy being born are busy dying."

The labor movement, along with other flourishing segments of our diverse, pluralistic society, is "busy being born" as it confronts an array of stimulating options. We see the future as a chance to seize the initiative for improving the quality of the life that was given to us and for ensuring that it will be lived with dignity in a sustainable world. □

National Park Service, U.S. Department of the Interior

"It's Himself, on Extension Three."

Religious Life, Thought, Institutions:

Technology and the Transformation of Religion

By the Rt. Rev. John Thomas Walker

Religious institutions have been reeling under the impact of science and technology for years. They have undergone a great transformation in thought and activity as a result.

Leaders of institutions such as the church that focus on human life and behavior are forced in times such as ours to analyze the impact of technology on their institutions. They must look at its impact on the individuals involved in their institutions as well.

Technology and New Options for Individuals

Technological impact on human thought and behavior: During the 1920s, the prohibition movement and the Women's Christian Temperance Union based their activities on a simplistic notion of morality rather

than an in-depth understanding of the potential long-range physical effects of alcohol on the human being. Similarly, smoking was considered a sin because it somehow seemed wrong, not because anyone suspected that smoking was a serious health hazard. Medical technology then tagged along afterward, giving some a way to justify a concept of sin which had its origins in Biblical fundamentalism.

The sexual revolution is quite different story. For centuries, condemnation of premarital and extramarital sex was based on the biblical commandment concerning adultery and on a concept of purity. Behavior, however, was probably motivated more by fear of pregnancy. When technology produced the pill, that fear of pregnancy disappeared—and the sexual revolution began.

A corollary development in society produced a change in abortion laws, and the sexual revolution was complete.

In the development of a religious-ethical structure, certainly all of these matters are of importance. However, with the possible exception of abortion, they all require relatively simple decisions on the part of the individual. In the case of smoking the question for the individual is whether he or she is prepared to risk cancer.

The decision is direct, personal, and generally uncomplicated. The same line of thinking might be applied to drinking, consensual sex, or any number of other problems. Even the issue of abortion was, and is, primarily related to the individuals involved.

Technological and Ethical Frontiers

Technological and ethical frontiers: Beyond the transformation of common every-day moral decisions by new technologies, many of our technological frontiers are also ethical frontiers. At the moment, no decision is required of the average individual. For example, *in vitro* fertilization and cloning are largely unknown to the layman, and may lie so far beyond the understanding or experience of most people as to be non-problems.

But religious institutions are concerned with what is happening at the moral frontiers of human choice and decision-making. For example, during the past several years there have been

many discussions across the country between experts in genetic engineering and religious leaders. I might cite the symposium held at the Washington Cathedral that produced the book edited by Rev. Canon Michael Hamilton, entitled *The New Genetics and the Future of Man.*

Transplanting human organs opens up the danger of possible abuse. Who determines when a donor is legally and medically dead, and by what test—heart beat or brain wave?

And when shall a person be kept alive by extraordinary medical and technological means? These and similar questions require a redefinition of life and death as well as profound ethical reflection about what the right decisions are in such matters.

Technology as ethical stimulus: There are many other technologies which, like medical technology, have stimulated in religious institutions a new and critical examination of both human behavior and theology.

Consider, for example, the impact of television and electronic communications upon our perception of war. It has been said of the Vietnam War that, for the first time in history, a war was fought in the living rooms, dens, kitchens, and bedrooms of America. The immediacy of television's portrayal of how military and defense technology had changed the fighting of a war created problems for several national administations—and for the church as cultivator of the nation's conscience as well.

Religious Renewal and Technological Change

The circular nature of social causality: It would be a mistake to assume that religious institutions and thought were only recipients of technological impact. Similarly, it would be a mistake to think that technology alone accounts for the recent and continuing transformation of religious thought and institutions.

We can see the circular nature of social causality quite clearly in case of the sexual revolution. Yes, better safeguards against pregnancy were developed, and these made it easier to engage freely in sexual relations. But there had been underway in various theological circles a concomitant development called "situation ethics," which was moving beyond universal laws and commandments to address the unique nature of many moral situations, particular in medical practice. The popularization of situation ethics in the 1950s and 1960s joined with advances in birth-control technologies, and influenced the thinking and sexual practices of many younger and older Americans during the 1960s and 1970s.

Similarly, the transformation of religious thought and institutions has been a centuries-old process. It does respond to such influences as technological advance outside of religious institutions. Galileo and Darwin are examples from other centuries of such advance which had a major impact upon subsequent religious thought.

But religious renewal and advance is also generated from within the religious community. Such figures as Reinhold Niebuhr in the 1930s through the 1950s and the "death of God" theologians in the 1960s have had an impact not only upon religious life and institutions but also in society.

Technology and the future of religious institutions: Historical perspective is helpful here. It is easy to point out that there has been a drop in membership in the "main line" Protestant denominations (Presbyterian, Lutheran, United Methodist, and United Church of Christ) and the worldwide Catholic and liturgical churches (Roman Catholic, Anglican (Episcopal), the Orthodox churches, and the various national Catholic churches).

On the other hand, the Baptist, pentecostal, and charismatic movements have been experiencing almost continuous growth.

Looked at from another viewpoint, it is clear that fewer Americans attend churches and synagogues today, and fewer indicate any religious affiliation than in the 1950s and early 1960s. The reasons are not altogether clear.

It is the old question of the chicken and the egg. Did science and technology induce the major shifts in theological view that led to the "death of God" debate? Or was that debate already inherent in the works of such theological thinkers as Dietrich Bonhoeffer, Paul Tillich, and Reinhold Niebuhr? Social causality is such that probably both are true.

Religious Adapting—and Co-opting

A long history of coming to terms with changes in thought and life in human culture: From the 18th century Enlightenment onward, Judeo-Christian religious institutions in the Western world have been forced to come to terms with both scientific and technological advance. But the Enlightment—and earlier the Protestant Reformation of the 16th and 17th centuries—had diminished the power of religious institutions over the individual, and new religious leaders emerged and gave new direction to theological thought.

On the other hand it can also be argued that modern science, scientific philosophy, the Industrial Revolution, modern technology, and secular giants such as Karl Marx and Sigmund Freud, all grew from within a culture that was itself religious. The point is that none of these can really be viewed as separate phenomena.

The waxing and waning of religious life and institutions and influence: From St. Augustine and the fall of the Roman Empire in the 5th and 6th centuries until the present, Western history shows clearly that the vitality of religious life and the power and influence of Judeo-Christian institutions wax and wane.

The Threat and Potential of Change

Then given that background, can we say we have reached a crisis point in religious life, thought, and institutions? I will speak from this point on about what I know best, the life and institutions that are specifically Christian.

Religious institutions in some cases face schism and possible disappearance as they confront change. In other cases, they move proudly toward unity with a strong faith in their future. There is for many of these institutions little growth in numbers of churchgoers. On the other hand, financial donations to religious bodies have increased each year in spite of inflation and recession.

Will religious institutions survive? Or will they gradually disappear?

Albert Mollegen was wont to say that many nations and civilizations had struggled and hammered against the anvil of the Judeo-Christian tradition and found themselves destroyed—and that many more would do so before that tradition disappeared.

During the period following World War 2, the religious institutions of Christianity experienced a remarkably strong comeback. The late 1940s and 1950s were a time of extraordinary growth in churches, in church schools, and in the number of men and women seeking training as professionals within the church. An increasingly aware and active constituency of lay men and women was an accompanying phenomenon, as more lay men and women than ever before were more highly educated than ever in the history of the Christian church.

By the end of the 1950s as the post-World-War-2 baby-boom slowed, most churches began to show a levelling-off in membership. The civil rights movement burst upon the American scene beginning in 1959, and produced the first of many crises in the churches, crises which continue to the present.

It is impossible to know if, even without the crises of the 1960s and 1970s—the Civil Rights movement, the women's rights movement, the anti-Vietnam War movement, the gay and lesbian rights movement—the growth in membership in the churches would have come to a halt in any event.

The polarization of religious institutions in the 1960s and 1970s: What is obvious is that many local, regional and national religious communities were polarized by the increased participation on the part of clergy and laity in these movements. The polarization raised serious questions about the future of many local congregations.

The roots of this polarization extended back into the early decades of this century, when the church, or many parts of it, began to become radicalized both from without and from within in an almost systematic way. The roots of this radicalization harkened back to early 20th century, and the Social Gospel Movement in the churches and the union movement in industry. The church and U.S. society were coming to grips with the increasingly massive industrialization and urbanization of American life.

The Gospel of Renewal and Liberation

Voices calling for change: There were many voices calling out for change in church and in society. The voices of black people struggling for freedom called the church to recognize and honor the implications of the Gospel. The strong suggestion was that Jesus would not condone the evils of racism, segregation, and discrimination.

What at first was the church's fearful and half-hearted support of the NAACP, Martin Luther King, Jr., SNCC, and CORE, grew over the years to an army of supporters. What at first was a body of church people on the offensive and determined to keep their churches free of the evils of integration, lived on to become a group defensive of what was, at best, distorted Christian thinking and, at worst, the anti-Christ.

The struggle for black liberation lead the way for other liberation movements. The most prominent among them were for women's liberation, ethnic liberation, and—within the Roman Catholic and Anglican churches—liberation from rigid and stultifying liturgies expressive of the life, work, and thoughts of people who had lived five hundred to a thousand years ago.

Pope John 23rd opened the Roman Catholic church to the fresh winds of change in the Second Vatican Council in the early 1960s. In Protestantism, the ecumenical movement had been underway from the early decades of this century, and the Consultation on Church Union (COCU) was moving nine major Protestant denominations closer together than ever before. Organic unity is perhaps no more likely now than ten years ago, but there is within the nine a new respect for each other's life and ministries, and a sense that all are working toward a common goal. Anglicans and Roman Catholics have developed and agreed upon approaches to commonly understood concepts of priesthood (ministry), and Eucharistic Worship. Such ideas as "cross ordination," commonly understood membership, and generating communities ring through every ecumenical conference.

Technological Advance and the Arousing of Christian Consciousness

Technology has played a major role in young people becoming disillusioned with religious institutions. The communications media, particularly television, have helped Americans compare the claim of the Christian church—that it is in our midst as the reconciling body of Christ in the world—with historic as well as present reality. What the Christian church as well as today's young people see is clearly unpleasant.

Jesus Christ came to sow brotherhood, love, and peace. Yet the church, which calls itself the body of Christ, has in its various forms persecuted the Jewish people, black people, and fellow Christians who were members of other branches of its own body. Far from always freeing people, religious institutions have too often enslaved Christians under a new law of "Hate thy neighbor as thyself."

The churches have been able to justify almost every war in history. The churches in relation to both women and blacks has been able to accept a distorted understanding of humanity. The churches have had largely closed eyes to such horrendous crimes as human slavery, the slaughter of the native inhabitants of the North and South America, poverty, massacres, and the attempted elimination of the Jews of Europe.

The church did all this generation after generation—until technogical advance brought such matters into every home.

The transformation of religious institutions under the spotlight of communications technology: The portrayal of the many scandalous aspects of religious life and history have helped many to leave their childhood religious institutions.

Still others in the Christian community dug in their heels in defense of old power, status, and traditional views. These remained, vowing to fight every effort to change.

Still others remained, hoping to save their religious institution by changing not only its direction but its basic understanding of many of the central ideas embodied in its creed.

Civic pressures for change: There were still other outside factors pressuring the church toward change. There were extraordinary advances in scientific technology. Jet travel and rocketry seemed to reduce the size of the earth. Accomplishments in medical technology such as the contraceptive pill, organ transplants, and the like, all came with amazing rapidity.

L'Osservatore Romano

Christian institutions either had to readjust their thinking or reject science as a means of ultimate knowledge. The religious person was confronted by a revelation-based religion and a society-based "civil religion." When they were in conflict, the civil religion was often the choice.

Looking Backward: How the Church Copes

Coping by withdrawal: In times past, when the church has been confronted by threatening forces, it has developed ways to absorb them into itself, or it has fought them and lost.

In the 4th century during the reign of the Roman emperor Constantine, identification as a Christian was no longer grounds for persecution and martyrdom. Suddenly acceptability threatened the church's life, diluting the meaning of being a Christian.

Christianity itself became overly identified with the political and social interests of the church's new patron and friend, the emperor, and the Roman Empire. So, in the fourth century, the secularization of the church led to a movement of withdrawal, called monasticism.

Monasticism was a movement of withdrawal from a secularized church, and focused attention back upon a dedicated and disciplined Christian community—what today is often referred to as the church's "true agenda."

In subsequent centuries during what today we call the Dark Ages and the Middle Ages, the disciplines of prayer, study of the scriptures, and scholarship were central to repeated monastic movements to renew and reform Christian life.

Coping by fighting change: As the Medieval Period gave way to the Renaissance, the church again fought change. It used its secular power to keep church people in line.

The results were disastrous. The Reformation came, Western Christianity divided, and the Protestant force was established as a separate movement in Christianity.

Coping by absorbing change: Sometimes Christianity absorbed change. The Church of England after the Reformation took the power out of Deism by incorporating it into the church. But later, that same church would see itself split by its inability to incorporate the new forms of Christian discipline, "method," and organization that were to become Methodism.

Twentieth century responses: In more recent struggles churches have often been more flexible and able to bend with the times, and more able to be more inclusive in their internal and external relations.

During the 1930s and 1940s, the churchmanship battle was waged in the Episcopal churches. The more Catholic-minded sought to define the Episcopal Church in terms of its Catholic heritage. They argued for Eucharistic Worship; the complete restoration of oracular confession; a general use of incense and special vestments for communion; Gregorian chants as the normative music of the Eucharist; and, in some places, for emphasis on a celibate clergy.

The evangelical wing in the Episcopal Church focused on the more Protestant aspect of Episcopal Church life such as morning prayer and sermon; the occasional Eucharist, and a direct and personal confession without a necessary priestly mediator.

In time, other things come to seem more important: By 1960, the wrangling was over. The world outside had influenced the church in such a way that other priorities seemed far more important than such internal arguments.
■ The birth of the Consultation on Church Union assisted the liturgical movement in several churches which had been non-liturgical.
■ The Eucharist became the normative service of worship in an increasing number of churches.
■ A liturgical revival took place architecturally in many of the non-Catholic churches, and

■ the efforts at renewal in the Roman Catholic churches opened the door to new Anglican-Roman conversations and brought both Catholics and Protestants closer together.

Externally, the world's agenda brought about change in the level of social concern. The Methodists and Presbyterians, who traditionally have been far more deeply involved in social action than others, set an example that forced Episcopalians into that arena. The debate that ensued in the Episcopal church took the attention off its internal affairs and caused a closer look at the social mandates of the Gospel.

For some time, the church has argued over whether it is right or wrong for Bishops, Conventions, and Councils to speak forthrightly on the many social issues of the day. In the recent past, civil rights and the Vietnam war have been the main focus.

. . .And Changes

Effects of the upheaval in ethics and morals: It is extremely difficult to say which of all these many influences has had the greatest effect in forcing change.

But certainly the change in Christians' views of ethics and morals has caused upheaval in the life of the church. Development of "situation ethics" removed the daily behavior of the individual from the purview of the church. If the church was no longer viewed as the repository of effective ethical principles, if the church was no longer able to "put the fear of God" into people, then it had lost much of the leverage it formerly had or at least thought it had.

So, along with the advent of "the pill," the notion that changes in one's "situation" changed what was "right behavior," had an extremely profound effect on the life of the church as well as upon the behavior of individual Christians.

These developments, and then the legalization of abortion by the U.S. Supreme Court, threw many church people off balance.

The Roman Catholic church and its people have been most deeply affected.

But many other churches have also responded to these changes with great concern. This has been expressed as a "right to life" movement as well as a politically active "Moral Majority." Both of these expressions of concern appear to have had a profound effect in greatly assisting the election of President Ronald Reagan in 1980.

Structural changes: The confrontations and demands of the 1960s caused changes in the structure and policy of some religious institutions. Changes were made in church constitutions, canons [laws], and by-laws of national and local church groups as Black people, young people, women, native Americans, Hispanics, and regional groups have all demanded a place in the decision-making bodies of the church.

The demand of women to be ordained to the priesthood in the Anglican churches caused Episcopalians to re-examine their polity. What is the role of bishop, priest, and deacon? What is the authority of its ministry? Where does decision-making take place? Is the local congregation the focus of power? Is it in the hands of the local bishop and convention? Or does the Church's General Convention [triennial national legislative assembly of local bishops and delegates from local conventions] hold the ultimate authority? The answers to these questions will determine the future shape of that church.

Looking Ahead

Will these religious institutions survive, or will they gradually disappear? It is difficult to project very far into the future. The needs of people change and flow with the pressure of events, and often depend on inner and more personal stresses as well.

Who can predict, for example, how the generation of children who reach kindergarten age this year will respond to events of these early years of which they are vaguely aware, and which even their parents barely understand?

In the United States, how will they react to the excessive violence of recent years? We have never had a generation grow to school age watching war live on television during their evening meal.

What will happen to the psyches of those children in the Sahel, in Vietnam, in Cambodia, in Uganda, and other places who have watched people die of starvation or the direct effects of war?

And will the liberation movements cause frustrations not yet realized—and will such frustrations drive people toward or away from religious institutions?

Will a maturity finally come that will render all such institutions useless?

Let me hazard a guess. The signs do not portend the end of the church, much the less the end of religion. The church itself and its related institutions (schools, colleges, etc.) face some difficult times, but seem alive and well.

There will be a need for some retrenchment and a more careful use of resources. Schools (parochial and independent as well as primary and secondary) and colleges are in a serious financial bind. Many will close. Others will merge and live for another decade or two.

The elaborate church buildings may well disappear. But if they do, it would not be a disaster. The mood and drift of the church itself seems toward smaller, more economical buildings. The current emphasis upon personal pilgrimage and spiritual development may lead individuals to find spiritual fulfillment in smaller, more intimate units. If we take the conservation of energy seriously, the large metropolitan church building could become obsolete.

The positive signs, all around us, are:
■ the number of men and women seeking to serve through ministry,
■ the search of many young people for a new and viable expression of religious life,
■ the notion of the pilgrimage or spiritual development, and

Who am I? John Thomas Walker

Bishop Walker was born Georgia, and grew up in Detroit, Michigan, where he graduated from high school in 1943. In 1948 he entered Wayne State University, earning a B.A. in history in 1951. In 1951 he became the first black student at the Virginia Theological Seminary, from which he was graduated in 1954.

Returning to Detroit he was ordained and in 1955 he became rector of St. Mary's Church, a white parish in a racially changing neighborhood. He served there until 1957 when he became a teacher of religion and history at an independent Episcopal boarding school, St. Paul's, in Concord, NH.

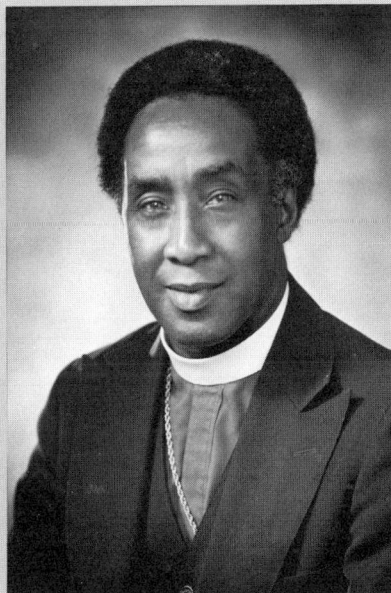

In 1961 he directed a summer training program for the Episcopal Church's national governing board in Nicaragua, Guatemala, and Costa Rica. This began what was to become a long involvement with the Episcopal Church's overseas programs. He later led similar conferences in Puerto Rico and Mexico.

During 1961 he met his future wife, Rosa Maria Flores. A native of Nicaragua, Mrs. Walker was then a resident of Costa Rica; they were married there in May 1962.

In 1964 St. Paul's School granted Walker a one-year sabbatical for him to go with his his wife and year-old son and teach at the Bishop Tucker Theological School in Mukano,

■ the maturing of the Christian charismatic movement.

These point to a further transformation of religious institutions, not to their death.

Churches know that their continued existence depends upon their ability to adapt to a world that itself is undergoing transformation.

Unlimited economic wealth for individuals is no longer feasible, if not to say impossible. The continued separation of the world into the haves and have-nots will end. The worldwide hegemony and influence of Western culture has already ended, and in the future Western culture may even descend to the level of one among many.

Ours is a very pluralistic world, and the church will henceforth be forced to find its place in such a world and undergo further transformation itself.

The appeal of traditionalist Christianity: Many people long for an age of stability, whatever that means. They have seen the church as the one unchanging, immutable institution left in the world. The tampering with liturgy, the translations of scripture and prayer books into modern vernacular language, the church's involvement in social and political affairs, the loss of interest in overseas missionary activity, the stress on liberation theology and on the role of women, have all shaken the foundation of the traditionalist Christian.

Traditionalist Christians would save the church by restoring it to its previous condition, in which a hardening of its spiritual arteries was bringing it closer to death.

But even this rigidity has its place and contributes to the transformation. What proponents of change must remember is that the church is not dead, religion has not disappeared from the earth, and we do not have to recreate the entire religious experience of humankind. Rather, we need to bring the church into closer relationship to the Divine Spirit that continually transforms our lives and also our institutions. □

This article is adapted from a lecture presented in the third Herbert Spencer Lecture Series on Technology and Society, February 1976.

"And what kind of a world would this be if everyone decided not to get involved?"

Drawing by John Corcoran ©1971 The New Yorker Magazine

Uganda, East Africa. Since that time the Walkers have been instrumental in helping Ugandan students in the U.S. attending high school or university. They have also aided political refugees, including Anglican priests and bishops.

In 1966 Walker came to Washington to serve on the staff of Washington Cathedral. As part of that ministry he began and hosted for four years a weekly television program focusing on urban, ethnic, and ecumenical concerns.

In 1977 he was elected suffragan bishop of the Episcopalian diocese of Washington, DC, and on June 12, 1976 he was elected to became the 6th bishop of the Episcopal Diocese of Washington.

Bishop Walker's continuing concern for problems of the urban centers of this country led him to join with other city bishops of the Episcopal Church in the formation of the Urban Bishops' Coalition of which he is chair. The group has held hearings in major cities throughout the United States and Panama and seeks action from the church and the government on problems which confront our cities.

Long active in ecumenical affairs, Bishop Walker led in the formation of the Interfaith Conference of Metropolitan Washington in 1978, and is now its first president. He has served on the Episcopal Church's Joint Commission on Ecumenical Relations, the Consultation on Church Union, was delegate to the World Council of Churches Fifth Assembly in Nairobi, Kenya in 1975 and presently chairs Africare, a non-profit organization dedicated to self-help projects in Africa.

Upon the retirement of the Very Rev. Francis B. Sayre, Jr. as dean in 1978, Bishop Walker became dean of Washington Cathedral, thus linking more closely the cathedral and the diocese.

MAKING IT HAPPEN:

A POSITIVE GUIDE TO THE FUTURE

Office of Technology Assessment

Action:

It's Happening

Commentary

We cannot wait for the world to turn,
For times to change,
  that we might change with them,
For the revolution to come
  and carry us around in its new
  course.
We, ourselves, *are* the future.
We *are* the revolution.

BEATRICE BRUTEAU,
Anima, Spring 1977,
quoted by Marilyn Ferguson in *The Aquarian Conspiracy*

As I write this page, I will be creating the future. As you read it, you will be doing the same. *We cannot choose whether or not to create the future, we can only choose whether or not to create the future we want.*

Making that choice and following where it leads, is what I mean by taking responsibility for our future—making that choice and going with it productively and effectively.

The people in the pages that follow are not exceptional people, except in one respect: they are people who have decided that they are going to make their lives make a difference in our world. And the future *will* be different because of their commitments to make it so.

I am struck by how far into the future many of their visions and commitments extended. This has reminded me once again that what happens tomorrow will be mostly determined by choices made months and years ago. Months and years ago we—

  built the buildings,
  wrote the contracts,
  chose the companions,
  conceived the families,
  gained the knowledge and
  experience,

  made the commitments,
  chose the leaders
that we will have at nine o'clock tomorrow morning.
What will
  we be like,
  our surroundings be like,
  our society be like,
  our world be like,
at nine o'clock in the morning on this date in the year 2000?

We cannot *predict* that world. But we can begin to shape it with our purposes, our intentions, and our actions. We are bounded only by those physical, geological, ecological, and social laws that are immutable, unchangeable. History —especially American history—has shown that, in the face of real commitment and effort, there are fewer "immutable" laws than we think.

MAKING IT HAPPEN:

Some people have a fear of flying. Many more have a fear of planning. Yet we will never be able to create a better future if we don't make plans.

Americans are very ambivalent about planning. Those holding negative views of planning often reflect the erroneous belief that planning necessarily limits freedom. In fact, planning *can* create freedom—so long as *we* create our own plan. What limits freedom is the imposition of plans on unwilling participants, and being rigid about plans, even when they turn out to be wrong. This is what limits freedom—not planning by itself.

It may also be that Americans' negative attitudes toward planning are left over from the early 1950s when it was automatically assumed that Planning = Central Government Control = Socialism, or even communism.

Even though many Americans have a negative "gut reaction" to the notion of planning, we should all recognize that a lot of planning is already going on in a great many settings in U.S. society.

Some corporate leaders oppose planning in the public sector. But no major corporation would be without its strategic and operational planning groups. Even though he or she may choose to ignore it, a policy-level official in the private sector would not consider conducting business without at least a five-year plan. Even in the federal government, a lot of planning goes on, though it is much more fragmented than it should be.

In 1976, John Gardner, the founder of Common Cause, discussed the need for a new view of planning in a brief paper written for the Advisory Committee on National Growth Processes. Here is a brief excerpt from what he said:

"[Planning is a subject that] stirs apprehension in the minds of many Americans. Much of the apprehension stems from the fact that people envisage a small group of technocrats, insulated from criticism, achieving centralized control and imposing a rigid program on an unwilling electorate, destroying all private sector freedom and market mechanisms in the process. Obviously, no one who cares about our liberties could possibly relish such an outcome.

"But there's nothing in the nature of planning that requires such an undemocratic solution. Proponents of planning have failed to make clear how we can and must avoid the dangers that frighten so many people.

"[I] will argue that the dangers will be kept at a minimum:

■ if the process is open from start to finish;

■ if there is adequate provision for public debate;

■ if the final recommendations receive orderly consideration by our democratically accountable institutions of self-government;

■ if we centralize only those portions of the process that cannot be dealt with in any other way; and

■ if there is adequate provision for monitoring and grassroots feedback.

"It isn't as complicated as it sounds. We can resolve that any process we create will be compatible with freedom and will preserve, to the greatest extent possible, the widely-dispersed initiative and creativity we care so much about. The oppressively technocratic and centralized atmosphere that has surrounded the image of planning can be put behind us."

Facing A Changing World:

Planning—And Learning from It

By Donald N. Michael

Coping with change can be an exhilarating experience. It can also be profoundly terrifying.

Often, it seems that twin desires—to soar into the future and to cling fearfully to the past—are at war within us and within our society. The outcome of this war will shape the future of humankind. It will also teach us a great deal about ourselves, through the choices we make.

Our choices: One choice is to withdraw from the burdens of an open society, to retreat to the illusory security of authoritarianism, and protect our identity behind walls separating "us" from "them."

But doing that would also create impediments to building an enriched and more satisfying society at home. In denying a better life to the peoples of the Third and Fourth Worlds, we would also be disenfranchising people like ourselves in the First and Second Worlds who are stimulated and challenged by an open society and books like this.

An alternative choice is to accept the years ahead as a challenging and exhilirating transition to a more humane and sustainable world. If this is our choice, then—

■ We must recognize that neither we nor anyone else can offer simple solutions to our problems. We must start with candor about our uncertainty and ignorance.

■ We must have a vision of what the new global order can be, and confidence that we have the power to attain it.

■ We must have the hope and the humility to become learners. A time of transition is inevitably a time of unlearning and learning anew. It is a time for discovery of new norms, new goals, and new modes of private and public conduct.

Profound relearning of this kind has occurred before. The transformation from feudal society to modern civilization is a vivid example.

But in contrast to earlier transitions, our relearning this time must be carried out self-consciously and deliberately, with continuous attention to process and to humanitarian purpose.

Our relearning also must aim at making *present* life more meaningful, in part by deliberately creating and seeking to attain *desired* futures. The human costs and dollar costs of indifference, unreflectiveness, and expedience, will be too great to allow any hope that we can merely bumble along to our goal.

Learning new perspectives and processes: We speak about "interdependence." But how many of us actually accept the fact that everything really is connected to everything else, and more tightly connected now than ever before? Interdependence means mutual dependence.

A mutually dependent world requires perspectives and processes that take into account the whole as well as the parts. This is all new to most of us. In our society, the emphasis has been on compartmentalization, specialization, and division of labor. We must learn the new perspectives—the new ways of seeing people, things and relationships—that are essential to survival in a humane and sustainable global order. Such perspectives rely on discovery, evaluation, and learning, and can only be attained through planning.

Needed—a new kind of planning: The planning that is needed must be based upon an acknowledgement of our present *ignorance*.

Thus, the approach I am proposing is contrary to the premise that undergirds all the conventional planning, which is always done in an engineering mode. Such planning presumes that we know what we are doing and how to do it.

That mode works well, for example, when we are going to the moon. We know what we need to know to get there, or at least we know how to find out what we need to know, but don't.

Acknowledging our ignorance: Planning to deal with the present and anticipated human condition is quite different. Underlying all else is the need to recognize and accept the extent of our ignorance about our situation.

It is not enough to acknowledge that the future is full of uncertainty and unpredictability. The fact is that we also do not understand our present situation very well. For example (and very important in this connection), we do not yet have an adequate theory to explain and predict the processes of social change. What this means is that we do not yet have any theory that can reliably direct us. A theory is used to identify the significant factors in what we see

happening, and to estimate future consequences.

All this is not to say there are no such theories. They abound and are regularly applied by their proponents as if they were true and perfect wisdom. All ideologies assume such theories. They are implicit in all future studies, technology assessments, environmental impact statements, demographic projections, and economic forecasts. But none of these theories of social change has yet been conclusively proved right or even adequate.

The depth of our ignorance: Three examples, of particular pertinence to the subject of this book, will demonstrate this ignorance.

■ *We have never been able, nor are we now able, to predict birth rates.* This fact alone indicates how little we understand about individuals, groups, or institutions and their interactions over time.

■ *Economists are unable to agree on appropriate fiscal or monetary policy, and even their best projections of critical economic indicators may be correct for, at most, the next three quarters.*

■ *A more abstract example: we don't know, with any conceptual rigor, how small societal events generate large ones or how large societal events influence small ones.* Or, putting it another way, do great individuals make history, or does the thrust of history "create" great individuals? To answer "Both" says nothing.

This is not to say we know nothing at all. For example, the evidence in this book proves that we possess some knowledge and experience—and that, at times, we have the good sense to realize what we don't know.

It is that knowledge of our ignorance that provides the impulse and the potential to plan and learn our way through the years ahead.

Planning, then, is the mode in which a complex social organism can learn what it seeks to become, perceive how to attempt to do so, test whether progress is being made, and reevaluate along the way whether the original goal is still desirable.

Planning, in this definition, means societal learning, organizational learning, personal learning. Specifically, such planning can provide procedures and a context for pursuing the transition to a better future so often postulated in this book.

Which human requirements must be met if we are to become learners under the turbulent and complex social conditions of today and tomorrow?

In what follows, I want to describe some of those I consider most critical. They will be very difficult to attain and sustain.

If our situation were less serious, we might try to muddle through as in the past, occasionally essaying a more self-conscious and risky change. But this book as well as many other contemporary observations on the human condition leave little doubt about the gravity of our situation: conscientious

DRIVE
SAFELY

MAJOR
DICHOTOMY
½ Mi. AHEAD

Drawing by Ed Arno ©1981 The New Yorker Magazine

MAKING IT HAPPEN:

and informed persons have no choice but to accept the prospect of profound change.

If we are to shape, rather than be shaped by, that change, we face the task of becoming learners, as individuals, organizations, and societies.

Living and Acting Compassionately

With the acknowledgment of our ignorance comes the first requirement for learning, indeed its justification: to act compassionately.

Acting with compassion means acting in recognition of the reality that: (1) none of us, including you and me, really know what we are doing in terms of the *ultimate consequences* of our acts; and (2) all of us, to a very great degree, are living in a world of illusions, believing in the "facts" that comprise our world—instead of recognizing that

Achieving "New Competence"

There are several specific norms of performance which are integral to this compassionate posture. Altogether, I call these the "new competence" because they differ importantly from conventional definitions of what constitutes competent performance for leaders, intervenors, and agents for social change.

1. Acknowledging and sharing uncertainty: The first characteristic (and these are not in order of importance) is the need to *acknowledge, to yourself and to others, that you share with others very high levels of uncertainty.*

Here I do not mean that qualified uncertainty associated with estimates of probability. I mean that uncertainty that accompanies the realization that you simply don't know..., that anxious awareness which haunts us in the dark of the night, makes our stomachs sink,

we live in a *constructed* social reality (even though it may not have been consciously constructed).

This means, then, that we need all the clarity we can muster regarding our ignorance and finiteness, and all the support we can get in order to face the implications of what that greater clarity reveals to us. A compassionate person is one who, by virtue of accepting this situation, can assure others *and self* of such support.

Living compassionately can free people from the pressure to act as if they really know what they are doing and how to do it.

In particular, living more compassionately can reduce the need to hide errors of the sort that arise from actions based on shared and acknowledged ignorance. And it can reduce the need to act overcautiously and conservatively out of fear of being caught making a mistake. Acknowledging our condition of ignorance and its associated vulnerability can eliminate those defensive, self-protecting, interpersonal posturings that make it so hard to act responsibly and compassionately.

produces headaches, high blood pressure, and ulcers, and eventually heart attacks and strokes.

But why should an individual or organization run the risks of sharing such uncertainty?

■ First, such acknowledging and sharing is intrinsic to learning. Neither you nor your associates, nor others you need to involve in a process of change, can truly learn if you begin with the assumption that you already have all the facts, are certain about the issues, know what the outcome should or could be, and can judge accurately whether the preferred outcome is being attained.

■ Second, sharing uncertainty increases your capacity to live with that uncertainty and learn from it.

No one knows how much uncertainty a person can usefully sustain. Certainly there is some limit. But when you have

others with whom to share it, you can sustain much more uncertainty. It's a commonplace to say that misery loves company; but shared misery can also increase both individual and group capability.

■ Third, when dealing with complex social issues, to act as if you are certain of what you are doing simply increases distrust.

Some kind of shared belief—a basic if qualified trust—in the capability, reliability, and responsibility of institutions, is a critical requirement for governance (of which government is one part). Growing distrust, studies show, destroys these qualities.

The very act of acknowledging uncertainty can help greatly to reverse this downhill trend. Heightened trust makes it easier for all parties to accept risk, to take chances in learning and discovering, and to develop new potentials in ourselves and in our organizations for working and learning our way into a better future.

2. Embracing Error: A second characteristic of the new competence is what I call embracing error. Neither individuals nor organizations can learn if they fail to perceive the positive benefits of the errors that will unavoidably accompany planning over the years ahead.

Error is not synonymous with failure.

Historically, the tendency to equate the two derived from the belief—so characteristic of the white, Western male—that the only truly competent person is the one who is in control, who fully understands the situation, and therefore doesn't make errors. If one does make errors, one is not competent: one is a failure.

But *in coping with complex problems, we will be wrong much more often then we're right. The only way to learn is to reach out to discover our errors, embrace them, and use them.*

The truly competent person, by this definition, is the one who has worked beforehand to develop a capability to understand what is going right or wrong in the system of which he or she is a part, and to use subsequent information—

177

including information gleaned from error—to relearn, revise, and experiment anew.

Error-embracing also helps a leader to engender needed trust. And sustained by that trust, the leader can elicit greater willingness to experiment and to explore openly what this nation, this world, might become.

3. Responding to the Future: A third requirement for learning, is **to be future-responsive, i.e., to make the future always a part of the present.**

■ **Future studies** are usually thought to deal with what lies ahead, "out there" in the time to come. **The true usefulness of future studies is for learning about our assumptions and our ways of acting in the present.** Future studies unavoidably bring to the surface ethical issues, questions concerning what we are seeking or avoiding through our present actions. They can confront us with questions and ideas that help clarify the gaps between where we are and where we want to be. They can show us the degree to which one or another of our actions may already be obsolescent, counterproductive, or wasteful.

■ **Goal-setting:** Being future-responsive also means **taking seriously the setting of long-range goals at a level of explicitness that forces us to face value preferences and priorities. This book is such an effort.**

In the learning mode, goal-setting is not an engineering activity, in which we set our goals, put our heads down, and drive ahead. Instead, goal-setting becomes a means for continually reexamining who we are now—as individuals, organizations, and societies—as we move into the future. In this case, it is also a means of measuring our progress in creating a more human and sustainable world.

In addition, goal-setting has the enormously powerful and important function of engendering visions that commit us passionately to what we might become—or want to avoid becoming. We will need such visions to carry us through this transition and reinforce our creativity.

In summary, **because future-responsiveness forces us to concentrate on who we are and what we are doing, it**

Drawing by W. Miller ©The New Yorker Magazine

"Beg pardon, Captain, but me and some of the boys would like to sing you a little chantey we just composed about being so off course we don't know where the hell we are."

can encourage community, trust, and openness, thereby stimulating additional forms of human potential.

The surfacing of value conflicts can, of course, produce the contrary too. Learning is always risky. But, in our situation, not learning is riskier still. If we do not learn how to make the transition to a world in which essential human needs are met, we face disaster.

4. Becoming Interpersonally Competent: Constructively accepting uncertainty, embracing error, and facing value differences all lead to a fourth requirement for becoming learners: interpersonal competence.

For example, few of us listen well: we are too busy preparing our own statement. Nor are we skilled (compassionate, empathetic, nurturing) at supporting one another and empowering one another as we take risks by expressing our hunches, intuitions, doubts, feelings, and values as we risk learning.

The kind of interpersonal incompetence I am referring to here is often encountered in task force, staff and committee meetings that are not "touch-feely" encounter groups. We all, both women and men, hide our incompetence behind the old macho facade of super-competence. We are

MAKING IT HAPPEN:

"tough-minded," and we "protect our turf." But it is precisely such tactics that discourage the human potentialities needed for a true planning capability.

We are also inept at coping creatively with value conflicts. This is a major reason why we try to separate values from substantive issues and preoccupy ourselves with hard data.

Instead, we pretend that issues can be managed without giving attention to intense feelings in ourselves and in others. In doing this, we confirm that we're really not very serious about the task, since each of us knows deep down that those value issues are fundamental.

Our depression and our exhaustion as we face complex problems is, in considerable part, the result of this self-deception. In denying the validity of value questions, we leave our vitality entrapped within us, and the well-springs of personal caring and motivation denied and inaccessible.

Overall, our incompetence at listening, supporting, coping with value conflicts, nurturing, role-playing, and empowering contribute to the appallingly low efficiency and level of success of task groups.

We cannot continue to afford such incompetence in the turbulent times ahead. Most of us can learn these skills and we must do so, if we are to plan well.

5. Gaining Self-Knowledge: To be interpersonally competent one has to know oneself. This is another characteristic of the new competence.

The Greek oracle counseled, "Know thyself." Socrates said, "The unexamined life is not worth living."

Learning about self means confronting one's value conflicts and making constructive use of them (since they seldom resolve themselves). Learning about self, for men, means learning about their feminine qualities, and for women, about their masculine qualities. Being able to rely on both enriches whatever we do on the job. Learning about self improves our ability to keep our bodies healthy and opens up direct ways of imagining, thinking, and reasoning unavailable through words or numbers.

For risk-taking as well in planning or learning, this life-long learning about self is critical. Self-knowledge increases our responsiveness and resilience, and reduces our inclination to use other competences exploitatively. Then each of us has more arms and legs, heads, eyes, ears, and skin to pick up the clues—recall the Eastern statues so sculpted—and we can make better use of those clues to learn.

Self-knowledge also helps us to cope with the overriding fact of living as a learner: being vulnerable. There is no way to be a learner without being vulnerable, open, and willing to take risk. To be vulnerable requires the kind of strength only self-knowledge affords, as all the sages of history attest.

Accepting Responsibility

These performance norms of the "new competence" are only plausible if we are willing to accept much heightened responsibility.

Responsibility has a respectable past in the Western tradition—we are familiar with being our brother's keeper, and doing unto others as one would have done unto oneself.

But, as a means for social control or social guidance, responsibility has had second-class status over the last 200 years in the West. Instead, we have depended on the "invisible hand," believing that, if everyone "did his own thing," the result would be social good.

This belief in our society in the beneficent effect of the "invisible hand" has resulted in an emphasis on *rights* rather than on *obligations*. That emphasis has unavoidably reduced the role accorded to responsibility as a social value.

But in our increasingly interdependent world, greater individual and social responsibility will be imperative. We confront an imminent need to conceive, design, and operate all our systems so they are based on constant feedback of information from human and natural environments. This is necessary in an interdependent world so we can detect the consequences of our actions.

ACTION

Who am I?   **Donald N. Michael**

My undergirding need is to nurture—which means to help others understand.

For me, the world is always potential, self-transforming, problematic, unavoidably creating and destroying itself simultaneously. My basic image for reality is a fruit: the seed fulfilled—which includes the seeds remaining to be fulfilled.

The ways I live my need and image are to link persons to persons, and persons to ideas; and to teach and learn myself. My areas of professional interest that give substance to these ways are the processes and circumstances of social change, future potentials and problems, and planning as a learning process.

I express these through the written word, through one-on-one relationships, and by designing and facilitating task group activities. These are intended to help persons and organizations become learning systems that will be better able to help keep this turbulent world creatively open.

My goal is to help assure that, over the difficult years ahead, we will have the chance to discover what we can become.

A pervasive sense of responsibility is an essential precondition for accepting such an obligation. That is to say, our responsiveness is an expression of our responsibility for maintaining the well-being of the systems of which we are a part.

Exercise of greater responsibility contributes powerfully to the legitimacy of individuals and organizations. It is part of the "new competence."

A sense of legitimacy, in turn, encourages more reliable and predictable behavior for the future. If organizations are not accepted as legitimate, their behavior tends to become less predictable; it is not reinforced and circumscribed by a constituency that has come to expect a certain level of performance.

Moreover, if organizations lack legitimacy, the behavior of the individual is no longer guided by fixed expectations growing from an established relationship to those organizations.

Willingness to Collaborate

For Westerners accustomed to being "in charge," this is perhaps the most radical requirement. Planning as a mode of learning depends on *collaboration* among parties, rather than control or subordination of some by others.

The justification for a control stance, other than the ego satisfaction of exercising raw power, is that the controller—
■ knows the relationships between cause and effect,
■ knows what effects are desirable, and
■ knows how to produce the requisite effects.
But these claims, and indulgence in the exercise of raw power for its own sake, are inappropriate for the transition ahead.

There are great tasks of transition, and we have much to learn about how to collaborate on them. Fortunately, there have been many new experiments in collaboration on a smaller scale in recent years. Moreover, we can draw upon the experiences and methods of

other cultures, especially those of non-Western cultures.

Here in the United States, there are the underutilized skills and perceptions of women to draw on. Although women have traditionally been without power, they are aware that cause and effect are infinitely more subtle than acknowledged in the male world of technology, and they bring a generations-long heritage of insight and skill to learning-how-to-collaborate-for-planning in a transition. And men also—to the extent they will draw on the feminine in themselves—can cultivate these skills.

It is an exciting challenge to learn to use these enormous, essentially untapped pools of resources and talents to supplement those that, by their very successes, have created a world they can no longer sustain.

Learning through planning is essentially a nurturing process. So its benefits are, by definition, shared.

This should be a great relief and comfort to those of us in the West. It is not only the Third and Fourth Worlds that have unmet human needs. In this mode of creating a better future, we can best meet our own needs by assuring theirs. □

Who am I? **Martha Stuart**

Martha Stuart makes television as if people mattered. She is an independent video producer, a photographer, a mother, a woman business owner, and a change agent.

She is probably best known for her video series called "Are You Listening" and for her work around the world teaching and using videotape as a development tool. She is proud of—

■ opening broadcast communication about birth control,
■ opening public broadcasting to independent production,
■ letting people speak for themselves on the air
and especially of Sally and Barkley Stuart who now produce, teach, and edit with her.

A Guide to Doing Good Work

■ **Get an atlas and some colored felt pens,** and spend weekday evenings for three months marking up the atlas to connect real people with real places. The world will look entirely different to you.

■ **Whenever you learn about some interesting project,** think of it as part of a specific mini-economy in terms of what is produced and used, where and how it is produced, and what part it plays in which sector both of the mini-economy and of the specific local economy. Think too of the other corners and other "markers" in that mini-economy, whom it could buy from or sell to (or barter), where needs and opportunities may coincide, where you might go to work.

■ **Use your purchasing power selectively, both to inform yourself and to support good work in being.**

Think about how a given purchase or transaction serves to strengthen the meta-economy or the exhausting economy, how it can be targeted to strengthen something or someone you want to support. Remember Gandhi's remark that if your village barber gives a bad haircut, instead of going to Madras for a haircut from a city barber, it is better to patronize the village barber and persuade him to learn how to give a better haircut. All of these things take effort as they become conscious, deliberate economic acts; they also take on reality in your own mind and give meaning where none existed.

■ **Pay dues to the half-dozen groups closest to your place** (where you are or where you might want to move) or to your specific interests as you start to identify them through daydreaming.

Get yourself invited to one of their work weekends. Do anything that

Learning to Listen

In the first chapter of this book, I expressed concern over Americans' lack of confidence in their political leaders. This is reciprocated by leaders' lack of confidence in the American people.

"Why don't they listen to us?" say the leaders.

"Why don't they listen to us?" say the people.

"Why don't they believe us?" say the leaders.

"Why don't they tell us the truth?" say the people.

"Why don't they approve of what we do?" say the leaders.

"Why don't they do what we want?" say the people.

A big part of the problem may be faulty communication. Martha Stuart's contribution to creating the future is a fundamentally new approach to human communication using video technology.

Although the approach is new, the principles upon which it is based seem timeless:

- *Information must be viewed as the raw material of change.*
- *There must be equality between sender and receiver.*
- *We must start where people are.*
- *We must deal in feelings as well as thoughts.*
- *We must tell the truth.*

Several years ago I made a videotape in Bucharest, Romania during a United Nations Population Conference. My crew for the production was Romanian and we had very little language in common. Mostly our exchange involved a lot of pantomine leading to a "yes" or "no" response. More precise distinctions were impossible.

Because the project was small and quickly completed, this inability to reach precise understanding was never particularly important, though it was often frustrating in small ways. After the production was finished, I wanted to

Getting Beyond "Trickle-Down" Communication:

Social Change Through Listening

By Martha Stuart

needs doing on the first day; it may be rough or boring, but you thereby pay your dues so you can spend some time the next day poking around and asking questions.

Find out what things they wish they could do next "if only." Think constantly in terms of mini-economics, focal economies, and diversifying personal and family microeconomies (your own and others'). Identify where you might provide or help find the "if only" for them.

Add more pages to your notebook, and mark up your atlas some more as your own map of reality, conceptual and factual, starts to feed on itself and to grow and reach out.

- **Remember the three different groups of homecomers—**
- those who remain within the macro-institutions,
- those who work on them from the outside, and

- those who go off into the meta-economy—

and realize how much they need to work with each other.

The second category often provides valuable skills for reducing constraints in any sector or "market" of a mini-economy: getting county commissioners to give a variance or change a regulation, for instance. You will need to understand the strengths and capabilities and mind-set of each to help bring them together where you can.

- **Don't be put off by** the number of people whose professional expertise causes them to focus on a problem rather than on the potential resources to solve it or prevent it from arising in the first place; that is one of the problems with professionalization.

And don't be put off by the extraordinary number of people with good motivation and underused vital

energies whose initial idea of the way to make a constructive contribution is criticism.

- **Keep in mind the lethal summary of our whole situation** that Hazel Henderson encountered in a bona fide, serious question after one of her talks: "Where do you get federal funding for projects in self-reliance?"

Our unconscious dependence on or at least deference to large organizations, the legacy of the assumption that nothing effective happens except through their participation, is in our bloodstream. Self-immunization takes prolonged and constant attention to unexamined assumptions, questioning, clearing away, letting the new and stronger emerge.

- **Combine your informing and supporting activities with others as you find them,** pooling information and resources, ideas and energies and questions.

show the videotape to the women leaders who had participated in the program. An evening showing was arranged, with the proviso that if an anticipated event interfered, the screening would be postponed.

Of course, I wanted the crew to come, too. But there was no way I could make a flexible arrangement with them across the language barrier. It was either come or not come. In the end, I decided to ask them to come, hoping the screening would not be rescheduled. I was lucky and it wasn't.

The Romanian experience taught me the lesson that **poor communication forces us to deal in absolute alternatives.** There is only the choice between yes/no, on/off, go/no-go. All gradations in between are lost. Understanding is minimal.

No wonder computers, which only deal in sequences of yes or no choices, frequently prove incapable of coping with individual human circumstances. Good communication enables you to deal in variables. You can talk about the *whys* of things as well as the *whats*.

Why "Trickle-Down" Communication Does Not Work

Unfortunately, I think we must classify most communication in the field of development as poor. It tends to limit choices rather than expand them.

The scale is so huge, however, that the costs of this poor communication far, far exceed the tiny inconveniences of my Romanian example. Instead of a few individuals possibly wasting an evening's time, this waste is measured in the lost growth and productivity of whole populations.

Why do the traditional forms of communication used in development work work poorly and at high human cost?

A one-way flow: First and most visibly, development communication usually proceeds from the top down, from the government to the people, from the expert to the worker, from the central authority to the local outpost, from the educated to the uneducated, from the city to the village.

One might call this the down-and-out principle of communication—and the echo of impoverishment is entirely accurate and appropriate. This process assumes that all knowledge, authority, understanding, and resources are located centrally and can be dispensed according to stipulated bureaucratic procedures.

Presumably, nothing of value exists to travel in the other direction. The transmitter of information, in this view, is the unquenchable source of truth; the receiver exists only to accept and act on the transmitted truths.

Reliance on the written word: A second characteristic of development communi-cation is its reliance on the written word. This arises from the bureaucratic necessity to put everything into writing before it can be either formally conveyed or permanently recorded.

This leads in turn to what I call "report conceit," which assumes that once an experience has been committed to words and placed in a report, it has been officially been made available for replication elsewhere. The report becomes the primary reality and the situation from which it was abstracted, comprised of real people and real events, is consigned to a paradoxical shadow reality.

All this turns upside down the familiar biblical proclamation that the word was made flesh and dwelt among us; in development, the flesh is routinely made into words.

Needless to say, this orientation makes literacy a basic ground rule of the development game—without it you cannot be a player, only a pawn.

The blueprint fallacy: The third characteristic of development
ation follows from the first two: it is the view that communication exists to tell people what to do.

By this reasoning, communication provides the means by which those in

■ You can contribute up to 10 percent of your income to existing nonprofit organizations (or new ones you form).
■ You can invest more money and have it deductible by "losing" it in some kind of business enterprise that is pointed toward becoming a viable part of some corner or some sector of some mini-economy—so long as the endeavor makes basic economic sense and is making progress toward break-even.

Good, imaginative, and principled lawyers and accountants love to help on projects like this, where the government subsidizes your work whether they like it or not.

■ ...I would add another component to Schumacher's urgent dictum "Take back the value added," namely "Take back the imaging function."

By imaging I mean that aspect of imagination which seeks a resulting action in the real world. As much as humanely possible, the crucial imaging function must be conducted by those who will actually make the entrepreneurial leap from thought to action, venturing their energies and resources and often their working lives.

Professionals and specialists typically think that it is a regrettable waste of everyone's time when people "have to reinvent the wheel." The essential fact to the contrary is that professionals, specialists, and experts (few of whom, we might note, also have responsibility for any real action or risk-taking) have eliminated the imaging function....

...*Going through that imaging process is an essential precondition for the mobilization of thought and action and the self-discipline required to carry through anything of substance and complexity,* most particularly any real business or any other productive economic process.

PETER GILLINGHAM,
in *Rain* magazine, October 1979
and subsequently an epilogue to *Good Work,*
by E.F. Schumacher (1979)

Specified excerpt from "The Making of Good Work" (pages 208-211) by Peter N. Gillingham, in Good Work by E.F. Schumacher. Copyright © 1979 by Verena Schumacher. Reprinted by permission of Harper & Row Publishers, Inc.

power educate, direct, or manipulate those who are the object of the development effort. The people, in fact, are little more than targets at which policy-makers throw information decked out as instruction.

Success is measured according to whether people do as they have been told. No one is particularly concerned with ascertaining whether they have been told the right things or not; that is taken for granted. The plan rules, not the local reality.

Not to raise questions but to deliver answers: In the end, it always comes down to some version of a single choice. "Do it" or "Don't do it." There is little provision for feedback or course corrections. There is little effort to encourage alternatives or options or innovations. The point is not to raise questions but to deliver answers. It is business conducted by pure yes-or-no accounting.

Overall, this adds up to plain poor communication, and the liabilities of communication in this mode are both operational and philosophical.

■ **For transferring human experience from one locale to another** the record shows very clearly that this style of communication does not work very well. An endlessly recurring disappointment in development work is the seeming impossibility of transporting a successful project from one village or province or country to another.

Seedlings of human enterprise are extraordinarily delicate. Usually, the transplant withers and dies. If it survives, it is often because it grows in an unexpected direction.

Chaff from wheat: Communicating human experience in this fashion is not simply a matter—as the conventional approach has it—of separating the wheat from the chaff, committing the seed to written reports, and then scattering these words on other likely soil.

Most of the time, what is preserved and is nothing more than handfuls of chaff. The spirit of the thing is somehow left behind, lost in the process of abstraction. It is hardly a surprise that nothing grows.

The fact that traditional communication hasn't worked is no doubt why

communication projects fare so poorly with funders. The United Nations Development Program, for example, spends only 1 percent of its budget on communication projects. Funders tend not only to avoid communication projects but also to slight the communication aspects of the projects they do fund, especially the matters of evaluation and pass-along.

Communication to Empower People

At the very heart of the development effort there needs to be the ability to transfer successful human experience from one area of the world to another. Doing this provides our only hope for extending scarce resources across the chasm of need.

We simply cannot afford to start things from scratch each time. We need communication that can transport results from place to place. Without that, we have nothing.

Even with unlimited money, there would not be enough programmers and designers to convey the critical ideas concerning birth control and farming methods and nutrition to all the people who need to know these things in order to improve their lives. The need is vast enough to swallow up all the policy-makers in the world.

The only thing that possibly can meet the need is a communications that empowers people, by giving them tools and ideas and the experiences of others, and inviting them to create their own solutions.

Starting from a different assessment of human potential: Communication that empowers clearly involves a different view of human nature, treating people more as collaborators to be joined than as objects to be moved.

What has been assumed by the conventional model of communication is based on a very narrow picture of human potential. The conventional model of communication undervalues the people being "developed."

Its assumptions are reminiscent of the colonial hauteur that conceived its mission to help the poor natives become more like us. It encourages the false and

But the failures that have given rise to this skepticism are not inherent in communication itself, only in the way it has traditionally been conceived and pursued.

debilitating view that a woman who pounds grain by hand to make flour cannot be wise, or that a woman who has never drawn hot water from a tap cannot have dignity.

Learning how to listen: Because people are not stupid about how others regard them, communication according to these principles gets people's backs up. It makes them far more likely to think of the reasons why they cannot do what is recommended than why they can. It is much more effective at creating resentment than change.

Conventional development communication approaches people at their lowest level—the fear of authority and power—rather than at their highest—the exercise of their creative functions. This is not only bad psychology, it is out of step with contemporary realities.

The world as a whole is moving away from authority/control forms of governance and toward information/choice forms. This is evident in the family, where strict role definitions are being replaced by more democratic kinds of interaction. It is evident in the relations between men and women, where individual choices are dictated less by biology than by what each partner desires for him/herself and for the relationship. It is evident in business, where workers now sit on boards of directors.

At the growing edge of nearly every sector of society, there is a new regard for people sharing information and perspectives in order to arrive at mutually satisfying choices. We are learning how to listen to the people with whom we are in partnership.

Shared concerns: Applied to development, this means that instead of telling people what to do, you elicit their involvement.

At first glance that looks like a much more difficult, unwieldy, unpredictable and inefficient way to proceed. It may indeed be all of those things. But it is also the best way to arrive at solutions in which people are willing to invest their energies and their futures.

Development has to be based on shared concerns—whatever the people want for themselves is just as important as whatever is on the agenda of the central authority. Ultimately, development is—or should be—teaching people that they can design their own lives, and then giving them the tools to do it. A psychic balance is preserved; people are giving and taking at the same time.

If you can find out what things have the most meaning in a person's life, and give him or her the experience of making decisions about these things, then you have given this person a genuine control over his or her own life.

By this "empowerment," you enable the person to go on to do a great deal more than if you had merely "convinced" him or her of something in the traditional manner. People change more deeply and more happily as a result of a concrete experience demonstrating where their advantage lies than as a result of an abstract argument to the same effect.

This means seeing information not as a means of control but as the raw material of choice. Communication is not a matter of one-directional delivery of finished goods in the form of policies and directives. It is a multi-directional network that sends raw materials in many directions at once, assuming they will be assembled into different products in different locations.

This image is of an open marketplace with lots of word-of-mouth exchange, as opposed to a dispensary line where all the goods are standard issue and announcements are broadcast by a single loudspeaker.

This is the kind of communication I do. It offers an alternative model to the standard form of development communication, one that operates from the belief that you make social change by fostering human exchange.

Not "Trickle-Down" But...

■ **Equality between sender and receiver:** The new style of communication can be distinguished from the old in several particulars. The first principle is equality between sender and receiver.

For a true act of communication to occur, both parties are equally important; neither can complete it alone. The most obvious signal of such equality is the willingness to listen as well as talk.

The idea of listening does not even occur to development people working in huge countries like Indonesia or India because scale alone makes the undertaking seem so hopeless. How do you listen to a population of such immense size?

It can be done, as I will show a little later. What is required is first, commitment, and second, a different mental set. It also helps to have the right technology, but technology alone is not the answer.

I sometimes wonder whether the current rash of kidnappings and hostage-taking everywhere in the world is not an indication of the desperate lengths to which some people feel they have to go in order to get the attention of those in power. Once the so-called terrorists have our attention, they mainly want to be heard. While policy analysts in Washington say that the Iran episode reflected on the status of our military might and level of respect in the world, I would say that, in part, it showed what poor listeners we are.

■ **Starting where people are:** The second principle of the new style of communication is to start wherever people are. You don't have much mutuality when you constantly require people to accept your assumptions before they can join your conversation.

If communication is truly to make connections, it must find people where they live and speak to them on that ground. The gaps in background and experience between development personnel and the constituencies they serve make this difficult.

The development officers live in urban areas where most of their information comes through the government-controlled media rather than through other people. They do not usually know or talk to their neighbors. They do not work with their hands—nor, in many cases, do they have friends who do.

When these people enter village life, they frequently are prisoners of their own orientations, expecting the change processes to operate in the same way they do in the environment they know. As a result, they rely on an intellectual approach where a visceral approach is needed.

■ **Dealing in feelings as well as thoughts:** This leads in turn to the principle that communication must deal in feelings as well as thoughts.

The traditional style of communication was to sanitize information by removing any vestige of emotion or feeling. But feelings, by and large, offer a much stronger and more trustworthy way to identify common concerns than thoughts. Changes in feelings are generally what makes changes in thought possible.

Organizations do not deal in feelings; individuals do. We need an approach to communications that can bridge that gulf.

■ **Telling the truth:** The final principle of the alternative communication philosophy is the willingness to deal in truth.

The temptation exists in any political activity to be more concerned with how things look than with how they really are. But if develoment efforts are to succeed, they must be pursued with larger motives than political safety or public relations. Communication that attempts to deal in images rather than truth is eventually strangled in its own lies.

Truth is, I should add, more than the mere avoidance of lies. It requires active effort to get behind stereotypes. It means looking beyond the immediate moment to long-term effects. It includes opening yourself to the other person's truth as well as your own.

Fortunately, there are leaders in the world who are beginning to understand that their power comes from encouraging exchange and communication rather than from attempting to control what people think and do. They are open to truth-telling in a way that traditional leaders seldom were. They feel it is good to know when something is wrong, so you can fix it; and it is good to know when something is right, so you can spread it.

A Technology to Serve These Values

This alternative communication philosophy is made truly powerful by the fact that there is a technology available that is ideally suited to serve these values. That technology is videotape.

Video communication can be multi-directional, person-centered, locally-originated, and feeling-sensitive. Because it is simple to understand and operate, relatively inexpensive and durable, it can also act to democratize communication activity in a profound way.

Video's unique strength is that it does not require central processing—as do film, print, television and practically every other medium. So videotape opens up many different kinds of horizontal exchanges.

Material produced in one place can be taken and shown directly in another place, with no necessity of going back up a pipeline to a central laboratory or clearinghouse. The liberating potential is simply enormous. Central systems everywhere are an overload; at best, they are difficult places to exchange ideas. Video allows and encourages direct communication from woman to woman, from doctor to doctor, from village to village.

Videotape as literacy tool: Videotape provides for people who neither read nor write a means for sharing ideas and experiences over distance. It puts in their hands a way of extending themselves, of sharing what they know, which was never before possible. Video technology breathes new electronic life into the oral tradition.

The user is in control of the videotape, so he or she can take in at a comfortable rate unfamiliar or threatening material. A videotape can be played over and over again, it can be stopped in the middle and restarted, it can be rolled backwards and then forward again—all flexibilities that help to make it an ideal personal learning tool for use either individually or in small groups.

The absence of intermediary subjectivities: Because videotape can serve as a straightforward recording medium, it gives the viewer direct access to an event without any filtering of the experience

ACTION

by intermediary subjectivities—as a newspaper reporter, teacher, TV newsman, or messenger would do.

Also, no intervening experts, brokers, or interpreters are needed. The viewer can see for him/herself what is happening, deal with it, confront it, integrate it on a personal basis. The viewer also has access to the full feeling-tone of what transpires, not just a disembodied record in words alone, pictures alone, or edited snatches of both together.

In short, people can trust and act on the basis of a videotape record of an event, discussion, meeting, or decision-making session in a way they could not if they were dealing with someone else's report of what was happening.

A tool of communication, but not the communication itself: Videotape does not, by itself, magically reshape the quality of communication. Like any technology, it is only a tool.

But it will produce nothing out of the ordinary in the hands of a person who needs to keep control. And in the hands of a person who enjoys watching other people grow, and who sees videotape as a means to inspire people and draw out their creativities, it will honor specific circumstance in a way no other medium can.

Nation-Building by Promoting Two-Way Learning and Communication

Nation-building: When videotape technology and the desire for democratic communication are sensitively and creatively joined, phenomenal things can happen. Small-format videotape, used in combination with national television, can stimulate an unprecedented degree of exchange within a country, giving people of diverse cultures, circumstances, and backgrounds a way to know each other.

Governments need not think of the broadcast air as a resource to be carved up into small pieces like the land. And when governments respect their

citizens' capacities to be initiators of ideas about themselves and their ways of life, then videotape communication can become an incredibly exciting and important kind of nation-building.

The nation-building isn't xenophobic—jealously protecting national prerogatives—but is nation-building in the joyful sense of finding and exploring people's similarities and differences.

Many developing countries—quite wisely, I think—are indicating they do not want to adopt Western models of national communication systems. They want the benefits of technology, of

course, but in ways that will complement, rather than compete with, their own traditions.

These countries also want to develop in ways that will establish them as "learning" cultures on their own, rather than as dependent "nursing" cultures fastened to the tit of Western commerce.

Videotape, especially in conjunction with broadcast television for wide dispersion, is proving to be extraordinarily attractive to leaders looking for alternative systems of national communication. In this respect, video is at the forefront of an emerging global communications revolution.

Videotape in Indonesia: To show how the principles of this new communication philosophy can be embodied in a concrete way, I would like to report on my work with videotape in Indonesia over the past two years. The Indonesian case study builds on international work with videotape as a develoment tool that I have been doing for over a decade.

As my most recent, large-scale application of these principles, Indonesia has a greater vividness and freshness than some of my earlier work.

And Indonesia itself is a fascinating country. It is large enough to experience the enormous difficulties of bringing development to a huge population dispersed over an archipelago of islands. Yet Indonesia is not so disillusioned as to believe the task is neither manageable nor worthwhile.

Assisting Family Planning in Indonesia

Dr. Suyono: My contact with Indonesia began when the Ford Foundation office in Jakarta sent the deputy chairman of the family planning program, Dr. Haryono Suyono, to see me. Haryono was preceded by his reputation as a communications genius.

Family planning in Indonesia works to an unprecedented degree. Haryono's technique was to create lines of communication that began in countless small apsaris or women's groups in each locality, and extended upward through villages, groups of villages, regions, provinces, and finally to the national ministry for family planning, the BKKBN.

Haryono's approach, provided for discussion at every level of organization, and had helped bring about a dramatically large and rapid shift in traditional habits and attitudes concerning birth control. Even more impressive, these changes were documented in a statistical reporting system that functioned admirably.

Getting from "whats" to "whys": Dr. Haryono, despite his successes, had several concerns when we met. He and his colleagues knew a great deal quantitatively about the family planning program—who in what village was practicing what form of birth control. But they did not know much about the whys.

Why were some people so committed? Why were others not? Why were people dropping out? Why would people decide to change their minds and habits?

In trying to get answers to these questions, Haryono had been running himself ragged going to sessions all over the country with individual groups. He was interested to see whether videotape could help provide feedback on a larger scale and with greater effectiveness. He also wanted to find ways for the family planning program to get on TV in Indonesia, so they could bolster their lagging urban program.

We talked at some length about the powerful impetus for social change that can be provided by ordinary people talking about their own attitudes and experiences. At the end of this first meeting, both Haryono and I were excited at the possibilities videotape seemed to offer the Indonesian family planning program, but we still had to figure out what we would do, and how.

Next I went to Indonesia myself, where I visited a number of villages and listened to what was going on. This exploratory process was very exciting and invigorating. I was fascinated by the differences I saw. Indonesia is not one culture, but many cultures coexisting in a shifting relationship of isolation and mutual enrichment.

Because it was colonized for hundreds of years, Indonesia blends a very deep sense of its own traditions with a surprising degree of Westernization. The effect of all these cultural cross-currents had been to establish the Indonesians as people used to learning from each other. I began to perceive some of the human dimensions of how communication worked in the country.

I had thought, when I first arrived in the country, that I I might prepare a broadcast-quality "Are You Listening" videotape with women who were using birth control, and then conduct a brief workshop in a small-format videotape.

But after exploring the country for a while, I wanted to do more than that. I wanted to put much more emphasis on the workshop in a small-format video. In that way, I could leave behind an ongoing capability for people to use the technology to speak to one another across the boundaries of distance and cultural difference. This ripple effect could extend my own activities a hundredfold—or even a thousandfold.

Generations Teaching Each Other

As I traveled and talked with people, especially women, I was extremely interested in the ways that generations were teaching each other. With family planning in particular, there was a reversal of the usual pattern.

Martha Stuart Communications

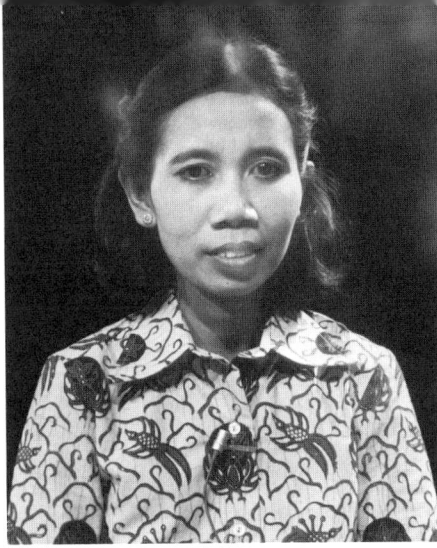

Here the younger generation was teaching the older, and with a degree of love and respect that was touching to witness. And because there was no denial of tradition, there was less fear of change. Drawing on the unusual quality of this generational exchange, I prepared a powerful "Are You Listening" program entitled "Three Generations of Javanese Women."

I was also impressed by the dignity with which the Javanese and Balinese Indonesians dealt with their sexuality. Loving someone—physically as well as emotionally—was accepted as an important and valid aspect of life everywhere I went.

The security provided by this loving connection contributed a great deal to people's self-esteem. This attitude comes through clearly in the refreshing sexual frankness of the videotape program.

The Ford Foundation later sponsored a second trip to Indonesia for me specifically to encourage Indonesian television, TVRI, to work with the Indonesian family planning program. I was successful in this mission, but partly due to my own efforts and partly due to a fear among Indonesian television people that their grip on information technology in the country was slipping somewhat.

The Javanese government had recently given the BKKBN [national ministry for family planning] a small-format video studio along with 400 recorder and playback units. Suddenly, the BKKBN looked like a rival network. That was enough to make the Indonesian television people willing to join in our project.

Together, we designed a two-week workshop with 15 BKKBN people and 15 TVRI people, using the TVRI training center, which proved an ideal location for the project. It also enabled the "Are You Listening" crew to demonstrate some of the finer points of the new television equipment to the Indonesians. The workshop was made possible by grants from the Ford Foundation, World Bank, UNFPA, and USAID. There were also contributions of technical consultations from Sony and of equipment and training from JICA, the Japanese AID.

When the workshop finally convened in addition to the 30 television and family planning people, there were several additional participants from non-governmental agencies, and a number of observers. After theoretical discussion about the uses of videotape as a development tool, we quickly moved on to give them hands-on experience with the technology itself.

None of the participants had ever worked with small-format video. The most interesting aspect of the workshop was to watch people who had been skeptical or even defensive at the beginning slowly change their minds and attitudes as they worked with the equipment and the ideas.

The workshop produced 10 videotape programs with titles such as "Youth" and "Doctors." Two of the participants—both from the family planning bureau—exhibited unusual fluency with the equipment; one was a near-genius with the camera, another at editing. A music producer from one of the television districts, who initially did not wish to join in the workshop, eventually become totally involved and made a beautiful videotape on fishermen.

The workshop process familiarized the participants with all the equipment involved in producing small-format video programs. But, beyond that, it sensitized them to the different ways

Indonesia Minister of Family Planning and Health works with Barkley Stuart in a workshop on "Videotape as a Development Tool."

Informal discussion after a day of camera work.

video technology could be used as a tool of human exchange. We attempted not only to give them mastery of certain basic video equipment and production procedures, but to give them a new perspective on communication.

At the end of the workshop, the "Are You Listening" crew came to Indonesia and we made the program "Three Generations of Javanese Women." All of the women on the tape came from two remote villages. They had never before ridden on an elevator or escalator or seen a building with more than a stair, much less the inside of a television studio.

The conventional view holds that women from such rural, economically limited backgrounds, lacking in formal education, have little of value to say to other people. Yet, by the end of our taping, these women had covered a great deal of important ground about the status of women and women's development in Indonesia. One of the participants phrased their conclusion this way: "Women shouldn't just be

listeners or observers, they should be equal partners. This program will benefit women in the villages by showing them that women have valuable things to say and should be heard. This will help contribute to the success of all sectors of women's development."

No one who sees this program can doubt that the issues of women's development have penetrated to the most rural and isolated areas of the world, where they are being dealt with creatively and humanely with the intent of expanding the potential of individual lives. There are few messages more heartening or hopeful.

Once the editing was completed in New York and the program in final form, I returned to Indonesia. I wanted very much to show the program first to the women who had participated in it, and that meant traveling to their two remote villages. My emotions were mixed: while I was proud of what I had done, I was also worried that it might cause problems for the women who had

been so open and helpful on my behalf.

When I got to the first village after a four-hour drive, the gong that serves as the community call was struck and the people begin to assemble. As the tape was shown I was anxious to gauge its reception. After a few minutes, my trepidations were put to rest—the lurah or village leader, who was also the husband of one of the participants, gave me a thumbs-up signal of approval.

After this showing, we departed for the second village, where a higher echelon of leadership was convened, including the bupati or regional governor. Within a few minutes after the second screening had begun, the bupati was laughing heartily. I asked what amused him. He said, "That woman just said something very nice, something a man likes to hear. She said that even if she didn't have birth control she would have eight children again because she enjoys making love."

When the program was over, the bupati was generous in his praise. He described the program as helping

MAKING IT HAPPEN:

Learning to lay an audio track superimposing one dialect on another.

Teaching officials of Indonesian television that ordinary people can be interesting.

women see many different women doing different things, and functioning as spokespersons. After all, he concluded, birth control is working because of women, not men.

From there I returned to Jakarta and showed the program to a number of other groups. I was struck by how the reactions shifted as I moved further away from the people and into organizational structures.

■ The head of the Women's Bureau in Indonesia (who screened the program with her five male deputies) said she loved the program and asked to present it at the UN Women's Conference in Copenhagen as another "poem" from Indonesia.

■ The population planning division of the AID office responded very positively to the program. One man said it gave him goosebumps and made him feel his work was worthwhile.

■ The Indonesian telvision people got very nervous when they saw the program and the frankness of the discussion. They were quick to say that

only film, not videotape, could be broadcast on television! Now I hear they are planning to air it.

Perhaps the most curious and revealing reaction came when I screened the program for a group of foundation people and funders in New York, most of them involved in population planning work. After watching the program attentively, they made a number of comments reflecting an attitude of criticsm and even personal discomfort.

Having thought about it since, I think their discomfort with the program was based on a feeling that they realized they had lost control. The women in the program made birth control and the decision to use it seem easy and natural, whereas these planners were used to thinking of it as a difficult choice for people to make, one that required a substantial education/communication effort.

Suddenly, here were local women saying, in effect, that people don't resist change so long as there is something in it

for them. That whole orientation was foreign to this group of planners. They may also have been put off by the intimacy of the discussion, not only in substance but in style.

But the price of this approach to communication, quite frankly, may often be discomfort for those who still think about development communication in the old mode of authority/control. These people will not always hear what they expect to hear or what they want to hear.

They will get some surprises and some of them may be unpleasant. Unfortunately, planners hold it as an article of faith that any surprise is bad. That just is not so. No learning ever occurs without expectations being violated.

If these planners were willing to think of themselves as students as well as teachers, as people with lessons to learn as well as to give, they would not feel so afraid of exposing themselves to the unexpected.

A POSITIVE GUIDE TO THE FUTURE

The Value of Direct Human Feedback

The most important place to begin using this new communications approach, I am convinced, is in project evaluation.

■ Most project evaluation is now purely quantitative. But, **in development terms, the most important questions usually are qualitative and motivational. Only these questions really indicate what the source of the change is, what people are learning, and how deep their commitment is.** Statistics help, but you really need to know what is happening in people's hearts and heads.

■ **We deny those who are aided the opportunity to be honest with us, if we know about them only through the reports of others.**

■ **And that, in turn, denies us the chance to get new ideas or modify our existing ideas and programs.**

Filtered feedback commits development to a lock-step approach of continuing to do what has already been done. Direct feedback opens the door to a creative, two-way learning process in which development becomes a truly collaborative enterprise.

■ **Only with communication in this new videotape mode can you begin to release the energies of people to find their own solutions.** There is, I think, a greater need for tools than for directions. I use videotape as such a tool, a technology that provides a far more effective way for people to exchange experiences and ideas than through the maze of bureaucracy or piles of papers.

■ I also think it is **important that we view the information exchanged between people as a renewable expanding resource—rather than as a commodity in limited supply. Information is a raw material that can be used in different contexts in different ways.**

■ **Information is often embodied in the form of individual experience, and since it is a wealth rather than a scarcity, it is not necessary that we agree, only that we share.**

Sharing opens an infinity of choices, and such sharing is the only kind of communication that will truly contribute to human growth and development.

□

Javanese women watching a videotape in which they were participants

Seat Pleasant, Maryland: Learning by Building at Central Senior High School

In the winter of 1976, some students and teachers at Central Senior High School in Prince George's County, Maryland, learned about the energy crisis the hard way. Due to overcrowding, many classes were held in temporary, prefabricated propane-heated buildings which were shut down because of fuel shortages.

Learning from crisis: But a couple of enterprising Central High teachers decided to turn the energy crisis into a learning experience for students. Jerry Silver, a science teacher, and math instructor Kurt Johnson created a project for math, science, drafting, and other students to design, construct, and install a simple solar collector to provide heat and slash the amount of propane fuel needed.

"Probably the strongest message that students receive from their school about energy is the example set by the school itself," Silver and Johnson wrote in a 1977 *Today's Education* article. "The types of energy choices made by an educational institution influence students' perceptions of what is appropriate use of energy."

Developing plans: In class twenty students and the two teachers discussed and evaluated ideas and agreed on a design to capture the sun's energy—an efficient but simple solar heating system for their classroom. The 8-by-24 foot collector is made from six plywood boxes—or panels—painted black inside to absorb the suns rays and filled with aluminum cans to collect the heat. Fiberglass covers the box to keep in the heat. The panels are connected, creating a long single solar collector which faces the sun. Air is circulated through ducts by two blowers, one pumping solar-heated air into the room and the other pulling the room's air into the collector for heating.

Getting started: The teachers persuaded the local utility to donate lumber. School maintenance personnel and a local electrician and sheet metal worker offered their expertise. The Board of Education kicked in $800 for other materials such as paint, nails, insulation, and fans.

With resources in hand, the students tackled the project. Drafting students drew up plans for the collector. Others gathered, cleaned, and painted 1,200 aluminum cans and calculated room dimensions and volume to determine energy needs.

Building and installing: With materials ready and two textbooks for reference, the crew of students, teachers, and technical helpers began work one March weekend. By the end of the day, three of the collector panels were completed and within a few weeks all six were finished. By May, the solar collector was operational.

Valued at $2,000, the solar heating system, which is controlled by an automatic thermostat, costs about $10.40 a year to operate. On winter days, the collector's temperature reaches between 140° F and 180° F. So even on cloudy days when the sun's rays are harder to capture, heat from the collector is capable of boosting room temperatures from 5 to 30 degrees above those outside.

Second solar project: In 1978, Central High students tackled another project—a solar heating system for the William S. Schmidt Environmental Education Center in Orme, Maryland. Funding again came from the Board of Education. And because the Center is so well insulated, the system provides nearly all heating needs on clear days. "The projects gave us a chance to interact with students in a new context and provided a vehicle for students to tie in what they were doing in other classes," Johnson and Silver wrote in the *Today's Education* article. "For example, students in woodworking classes used their skills in building

the first collector. It also gave us many opportunities to present concepts that are part of our regular math and science curriculum."

And Silver has a tip for other teachers planning a similar project. "You should involve as many different teachers and program areas as possible," he suggests.

—from *People Power*, U.S. Office of Consumer Affairs

Jerry Silver

Central Senior High students attach the solar heating system to the schoolhouse.

New Alchemy Institute

Serving our Dreams and Values:

Appropriate Technology

By Harriet Barlow

The applecart is overturned: The quest for appropriate technologies began in the early 1970s. It has become a movement that joins a wide range of people who seek guideposts to a more equitable and sustainable society—social philosophers, planners, scientists, technicians, activists, and ordinary citizens.

Appropriate technology represents a rethinking of the relationship between one's context and the design, development, implementation, and management of hardware and process technologies.

Tom Bender, the founder of *Rain* magazine, wrote, "Appropriate technology reminds us that before we choose tools and techniques, we must choose our dreams and values, for some technologies serve them, while others make them unobtainable."

Thus, the applecart of technology is overturned.

Our approach to technology has moved from one that expects people to adapt to technological development, to one which places cultural, environmental, and ethical considerations first, demanding that technology be consistent with those considerations.

The origins of appropriate technology: This sort of approach to technology began in the developing nations. Those working for community development had observed many of the new projects to be counterproductive. Large-scale projects such as the Green Revolution in agriculture and the massive construction projects (such as the Aswan dam at the head of the Nile) were observed often to involve large-scale surprises, in the form of adverse and unintended consequences.

In addition, these community development leaders could see, in retrospect, that it had been a devastating mistake to replace so much

human-, water-, and animal-powered machinery—which had been widely available, simple, and inexpensive—by oil-dependent machines that were costly and complex, and required often-scarce gasoline.

So in the developing nations it was becoming clear that many developed-country technologies did not match the resources available within the less developed countries. To some, they seemed a form of technological imperialism, renewing old patterns of dependancy and control.

These imported technologies tended to be capital-intensive when the countries had a shortage of capital—and a surplus of labor. They required professionals for construction and maintenance when the countries lacked engineers and Ph.D.'s—but were rich in semi-skilled labor. The imported technologies were characteristically large in scale—and required vast markets and social support structures where none existed.

The most serious deficiency lay in the social effect of the technologies. In countries where community developers were struggling to balance growth with social justice, these technologies tended to widen the gaps between economic classes.

To address these problems, the predecessors of the appropriate technology field sought new approaches. They would utilize local resources. Their approaches would be labor-intensive. They would require little capital. They would be easily maintained. And they would contribute to equity.

192

MAKING IT HAPPEN:

Three principles emerged:

- **human scale,**
- **democracy, and**
- **decentralization.**

The closer a technology was to human scale, the greater its chances of being responsive and sustainable. And the more democratic and decentralized the structure of a system, the more accountable and maintainable it could be.

Rethinking and restructuring the relationship between technology and society: In industrialized nations, such thinking sounded a responsive chord among those who were concerned with resource depletion, social inequity, and environmental pollution. Theoreticians and practitioners in America, Europe, and Japan felt that the institutions governing their social, economic, and political structures had grown too large, too bureaucratic, and too remote. There was a shared sense that our production and distribution processes and systems had become, in themselves, increasingly authoritarian and exploitative.

Those who first expressed these concerns have been joined, in the past decade, by people from every sector. Our goal is a rethinking—to be followed by a restructuring—of the relationship between technology and society. Peter Henriot and others at the Center of Concern wrote a memorandum in preparation for the 1979 United Nations Conference on Science and Technology for Development [UNC-STD], in which they expressed the essence of this new point of view. The goal of universal and long-term satisfaction of individual and collective requirements and needs should guide science and technology—and not the other way around.

For our purposes here, we can identify five basic values that express the essence of this new concept of development:

- **Human Dignity:** Each person—female and male, adult and child—has basic rights and needs that are to be respected and satisfied. Each person is to be given the opportunity to develop to her or his full potential. And each culture, with its own particular traditions, symbols, religious expressions, social organizations, and modes of behavior, is to be respected and its heritage preserved.

- **Societal involvement:** Each person should be given the freedom to be an active participant in the planning and decision-making processes that directly affect him or her. This requires social structures that provide interested persons with access to information that allows them to enter as equals into the process. Moreover, income-generating employment is a key element in the development process.

- **Social justice:** All peoples and nations are interdependent and should share fairly in the fruits of the earth and the development process. No economic or political structure or ideology should be allowed to oppress or marginate individuals or groups.

- **Ecological sustainability:** There is a bond between humanity and the physical environment that must be respected. This requires a recognition of the finiteness of resources and the fragility of the global ecosystem. The future impact of actions taken today should always be weighed.

- **Self-reliance:** Nations and peoples should have the capacity for autonomous decision-making and implementation in all aspects of the development process, as opposed to all forms of dependency. The main responsibility for solving the problems of the developing countries lies with these countries themselves. This is not, however, autarchy [complete withdrawal from contact and commerce with other nations and regions], and it requires new modes of incorporating the developing countries into the international order.

Toward a technology serving human values: These five values provide a foundation upon which to base all recommendations for action on a science-and-technology policy for development, whether in a developing nation or in our own communities in the United States.

If you takes as your context a development process that is doing all of these things—satisfying basic needs, guaranteeing public participation, promoting greater equity, respecting the environment, and ensuring national self-reliance—then the technological means in such a culture have *social* functions to perform beyond their obvious technical ones. So all proposals relating to science and technology can be "tested," not simply in terms of their economic costs and benefits but also their human and social impacts.

U.S. Centers of Alternative Technology

In the United States, a number of organizations have sprung up in both rural and urban areas to design alternatives to centralized, high-technology development. These were the pioneers.

- **John and Nancy Todd and the New Alchemist Institute on Cape Cod** created an oasis of sustainability in their Ark, combining shelter, solar energy, and food production under one roof.

- **On East 11th Street in New York City,** solar collectors, a Jacobs wind generator, and a cooperative garden emerged from burned-out slums through the combined talents of sweat-equity labor and solid technical assistance.

- **In the Ozarks, Ted Landers** experimented with methane digesters and tree crops.

- **Bill and Helga Olkowski** co-founded the Farallones Institute in the San Francisco Bay area and parented the science of Integrated Pest Management in an urban context. At the Integral Urban House in Berkeley they demonstrated the relationship between household life-support systems. At the Farallones Rural Center in Occidental, California, they designed techniques for living gently on the earth.

- **The Institute for Local Self-Reliance,** our organization, was also there at the beginning. ILSR was founded by David Morris, Gil Friend and Neil Seldman. Our mission was to foster equity in urban areas.

Rethinking Urban Economics

Urban self-reliance—beyond "welfare": The staff of the Institute for Local Self-Reliance realized that the welfare approach to social justice was not working. So we undertook to rethink the basis for providing goods and services within an urban context.

Our objective was to evaluate whether it was technically feasible for city neighborhoods to become self-reliant communities. The assumption underlying our work was that natural resources constraints were going to redefine the presently assumed American definition of efficiency. Rising energy costs would make it inefficient to produce goods and services far from their markets. Materials scarcity would make recycling a common enterprise everywhere. A Conserver Society would emerge, emphasizing quality of life and quality of products.

Communities would begin to use their wastes as raw materials, and develop "closed-loop systems." That is, goods and services would be produced locally, from local resources, for local consumption. The city, the unit of government closest to most of the people, would expand its political authority, and begin to define itself as a nation—not self-sufficient, nor isolationist, but a community that took its boundaries seriously and developed a sophisticated planning capacity and economic development responsibility.

Within this framework, neighborhoods would become the planning and delivery mechanisms, with equity and environmental health as the primary considerations.

Implementing a Conserver Society: The Institute's program began with small demonstrations such as community gardens, recycling centers, and home-made solar collectors as points of definition for our broad vision. During more than five years the program has evolved to spurring and enabling actual implementation of the Conserver Society on a neighborhood and municipal scale.

Many of the ideas we foster, such as conservation and solar retrofit, are now financially cost-effective. Given that our objective is to move decision-makers from capital- and energy-intensive technologies to alternative labor-intensive and renewable-energy systems, we organize our program to address the concerns of the businessmen, politicians, and planners who make decisions at the federel, state, and local level. That means talking to planners about the tax base, to bankers about returns on capital, and to politicians about votes.

The Institute's task is both to challenge and to aid city governments in making the conceptual and policy changes necessary to implement self-reliance on the local level, and to link the response of cities with the aspirations and abilities of their local residents and their neighborhood organizations.

Research—plus advocacy: There is a common pattern for Institute projects, which has evolved as we have learned the balance between advocacy, research and implementation.

New York City: Raising a Windmill on 11th Street

Origins: The 519 Housing Co-op began in 1973 when Freedberg and Roberto (Rabbit) Nazario, director of Inter-Faith Adopt-a-Building, a nonprofit group dedicated to restoring the impoverished Lower East Side area, began organizing unemployed residents to buy and renovate the abandoned building.

Once organized, the group had no money for the hefty down payment needed for a loan to buy and restore the dwelling. But a revolutionary city program called "sweat equity" came to the rescue. Sweat equity [the difference between the normal labor cost of building rehabilitation and the small amount paid renovators] allows low-income residents to use their labor as a down payment on city loans to buy and renovate deteriorated dwellings.

"Sweat equity produces housing for low-income people at half the cost of conventional methods," Freedberg says. As a result, residents become co-op owners in the renovated building at payments they can afford.

In 1974, with backing of Inter-faith Adopt-a-Building and the nonprofit Urban Homesteading Assistance Board [UHAB], the 11th Street co-op won a $177,000 sweat equity loan from the city. And the propective tenants began the hard work of renovation. (Although not available in time to assist the group, co-opers may now qualify for technical and financial assistance from the newly created National Consumer Cooperative Bank.)

Installing Solar Savers: Meanwhile, at a UHAB meeting Freedberg met Travis Price, a solar architect from New Mexico who had learned of New York's sweat equity program and realized its potential for cutting solar installation costs for poor residents.

The two got together at 519 in the spring of 1974, and Price was given the green light to apply for funds and design a solar system for the building.

Funding: In October of that year, Price began teaching the co-op members how to weathrize the building by installing storm windows and insulating exterior walls. A $43,000 grant from the Community Services Administration's [CSA] Emergency Energy Conservation Services Program paid for solar hardware, insulation, and technical consultants.

Meanwhile, Price and several youth architectural students formed the Energy Task Force, a nonprofit technical assistance group which, for three months during the cold 1975 winter, worked with co-op members in building the solar heating system.

"There we were up on the roof Saturday nights working by drop-light, the wind whistling through our

When we perceive an inappropriate technology (nuclear power, the burial in city dumps of urban wastes, franchised fast-food stores, etc.), we develop or adapt and introduce an alternative technical solution in a demonstration project. In the process, the state and federal policies that deter the rapid spread of a working technology are pinpointed and criticized. And through information, training, and technical assistance the people-base is strengthened to support the change.

In 1976, for example, three people from the South Bronx invited us to talk with them. They had read in *Audubon Magazine* about the Institute's work and were interested in the concept of local self-reliance. They wanted to do development work in their own neighborhood, an area of gutted and fire-ridden shells of buildings. They had no money and no organization.

Their principal resources were—
■ access to 400 acres of vacant land strewn with brick and rubble,
■ a large unemployed labor force, and
■ the Hunts Point Produce Market, the wholesale food distribution point

for New York City and a generator of large volumes of organic waste.

In appropriate technology there are no quick fixes. Institute staff members—including an urban planner, a horticulturalist, a community organizer, an engineer and an economist—worked for 18 months to conceptualize and implement the use of that organic waste from Hunts Point Produce Market as an economic development venture.

To organize the venture, the Bronx Frontier Development Corporation was ultimately established, and, by the end of the first year of operation, it was producing 70 tons of finished compost a week. The compost was used to restore the soil for community gardens in the South Bronx.

To reconceptualize or rethink the use of our physical, fiscal, and human resource base is an on-the-job learning process. In the Bronx, as with other projects, we found that everything takes twice as long, is twice as expensive, and is twice as complex as was anticipated.

Such frustrations and the lessons learned from them are the foundation of experience and learning upon which we

ACTION

are constantly building. For example, we were moved to look at the entire regulatory system, local and federal when it took us 12 months to secure the health permits for the composting project. We knew that similar difficulties and delays were being experienced by groups elsewhere when they applied for permits for waterless (composting) toilets.

What was happening was that the regulatory system had developed in response to the strategies other than those we were proposing, and thus was not amenable to them. As citizens have begun to retrofit homes for solar energy systems, similar problems with housing codes, tax laws, and the issue of solar rights have surfaced.

How things build upon one another: Today the Bronx Frontier Development Corporation has a larger budget than the Institute for Local Self-Reliance. It has itself become a source of expertise and creativity for other urban-based, minority-oriented orga-

---

ears, our fingers freezing off as we fitted the pipes," Price recalls. By March 1976 the solar water heating system was complete and the co-op owners moved in.

The Windmill: But the work still wasn't over. During the building's reconstruction, the 11th Street group had tangled with Con Ed over a $1,000 electric bill. The dispute led Price to an alternative energy conference in New York where Ted Finch, a recent college graduate with a major in wind energy, lectured. Price asked Finch to take a look at 519 and offer suggestions. On the day of Finch's visit, Con Ed pulled the plug on 519, cutting off the building's electricity and causing the solar collectors to overheat.

Finch reacted instantly. Determined to minimize the co-op's dependence on the large utility company, in October 1976 he acquired a $4,000 secondhand, 2,000-watt windmill that measured

14 feet in diameter. And, with another small CSA grant from the Emergency Energy Conservation Service Program, construction and intallation of the windmill was completed.

Hoisting the windmill: ETF and 11th Street co-op members prepared for the windmill by constructing a concrete base and reinforcing the roof to hold the structure tightly in place. Scaffolding material was borrowed from the Cathecral of St. John the Divine, a local Episcopal church [sic.], to hoist the windmill onto the roof. And a rugged pulley system was attached to the side of the building.

Mustering all the know-how and ingenuity they could, a group of about 40 neighborhood residents managed to hoist the two 20-foot windmill sections to the top of the five-story building, as Freedberg recalls, "with a lot of luck, sweat, and muscle power."

Once the windmill was in place, the group used wire to secure it to the reinforced sections of the roof.

Bronx windmill: Solar systems and weatherization techniques have spread much more rapidly than windmills on New York's Lower East Side. But the small demonstration windmill on 11th Street led to another impressive project in the Hunts Point section of the South Bronx. The 64-foot structure is the first commercial windmill of its size in New York. The windmill—constructed with ETF's technical assistance—is part of an innovative plan dreamed up by the Bronx Frontier Develement Corporation, a nonprofit community group, to "green over" some of the beleaguered borough's worst rubbled areas. The windmill provides low-cost electricity for the nonprofit group's composting operation, which occupies four acres near the Hunts Point sewage treatment plant.

—*People Power*, U.S. Office of Consumer Affairs

nizations. BFDC has a variety of programs and proposals, including now a wind generator that provides electricity for the compost project. And they, in turn, are benefiting from the experience and legal precedents of others.

The East 11th Street project, when they constructed their roof-top wind generator, became energy producers as well as energy consumers. They had bought electricity from Con Edison when they needed more, and now they sought the legal right to sell any excess back to Con Edison. When Con Ed rejected their initial offer, they turned to the courts in a classic David-and-Goliath contest. The courts found for the local Puerto Rican and Black residents.

So subsequently the Bronx Frontier could build on that precedent and backfeed—and sell—its excess electricity to the utility. This New York-based right of small energy producers to sell their excess electricity to utilities has subsequently been extended to all states by Federal legislation. In fact, utilities are required to buy those kilowatts at the price they would have cost the utility if the utility itself had constructed that additional generating capacity. *That's* decentralization in action.

How Appropriate Technology Spreads

The South Bronx project is one example. Some are new, some are old. Farmer cooperatives and direct markets, parent-run day care centers, walk-in preventive health clinics, car pools, bike paths, user-supported media—all of these utilize "appropriate" technology in that they stress individual initiative and are cooperatively joined in the community interest. Every community in America has projects that conform to the criteria of "appropriateness," and participants in these projects are using less and wasting less in an age of limits. And they are teaching others how to do the same.

Practitioners of community technologies share an impulse to pass on their experience. There are scores of newsletters, mini-conferences, computer data bases, and a lot of old-fashioned letter writing. We all consider it a part of our work to ignore the tradition of withholding as "proprietary information" what we have learned. We have avoided the wheel reinvention syndrome and have built a community-based network that spans the continent.

Take the case of Hal Conklin and his friend Paul Relis. They live in Santa Barbara, California, a community which, like all American communities, considered its solid waste a public problem. Santa Barbara taxed its residents for garbage removal, which was then buried at a site, which also required tax dollars for its purchase and maintenance.

In 1969, Hal and Paul started a recycling center. The community responded. Business boomed. Hal and Paul joined forces with other local visionaries to establish the Community Environmental Council [CEC]), which in their words "is dedicated to building an ecologically based society. Such a society can arise when people of varying ages and backgrounds work together to learn and teach one another the dynamic relationship between natural resources and human needs—to bridge the gap between conservation theory and practice."

Their work has grown from a single recycling bin until now it includes several recycling centers, an ecology lending library, community gardens, energy-efficient buildings that are solar-heated, and bio-intensive agriculture. In 1977 alone, they collected over 100 tons of paper material per week for recycling, and disbursed more than $100,000 to over 200 participating community organizations in the area.

They have reduced the tax burden, and they provide jobs for area youth and raw materials for regional manufacturers. Hal Conklin is now a member of the Santa Barbara City Council.

To translate their experience into local, state, and national policy, CEC and the Institute work with other ecology and community development organizations across the country. If

consciousness is to be translated into accepted social convention, this extension from the individual to social institutions to various levels of government must occur.

"Soft Path" Energy Strategies

Appropriate technology and the "energy crisis": Despite the eightfold increase in the price of world oil since 1973, it is still necessary to argue for the merits of government policies favoring energy conservation and solar energy. Ill-conceived federal programs have emphasized high-technology alternatives to imported oil.

Those of us who advocate what Amory Lovins has termed the "soft path" have had to scramble to articulate and demonstrate its efficacy. Our strategy at the Institute for Local Self-Reliance has been to build a soft-path model in a local neighborhood, and in mid-1978 the ILSR completed an evaluation of the potential for the District of Columbia to achieve energy self-reliance.

Based on aggressive implementation of conservation and renewable energy measures, ILSR estimated the District of Columbia could become 75 percent self-reliant by the early part of the next century in non-transportation energy, and could supply more than 40 percent of work-related transportation energy if the system were electrified, and solar cells were used to generate the electricity. The program would reduce the outflow of energy payments fvom the local economy by several hundred million dollars, and would create thousands of local jobs.

In that report, *Planning for Energy Self-Reliance: A Case Study of the District of Columbia,* ILSR recommended that city energy policy be implemented at the neighbnorhood level, using the strong, existing formal and informal community organizations in the District.

During early 1979, the Anacostia Energy Alliance was established in southeast Washington, D.C. During that year, more than 1,000 low-to-moderate income black residents of the Uniontown neighborhood had energy audits of their homes. More than 100 participated in workshops, where they learned about conservation, and subsequently built and installed solar domestic hot-water systems. Six solar systems were built and installed by the neighborhood, and the largest Trombe [passive solar heat-storage] wall within a three-state area was installed by 150 residents over two days.

Merchants gave 10 percent discounts to holders of energy-audit cards, and local housing rehabilitation contractors began to integrate conservation into their work.

Until more winter seasons have passed, it will not be possible to evaluate the project completely in quantitative terms. But the first results appear to show that the project has effected major energy savings through citizen education and actions.

The success of the project has enlisted the support of the city government, which has now recommended widening its scope by establishing local energy and technical assistance centers in neighborhoods throughout the city.

The Anacostia project—like demonstrations by citizens and technologists in Fitchburg [Massachusetts], Memphis [Tennessee], Davis [California], and scores of other cities—shows what can be done with adequate education and simple self-help tools.

Is "Profit" the Real "Bottom Line"?

Rethinking the "Bottom line": There is overwhelming evidence that prevention, conservation, efficiency, and carefulness are productive and life-sustaining principles. The obvious question that must be asked, then, is why do we persist in expending capital and natural resources to support policies and programs in defense, energy, agriculture, health, and transportation that defy such awareness?

The issue of profit is at the heart of the problem. Many business and political leaders accept without question that large cars are more "profitable" to manufacture and sell than small cars, that use of pesticides "profits" industry more than do integrated pest management technologies, that the medical profession would lose "profits" if preventive health care were the norm, that interstate highways "profit" builders more than do bike paths, that the energy industry "profits" more from synthetic fuel production than it can from conservation. . . and so on.

The accounting systems used in measuring such profits do not take into account the social and environmental costs for which this and future generations must pay.

Appropriate technologists do not oppose the notion of profit in itself. Many, in fact, are small business people. But all have watched as the solar industry was absorbed by the oil companies, as small farms were purchased by agribusiness corporations, and as independent breweries, bakeries, newspapers, and dairies were bought out by conglomerates. We see such centralization as fostering the unthinking notion of profit solely for profit's sake—which costs in social and environmental costs so dearly.

Appropriate technology and the politics of change: We cannot talk about appropriate technology without talking about economics and politics.

If the criteria for appropriateness are generalized to the way in which we as a nation do business, we will necessarily undergo significant structural change. But the change will be toward a strengthening of democratic tradition and a reduction of dependence. The change will be toward a social mentality closer to that of the Ojibwa Indians, who asked of each pending decision, "What will it mean for the seventh generation beyond us?"

It will not be an easy transition, but the models and resources exist, if we have the wisdom and will to heed them. □

ACTION

Who am I?   Harriet Barlow

Shaping a better future requires facing up to the present. I find that difficult. But paying attention to the present—the world as it lives, the place and the people on it, how they affect one another, as well as my own role in the scheme of things—is what I see as my life work.

I am way behind, both in perception and action. I still "save time"—an irrational concept, if there ever was one—by driving rather than walking. I continue to eat meat frequently, although I understand the protein profligacy in which I am indulging. I am often quiet when I should speak truth to power. Or I am too talkative when I could learn by listening. As I come more to understand which personal steps could lead to, or at least represent, the goal of a more equitable and healthful globe, the worse I look to myself.

All this could be a grim unrelieved business, if it were not for the constant intrusion of elements human and divine. I take regular doses of the great equalizers—children, music, ice cream. I revel in natural and historic mysteries, great and small. I pay very close attention to the absurd behavior of people who think that they, rather than life itself, are the Bingo.

In short, I gallop along, thinking a lot about what needs to be done, doing a bit, and trying to stay on the side of Light. And laugh a lot.

Seattle: Putting Garbage to Good Use

The cost of waste: Americans pay a staggering $4.5 billion annually—and untold time and energy—for sanitation trucks, employees, landfills, and dumps to collect and dispose of our garbage.

Those costs can be cut by boosting public interest in separating and selling reusable trash. About half of all garbage—glass, aluminum, newsprint, bottles, and other reusables—can be recycled by manufacturers and industries. And they can then be turned into new products less expensively and using less energy than with raw materials.

Paying for trash: By putting a price tag on trash, recycling businesses across the country are beginning to prosper while prodding residents to build trash-separating habits which benefit themselves, their communities, and local governments. For instance, the for-profit Seattle Recycling, Inc. (SRI) in Washington is making a significant contribution to the city by reducing garbage and decreasing the need for costly landfills.

Recycling-conscious residents earn an average of $10 to $15 per SRI pick up, getting as much as two cents a pound for newspapers, 26 cents a pound for aluminum cans, and from 35 to 50 cents for a case of beer bottles.

Moreover, SRI has helped about 100 church, school, and other nonprofit community groups raise funds by encouraging them to launch reusable garbage drives. Not only are the groups paid for the recyclables they collect from residents, but they also get a 10 percent bonus for their organizations. Since SRI began in 1976, over $100,000 has been paid to community groups.

Origins and first funding: It all started in 1975 when two environmentally minded enterprising young men, Don Kneass and Jim McMahon, set up a toll-free, statewide Recycling Information Hotline to give Washington residents information on recycling reusable garbage [funded with a $500,000 grant from the State Department of Ecology]. After one year, the successful hotline was taken over by the State Department of Ecology.

Convinced that Seattle needed another recycling operation, Kneass and McMahon formed Seattle Recyling, Inc. They wooed $14,500 from private investors and kicked in $2,500 of their own money to launch their business in a low-income Seattle neighborhood.

Rocky times: They had little trouble finding buyers for the reusables. Paper mills were eager to save lumber and pulping expenses by buying old newspapers to produce paper goods, and large aluminum companies like Kaiser were anxious to purchase cans to shred for their products.

The men soon learned that this was not enough to ensure success. They knew they had to attract a large volume of customers to get the quantity of reusable materials needed to put SRI in the black.

Capturing public interest: So, in the summer of 1977, determined to build a strong business, the men launched a public awareness campaign. They advertised in local newspapers, held workshops, and met with school assemblies and other groups to push the recyling concept. Within a year, SRI's sales to manufacturers totaled $61,000, allowing Kneass and McMahon to draw a small salary for the first time and hire a part-time helper.

That year SRI collected 75 tons of aluminum cans, 427 tons of newspapers, and dozens of other items such as corrugated cardboard. They paid out almost $42,000 to area residents.

In 1979, SRI collected about 1,800 tons of newspapers and 264 tons of aluminum cans, boosting their sales to $500,000 while paying out almost $200,000 to conserving citizens.

Moreover, they have provided jobs in the low-income area in which their operation is based by hiring most of their 18-strong staff from that community.

City demonstrates support: In April 1978, the city tipped its hat to SRI by enlisting them as partners in a $185,000 pilot project aimed at saving city trash-removal costs while increasing resident awareness about the value of reusable wastes. The city-administered program, Separate Our Recyclables from Trash [SORT], offers lower garbage collection rates to about 5,000 families in 20 targeted neighborhoods who are willing to separate glass, tin, and other reusables from their trash. Eligible families pay a per-trash-can rate for garbage collection, and the city pays SRI to collect and market the reusable materials—and to continue its recycling education program. SRI estimates the city will get about $40,000 from the sale of the reusables to manufacturers and save an untold amount in waste removal costs.

Drop stations: SRI continues its efforts to make Seattle's residents responsive to recycling. In May 1978, the group installed a mobile recycling drop station 25 miles from its headquarters. On designated days, residents can get on-the-spot cash for reusables. The success of that station led to two additional mobile stations, and eight more strategically placed sites across the city are planned by March 1980.

—from *People Power*, U.S. Office of Consumer Affairs

December 1977:

Last Rites for Small Pox

The end: In 1974, India had 188,003 smallpox victims, of whom 31,262 died.

In 1978, India had no smallpox victims.

[Macaulay, describing 17th-century England, wrote:]

"The small pox was always present, filling the churchyard with corpses, tormenting with constant fears all whom it had not yet stricken, leaving on those whose lives it spared the hideous traces of its power, turning the babe into a changeling at which the mother shuddered, and making the eyes and cheeks of a betrothed maiden objects of horror to the lover."

On December 14, 1977, an international commission of public health experts from nine countries signed the death certificate for one of the most terrifying human afflictions ever known: *Variola major,* smallpox.

Meeting in Dacca, the capital of Bangladesh, two years after the last case of the disease had been detected, the experts certified that sufficient time had elapsed without traces of smallpox to safely say that the disease had been eradicated from that country. Since Bangladesh was the last place in the world known to harbor *Variola major,* the most lethal form of smallpox, this declaration fulfilled a hope that began with Edward Jenner's 18th-century discovery of vaccination.

The commission's decision came after a painstaking review of the Bangladesh smallpox campaign, which included an elaborate house-to-house search throughout the country for any outbreaks that might have been missed. Satisfied that no case could have eluded the search workers, who made eight visits to every house in the country during the last two years, the commission concluded that "smallpox vaccination will soon become redundant" throughout the world.

Smallpox had been a seemingly inevitable part of the human condition. The eradication of smallpox provides an inspiring example of what has been done to eliminate a scourge which had seemed inevitable.

Hunger and smallpox are different in many respects, but those committed to the end of hunger take heart from the smallpox experience.

The start of a dream: That dream goes back to a 1958 meeting of the policymaking World Health Assembly, which represents most of the world's nations. At the meeting, Dr. V.M. Zhdanov, a leading Soviet health official, introduced a resolution urging the World Health Organization (WHO) to launch a global campaign to eradicate smallpox from the face of the earth. If WHO led the way, Zhdanov predicted, smallpox could be wiped out and vaccination would become obsolete. Although his resolution was adopted, the campaign remained dormant until 1966, when the United States, the U.S.S.R., and other nations finally put up the necessary funds. At that point, some visionaries spoke of finishing the immense task within 10 years.

Few believed that such a feat was possible. Smallpox had a tenacious grip on 33 countries where it claimed 2,000,000 victims each year. The technical and administrative obstacles seemed insurmountable. Previous efforts at "international cooperation" had bogged down in Cold War rhetoric.

WHO, a United Nations agency, drafted Dr. D.A. Henderson from the U.S. Center for Disease Control in Atlanta to head up the campaign. Henderson, in turn, mobilized an army of top epidemiologists and health administrators from 50 countries who worked feverishly to stabilize the quality of locally produced vaccine, help coordinate national governments' programs, and research better strategies for combating the virus. Soon the disease began to yield its secrets.

Refinements in technology and strategy: Reminiscent of other world wars, new technologies were speedily developed to conquer the enemy. A freeze-dried vaccine, stable in the scorching heat of tropical countries, eliminated the need for refrigeration. A bifurcated needle, holding just the right amount of vaccine in its two-pronged tip, enabled inexperienced volunteers to carry out rapid and safe vaccinations in thousands of infected villages. Lessons learned in one country were applied to others.

One key breakthrough was the shift away from mass vaccinations to a more scientific strategy of "surveillance and containment," which focussed all vaccinations on people directly exposed to infectious cases. This concept later ripened into house-to-house searches by hundreds of thousands of health workers who combed the most inaccessible villages of the Indian subcontinent, where the last battles against *Variola major* were fought.

In October 1975, seventeen years after the World Health Assembly resolution, Rahima Banu, then three years old, became history's last case of Asian smallpox. Her mud-and-bamboo hut on Bhola Island at the southernmost tip of Bangladesh quickly became a universal symbol of international solidarity against disease. Since smallpox can be passed on only by human beings who actually have the disease, Rahima Banu's recovery from her illness broke the chain of transmission, and the disease ceased to exist.

With the total extinction of smallpox, millions of lives have been spared; countless children have been saved from blindness or from hideously scarred faces. Macaulay's description of 17th-century England has been consigned to a footnote in human history.

Agbeko Davis and Hunger Project executive director Joan Holmes on a fact finding mission in East Africa

Werner Krutein Productions

Ending Hunger by 1997:

The Hunger Project

Commentary

Many of the principles discussed in this book are being put into practice by the more than 1.5 million people in more than 80 countries who have enrolled themselves in the Hunger Project.

I first heard about the project in 1977 and reacted with skepticism to the concept and to the project's close association with the founder of *est,* Werner Erhard. But when I learned that a number of my most respected personal and professional friends had enrolled, I decided that my initial snap judgment was not sufficient. I carefully reviewed the written materials describing the project, including the project's finances, and, after enrolling in the project, attended a board meeting.

In March 1981, I was proud to become a member of the Hunger Project Advisory Council. Like others who have enrolled in the Hunger Project, I am committed to creating a future in which every human being is nourished sufficiently and sustainably.

Most people, including many experts, don't believe that it is possible to end hunger in the world by 1997—or ever. Most people didn't believe that it was possible to eradicate smallpox either.

The description of the Hunger Project that follows is, in my opinion, one of the most objective and accurate available. It is excerpted from *The Aquarian Conspiracy,* by Marilyn Ferguson

Ending Hunger—
Creating a Paradigm Shift

Historically, movements for social change have all operated in much the same way. A paternal leadership has convinced people of the need for change, then recruited them for specific tasks, telling them what to do and when to do it.

The new social movements operate on a different assumption of human potential: the belief that individuals, once they are deeply convinced of a need for change, can generate solutions from their own commitment and creativity. The larger movement inspires them, it supports their efforts and gives them information, but its structure cannot direct or contain their efforts.

The power of individuals to generate broad social change is the basis for the Hunger Project, an international charitable organization launched by *est* founder Werner Erhard in 1977 and headquartered in San Francisco. The Hunger Project's goal is to speed up a solution to the world hunger problem by acting as a *catalyst*. It is an intense, sopisticated large-scale effort to hurry a paradigm shift—to "make an idea's time come," as the project's organizers put it. The successes of the project and the ways in which it has been misunderstood are instructive.

The Hunger Project assumes that solutions do not reside in new programs or more programs. According to the best-informed authorities and agencies, the expertise to end hunger within two decades *already exists*. Hunger persists because of the old-paradigm assumption that it is not possible to feed the world's population.

In less than two years, *seven hundred fifty thousand* [by January 1981, nearly two million] individuals in dozens of countries have pledged their personal commitment to help end world hunger by 1997; enrollment in the Hunger Project is increasing at the rate of more than sixty thousand per month. Three million dollars has been raised explicitly to increase public awareness of the tragic proportions of the problem, the available solutions, and the ways in which individuals and groups can accelerate an end to hunger and starvation.

MAKING IT HAPPEN:

The Hunger Project does not compete with older hunger organizations; rather, it publicizes their activities and urges enrollees to support them.

The project draws all concerned parties into its efforts. Just prior to the launching of the foundation, a delegation that included world food distribution experts met with India's prime minister. Advisers to the project represent many nations and existing hunger organizations; Arturo Tanco, president of the World Food Council, is one. Government data, like the National Academy of Sciences report on the means to end hunger, are promulgated.

To create a sense of urgency, the project draws on the power of the symbol and the metaphor, describing the toll of starvation as "a Hiroshima every three days." When a Hunger Project relay of more than one thousand runners carried a baton from Maine to the White House, they did not ask the government to solve the problem. Rather, their message spoke of their own commitment to help end hunger and starvation.

The project uses models from nature and scientific discoveries as metaphors; the hologram, for example, is "a whole within a whole." Everyone who enrolls is the "the whole project." The project is "an alignment of wholes." Everyone who signs up is told to "create your own form of participation."

■ Some fast and contribute to the project what they would have spent on food.
■ Many businesses have donated a day's receipts.
■ A team of forty runners generated pledges of six hundred twenty-five

thousand dollars for running in the Boston Marathon in 1979, and twenty-three hundred spectators were enrolled along the way.
■ Eighty-eight fifth graders in a California school sponsored a Skate-a-thon and raised six hundred dollars; when they designated their funds for "the boat people," the Hunger Project put them in touch with Food for the Hungry, an organization directly assisting the refugees.

Everyone who signs up is encouraged to enlist others. Enrollees are told how to capture the interest of clubs, school boards, lawmakers; how to direct letters; how to make public presentations. Each enrollee is asked to become a teacher.

People Who Are Making It Happen Through Their a Commitment to Ending World Hunger

These case studies have been selected from a much larger number. In fact, there are thousands of stories of individuals enrolled in the Hunger Project who have made a difference in their lives, and the lives of others, through their commitment to ending hunger.

The research and writing up of case studies was a contribution of Hunger Project volunteers Cheryl Jacobs, Shannon Kepp, and Melody Leo, who chose this as one way to take responsibility for creating their future.

Russell Lee: Los Angeles
A Program to End Hunger in Los Angeles

Out of his commitment to end hunger in Los Angeles, Russell Lee, a former professional musician and business owner, founded ECCA (Ecumenical Coalition of Concerned Americans), a group of concerned citizens and major corporations who are cooperating to establish a massive food distribution center and job training program in a 100,000 square foot building.

The results ECCA intends to achieve are:
■ To have Los Angeles be the first major city in the western hemisphere to state publicly that it will take responsibility for adequately feeding its undernourished population.
■ To have worked out the details, logistics, and distribution and accomplished getting food to the needy of Los Angeles on a continuing basis, prior to the beginning of the 1984 Olympic Games.
■ To have local volunteer groups and food distribution centers in each of the 15 council districts operating prior to the 1984 Olympic Games.
■ To have an on-going volunteer organization comprised of inspired individuals and agencies.
■ To have created an on-going self-supporting job training and placement assistance program.

From music to ending hunger: Russell used to run a urethane manufacturing business in Los Angeles. He has travelled around the world performing a variety of music with major musicians such as Elvis Presley, Nat "King" Cole, and Frank Sinatra.

About 3½ years ago, after completing a movie and finding himself between shows in Las Vegas, Russell took a job at a warehouse. His experience with the loading of food for transportation was the impetus for the process that inspired him to devote his life fully to the end of hunger.

Accidents in the warehouse would occur, like a carton of ketchup toppling off a forklift pallet. There might be 24 bottles of ketchup in the box and only three broken, but it was financially unfeasible for the company to dismantle and repack the box; so the entire container had to be destroyed.

Russell knew that there were needy people in his own city who could utilize some of the food he saw misplaced, and he was determined to find a way to make some of that food available to them.

Enlisting help: Moved by his religious faith and by a Hunger Project presentation that he heard in 1978, he decided to create a coalition of concerned citizens, businesses, and churches to create a food distribution program that would target Los Angeles as the first major city to end hunger.

Russell now devotes all of his time to the massive task he has taken on.

Seminars emphasize the power of a single committed person, like the man in New Rochelle, New York, who enrolled his mayor, school superintendent, city manager, governor, and lieutenant governor; and the Honolulu woman who signed up the entire congressional delegation, governor, and most of the state legislature. At her urging, the governor proclaimed Hunger Week, and state legislators passed a resolution to encourage Hawaiian agricultural research to help alleviate world hunger. A Massachusetts couple enrolled *fifty thousand.*

Prisoners have been among the most dedicated supporters of the Hunger Project. A prisoner in the correctional facility at San Luis Obispo, California, enrolled fifteen hundred of the twenty-four hundred inmates. A Leavenworth prisoner not only became involved in the project; he and seven other inmates also pooled their money to sponsor two Vietnamese children through Save the Children. A long-term prisoner in a Virginia women's penitentiary said, "The women get bitter and critical in here, the walls close in. Each day grinds. Finally you give up and close in on

yourself.... I realized the Hunger Project is a way to out of the trap—by reaching out to hold others."

The need to confront painful knowledge: So long as we thought we couldn't do anything about the world's starving millions, most of us tried not to think about them; yet that denial has had its price. The Hunger Project emphasizes a key principle of transformation—the need to confront painful knowledge:

"We have numbed ourselves so that we do not feel the pain. We have to be asleep in order to protect ourselves from the horror of knowing that twenty-eight people, most of them young children, are dying this very minute—twenty-eight people no different from you or me or our children, except that we have food and they do not.

"We have closed down our consciousness and aliveness to a level where it doesn't bother us. So if you wonder if it costs us anything to allow millions to starve, it does. *It costs us our aliveness.*"

Within a year after the launching of the project, ninety committees had been organized in thirteen countries.

Celebrities spoke out for the cause, sometimes without specific reference to the project, much as movie stars helped sell war bonds in the 1940s.

Singer John Denver made a documentary film on world hunger. He told a newspaper interviewer, "We're at a point in this planet where we're going to have to make a specific shift in attitude, in how we lend ourselves to life. Up until now it's been, "If this were the last cup of grain, my very survival depends on my keeping it for me and my own." Now we're at a time when we will shift to "My survival depends on my sharing this with you. If this isn't enough for me, my survival *still* depends on my sharing this with you.'"

Denver, who served on the Presidential Commission on World Hunger, wrote "I Want to Live," the title song in a gold-record album, for the Hunger Project. Its theme: We are on the threshold of the end of war and starvation. "It is only an idea—but I know its time has come."

Comedian Dick Gregory gave the project one of its most dramatic images:

"When people ask me, 'Well, what do you think is going to happen with

ECCA is run totally by volunteers with Russell as President and Chairman of the Board, a position that is also volunteer. Volunteers from the local Hunger Project participate by serving on the Board of ECCA.

ECCA has made major progress towards achieving its goals. It has convinced the State of California to donate the old National Guard Armory on Hope Street—a four-story, 100,000-square-foot building —to house the project. The Greater Los Angeles Grocery Industry has already donated over $2,000,000 worth of refrigeration, grocery, and training equipment; members of the California food industry have already committed to supply over a half million tons of surplus foods for distribution to the needy and elderly in Southern California. ECCA currently owns one diesel truck and is seeking to acquire more to transport

food to their food distribution and feeding programs.

Los Angeles Mayor Tom Bradley is also supportive of the ECCA program. At one point last year, he had several tons of food stored in his mansion in such large quantities that foreign dignitaries were forced to hop over the boxes while visiting him.

Making a difference: Russell himself is working in the meat department of a major supermarket chain; studying and working with meat, studying how it is quartered, cut, processed, and handled. He learns about the source of meats and relates the information to the ECCA food programs.

One example he cites is the processing of hot dogs. Hot dogs are all required to be similar in size and shape prior to packaging. If they weigh too much or too little, they are discarded, again due to the

unfeasibility of reprocessing. Rather than allowing the food to be destroyed, Russell convinces the meat packaging company to donate it to the food program.

He is convinced that large industries want to contribute and make a difference to their community. They just do not have the knowledge or the resources to set up community relations programs. Therefore, it is up to individuals in the community to create programs as vehicles to permit corporations to relate and contribute to local people.

ECCA is also establishing nutritional education and job training programs to train people for work in the food industry. With the dedication of Russell and ECCA volunteers, the stage is set for ending hunger in Los Angeles. The opportunity is also availiable for individuals and corporations to serve and experience the fact that they can make a difference in the quality of life in their community.

hungry folks?' I give them the kind of answer the fire marshal gives to the TV reporter when a forest fire is burning out of control: 'It's out of our hands now. If we don't get a shift in the wind, we can't save it.'

"For a while it looked like we weren't going to make it unless we got a shift in the wind. But I left leeway for that which controls all winds to step in.... Our Hunger Project is that shift in the wind."

A world transformed: A key point is made to those who sign up: A world in which hunger has ended will be not merely different or better but transformed.

And those who take part will be transformed by their own participation by telling friends, family, and co-workers of their own commitment, even if they feel self-conscious; and by searching for answers.

Robert Herstek and Russell Lee distributing surplus food

Vanguard Photographs

Agbeko Davis: Los Angeles: One Man's Self-Sufficiency Program

Out of commitment that he made in 1977 to help end starvation in the world, Agbeko Davis, a Los Angeles attorney, initiated a ten-year farm project in Ghana to assist a village in eliminating malnutrition and becoming self-sufficient.

As assistant provost at Oberlin College several years ago, Agbeko used to take groups of students to Africa during the summer to live in host villages for six weeks as part of the school's African Community and Student Development Program.

Agon Duakwa, the site of the pilot program, was one of the villages where Agbeko established a strong friendship with the people. While in Africa, Agbeko made a promise to himself that someday, somehow, he would find a way to make a contribution to the lives of the villagers who had so warmly welcomed him into their homes.

His opportunity materialized when he enrolled in the Hunger Project. In the summer of 1979, Agbeko went to Africa to present his idea—a 10-year farm project that would enable Agon Duakwa, a village of 10,000 people of whom 7,000 are below the age of 21, to raise enough of the right kind of food to feed everyone in the village.

Research that Agbeko had done during past travels on the African continent had led him to discover what was necessary to make a village self-sufficient in food. The potential for enormous wealth exists in Africa, enough to "feed the entire world" if it were properly developed, according to Agbeko. The land is rich with vast resources of oil and minerals, while the fertile rain forests produce plentiful tropical fruits and vegetables without cultivation.

Yet, in the midst of this abundance, Agbeko saw signs of gross malnutrition among the children in the form of bloated stomachs and thin little legs. He realized that the African diet—

composed entirely of starch or carbohydrates—was severely deficient in protein. The land was once teeming with animals, but most of the animal life has been devastated by the effects of colonialism, slave trade, hunting for sport and commerce, and droughts—forcing the people to subsist on substandard diets. The first part of Agbeko's plan was to create new sources of protein, such as the raising of rabbits, chickens and fish for food.

Convincing the village elders to allocate 550 acres of land with a 50-year lease, Agbeko also invited a number of Ghanaian businessmen and journalists to participate with him in the project. The villagers began by clearing the land allotted, building hutches for the animals, and raising crops to provide feed. Agbeko had put together the finances to purchase small hand tools—shovels, picks, hoes, and other implements—to clear the brush.

When Agbeko returned to the United States at the end of the summer, he left the directorship of the project in the capable hands of Kojo Yankah, a journalist who is a member of the village as well as Director of Public Relations at Ghana Industrial Holding Corporation. Much of the land has been cleared and hutches to house animals have been built. The villages are currently raising rabbits, pigs, ducks, chickens, and turkeys. In the near future, a windmill and fish hatchery will be installed.

Part of the project's goal is to develop an industry for the village. When the farm begins to produce more than the village needs, the people will market their crops and buy larger and more sophisticated equipment to clear more land and raise more animals. As the 10-year plan continues to unfold, it may expand to include the development of tourism and the export of African artifacts to the United States to generate funds for the community.

Agbeko travels to Agona Duakwa annually to contribute to each phase of his farm project. He is currently working on some legal aspects, and is seeking financial support from private investment funds and foreign aid programs in both the United States and Ghana. A business partner in the United Sates, Frank J. Satterwite (Omowali), with the Institute for Community Economic Development in Palo Alto, California, assists him in formulating ideas and writing proposals.

Over a 10-year period, Agona Duakwa is expected to become totally self-sufficient, and to serve as a model to be replicated from one village to the next through out Ghana. "Their individual efforts never produced any real volume," Agbeko says. "This project is partly a process of exposing them to cooperative efforts which will benefit the village, Ghana, Africa, and ultimately the world. They could do it without me or anyone else. I'm providing a perspective, a focus around which their efforts can be organized."

The Solomon Family, Pompano Beach, Florida:
Promoting the Idea of Ending Starvation

In 1977, Leonard Solomon, president of Budget Rent-a Car in Miami, Florida, attended the first major presentation of the Hunger Project. The presentation gave Leonard the opportunity to think what he could do as an individual and as a businessman. His choice was to promote the idea of ending starvation in a way that inspires others to take action; and to raise funds for the Hunger Project.

He began by enrolling his immediate family in the notion that they, in their everyday life, could express a commitment to end hunger. His wife Roz, his sons Harold and Mark; Harold's wife Jan; his daughter Barbara and her husband Jeffrey Liss, all pledged to participate in their own way.

Leonard's son Harold is one of the top-ranking tennis professionals in the world. To raise money to support the work of The Hunger Project in 1977, Leonard sponsored the "First Annual Tennis Festival for The Hunger Project" in Fort Lauderdale, Florida. Participants included Harold Solomon, Eddie Dibbs, and Brian Gottfried. Dick Gregory gave the opening speech, and members of the Miami Dolphins and their coach Don Shula came to support the event.

This first major fundraiser generated $8,000.00. The following year, a second Tennis Festival at the Woodmont Country Club raised $10,000.

In 1979, Jan decided, personally, to support the expansion of the Hunger Project while traveling on the tennis circuit with Harold. She gave the Tournament Directors Association a presentation on the Hunger Project and was granted permission to open a booth at all tournaments that Harold participated in.

In the cities where the tournaments were held in 1979 and 1980, Jan contacted local Hunger Project volunteers and turned the booth over to them to communicate with other people about their commitment to end starvation. Anywhere a crowd forms to obtain Harold's and other players' autographs, Jan has made sure that Hunger Project volunteers are also in their midst, talking with people about the problems of persistent world hunger. Anytime Harold is interviewed by the media about his tennis, he mentions that individuals have the opportunity to end starvation on the planet.

The Solomon family's commitment is so great that when Jan calls home, Leonard and Roz do not ask if Harold won the tournament, they ask, "How many people did you talk to about ending hunger today?"

In addition:
■ In 1979, Jan flew to Seattle to support a community conference, sponsored by the Hunger Project, on "Ending Starvation—What Will I Do?" She moderated a panel of

The Hunger Project

speakers who reported on world hunger to 250 individuals who participated in the day-long conference.

■ In August 1980, when Harold won a tennis tournament in Cincinnati, his father Leonard was riding a bicycle from Atlanta, Georgia, to Miami, Florida, in a journey called "A Bike Ride for Life". The trip took seven days, one hundred miles per day, and raised $17,000 for The Hunger Project.

■ In December 1980, the "Third Annual Tennis Festival for The Hunger Project" in Miami generated $30,000; Dr. Wayne Dyer, author of *Your Erroneous Zones,* served as master of ceremonies, and participating tennis professionals included: Jimmy Connors, John McEnroe, Vitas Gerulaitis, Harold Solomon, Eddie Dibbs, and Andrea Jaeger. The tournament was so successful that it played to standing room only, with people turned away at the door.

■ Plans are already being completed for a "Fourth Annual Tennis Tournament for The Hunger Project" in 1981. Leonard is also in the process of organizing a bike ride across the United States.

The Solomon family participates wholly in expressing their commitment to end starvation. Mark was a contact person at Greensborough while he was going to school there. Barbara and her husband Jeff always come out to support the Tennis Festival by taking care of logistics. Leonard has also put bumper stickers on his entire fleet of 3,000 rental cars, with a message reading: "The end of starvation—An idea whose time has come," and the phone number for The Hunger Project International Office in San Francisco, California.

Leonard Solomon sees the universe as family and he intends that his family will set an example for others to participate by expressing their support for the idea of ending world starvation.

ACTION

Starting Where You Can

A study group in "applied religion": The Sunday Morning Seminar at the Annandale (Virginia) United Methodist Church has been a part of our lives since the mid-1960s. It has provided thought-provoking insight into today's complex world and been a sort of study group of "applied" religion.

In early 1980, Eleanor Morrow, the seminar coordinator, suggested that we attend "The Human Side of the Energy Transition," a conference of the U.S. Association for The Club of Rome. This turned out to be quite an experience, offering us firsthand views by experts on a subject that had concerned Dave for some time.

Returning to our own seminar, we set out to share some of the ideas with the rest of our group.

Working with Eleanor, we decided to focus on energy, but also to touch on other dilemmas facing us in the next two decades, since many overlap. The obvious beginning was for Dave and me to sift through our voluminous notes on the two-and-a-half-day conference and lead the first session ourselves.

For the next Sunday, we invited our Congressman, Joseph Fisher, to come and give us the energy picture as he saw it from Capitol Hill. On succeeding Sundays, other speakers came. Dr. John Malcolm, from the Agency for International Development [AID] in the State Department, spoke to us about the long-range implications of the way we are using our soil today.

Someone in the church offered to

Good News: People Who Are Making It Happen

I want to share with you an idea that came to me in the course of putting this book together: a publication, and possibly a television series, which would be devoted entirely to good news.

By *good news,* I mean news about people who are taking responsibility for their future and making things happen, people who are committed to a world that is more humane and sustainable. Two years ago, I didn't have any idea how many people like that, from all sectors of our society, there were. But there are many, already making a difference and thereby creating their future.

Perhaps you are one of them. I am certain, in any event, that one of them lives within a mile of where you live.

I envision on everyone's desk or writing table orange envelopes—the color of sunshine—addressed to "Good News." Each person would be encouraged to look for and create good news in the world around him or her. The results of these efforts would be communicated to me and I would, in turn, communicate it to others.

Here is a small sampling of some of the stories of good news that we have collected in the course of producing this book. To cover them all would require not one book but several.

The idea of taking responsibility for creating our future is not impossible or purely visionary. It is happening.

Melissa Wells: Fighting Starvation Among Ugandans

The tall woman clutched the starving, nearly naked waif to her and, fighting back tears said: "His body feels thinner than ones I've buried."

The child, an emaciated 6-year-old victim of the Karamoja drought in northeast Uganda, just held on tight to her benefactor. She was the latest recipient of an unusual, personal kind of care from the United Nations.

An unusual kind of care from the UN: The world organization, often known for its abundance of bureaucrats who remain rooted to their desks, has a different image in Uganda, at least, as a result of the tireless efforts of Melissa Wells, the head UN official in the country.

Wells, trying to help save tens of thousands of starving Karamojong, has put the limited number of UN personnel in the country to work directly in the field to distribute badly needed food. She frequently visits missions and hospitals doing relief work in the province to check on needs and boost morale.

Normally, the United Nations simply arranges for donors and provides the aid to the government to distribute. In Uganda, however, there is scarcely any effective government, following the overthrow of Idi Amin and two of his successors in 13 months.

So Wells, a former American ambassador on loan to the United Nations from the State Department, has stepped in with her own personal form of diplomacy. It ranges from passing her "begging bowl" among the international community to nurturing of starving children.

It also sometimes involves helping to bury the children who no longer can be helped.

The title given to Wells in Swahili by her drivers and guards probably best combines the personal and professional aspects of her work.

It literally means "mother ambassador of all the nations of the world." That is the closest Swahili comes to UN Development Program resident representative, the position Wells has held since last September.

As one of the State Department's first women career ambassadors, Estonian-born Wells, 47, came up through the ranks in a fairly routine manner. She became Washington's first envoy to newly independent Guinea Bissau in West Africa in 1976 and later was appointed the U.S.

invite a personal friend, Dr. Gerald Barney, Study Director of *The Global 2000 Report to the President,* to give us an inside look at its findings and projections. James Stephens, one of our members, told us something about the outlook for technology, developing countries, and religion from the perspective of the World Future Society Conference he had attended in Toronto during July 1980.

A Jesuit priest and activist, Father William Millerd, came to our seminar representing the Interfaith Coalition on Energy. It seemed fair to offer our local energy company, Virginia Electric Power Company, a chance to give its viewpoint, so we invited them to send a speaker, too. We called the Solar Institute of America and the National Center for Appropriate Technology, both of whom provided speakers equipped with slides and films.

Reassessing the things we value: Our seminar seemed to be living up to its theme: "A Guide to Living in the 1980s within the Context of the Church." Over and over, running like a thread through the presentations,

was the urging by speakers that religious groups such as ours become more interested and aware of the changes we face in the next decade or two.

There was a remarkable agreement among our speakers: we are going to have to reassess the things that have value to us. Religious institutions, as custodians of society's values, can make a great contribution in this as we consider our lives in a rapidly changing world:

■ Who is our neighbor?

■ What is our responsibility in this, one of the most exciting and challenging periods in human history?

■ What are the constants? What must be adaptable?

■ How can we best act as stewards for our dwindling resources so that our children and our children's children may enjoy the state of "well-being" the church proclaims as the right of each individual?

We used a film on value-forming, Dr. Morris Massey's "What You Are Is Where You Were When," to help us consider what goes into working out problems and communicating across generations. The program

director of our church, Shirley Nelms, brought us up to date on some of the latest thinking on how the church teaches moral values today. We participated in "moral reasoning" games as we discussed the stages individuals go through in developing their sense of morality.

Even a Thanksgiving Sunday speaker, with no direct association to our theme, seemed to fit into the mosaic we were building. Bonaro Overstreet—psychologist and philosopher—talked about humankind's infinite capacity for caring. We take for granted the benevolent organizations and humanitarian laws which are so much a part of our society today, but, he pointed out, all these are a relatively new feature of life in our world.

One of our members, Jack Underhill, reported on his attendance at a conference in Cairo, Egypt, on "Urban Planning and Energy on a World Wide Basis."

Finally, Dave and I held a wrap-up discussion with the seminar to encourage them in their ideas for future consideration by the seminar.

---

representative to the United Nations Economic and Social Council in New York.

Wells is probably the only ambassador who worked in a Las Vegas chorus line. An athletic, 5-foot-11 southern Californian, she was a star swimmer as a teen-ager. That got her a part in the "Aquaparade of 1953," which combined Esther Williams-style synchronized swimming and standard Las Vegas musical fare.

The "Aquaparade" led Wells to an unusual first contact with the Foreign Service. The group embarked on a year-long tour of Europe, went broke and had to be repatriated by the State Department from Paris.

Five years later, she began training in the Foreign Service after graduating from Georgetown University.

In those days it was difficult for a woman to break into the State Department. "If you told them you'd like to be married some day," Wells said, "the examining panel would just say, 'Go away, little girl'."

She said she replied, "Look, I'm six feet tall and weigh two pounds more than Sugar Ray Robinson," then the world welterweight (147 pound) boxing champion. "They laughed and dropped the subject," she said.

However, she did marry—a foreign service officer, Alfred Wells.

They divorced in the 1960s but got back together later, although they have never remarried.

Alfred, now a housing consultant for the United Nations, lives in Nairobi, Kenya, with their younger son, Gregory, 13. Christopher, 19, their other child is a student at Columbia University in New York.

Melissa is a frequent commuter to Nairobi.

"If feeding these people doesn't make sense, then...": Explaining her preoccupation with Karamoja, she said, "I must take these trips—it's like a rope, a lifeline."

With unrest in the province growing, the trips are becoming more and more dangerous. Wells always travels with an armed guard, but she would be no match for the raiders who are terrorizing the area.

Asked if she has any difficulty with UN headquarters over her trips, she said only that "Occasionally I use some four-letter words."

In a firm voice, she added, "If feeding these people doesn't make sense, nothing does."

—From the Washington *Post*, June 9, 1980

Attendance at these Sunday seminars had ranged from 30 to 100.

Thinking about doing this in other settings: We were fortunate in our metropolitan location. We have many individuals and resources to turn to for our seminar sessions. As we discussed it, we wondered how we would approach session plans on energy and other concerns for the future if we had been more distant from Washington.

We decided we'd turn to the nearest college or university and seek out an interested professor. Business leaders could be a contact. The yellow pages of the telephone directory can often be a gold mine. We'd certainly try our local library. We'd talk to our Congressional representative. There are also networks of interested (and interesting) people all across the country, and we'd try to get in contact with them.

Organizations can often help with information packets, films, or suggestions for resource materials or speakers. We would contact groups like the Solar Institute of America,

National Center for Appropriate Technology, Department of Energy, and U.S. Association for The Club of Rome.

It might also be good to start a bulletin board and post magazine and newspaper clippings as well as relevant brochures and posters. We also had a table for sharing books we'd found helpful.

Most of all, we'd urge that the future not be looked on as just too "scarey" to talk about. The more we find out about "grass roots" actions, the more hopeful we become that we, the ordinary citizens, can help to provide a navigable course through one more critical turning point in human history.

By David and Vivian Smith

Mechai Viravaidya: Thailand's One-Man Population Program

As it does in the States, the tinkle of the ice cream wagon's bell brings children flocking from the crowded houses along the canals, from the street markets and tiny alleys of this jammed city.

But this ice cream wagon asks a different price for its wares. Any child may have a free Popsicle if accompanied by a parent willing to accept a condom, a month's supply of birth control pills, or a vasectomy.

The gaily painted wagon which carries both ice cream and a mobile birth-control clinic is the latest of a vast array of lures thought up by Mechai Viravaidya, an economist turned super-salesman.

Economist turned super-salesman: The 38-year-old Mechai, graduate of the University of

Melbourne, cousin of the king of Thailand by marriage, son of a Scotch mother and a Thai father (both distinguished physicians in Bangkok), has taken on, with evangelical fervor—and much humor—the task of reducing his country's birth rate. And he is succeeding. Indeed, the local colloquialism for a condom is a "Mechai."

In a country burdened with too many people for its meager resources and recurrently inundated by Indochinese refugees, the limiting of new births is crucial.

In the early 1970s, the birth rate of Thailand, like that of most Third World countries, had skyrocketed. The combination of more food from the new grains of the Green Revolution and improved health care resulted in far fewer infant deaths. The population was about to double in a 20-year period.

Rural families traditionally had 18 or 20 children, but before World War II many children died of tropical diseases and infections. Now most live.

"We became," says Mechai, **"a nation unable to provide for our children."** Only half the children in Thailand could attend school even though the schools went on double schedule.

This year, the statistics show what nationwide planning can accomplish. There were 41 percent fewer pregnancies than five years ago. A recent questionnaire sent to 8,000 villages found that there were almost no unplanned births.

"When I was in the government planning office," explains Mechai, "with my degree hanging smartly on the wall, I was director of a team that made marvelous plans for Thailand.

"I saw that we were advancing economically, but all our gains were being eaten up by overpopulation. I realized we would have to adopt a radical new approach to this most terrible problem.

"We had to change the Thai's puritanical view of sex, make the whole business of how many children a family had a subject easily discussed and thus acted upon. I wanted to remove the taboos, take birth control out of the realm of the secretive, make it fun."

"Many births cause suffering": In 1974, Mechai founded the community-based, nonprofit Family Planning Services and launched his extraordinary campaign to curb family size by handing out his calling card everywhere, from formal state dinners to vendors at the city market. It is a brightly colored contraceptive attached to an order form which features a Buddhist scripture, "Many births cause suffering."

An alternate card tells people just how much an extra child will cost them and in a series of drawings explains use. The tear-off card bears this commercial: "Plan your family with rainbow-colored Mechais. Bright colors, safe, easy to use. Reduce anxiety. No side effects.

Highly effective family planning..."

In less than a decade, what was once the province of staid physicians, a subject eschewed by peasant families and certainly not mentioned in polite circles, is part of everyday Thai life as a result of Mechai's strenuous and imaginative campaign.

Contraceptives can be bought from rice farmers, taxi drivers, and hotel porters. Bus fares, theater tickets, and tips can be paid in them. The national soccer team wears a shirt emblazoned with the motto "Too many children make you poor." In rural areas, new shipments of contraceptives are blessed by Buddhist monks before they are distributed.

The interest on a bank loan may be halved by the borrower if his wife is sterilized or he has a vasectomy.

In other villages, baby pigs are given to those who practice family planning. "Accomplishing two things at once," says the energetic Mechai, "improving the diet and popularizing birth control."

School children throughout Thailand sing a song, based on a popular tune, that describes the hardships of having too many children and thus not having enough for everyone to eat. It ends with a happy refrain, reminding everyone there is no need to worry as the local family planning agent can tell their parents where to get a condom or an IUD or a vasectomy.

"If parents hear this often enough from their children it becomes part of their thinking," says Mechai. "Anyway, it is good to give these kids an early start. They will be parents soon enough."

In the field, Mechai operates like an old-time medicine man. He pulls up his van near a country market, spreads out his wares: T-shirts, bikini pants, bed sheets, and pillow cases all bearing the message that too many children make people poor.

There are also sideshows where ovulation charts are used as dartboards, and other games demonstrate devices.

The audience is ragged—but eager.

Later, Mechai explains his merchandising technique to a foreign visitor. "Once people accept the idea that contraceptives are just one more item you can buy easily like soap or toothpastes or dried fish, they will be more likely to use them. Thais are a thrifty people. If you can show many uses for a product, you are more likely to get a buyer. If I can accomplish that by blowing up balloons or filling condoms with rice, I will do it. Acceptance is the name of the game."

"There was a time," Mechai adds with evident pleasure, "when my methods shocked people. I verged on becoming a social pariah. It was especially awkward for my wife, who is the personal press aide of the King of Thailand."

The apex of Mechai's shock program came in 1975 when he crashed the first state dinner given for the North Vietnamese vice-foreign minister by the Thai government. Thai officials, already tense about the occasion, were traumatized when they entered the formal dining room to find the ubiquitous calling card placed carefully at each place.

Mechai appeared personally to pass out T-shirts with birth control messages printed across the front. The austere Vietnamese, thinking this was Thai custom, dutifully donned the shirts and subsequently asked Mechai to discuss his program with them.

"I told them," he says with pride, "that population control is the most important war to win. Their current answer, exporting human beings wholesale, is not what I had in mind."

Now Mechai has become something of a national hero. The mention of his name hastens visitors through customs, brings a waiter scurrying in a Bangkok restaurant, guarantees space in crowded provincial hotels. The Thai government has adopted many of his ideas and vastly expanded its own family planning programs.

ACTION

"Mechai," says an American observer, "leads the way. He persuades someone to have his vasectomy televised, everyone is officially shocked, and a few weeks later the number of vasectomies being performed in government clinics had quadrupled."

■ *"Vasectomize the man of your choice":* A diplomat's wife regales the visitor at a large dinner with a description of how Mechai celebrated International Women's Year by inviting middle class ladies of Bangkok to donate $10 to "vasectomize the man of your choice." "It worked," said the foreigner. "And what's more, some of us joined in the game."

One wonders what makes Mechai run, but run he does, all the time. During one lunch he gave a formal scholarly talk on the concept of community health and nutrition centers as a starting point for rural social change. A moment later he described with glee how he had found a way of perfecting the size of the product that carries his name—by enlisting the aid of Bangkok massage parlors.

"I am, in the vernacular, a good-doer," he says, "but I abhor the cant. I think the words of economists and sociologists often obscure the objective. For example, what does 'World Population Year' mean? What we should have is a simple, 'No Baby Year.'

"You can do anything in a country if you let people have fun learning about it and let them do things in their own way. If you stay away from preaching, from theoretics, and allow people to do one thing at a time, you can bring about, slowly, real social change.

"We don't need to send social workers to our villages. The villagers can be their own social workers once they understand the pragmatic advantages of progress, be it fewer children, better nutrition, or better health."

There are days traveling with Mechai when you think you can't abide one more imaginative gimmick, like having a school band play the national anthem for the first child who swallows all the dreadful tasting anti-parasite medicine. But then as you progress through the villages, you see that, in the wake of the medicine man with his wares, his squealing pigs, and worshipping young staffers, there is solid method to his apparent madness.

"I looked," says the social reformer, "for ways to get participation that involved little training and less money. I decided sex was a good place to begin. You don't need a PhD to understand it."

Mechai's organization supplies contraceptives but insists local people be the providers and motivators. "And once their credibility is established, we are able to move into a series of health and development programs.

"We regard the family planning program as only the first step in a long war. It teaches people that, if they participate, it works to their benefit."

Seeing the benefit: "The consumption pattern in poor countries like Thailand is such that people don't see immediate benefit from not having a fifth or sixth child. We set out to provide some immediately tangible benefit from taking up family planning—almost as fast as they swallow that pill. We call it our 'better market' program."

Participants in the program can use the family planning organization as agent to sell their nonperishable products like coconuts, pumpkins, silk, and handicrafts.

"We cut out the middleman," said Mechai. "We find the markets, arrange the transportation, and the villagers get at least 30 percent more for their produce. How's that for proving that family planning is worthwhile?"

Mechai is proud that his small clinic in Bangkok and the expenses of his field staff are more than half paid for by the sale of products. The rest of his money comes from grants from the Population Crisis Committee, International Planned Parenthood, and a Japanese government-sponsored foundation. The Agency for International Development [AID] has given money for specific projects.

"If other Third World countries had a Mechai," says Frederick Pinkham of the Population Crisis Committee in Washington, whose organization finances family planning throughout the world, "we would see a substantial drop in population figures. It takes someone as tireless and imaginative—with the kind of access to power—that Mechai has.

"One cannot avoid the fact that a man already established in his own society can take more radical action and remain acceptable and thus effective. There are very few social scientists anywhere who would be pleased to have their smiling faces plastered on every taxi-cab advertising a contraceptive. It takes a special self-confidence and rare dedication."

—From the Washington *Post,* November 11, 1979
Copyright © by Marie Ridder

The Washington Sewer Ladies
By FAYE BEUBY

Twenty women: The common denominator of "parenting" brought together a group of about 20 women in the Washington, DC, suburban area.

Each had her own community concern and represented a different suburban locale. Several had launched their voluntary careers as political activists in 1970 in the effort to preserve a 336-acre plot of land from development and put it to use as a northern Virginia district park.

Another began in the late 1960s by single-handedly energizing her local community to halt the construction of a twelve-story office building in a residential neighborhood. Petitions and attendance at county meetings succeeded in modifying the building to a height of two stories.

Another Virginian, through the League of Women Voters, helped develop the Fairfax County Master Plan which became the basis for all county growth and planning until 1976. In 1976, she also created, with another "involved" woman, a newspaper, the Washington *Metropolitan Examiner.* The paper became a vehicle for conveying the group's stand on issues of transportation, water resources, higher education, nuclear power, population, growth, land use, and the justice system. With only meager contributions and a small grant, their money soon ran out. The last edition went out only 14 months after the paper's founding.

Step by step, these women became influential; people began listening to them. With that attention, they built their own constituency and became "unofficial" city and county board members.

Their involvement taught them that they could win. Ordinances were often modified due to their efforts and, thereby, policies changed. Many areas of concern have become local election issues because of their pressure.

They operated under no budget or budget constraints. The time they had, and willingly donated, replaced financial backing. Within the group there is a great deal of cohesion, and there is probably no more efficient "grass roots" organization.

Among their many accomplishments was the creation of a bicycle trail along the Potomac River in northern Virginia.

Another was the establishment of the Farmer's Market in Arlington, Virginia. The latter was primarily due to the work of a journalist in the group who, every six months for a period of five years, wrote in her weekly articles in the county newspaper of the desirability of such an enterprise. The goal was not only to serve consumers but to preserve farm land around major metropolitan centers. These markets also provide a financial incentive to local farmers.

Water and water sewers: Recently, the group's concern has been focused on improving of the water resources of the Washington, DC, area. They have clearly identified the problems and constraints involved in providing cities with a clean and readily available water supply.

This coalition is now attempting to surmount the many obstacles in its path, and has even become a plaintiff in law suits to acquire otherwise unobtainable information and call attention to its cause. Individual members have been influential in many cases involving sewage plant construction and location and sewage allocations. To further the group's goals, one individual has devoted the last three years to completing law school.

These women—mostly wives and mothers justly take pride in their accomplishments; they can look around their communities and see positive changes they have helped make. They have had, and continue to have, a profound effect on policymaking in the Washington, DC, area. Individuals from private citizens to federal agency directors and cabinet officials now routinely seek their advice and counsel. □

Robert Bainum: Vacations Spent Aiding Boat People

By JANIS JOHNSON

While riding in his car last August, Robert Bainum was listening to a sermon about how 40,000 Indochinese boat people were perishing in an "Asian holocaust."

"I kept thinking about that and said I needed to go over there and see if I could help," Bainum said the other day, as he prepared for his fourth trip to Asia to aid in refugee relief.

"For two months, I wrestled with it. Finally I bought a ticket and went to Hong Kong. I talked to people and decided I needed to go to Bangkok. There I was told I could find plenty to do."

Getting his own church to start a refugee relief program: Bainum, a Silver Spring resident who works in Fairfax County, came home the day before Christmas 1979 with a plan: the Church of the Savior in Washington, of which Bainum is a provisional member, should initiate its own refugee relief program.

Through a new project, COSIGN [Church of the Savior International Good Neighbors], the socially activist congregation at 2025 Massachusetts Avenue, N.W., has sent about two dozen volunteers—who give up their vacations—to assist refugee camps along the Thai-Cambodian border.

"This time I had no excuse": Bainum says the primary reason he became involved in the relief work was because he felt he should exercise some social responsibility.

"When I was a young man, Hitler was doing his thing and I felt powerless to do much," said Bainum, who is 55. "During the civil rights marches, I was married, had five young kids, and a big mortgage. I felt it was irresponsible for me to risk my life even if I wanted to. This time I had no excuse."

A co-founder of the Manor Care nursing home chain and administrator of Fairfax Nursing Center, Bainum has been a major financial

contributor to the relief project, although he declined to say how much he has given. While he's away, his wife and daughter manage the nursing home.

Bainum's organizational skills, say those who know of his work, have been his primary contribution to the relief effort. One of his first projects was to help establish an 80-bed hospital at a refugee camp in Thailand.

On another visit, the first thing Bainum saw at one camp was a family of three cooking three small fish "about an inch and a half long" on a stick. The fish, Bainum said, were the entire meal.

"I'd say there were hundreds of people lying on their beds in their huts shivering from hunger," he said. "The ones well enough to be up had huddled over and squatted in the sun for the warmth. We gave them what we had—medicine for malaria and dysentery."

"They said they needed more medicine and doctors and nurses. They figured at least 2,000 people in that camp needed immediate medical care and 80 percent of the 5,000 or 6,000 people were sick, but not critically."

Eighteen members of the church are currently working in Thailand for one or two months. Among the church's contributions have been 19 wells dug in three villages, purchase and delivery of a trailer of rice, and a shipment of old tires and inner tubes for sandals.

The church arranged for the delivery of 30,000 doses of vaccine in one camp, and volunteers have been teaching English to refugees destined for the United States, Great Britain or Canada. Volunteers have bought tools, bicycles, and motorcycle fuel for the refugee camps.

—From the Washington *Post*, July 24, 1980
© The Washington *Post*

Making it Happen and The Club of Rome:

Epilogue

Creating Global Consciousness: The Club of Rome

To understand the background of *Making It Happen*, one must know something about the U.S. Association for The Club of Rome. But to understand the U.S. Association and its purposes, one must begin with The Club of Rome itself. This unusual organization is comparatively well known in Europe, but most Americans have never heard of it.

In April 1968, a group of thirty people from ten countries—scientists, educators, economists, humanists, industrialists, and national and

---

Guiding Principles of The Club of Rome

Peccei describes in *The Human Quality* the guidelines developed by the members of The Club of Rome for its development:

■ The Club of Rome had to remain small, with no more than 100 members, in the expectation that this would allow for a minimum of communication among them— which is not easy anyway.

■ It was to be a non-organization— there are already so many organizations of all kinds in the world which it could use when necessary without being one itself.

■ It had to live on the leanest budget, in order not to depend, even remotely, on any provider of funds.

■ It should be really transcultural— drawing on all relevant disciplines, ideologies and value systems, without being bound to any of them.

■ It should be non-political.... [See below.]

■ It should be genuinely informal, and try to promote the freest exchanges among members.

■ It should, finally, be prepared to disappear when its time is over— nothing is worse than ideas or institutions which outlive their usefulness.

Furthermore, the Club was conceived not as a debating society but as an action-oriented one. Schematically, two main objectives were defined, which it should pursue gradually.

■ The first objective is **to promote and disseminate a more secure, in-depth understanding of mankind's predicament.** This objective obviously includes a study of the narrowing and uncertain prospects and options which will be left if present world trends are not urgently corrected.

■ The second objective is then—on the basis of all the knowledge available—**to stimulate the adoption of new attitudes, policies, and institutions capable of redressing the present situation.**

To serve this dual purpose, The Club of Rome has endeavored to become a cross section of progressive mankind. Its members are prominent scholars, scientists, civil servants, educators, and managers from more than thirty countries. They are of different training, experience, condition, and convictions....

By its nature The Club is not supposed to serve any national or political party interest, and has no ideological identification; by virtue of its composite membership, it cannot either, as a body, take sides on controversial matters which divide mankind.

No single value system or consolidated view can be attributed to it, nor can it speak with one voice. The projects it sponsors express the findings and ideas of the scientific teams which develop them, without in any way being construed as representing The Club's position.

In spite of this, The Club is in actual fact political and very much so in the true etymological sense. The analysis and clarification of the long-term interests of humanity it promotes are indeed aimed at establishing new and sounder bases to permit those who have the tremendous responsibility of making major decisions to make them more responsibly.

international civil servants—gathered at the Accademia dei Lincei in Rome. They met at the invitation of Dr. Aurelio Peccei, an Italian industrial manager, economist, and man of vision, to discuss a subject of immense scope—the present and future predicament of humankind.

After a series of meetings and discussions over a two-year period, The Club embarked in 1970 on the project which, two years later, produced *The Limits to Growth.*

At the same time, The Club's founders agreed to a few unwritten but stringent guidelines for the organization's development. [See box.]

The Club of Rome is best known in the United States for its pioneering project on global modeling, which in 1972 led to the widely publicized book *The Limits to Growth.*

This brief and highly readable volume was based on a computer simulation model developed at the Massachusetts Institute of Technology by Professor Jay Forrester and later refined by an international team of young scholars under the direction of Dr. Dennis L. Meadows.

In essence, the authors concluded that:

■ **If the present growth trends in world population, industrialization, pollution, food production, and resource depletion continue unchanged, the limits to growth on this planet will be reached sometime within the next one hundred years. The most probable result will be a rather sudden and uncontrollable decline in both population and industrial capacity.**

■ **It is possible to alter these growth trends and to establish a condition of ecological and economic stability that is sustainable far into the future. The state of global equilibrium could be designed so that the basic material needs of each person on earth are satisfied and each person has an equal opportunity to realize his individual human potential.**

■ **If the world's people decide to strive for this second outcome rather than the first, the sooner they begin working to attain it, the greater will be their chances of success.**

Since publication of *The Limits to Growth,* The Club of Rome has sponsored and published a series of eight additional studies focusing on different aspects of the human predicament. A brief summary of these follows on a subsequent page.

The rise of national affiliates of The Club of Rome: The Club of Rome is continuing its activities much as before, but in recent years The Club's activities have been augmented by a growing number of affiliated national organizations and associations.

Since The Club of Rome is itself a non-organization, its ties to the national organizations are informal and philosophical, rather than administrative, legal, or financial. Aurelio Peccei provides the principal linkage through

EPILOGUE

his frequent travels, reports, letters, and telephone calls.

Moreover, each national organization is different. But in their separate and diverse ways, all of them are committed to understanding and disseminating information about the human predicament and to creating new attitudes, policies, and institutions capable of improving on our present situation.

One of the most active of the national organizations has been the U.S. Association for The Club of Rome, whose members are responsible for this book. □

The Human Predicament: or, The Problem of Our Problems

The human predicament, or *world problematique* as it has come to be called, was described in this way by Aurelio Peccei in his book *The Human Quality:*

Man does not know how to be a truly modern man. Other species do not have similar failings. A tiger knows how to be a tiger. A spider lives like a spider. A swallow has learned what it takes to be a swallow.

By the use of natural wisdom, their species are continually readjusting and refining their survival qualities, adapting them to the modifications of their environment. Their success is proved by their very existence, as the present-day end-product of age-long evolution.

Now they are in danger because their deadliest enemy, the enemy or tyrant of most forms of life—man—moves ever more against them. Man invented the story of the bad dragon, but if ever there was a bad dragon on earth, it is man himself.

Man has many things in common with these other creatures, but apparently lacks their wisdom for survival. Already at the dawn of history, he began to forsake his natural capacity to adapt and survive, finding it expedient to trust his lot more and more to his brain, that is, to his technological capacity and, by it, to modify the environment instead. Thanks to his cultural uniqueness, he then rose to stardom in the world. In an eyeball-to-eyeball struggle with other species, he would have been an easy loser; but shifting the field of competition to his home ground, he became invincible.

There are, though, limits to which the entire world can be bent to please him and every time he forged a higher rung of his ascent, he had to learn how to live with it. Here we have the human paradox: man trapped by his extraordinary capacity and achievements as in a quicksand—the more he uses his power, the more he needs it, and if he does not learn how to use it, he just becomes its captive.

In recent decades, he has put on a spurt and made some quite exceptional technological jumps, but has not had time to master them or to adjust to them. He has thus lost the sense of reality, is even unable to realize the place and role he occupies in it.

The entire reference base which his ancestors had painstakingly constructed during the preceding ages and eras to keep the human system together, and regulate its intercourse with the ecosystem, is no longer valid. His traditional outlook of himself and of his fellow humans, of family, society, and of life itself, has to be profoundly revised—at a global scale—but he has yet to learn how to do this.

The U.S. Association for The Club of Rome

Beliefs

The rise of independent affiliates of The Club of Rome: It is not surprising that a number of national organizations supportive of the work of The Club of Rome have been founded, since The Club has a record of innovative study of global issues that affect every society. There are now groups affiliated with The Club of Rome in fourteen countries:

> Australia,
> Belgium,
> Canada,
> Finland,
> Greece,
> Japan,
> The Netherlands,
> New Zealand,
> Spain,
> Switzerland,
> Turkey,
> the United Kingdom,
> the United States, and
> West Germany.

The U.S. Association was founded in 1976 after five other national groups had been formed. It is important to emphasize that these organizations are sympathetic to and supportive of the efforts of The Club of Rome, but are nationally based in every case and for all purposes are independent.

The initiative for the U.S. Association came from a small group of concerned Americans, some of whom were members of The Club of Rome but most of whom were not.

They were motivated by the shared belief that, in virtually every major global problem, the United States has both a special responsibility and an unparalleled opportunity to join in finding solutions.

Few other countries have comparable advantages of great size and immense economic and military power, natural wealth and high material standard of living, widespread educational and technical development, and a national pride in working out practical solutions to problems.

In the United States, these characteristics are linked to a strong democratic political tradition, and a belief in the ideal—albeit not always observed in practice—of fairness, humane concern, and generosity in relationships with our neighbors.

These characteristics should lead naturally to active U.S. participation in cooperative measures for dealing with international challenges.

Primarily a catalyst of ideas: The U.S. Association is intended to serve primarily as a catalyst of ideas. It is not a mass-membership, lobbying group, and has no aspirations to become one.

USACOR will remain small. It was initially limited to 100 members. It is now expanding its membership to 500 so as to be more nationally representative.

It places basic emphasis on disseminating information to decision makers and the public at large. All of its activities are predicated on a trust in the power of ideas and information to shape the course of future events in a free and representative political system.

The Association offers no ready-made solutions, no panaceas, no messiahs. Its members are concerned first and foremost with improving the process of dialogue on critical issues as a first step toward timely political and social decisions.

In general, the goals of members of the U.S. Association for The Club of Rome are—

■ to help in the search for better ways of understanding the world of today and possible alternatives for tomorrow; and

■ to aid in the development of new patterns of activity, as well as new structures and institutions, to insure future human existence with dignity, equity, and security for the individual in a sustainable global environment.

While sympathetic to and supportive of the purposes of The Club, the U.S. Association retains for all purposes its independence of view and action.

There are many lively differences of opinion among the members of the U.S. Association for The Club of Rome (as there are among the members of the international Club). However, among the beliefs members of the U.S. Association tend to share are these:

■ **Major global problems and opportunities are closely interlinked, and they interact over time in complex and often unforeseen ways.**

■ **The goal of a sustainable future requires learning to live within constantly changing natural and social constraints, but humanity can change its patterns of growth and consumption of natural resources in ways that are compatible with the integrity and sustainability of natural systems.**

■ **An understanding of human values, perceptions, and motivations may be as important as scientific and technical data in the successful solution of shared global problems.**

■ **A long-range, wholistic view of an equitable and sustainable future, based on an accurate understanding of current realities and trends, is an essential foundation for timely policy choices that are responsive to the needs of the future.**

■ **The work of The Club of Rome has contributed significantly to global awareness of the human predicament, and provides an important stimulus for the goals and activities of the U.S. Association.**

Activities and Objectives

Activities of the U.S. Association include:

■ *periodic membership meetings,*
■ *an informal newsletter,*
■ *public conferences* from time to time, and
■ dissemination of *studies and reports.*

The basic objectives of these activities are:

■ to help disseminate information about the interlinkage of complex global problems, and the role and responsibility of the United States in these problems;
■ to stimulate discussion of creative policy alternatives for the future as a first step toward timely and appropriate public decisions in the United States; and
■ to provide a network of information, support, and personal encouragement for members as well as others in the United States who share similar concerns and interests.

The U.S. Association is a non-profit organization. To support its activities, it depends on membership fees, contributions, newsletter subscriptions, and grants.

Reports to The Club of Rome

1.

The Limits to Growth (1972): In the United States (perhaps throughout the world as well), The Club of Rome is best known for its pioneering project on global modeling, which led in 1972 to the widely publicized book *The Limits to Growth*. This brief and highly readable volume was based on a computer simulation model developed at the Massachusetts Institute of Technology by Professor Jay Forrester and later refined by an international team of young scholars under the direction of Dr. Dennis L. Meadows.

In essence, the authors concluded that:

■ **If the present growth trends in world population, industrialization, pollution, food production, and resource depletion continue unchanged, the limits to growth on this planet will be reached sometime within the next one hundred years. The most probable result will be a rather sudden and uncontrollable decline in both population and industrial capacity.**

■ **It is possible to alter these growth trends and to establish a condition of ecological and economic stability that is sustainable far into the future. The state of global equilibrium could be designed so that the basic material needs of each person on earth are satisfied and each person has an equal opportunity to realize his individual human potential.**

■ **If the world's people decide to strive for this second outcome rather than the first, the sooner they begin working to attain it, the greater will be their chances of success.**

2.

Mankind at the Turning Point (1974): The second report to The Club of Rome also involved computer simulation modeling, and was directed by Dr. Mihajlo D. Mesarovic of Case Western Reserve University in Cleveland, Ohio, and Dr. Eduard Pestel of the Technical University of Hannover, West Germany.

The global model used for their book, however, was divided into ten regional sectors. This allowed for a much higher degree of differentiation of data and more precise reflection of contrasting natural and historical characteristics, and levels of economic development.

In their findings, the authors concurred in the view that there are severe hazards in undirected and uncontrolled global growth. But they drew a distinction between such self-destructive growth and the balanced, "organic" growth that characterizes most human development—with periods of rapid activity and expansion leading gradually to a state of maturity, and eventually to some level of sustained equilibrium with the environment.

To achieve organic growth on a global scale, however, immense changes in understanding and outlook at the personal level will be required, as well as fundamental revisions in the ways in which individuals, corporations, and governments plan for and manage their future.

3.

Reshaping the International Order (1976): The third report to The Club of Rome was the product of an international study team, funded primarily by the Netherlands Ministry of Economic Development and led by the Dutch Nobel Prize laureate in economics, Dr. Jan Tinbergen. In effect, this book marked a shift in emphasis on the part of the Club of Rome from preoccupation with global growth processes and finite physical limits to analysis of the social, political, institutional and ethical problems that promise to become acute before the exhaustion of any major natural resource.

RIO makes a case for orderly transition to a more equitable sharing of resources, especially those of global commons areas such as the oceans and seabeds. Its authors also support the gradual introduction of new concepts such as an international currency, an international treasury, and other bureaucratic innovations that frankly would have the effect of transferring some sovereign powers from individual nations to a central authority for mutual global benefit. At the same time, the study points out, there must be major internal reforms in many of the societies of the Third and Fourth Worlds to insure that the benefits of increased international transfers would be shared more fairly throughout the population, and not siphoned off for the benefit of a tiny elite.

4.

Goals for Mankind (1977): The next report to The Club of Rome to be published in the United States, prepared under the guidance of Dr. Ervin Laszlo, took yet another tack. It was predicated on the belief that political and institutional changes of the future must begin with changes in human perceptions and goals.

Dr. Laszlo and an internationel team of collaborators **set out to catalogue the national goals held today in nations of diverse size, location, wealth, and governmental structure, and then to examine the ways in which such goals may be changed under the influence of tradition, religion, ideology, politics, and other factors.**

Finally, they attempted to chart the outlines of what they termed a "global solidarity revolution," which might be achieved by concentration on the most broadly shared human goals, characteristic of peoples in most societies, and deemphasis of other goals that are divisive or destructive of world peace and progress.

5.

Beyond the Age of Waste (1978): The fifth report to The Club of Rome—by Dr. Dennis Gabor (a Nobel Prize laureate in physics), Professor Umberto Colombo, Dr. Alexander King, and Dr. Ricardo Galli—was published in several languages in Europe before appearing in the United States. The project was stimulated primarily by the frequent assertion that the computer simulation projections for *The Limits to Growth* had failed to give sufficient importance to the factor of scientific and technological innovation.

A distinguished group of international experts from a number of disciplines set out to examine the prospects for technological advance in the areas of energy, materials, and food, which were selected as key indicators of our ability to meet the rising demands and aspirations of an expanding global population.

Beyond the Age of Waste **summarizes in considerable technical detail the working group's conclusions, identifying both positive and negative signs and, above all, making clear that scientific and technological progress are, and will continue to be, highly dependent on basic social, economic, and political decisions in each nation.**

6.

Energy: The Countdown (1979): This summary of world energy prospects, carried out in France, became the sixth report to The Club of Rome. The report was authored by Thierry de Montbrial, with an introduction and recommendations by Robert Lattes and Carroll L. Wilson.

The book surveyed authoritative studies of global energy prospects from sources as disparate as OPEC, the CIA, several major private banks, the OECD, and the Workshop on Alternative Energy Strategies (WAES) at the Massachusetts Institute of Technology. The approach was to compare the data bases, methodologies, and conclusions of these independent research efforts, and then to determine the degree of consensus in their findings.

The book highlights action implications, particularly for the developed, industrial nations, and describes the emerging world of energy as one in which the industrial democracies may "pay dearly for failing to remain in touch" with the reality of the current geopolitical situation, where critical decisions and changes take place with little relationship to broad public purposes and desires.

7.

No Limits to Learning (1979): This book—the seventh report to The Club of Rome—was based on a two-year research project on learning, with particular emphasis on the question of how the values, perceptions, and skills required to cope with the problems of the coming decades can be developed through national educational systems.

The project was coordinated from three centers: one in the United States at the Harvard Graduate School of Education; one in Eastern Europe in Bucharest, Romania; and one in the developing world in Rabat, Morocco. The findings of the study were presented at an international conference in June 1979, in Salzburg, Austria.

The authors—Dr. James W. Botkin, Dr. Mahdi Elmandjra, and Dr. Mircea Malitza—**argue that traditional educational structures are now almost totally oriented toward "maintenance learning." They strive to acquaint students with the skills, perceptions, and values historically developed within their respective societies.**

Traditional educational structures give insufficient attention to the kind of "innovative and participative learning" that would enable students to create more effective tools to deal with new situations, and fail to take account of the fact that many current problems demand solutions that lie beyond the control of any single nation.

8.

Dialogue on Wealth and Welfare (1980): This report, the eighth sponsored by The Club of Rome, offers a view of world capital formation that challenges traditional economic thought.

The author, Dr. Orio Giarini of the European Institute of Graduate Studies in Geneva, stresses the need to rethink many economic terms and the concepts that lie behind them.

■ **Can such factors as "savings" and "capital," which are very meaningful in the highly monetarized economies of the affluent, industrialized societies, serve as a useful guide to development in the largely non-monetarized economies of the Third and Fourth Worlds?**

■ **Indeed, does the discipline of economics suffice to define the totality of human effort and the rewards and benefits derived from it, or only that considerable fraction of the whole that happens to be measurable in statistical and monetary terms?**

■ **How would our thinking be altered if we were to take more account of other significant human and environmental factors? This book goes well beyond traditional economic analysis and leads the way into the social, philosophical, and ideological dialogue that determines so much of twentieth-century life.**

9.

How *Making It Happen* Happened

Road Maps to the Future (1980): The ninth report to The Club of Rome, comprising a more socio-political inquiry into the factors that determine the effectiveness of any society, was authored by Dr. Bohdan Hawrylyshyn of the International Management Institute (CEI) of Geneva, Switzerland.

As one who, through the hand of fate, has lived and worked under five dissimilar political regimes during his life, Dr. Hawrylyshyn may be uniquely qualified to discuss dispassionately the long-term inter-actions among societal values, structures of political governance, and economic systems—each of which is a critical element in determining the degree of harmony between a nation's internal organiza-tion and its physical and interna-tional environmental.

Dr. Hawrylyshyn also analyzes the current "state of the Nation-State" in a world characterized by rising population pressures, energy short-falls, political instability, sharpening demands for equity and economic development, and East-West ten-sions. In a concluding chapter, he proposes a set of indicators for measuring societal effectiveness.

By the end of 1978, the U.S. Association for The Club of Rome had been in existence for two and one-half years. During that period, it had grown almost to 150 members, and had become a close, collegial group. The organization was serving its broad goals, but lacked a project that could lead to measurable results.

"Wanted"—a project: In January 1979, at the Association's semiannual meeting, James Grant, the charismatic President of the Overseas Development Council (and now Director General of UNICEF), was the keynote speaker. He emphasized the importance of the "human needs" approach and described the pioneering work of the ODC in developing an index to measure progress in meeting basic human needs—the Physical Quality of Life Index, or PQLI. In the discussions that followed over dinner and in small workshop sessions, the topic was explored in greater detail.

But as the end of the meeting approached, the same concern about a specific objective surfaced once again. What, if anything, were we going to do? In the best American tradition, one member finally crystallized the sense of the meeting by placing a motion before USA/CoR: That the activities of the U.S. Association for The Club of Rome, for the next year, focus on the issue of meeting essential human needs in a sustainable world by the year 2000.

The motion passed unanimously. We all felt relieved. We had a concrete goal. But the question remained unanswered as to how to achieve this goal. A small

Commentary

Ever since it became clear *Making It Happen* would be published, it has been important to me to include a personal acknowledgement to many of the special people who made the book possible. Here is the way I have chosen to do so.

Thank you, **Linda Kovan,**
for sharing with me the joys and burdens of the project from beginning to end and never losing heart;
for typing and retyping the manuscript again and again;
for cheerfully spending innumer-able evening and weekend hours in order to do what needed to be done;
for always having a smile and a cheerful word.

Linda Kovan

committee, chaired by Jim Grant, was formed to explore this issue. It met once, to consider alternatives for the project.

Inspiration while shaving: Shortly after that first committee meeting, the idea for what has become this book came to me one morning while I was shaving. Essentially, my proposal was to try to express, in an edited volume focused on creating a better future, the remarkably diverse and collegial spirit of our U.S. Association meetings. Each interested member of the Association would be invited to comment on problems from his or her particular perspective—politics, ecology, economics, business, labor unions, women's issues, organized religion, and so on.

The range of experience among the members of the U.S. Association was broad enough that sketching an outline, with names next to appropriate chapter titles, was a simple matter. Producing such a book, I naively imagined, would be equally simple.

The idea of a book quickly received the endorsement of our steering committee and Board of Directors. Although they were very busy, many members agreed to write chapters.

Book concept (#1): At Jim Grant's suggestion, we decided in May 1979 to focus our initial attention on a presentation to delegates at the United Nations Special Session on the Third Development Decade to be held in New York in late August 1980.

We described the basic theme of our project as "Sustainability and Basic Needs: Emergent Issues of the 1970s."

Uneasiness: For several months this statement—which still sounds good to me—provided a focus for our project. But I knew from personal conversations with members that many were uneasy about the project. At a meeting of contributors to the book in October 1979, I found out why.

Twenty-one participants gathered at Marymount College in Arlington, Virginia, to review work in progress and plan the next steps for the project. The meeting was memorable partly because an unexpected snowfall and power failure reminded us, correctly, that humankind does not always control nature.

The agenda as planned was to be nuts and bolts—getting on with the book—and not a fundamental reconceptualization of its basic concept and objectives.

EPILOGUE

But, as the discussion progressed, it became apparent that we shared a major concern. In brief, it was a questioning about *why an organization in the United States should initiate a project whose primary purpose seemed to be telling other nations—especially Third World nations—what they should be doing.*

How, we were asking ourselves, could we do this at a time when we seemed to be coping so poorly with future-related problems in our own society? Did we really have anything to offer? Weren't many of the problems we were discussing directly related to policies and patterns of resource utilization here in the United States?

Redefinition: As we pondered these questions, it became clear that we needed to redefine the theme of the project as "Challenges and Opportunities for the United States in a New Global Order."

Commentary _____

Jan Richardson and her ceramic houses

*Thank you, **Jan Richardson,***
for always saying, "If you really think it is important, do it";
for providing the income which made it possible for me to work on this project;
for sharing in the process of design and layout;
for raising the children and taking care of the farm during the many days when I was out of town;
for always being incredibly capable, strong, courageous and considerate.
*Thank you, **Dana Meadows,***
for shaping many of the ideas which are reflected in *Making It Happen;*
for your unwavering faith in the ultimate success of the project;

for your help with writing and editing;
for introducing me to The Hunger Project and to Est;
for your collaboration on other books, which was so important in shaping this one;
for taking time from an incredibly busy schedule to share in the production process;
for your unflinching, unequivocal commitment to creating a better world for everyone and your courage in living that commitment every day of your life.
*Thank you, **Jay Harris,***
for your support of me and of the project even when none of us were really sure that it would succeed;
for your financial support;

**Book Concept #1
(May 1979)
"Sustainability and Basic Needs:
Emergent Issues of the 1970s."**

During the decade of the 1970s, two emerging issues—the sustainability of global society and the satisfaction of basic human needs—have increasingly occupied the attention of national leaders, the administrators of regional and international organizations, and scholars concerned with international affairs. Dealing with these issues knowledgeably, foresightedly, and humanely will be of critical importance to the future world role of the United States.

Today, however, the leaders of the United States appear ill-prepared to meet that challenge. Even more important, the U.S. public is insensitive to and poorly informed about the difficult choices which must be made in the next two decades.

Belief in the need for a sustainable global society has often been interpreted as advocacy of "no growth" and as fundamentally in conflict with the goal of meeting basic human needs. This has had the pernicious effect of seeming to pit environmentalists and humanitarians as well as "First World" and "Third World" leaders against one another.

But this interpretation is not only pernicious, it is wrong: the two goals are necessarily interrelated and complementary.

Today, a growing number of knowledgeable individuals believe that we are capable of achieving both objectives and that, indeed, we must do so. They argue that only a global society from which serious physical deprivation and human suffering have been eliminated, and in which the essentials of equity and human dignity are assured, can truly be called sustainable.

To achieve such a society, however, changes in political and social institutions will be required; technological feasibility is only one factor (and not the most important) in the process by which major policy initiatives are adopted and implemented.

Initiatives begin with leadership, a commitment to action and understanding of the process by which a

Commentary

Jay Harris

for your commitment to a book of the highest possible quality;
for your continued support in the face of postponements, changes in direction, missed deadlines and publishers' rejections;
for your open, sensitive leadership of the U.S. Association for The Club of Rome;
for your deep commitment to creating a better world for all of us, and for your willingness to act on that commitment.

Thank you, **David Dodson Gray,** for envisioning the format of *Making It Happen* more than a year before anyone else could imagine it;
for having the faith and the guts to undertake the task of design, typesetting and layout of a book of this size and complexity;
for taking me into your home and disrupting an orderly, well-balanced life to meet the needs of this project;
for your commitment to the highest standards of quality in the face of pressures to compromise;
for your willingness to compromise when you could be convinced that it would serve the goals of the project;
for your editorial adaptation of all the material for easy readability and magazine style, and your skill in carrying that task through to completion;
for your meticulous attention to detail;
for your unwillingness to lose sight of human considerations in the face of my drive to produce results;
for the richness of our friendship during the arduous task of book production.

Thank you, **Elizabeth Dodson Gray,** for serving as one of my most important intellectual mentors during the life of this project;
for always being there with a word of encouragement, love, and support when it was needed;
for cheerfully accepting David's long absences;
for sharing so generously from your cartoon collection;
for preparing nourishing breakfasts, lunches and dinners even when they "weren't on your diet" and you couldn't eat them;
for keeping us on track and on target.

David Dodson Gray

multitude of individual beliefs coalesce into national priorities. Often this process is described as the creation of "political will." In the United States, more than most nations, the effective exercise of political will requires—indeed embodies—a high degree of public understanding and acceptance.

Crystallizing the basic approach and themes: Following additional phone calls, meetings, discussions, and exchanges of memoranda, we had by February 1980 crystallized the basic approach and themes which you will find reflected in this book.

The occasion for setting these down was a seminar at the United Nations in New York, organized by the United Nations Institute for Training and Research [UNITAR]. We wrote then about why we should put the emphasis on the United States.

Redefinition of the Theme (October 1979)
"Challenges and Opportunities for the United States in a New Global Order"

Probably the most significant challenges and opportunities which the United States will face between now and the year 2000 are related to the emergence of a new global order. But the kind of role the United States will play is still to be determined.

It must not be the role of a privileged minority whose principal objective appears to be the preservation of an affluent, unsustainable, style of life. We have an obligation to preserve, as an option for humankind, the model of a diverse, open, adaptable, experimental society which has been our major contribution to history.

To face up to the future, we must first get our own values and priorities in order. The process of redefining our global role into the twenty-first century must begin now and it must begin at home.

By confidently building on our strengths, while candidly addressing our weaknesses, the citizens and leaders of the United States can

Commentary

*Thank you, **Don Lesh,***
for your consistent support of a project which often overburdened the limited resources of the U.S. Association for The Club of Rome and disrupted the orderly office procedures you had established;
for your friendship and understanding throughout the project;
for your careful editing of the entire manuscript;
for your participation in our joint—often fruitless—efforts to raise funds and find a publisher.
*Thank you, **Faye Beuby,***
for your volunteer work on the project even before joining the U.S. Association for The Club of Rome;
for your cheerful willingness to do whatever needed to be done, whenever it needed to be done;
for your effectiveness, commitment and creativity in these last months as executive director of the U.S. Association for The Club of Rome;
for lining up photos and permissions;
for helping with the production process.
*Thank you, **Anitra Thorhaug,***
for your help and support in conceiving, and organizing the project during its early stages;
for always doing more than was expected and before it was needed;
for your continued support, enthusiasm, helpfulness and effectiveness as a board member and contributor to *Making It Happen.*
*Thank you, **Carol Christensen,***
for your utopian thinking and dedication to inspiring others with the belief that utopia is attainable;
for your incredible efforts, along with those of your husband, David Ames, to provide us with the photographs we needed;
for your commitment to making this book and the U.S. Association for The Club of Rome the very best that it could become.

Faye Beuby, David Dodson Gray and John Richardson by the light table

effectively respond to the challenges we face on this diverse, finite, interdependent "spaceship Earth." Our response should be a more open, equitable, and sustainable society which, by its example, can provide humanity with one positive model for the shape of things to come.

Delays, surprises, and finally a completed manuscript: Initially, our plan had been to complete the book by September of 1980. But unforeseen events began to intervene.

■ Promised contributions were not forthcoming or required more editing than anticipated.

■ Another book on which I had been working required a major revision.

■ I took time off to write a report for the State Department on the Global 2000 Study.

■ And—before the book was really completed—we embarked on an exciting, but time-consuming, exploration of the possibility of doing a related television series.

Our fall membership meeting in November 1980 arrived and the typescript of the book was in-hand and "finished"—sort of.

But as potential publishers soon told me, it was not really a book. It filled three massive looseleaf notebooks (I needed a suitcase to carry it with me).

And the organization of the book, a vestige from earlier plans, didn't make sense.

One member of our board said, "Let's face it—this is a bad book; no one will buy it and no one will read it." I wondered whether he was right, and hoped to prove him wrong.

Still another reappraisal and reconceptualization: It was February 1981 before I faced up to the fact that something had to be done. I was convinced that the basic concept was sound, but we needed a new organization and a manuscript which was about forty percent shorter.

I asked myself, over an agonizing weekend, what the book would look like if we were starting from scratch with this concept and these materials. Three "books" emerged from this process. One of them seemed right, and we went on to what, at the time, I thought was final revision and editing.

Commentary

*Thank you, **Bob Stecker**,* for your calm, clear-headed support of the project and your willingness to offer wise counsel when it was needed; for the excellence of your editorial comments and suggestions.

*Thank you, **Lil Esselstyn**,* for your personal support and your financial support.

*Thank you, **Walter Hahn**,* for the excellence of your editorial comments and suggestions; for your support as a board member; for your willingness to offer wise counsel when it was needed.

*Thank you, **Lucy Cabot Smethurst**,* for the verve and effectiveness with which you got us moving on distribution and television opportunities; for your commitment to getting out the message of the book and the U.S. Association for The Club of Rome into the real world; for your warmth, enthusiasm and sense of humor.

*Thank you, **Roy Anderson**,* for telling us the truth about our book when it needed to be told.

*Thank you, **Joel Mazelis**,* for organizing pages of editorial comments and criticisms so that we could use them effectively.

*Thank you, **Dana Raphael**,* for your continued concern with editorial excellence, for your support, and for your tolerance of our oversights.

*Thank you, **Michaela Walsh**,* for your unflinching commitment to the principles upon which *Making It Happen* is based, and for your insistence that we live up to them.

*Thank you, **Beth Austin**,* for donating your Christmas vacation to the project and for producing exactly the photo-search results that were needed.

*Thank you, **Dave and Roberta Crocker**,* for guiding us through the intricacies of computer typesetting technology, and for your

unfailingly cheerful response to our needs and demands.

*Thank you to the entire staff of Crockergraphics, especially to **Don Haskel**,* for your care in producing high-quality photographic reproductions;

and to ***Rosemarie Morelli**,* for your invaluable assistance at the light table in the final days of paste-up.

Thank you to Nimrod Press, our printing company, for keeping to a very tight schedule and giving us every help,

*and especially to **Lynne Foy**,* for your skill in color design, and for your care and swiftness in the final preparation of our mechanicals for manufacture.

*Thank you, **Jean Lamuniere**,* for designing exactly the cover that was needed.

*Thank you, **Mark Gerzon**,* for your timely and helpful counsel on the front cover and internal structure of the magazine format.

Crystallization of the Basic Approach and Themes "Why Put the Emphasis on the United States?"

The focus on the United States is vital to an understanding of the project. The members of the U.S. Association have agreed that our purpose is not to lecture the Less Developed Countries—or other industrialized nations—about what they should or should not do, nor to attack past U.S. Government policies or the practices of multi-national corporations.

We do not wish to preach doom and gloom, nor to indulge in a search for scapegoats.

Rather, we want this book to provide a systemic, encompassing view of the global transition that is already under way, giving primary emphasis to the United States as an example of an advanced, industrial society that is beginning to face up to, and cope with, global trends that almost certainly will demand fundamental change in our own practices, institutions, values, and life styles as we strive to meet the imperatives of an increasingly interdependent world.

We will look less at the old patterns that are crumbling and more at the new ones being born. Maximum attention will be given to what is happening now, especially to the "success stories" of thoughtful and innovative developments, and show how it may be possible to facilitate the transition.

The approach will be positive, practical, and people-oriented—with clear recognition that we cannot expect quick fixes, and that the process of change may be difficult, but with optimism about the power of the United States to lead by the example we set at home.

In summary, we will steer clear of "Thou shalt" and "They must" while concentrating on "We ought to and can."

Commentary

Thank you, Gerry Vanderleun, for your guidance in composition and cover selection.

Thank you to all the contributors, for writing your articles so well, for getting them to me in reasonable time, and for being patient when my deadlines slipped and slipped again.

Thank you also for being able to trust the many layers of the editing process.

Thank you, especially, to those authors who wrote articles at my request—and which subsequent reorganizations of the book made it impossible to include.

I have been particularly grateful for your tolerance, understanding and commitment to the goals of *Making It Happen.*

Finally, thank you to those who deserve thanks but have not been recognized individually. Working with those named above and many not named has been an inspiring and enriching experience. I know I have incurred debts which I can never repay. *Making It Happen* is offered to all of you in partial payment.

"*Why, this broth we made is magnificent!*"

Going the rounds of editors and publishers Spring/Summer/Fall 1981: In the fall of 1980 a member who is also a small publisher, David Dodson Gray, had observed that what we were trying to do wasn't really a book, or even a book of essays; "It was a 'bookazine.'" What we had been thinking of as a book was also in major ways like a weekly newsmagazine. Like a newsmagazine, we were trying to lay out a broad mosaic of material for a popular audience, and to make sense for that audience of our world and lives—what was, is, and is going to be happening.

His suggestion had been that we do it as a bookazine ourselves. We had the know-how available, and it should look something like *Newsweek* or *Business Week* in size, page format, and design. "Make it like something everyone has seen. Make it read easily with lots of pictures and lots of headlines and lots of visual hooks to get people into it. People should be able to browse it the way they browse *Reader's Digest* or a weekly newsmagazine."

That idea had simply lain dormant. It was a possibility that I knew lay out there if all else failed.

What all of us wanted was the acknowledgement of an honest-to-god major editor and publishing house that what we'd done was good and that they wanted to sell it and make money while pushing our ideas.

And what we didn't realize then was that what we'd done hadn't been done before. It was new. And what many people in the publishing field need in order to survive personally and as an organization is do something that is like what sold very well the last time around. What we were showing them wasn't like anything else they had seen sell well. "It wasn't a book."

Through the spring and summer and fall of 1981 the manuscript was out to a variety of editors and publishing houses. We heard from one after another various forms of the word "No." Some simply weren't interested. Some liked the ideas but found the

Commentary

The two month sprint to produce a book: Any author or publisher will tell you that taking a book from manuscript to published volume takes, at a minimum, seven months. Our schedule was going to allow one month for manufacturing and two months for everything else.

David Dodson Gray agreed to be responsible for final copy editing, book design, production coordination, and introducing me to computer typesetting! David had foreseen that our magazine format would require a very readable nonacademic style that would be consistent among the many authors. It would also need short sentences, short paragraphs, and design of a comprehensive typesetting format to accommodate the thoughts of academics—who often write "laundry lists" [for example, items 1. through 10.]. He was the one who was going to make that particular part of this process happen.

Our place of work would be a 1910-style house in a Boston suburb, the home of Roberta and Dave Crocker and of "Crockergraphics." The Dodson Gray townhouse a few miles away (and already described on pp. 112ff.) would serve as a home away from home for me and as a second base of operations.

Here are some of the images fixed in my mind as I close my eyes and reflect on the hectic period from mid-December 1981 through early February 1982: ...the distinctive green color of the Crocker home ...the musty red of the 1968 Volvos in which we drove to and fro... New York Air cabin attendants singing Christmas carols on the late evening flight, two days before Christmas ...the International terminal at Boston's Logan Airport at seven o'clock in the morning and nine o'clock at night...my wife Jan meeting me at Washington National airport late on a Sunday night....

What I will most remember is the commitment, flexibility and kindness of the people who allowed me and the production of *Making it Happen* to become part of their lives.

Producing a book at Crockergraphics provides an opportunity to learn every phase of the computer typesetting process—and to practice good human relations in a small, highly interdependent human community. Computers and typesetting equipment are located in virtually every room of the Crocker home. At every hour of the day, from 9 A.M. until often well after the end of the Johnny Carson show [12:30 A.M.], several projects are often simulta-neously in progress. Computer typesetting machines as well as layout tables are interesting and important tools being used fervently by Crocker staff and by outsiders like ourselves.

On a typical day, David and I arrived in mid-morning and worked until about midnight, usually with a break for dinner. During the first weeks, our time was devoted to telecommunicating [transferring copy over the telephone to the Crocker main computer] from the U.S. Association word processor in Washington, DC. David spent long days for weeks on end at the computer terminal both copy editing and formatting the contents of the book according to his book design. I mobilized Beth Austin and many USA/CoR colleagues in collecting photographs, and spent a lot of time comprehending the full complexity and size of our task—and figuring out how to organize it in ways that would be helpful.

When we began typesetting in mid-December, we moved into our "project headquarters," a small, cluttered former sewing room off the Crocker upstairs hallway, and the book really began to take shape before our eyes. We moved in from the photographic department in the

Drawing by Wm. Hamilton ©1976 The New Yorker Magazine

"I tell you, the book has everything—sex, history, consciousness, and cats!"

Commentary

basement a light table [on which David would lay out and "paste up" the actual pages of the book]. We strung across one side of the room a "clothesline" of typeset galleys in the order needed for layout. A dresser top in the hall was partly cleared as my production center, from which I kept track of the various stages of the process. (Only one person could fit comfortably into the layout room).

One amazing thing was how help materialized just when it was needed. The Dodson Grays graciously took me along to a dinner party, at which we met Mark Gerzon, an author and former newsman, and he shared invaluable experience in trade publishing. His counsel on clarifying the internal structure of the book came just when it was needed. He also introduced us to his editor, Gerry VanderLeun, who spent a morning giving us valuable advice about book publishing and our actual selection of the cover.

Beth Austin, newly moved to Washington, DC, donated her Christmas vacation to collecting photographs—and accomplished miracles. Carol Christensen and her husband, David Ames, and Faye Beuby and her husband, Steve, were able to provide us with just the right photographs from their extensive personal collections. Dana Meadows came for four days and contributed ideas, as well as writing and editorial skills. My wife Jan Richardson spent four days after Christmas applying her considerable artistic talents to problems of photo selection, design and layout.

Elsewhere, other parts of the project continued to move forward. At the U.S. Club of Rome office in Washington, Faye Beuby and Linda Kovan lined up photographs and contacted publishers for the all-important permissions to quote. At his farm in Western Maryland, Jean Lamuniere designed the cover and conferred with me on my occasional trips home.

When we first planned the project, we thought we could lay out a page an hour. The expected 160 pages would take 160 hours. On good days, David could do as many as twenty

Roberta Crocker at the keyboard

Don Haskel at the camera

variety of authors and writing styles too varied to imagine in one book. One suggested that they'd like very much to publish a book based on all this material but written by one author.

We lived on with repeated submissions and renewed hope. We were comforted by Stewart Brand's experience. *The Whole Earth Catalogue* with its oversize format and its crowded pages "about tools" certainly was unlike anything else that had ever come along. It was a latter-day Sears catalogue. But finally it wasn't even that. It was what it was. So was what we were doing. And he had published and distributed his successfully. If we had to, could we?

"We'll do it ourselves, but...": In October 1981 the board of the U.S. Association met and heard the sad news about our latest forays with editors and publishers. Our president, Jay Harris, was still in favor of the project, as was the board. It could be done on our own without a great outlay of funds.

We were sponsoring a major conference early the following March in 1982 in Washington, honoring the 10th anniversary of the publishing of *The Limits to Growth,* and we all saw that this would be a good occasion to launch our now much-delayed book.

So the board decision was to go ahead. The Association would come up with the up-front money—but we were to continue to try to work out a possible distribution or co-publishing arrangement with a major publishing house or with a future-oriented one. Negotiations went on through phone and one meeting, but again there was a final "No" when we got down to what we'd provide, what they'd do, and what it would cost.

But by this time we were launched doing it ourselves. We were feeling more confident about being on our own, and now we were sure we could do it.

Commentary

pages. On difficult days, we would find we had mis-set something, or a needed passage would be missing (stopping everything), or we would be unable to find the "just right" photograph. Sometimes, it seemed to me we ended the day behind where we had started. After working one night until 1:40 A.M., David got an intestinal bug and had to spend a day in bed sick. The next two days were half-speed for him. I realized that strong commitment and intention to get things done might not accomplish everything. We were still somewhat subject to the uncertainties of fate.

In mid-January, the semester began at The American University and my schedule became more hectic. Thanks to a wonderfully understanding and supportive dean, William Olson, I was able to commute back and forth to Boston, in and around teaching my classes. The New York Air agents became familiar acquaintances. In one of the vilest winters on record, there were major plane crashes at both Logan International and Washington National Airports. Fortunately, I was able to read about them in the newspaper...enroute.

And finally...it was the end of January—January 30th, in fact. David was hard at work doing layout of the final chapter. Page mechanicals lay on the Crocker's bed, being checked by Faye Beuby. Machine time was being shared with a rush job on the Dover *Town Report*. Yet to be completed were headlines, some photograph corrections and the entering of proofreading corrections; also the table of contents and the writing of the conclusion to this epilogue.

It was clear that the book would be done in time for the March meeting. We had made it happen. I said to David and Faye, "This would be a good time for me to go to a quiet place and complete the epilogue." And I did.

But, of course, one can never quite complete the story of writing a book in the pages of the book itself. That would be impossible. All of us will discover the continuation of the story together.

David Crocker

MAKING IT HAPPEN:

How You Can Make It Happen

This may not say what you expect. Some reviewers of this book said they couldn't figure out what it was they or anyone else should do. I guess they were looking for exhortations to stop eating meat; drive smaller automobiles; or instead of driving, use public transit; recycle your cans and bottles; support (or oppose) foreign aid programs; write your Congressman; plant a garden; or buy a farm; or even move there and make it self-sustaining.

People interested in creating a better future seem to expect these sorts of very specific directions.

I do some of the things on that list, as do many of the contributors to *Making it Happen*. But I do not know for sure that they'll lead to the kind of future *you* want. You see, I don't know what kind of future you do want, even though I believe your vision would be in many ways similar to mine.

The future is uncertain. The consequences of any action you might take are uncertain. No one—whether the president of the United States or the head of a major multinational corporation or a high-powered futurist or a global modeler—knows how to make things turn out exactly the way he or she wants.

Recognizing this may become for you a source of anxiety for a while. But it can also become a source of power and freedom. M. Nicoll described the feeling well:

> I suddenly realized that
> no one knew everything, and
> from that moment
> I began to think for myself.

Living with uncertainty: The future is uncertain but you know perfectly well how to handle uncertainty. You do it all the time. You're not sure how to find the way to a friend's house, or what kind of tires to buy, or how to roast a turkey. So what do you do?

You experiment.

You don't press full-speed ahead, listening to no one, and advocating as the universal solution for all people and all times whatever you suspect might work. You go a bit slowly. You look for evidence that you might have gone wrong or that there might be another way. You prepare for the eventuality that what you do might not work the first time. And the first time you go to your friend's house you leave some extra time for finding it. And in case the first turkey you've ever cooked turns out to be inedible, you have a casserole on the side. That is nothing more than common sense.

Guiding principles: What are the principles you follow instinctively when you have to do a job you've never done before and you're not sure how to proceed? You learned these principles somewhere, sometime, and perhaps you have never really examined them. But if you do, you'll see some very useful principles that can help you create the future you really want.

These principles are not specific instructions that guarantee success, say, in making your first million, or ending the arms race, or creating a healthy environment. But they do describe for you an approach to new problems of greater-than-usuual uncertainty, an approach that has been widely used in various forms by you and others to produce results. I believe applying these principles will be very helpful in identifying for you specific actions which can lead you toward your goals.

1. Recognize that you are powerful and act accordingly.

None of us are without options. How you choose among the options open to you, and also create new options for yourself, will shape your future. You can begin to create the future you want simply by recognizing that you have the power to do so. If you decide to, your life can make the world a better place for yourself and for others too.

2. Describe clearly what you really want.

Many of us shy away from thinking about what we really want out of life—what kind of future we *want,* as opposed to what we *expect.* But creating a "vision," as it is sometimes called, is a very important early step in the process of changing your life and changing the world.

Kids create visions naturally. But many adults have lost the capacity to imagine, especially to imagine that things could be very different—and better—than they now are.

You can begin right now to picture clearly a world that would be exactly as you want it. Don't worry about what you assume is possible; look at what is the best you can imagine.

Once you have created your vision, stay in touch with it. Develop it. Don't work for a world you don't want, a world you feel lukewarm about and are willing simply to settle for. Keep working for the world that you picture in your truest, purest vision.

3. Be committed to your vision of the life—and the world—that you really want, but not to any particular method of obtaining it.

Keep your eye on your target. You know much more about your goals than about what path will actually lead to them. There may be several paths, or the path that you choose first may turn out to be wrong. Be committed to your goal. Be open to whatever paths might lead you there.

4. Start learning what you need to know.

In order to choose a path of action, you will need information about what is so in the world. You don't need to know everything in order to act effectively, but you do need to know something. Start finding out where information can be found. A good place to begin is your local library. Librarians are trained to help you find out things, and their skills are often underutilized. In most cases, they will be delighted to help, and you may even gain a friend or ally.

Another good place to begin is the local office of your Congressional representative. The phone number should be in the telephone directory. These offices are often staffed by someone who has grown up in your community and knows local problems well.

Don't limit yourself to information that is written down. One of the richest stores of information is the stories people tell about their experiences. You can tap another rich store by paying careful attention to the world that is unfolding before your eyes.

Asking questions is probably the most important part of collecting information. Become a living question mark. And continue to be one as you begin to take action. Be informed in as many ways, and from as many sides, as you can find. Ask the questions you really want answers to. If the question isn't answered or you don't understand the answer, ask again. There is no such thing as a dumb question.

As you begin to get answers, recognize that "facts" are often in the eyes of the beholder, especially "facts" about what can't be done. You must be the judge of what "reality" is. Use the wisdom and experience of experts—but be questioning and skeptical. Learn to seek out differing expert opinions, and choose among them.

5. Choose a path of action and begin to follow it.

Use the information you have gathered to describe clearly how things are right now. Contrast this description with your picture of how things should be.

Then, define a sequence of action steps that would begin to move things in the right direction. The steps should be easy and clear enough so that you can begin right now to do something that will produce some measurable result, no matter how small, tomorrow, next week, or next month.

Don't wait to know everything before getting started. You will learn much more by doing something, even if it turns out to be wrong, than by hesitating and trying to figure out which first step is exactly right.

You can't learn where a path leads without traveling on it for a while. Pick any form of action, any path that is accessible to you, any initiative which seems likely to move you the first small—and important—step toward your vision.

The path might be political or educational. It might involve your own lifestyle, or your work, or how you spend your spare time. It might involve supporting others who you think are on a constructive path. It might improve something on the other side of the globe or in your own neighborhood.

The important thing is to get started. Get started today, or tomorrow, or—at the latest—before the end of this week. See where the path you choose leads, what it teaches you, and what other paths it opens for you.

6. Find your partners.

Once you have a clear vision and are starting into action, you will be amazed to find out how many people share your goals and are already working on them.

Begin by seeking organizations nearby that are concerned about the same things you are. In larger cities, there is usually a bureau that can provide you with information about voluntary organizations. If you don't find a group that can help, start one, beginning in your own neighborhood. Your vision can become an inspiration and source of motivation for others.

7. Support others who share your vision but have chosen other means of realizing it.

No one knows for sure which of the many possible paths will lead to the world that you want. The faster all paths get explored, the more we will learn.

Don't spend your energy trying to pull everyone over to your way of doing things, creating obstacles for others, or trying to prove that your way is best. Recognize as your partners all who share even a part of the vision. They are. Honor those who try something that doesn't work, especially if they tell the truth about it. Encourage everyone. Learn from everyone.

8. Welcome feedback, especially "bad news."

When you begin, you can't know for sure whether your path is right. In traveling it, you will come across the information that will tell you whether or not it is.

Be watching all the time for that information. Be especially open to bad news, news that something isn't working right. Expect unforeseen events and mistakes. They are inevitable.

Be prepared to change your direction or abandon a path that clearly isn't working. But at the same time, don't give up too soon. Distinguish between the results of experiments [measured by real events in the world] and the opinions of other people about what won't work or isn't working. Often, negative opinions come from those on other paths who are trying to get you to see—or do—things their way.

9. Tell the truth, and share what you are learning truthfully.

There is no more difficult or important principle than this. Practice describing what you see and do. Describe it exactly as you experience it, not as you hope or fear it to be, nor as other people expect to hear it. Only accurate information will help you decide what is working and what is not.

Lies—communicating that something worked when it didn't, or comments that label something a failure when it wasn't—will lead to mistakes, bad judgments and wrong choices. Being truthful with yourself is even more important than being truthful with others.

When you have an experience from which others could learn, share it. Communicate your message clearly, concisely, truthfully, usefully. Maximize the likelihood that others will hear it, pay attention to it, absorb it and use it.

10. Have fun.

Do you have the impression that working and living in a way that improves the world for you and others must be a grim and cheerless business, involving deprivation and sacrifice? My experience, and the experience of many others I know, has been different. We have found that there is nothing more fun and fulfilling than living the process of creating a better world.

As you join in this process, do so with joy. Celebrate the joy of being human. Celebrate the diversity and greatness of your partners. Celebrate the beauty and richness of the planet upon which we live. Celebrate the opportunities that are unfolding—and celebrate, most of all, the opportunity to be alive today.

JMR ☐

Creating Our Future

The future always begins right now and is not predetermined.

I have the power to shape the future. What I do makes a difference and will shape my future. What I do will have an impact on the future of those close to me and even those distant from me.

My power provides me with the opportunity, challenge and obligation to become what I wish to become and shape the world as I wish it to become. This responsibility cannot be escaped or delegated.

I am responsible for what I do, and for who I am, and for the world around me. I would not have it any other way.

The exercise of power without vision has no meaning. Therefore, I must be very clear about the things I value and the kind of world I want to live in. I must decide what is most important and what is less so and live for what is most important.

I am capable of making these decisions.

The exercise of power without knowledge will probably be ineffective. It may even be dangerous. Therefore, I must strive to see the world as clearly and truly as it can be seen. I must understand the working of those parts of the world which affect the things of importance to me.

I am capable of gaining the knowledge I need.

I recognize that expertise exists and is important. Experts can help me to gain the knowledge I need. But I know, also, that the views of experts differ and may be colored by values quite different from mine. There is a difference between expertise and truth.

I must decide for myself what is true and act accordingly.

No one can take my power from me. This gives me the self-confidence to exercise power with humility and compassion. I can be open to new knowledge, and new ways of looking at things. While I can shape the future, I know I cannot plan it with certainty nor know all the consequences of my actions. Nor can I avoid errors. I know that human beings learn by trial and error, mostly error.

I must be a learner. I must not fear my errors nor be scornful of the errors made by others.

I await with excitement what I shall do, and learn and become.

Tomorrow.